THE PSYCHOLOGY OF
WORK AND ORGANIZATION
Current Trends and Issues

THE PSYCHOLOGY OF
WORK AND ORGANIZATION
Current Trends and Issues

Selected and Edited Proceedings of the West European Conference on
The Psychology of Work and Organization
Aachen, F.R.G., 1 - 3 April, 1985

edited by

G. DEBUS

and

H.-W. SCHROIFF

Department of Industrial and Organizational Psychology
Technical University of Aachen
Aachen, F.R.G.

NORTH-HOLLAND
AMSTERDAM · NEW YORK · OXFORD · TOKYO

ISBN: 0 444 70029 3

Publishers:

ELSEVIER SCIENCE PUBLISHERS B.V.
P.O. Box 1991
1000 BZ Amsterdam
The Netherlands

Sole distributors for the U.S.A. and Canada:

ELSEVIER SCIENCE PUBLISHING COMPANY, INC.
52 Vanderbilt Avenue
New York, N.Y. 10017
U.S.A.

PRINTED IN THE NETHERLANDS

PREFACE

This volume includes papers that have been presented at the "West European Conference on the Psychology of Work and Organization", held in Aachen (FRG) in April 1985. This conference was the follow-up to the "First North-West European Conference on the Psychology of Work and Organization" in Nijmegen, The Netherlands, in 1983. The papers of the first conference have been published by Koopman-Iwema and Roe (1984).

It is the aim of these conferences to promote the exchange of knowledge and experience as well as to encourage cooperation between psychologists of work and organization in Europe. The conferences are planned and organized by the national organizations of occupational and organizational psychologists.

The Aachen-Conference was planned and organized by colleagues from Belgium (VOCAP), France (SFP/APTLF), the Federal Republic of Germany (BDP), Great Britain (BPS), and The Netherlands (NIP): Karel de Witte (VOCAP), Albert Ripon and Gerard Scherer (SFP/APTLF), Helmut Methner and Horst Fischer (BDP), Chris Clegg (BPS) and Agnes Koopman-Iwema (NIP), formed the organizational committee. They were also responsible for the selection of contributions of their countries. The editors, Günter Debus and Hans-Willi Schroiff, members of the Institute of Psychology at the Rheinisch-Westfälische Technische Hochschule (RWTH) Aachen, were responsible for the local organization of the conference. They were asked to edit the contributions of the Aachen-Conference.

Content and structure of the present volume are strictly in accord with content and structure of the conference. The papers of all invited speakers (Sanders, Heller, Hacker, Goguelin, Jonkergouw, and De Cock) have been included in their full length. Of the total of 64 contributions 34 selected papers are presented in the volume. Summary reports on 4 out of 10 workshops have been prepared.

The editors' task consisted mainly in checking the papers with respect to the fulfillment of formal requirements. Since the book should mirror structure and content of the conference it was intended to avoid any rigid selection. The invited papers and the workshop summaries have been accepted without any substantial changes. The seminar papers have been checked more thoroughly with respect to their content by the editors as well as by a number of independent reviewers. In most cases the authors accepted the reviewers' suggestions and submitted a revised version, in other cases they did not. Others withdrew their papers upon being asked for substantial changes. In very few cases papers could not be accepted in the prepared form. Each author is fully responsible for her/his paper.

The editors are greatly indebted to a number of people who helped editing the book. First of all thanks are due to the authors for their contributions and their cooperation in the reviewing process. A number of independent reviewers have helped to improve the quality of the papers. Warmest thanks are expressed to Frau Dipl.-Psych. Marina Schroiff, postgraduate student at the Institute of Psychology in Aachen. Without her thorough editorial help the book would not have got its present form. They are also indebted to Frau cand. phil. Irmgard Haupts for her assistance in proof-reading and the re-typing of quite a number of manuscripts. Last but not least they want to thank the staff of Elsevier Science Publishers B.V. (North-Holland), above all Mrs. Inez van der Heide and Dr. Kees Michielsen, who have been most helpful in the preparation of this volume.

Günter Debus
Hans-Willi Schroiff

REFERENCE
Koopman-Iwema, A.M. & Roe, R.A. (Eds.) (1984): Work and Organizational Psychology — European Perspectives. Lisse: Swets & Zeitlinger.

CONTENTS

PART III: PROFESSIONAL PROBLEMS

INTRODUCTION

The Psychology of Work and Organization - Current Trends and Issues

Günter DEBUS and Hans-Willi SCHROIFF

Department of Psychology
Rheinisch-Westfälische Technische Hochschule Aachen
Jägerstrasse zwischen 17 und 19
D.51 Aachen, Federal Republic of Germany

This volume indicates general trends in the field of work and organizational psychology. It also uncovers specific communalities in research questions and research methodologies of European scientists in these domains.

General trends are

(1) an increasing interest and activity in the domain of applied psychology.
This is already indicated by the fact that the first conference in Nijmigen did not remain a unitary event, but was followed with increasing interest (as inferred from the number of participants) by the Aachen conference. The prospects for the future with regard to such a biannual meeting look rather bright: in 1987 the Belgian colleagues will be organizing the meeting which is supposed to be a regular event.

(2) increasing communication and exchange between basic research and applied research
It is our impression (as inferred from the institutions of the participants) that the Aachen conference was a forum for both practitioners and so-called academic psychologists. To us this seems a desirable development because -- and this holds particularly for the situation in the Federal Republic of Germany -- academic research in the area of work and organization has been undoubtedly neglected in the past decades. The rapidly growing interest of academic psychologists in psychological problems of work and organization is an essential precondition for a further fruitful development of our discipline. It not only stimulates basic research focussing at applied problems but also adds to the study programs for those psychologists who begin their work outside the university.

(3) increasing international communication and cooperation
This aspect is enhanced in expectation of the new technical developments in the area of work and organization by the promotion of internationally organized research activities (e.g. the European Economic Council) and similar internationally funded research projects in various European countries.

Specific trends may be seen from different points of view. In their introduction to the proceedings of the Nijmegen conference, Koopman-Iwema & Roe (1984) identified four major research trends concerning general social and political aims as well as recent technical and

economic   changes.   The four trends that determine the   relevant
psychological topic to a larger extent, are still valid today.

- "the shift in labor relations into the direction of a growing
  workers' participation and co-determination",

- "the trend towards humanization of work, with its increasing stress
  on qualitative, immaterial working conditions and outcomes apart
  from the physical aspects that have been of importance since the
  early years of industry",

- "the rapid introduction of new technologies in organizations,
  raising questions with regard to its effects on employment, qualifications, working conditions, etc., as well as its opportunities
  for organizational innovation and improvement·of the quality of
  working life",

- and "as a result of the economic recession, a growing interest in
  unemployment effects, and in alternative forms of work that may
  lead to a more even spread of employment throughout the population,
  and at the same time enhance initiative and flexibility".

These trends are still valid although they do bear a strong bias towards
organizational psychology and other forms of applied social psychology.
From our equally biased point of view we want to draw attention to some
other trends.   These trends concern the possible contributions that
psychology should focus on.

(1)   There is a trend towards a <u>need of psychological expertise</u> in areas
       where our discipline seemed to have lost ground. "Ergonomics" e.g.
       as a scientific discipline has been taken out of the hands of
       psychologists and is now strongly dominated by engineers although
       psychology has a lot more to offer with regard to systems   design.
       Experimental psychologists with a strong background in General
       psychology are getting more and more involved in a new   type of
       ergonomics that focusses on the adaptation of new information
       technologies to the human information processing system (see e.g.
       Sanders, this volume). The continous exchange of knowledge between
       basic research and applied problems will help to regain the lost
       ground here. In this regard it will be desirable that psychologists
       are not only involved in the a-posteriori-evaluation of new techno-
       logical systems,   but contribute to the very early stages of their
       design.

(2)   There is a trend towards <u>specialized expertise</u>. It is recognized
       that certain problems need specific sophistication in theory and
       methodology. With regard to the development of stress research e.g.
       there is an obvious stagnation in the area of work and organiza-
       tion.   Correlational studies taking into account psychosomatic com-
       plaints as well as stress and strain variables do not show any
       further improvement in predicting somatic diseases (see e.g. de
       Wolff,   this volume). Hence, psychophysiologists with applied
       interests are designated to become experts in these areas.   Whereas
       social psychologists investigate relationships between stress and
       strain variables, psychophysiologists may study those between
       strain variables and somatic diseases. Further examples can easily
       be given.

(3) There is also a trend towards an integrational_attack_of_existing problems. Despite of the need for expertise each psychological intervention in ergonomics and organizational counseling is nothing but a part of the solution of a more complex problem. This requires that psychologists in these areas should bring along a broad basic psychological knowledge and methodological skills in order to be sensitive towards various kinds of problems in an occupational and organizational context (see e.g. Goguelin, this volume).

The editors are convinced that a joint effort to accentuate these trends can contribute to the improvement of research on work and organizational psychology and will help to further develop our discipline.

REFERENCE
Koopman-Iwema, A.M. & Roe, R.A. (Eds.)(1984): Work and Organizational Psychology - European Perspectives. Lisse: Swets & Zeitlinger.

PART I

GENERAL ASPECTS OF WORK
AND ORGANIZATIONAL PSYCHOLOGY

THE PSYCHOLOGY OF WORK AND ORGANIZATION
G. Debus and H.-W. Schroiff (Editors)
© Elsevier Science Publishers B.V. (North-Holland), 1986

CONTEXTS AND CONFLICTS BETWEEN ERGONOMICS
AND INDUSTRIAL PSYCHOLOGY

Andries F. SANDERS

Department of Psychology
Rheinisch-Westfälische Technische Hochschule Aachen
Jägerstr. zwischen 17 und 19
D-51 Aachen, Federal Republic of Germany

At least partly, this address is built on the basis of a misunder-
standing. The original title that I had in mind, was "contacts and
conflicts between ergonomics and industrial psychology". As is clear
from the programme the word "contacts" was replaced by "contexts" due to
distorted information transmission somewhere along the line in between
the statement of the title and the printing of the programme. I dare to
add that the error occurred during auditory transmission since it is a
classical example of acoustic or perhaps articulatory confusion that
plays such a dominant role in theories on encoding and short-term memory
(e.g. Conrad, 1964; Crowder and Morton, 1969). The phenomena are well
documented and, at least for a psychological phenomenon, they are based
on a developed theoretical structure. Yet, actual practice teaches us
that it has not been sufficiently considered in communication lines so
as to prevent errors such as changing contacts into contexts.

At first I was dismayed about the error and about to start with a proper
apology. I changed my mind however when a colleague, present at this
meeting, convinced me that the erroneous title was in fact much better
than the original one. The contacts and the conflicts between ergonomics
and industrial psychology are probably based upon the different contexts
in which both fields have been traditionally operating. Hence, the term
contexts adds a further dimension and makes proper sense. In this way
the situation was saved, although it obviously does not argue in favour
of introducing intentional misunderstandings in communication lines.
This remains an important ergonomical problem which is still too often
neglected in actual designs.

So we will first discuss contexts. What are the traditional contexts of
ergonomics and of industrial psychology? With regard to the latter
subject I have consulted the classical text by Tiffin (1952) from Purdue
University who starts his account with a chapter about the significance
of individual differences in industry. "The mangagement of an expanding
industry may obtain new machines with reasonable assurance that they
will be equal in efficiency and capable of uniform output." Yet, this
depends on the human who is actually operating the machine and "people
are not alike by nature, training, education, and inclination" (Tiffin,
1952, p. 1). Hence the output depends on human mental abilities and
skills, so that aptitude testing and determination of people that fit
the job is relevant. Most of what follows in Tiffin's "Industrial
Psychology" is about tests of individual differences, even when fairly
general principles of perception, training and motivation are discussed.

I quoted the revised 1952 edition of Tiffin's original 1942 publication.
About five years later, in 1957, Ernst McCormick, also from Purdue

University published the first edition of his "Human Engineering", that was to become a classic text. Tiffin's book is quoted only once, although Tiffin is acknowledged for his "personal encouragement and helpful advice". McCormick starts by asserting that human engineering ".... can be thought of as the adaptation of human tasks and work environment to the sensory, perceptual, mental, physical and other attributes of people". The aim of human engineering is fitting the job to the worker, rather than fitting the people to the job, as was the predominant theme in Tiffin's book.

It is clear that this means diametrically opposed contexts. The one is primarily concerned with individual differences and the other with general features. The one is concerned with selection, the other with improving equipment. The one has its background in the study of personality and mental abilities – sometimes also in social psychology – the other in experimental general psychology, and these are quite distinct worlds.

There are additional differences in context, that are probably correlated with the difference in emphasis on individual differences and general functions. These additional differences are related to differences in actual job demands between industrial psychologists and ergonomists. The traditional job demands of the industrial psychologist concern selection, work satisfaction, merit rating, leadership, morale and social structure and conflicts in organisations. In itself these are wide areas of interest that, in my opinion at least, can be hardly expected from one individual only, but rather belong to the different expertises of persons in a team of industrial psychologists. Yet such a team is engaged with properly recognized branches of applied psychology. Although the outcomes of their work may be debated by management or physicians, the industrial psychologist has no real competitive disciplines to face, except of course in the areas of transition to management, social work, and occupational medicine.

In ergonomics the situation is very different. Ergonomics cannot be identified with applied psychology since it consists of elements of technology and physiology as well. There are representatives of each of these disciplines in actual practice. It is undoubtedly true that engineers, physicians and psychologists show distinct differences in orientation, but it is equally undeniable that they all have some rights to claim a part of the cake. Engineers, since they are the ultimate designers, physicians in view of their special anatomical and physiological interests and psychologists, since they are foremost acquainted with research on behavioral resources and limitations. Yet the representatives of the various disciplines, and in particular psychologists and engineers, have learned how to talk to each other and to appreciate each other's contribution. It is striking that among the five PhD students that I have guided or that I am still guiding during recent years, there are two engineers. At the same time I know of psychologists-ergonomists who took a PhD in engineering. The ergonomist has to be interdisciplinary in his outlook, and I guess he needs that more than an industrial psychologist.

There is a further difference in context in that many psychologists-ergonomists are strongly engaged with their background basic science, i.e. general experimental psychology. There are various well known psychologists-ergonomists that belong to the prominent researchers in subjects such as human performance theory, sensory perception, human memory, or motor skills. Paul Fitts was one of the founding fathers of human engineering, he was also prominent in human performance theory. The same can be said of researchers such as Mackworth, Broadbent, Welford, Baddeley, Poulton and Moray who are all dominant British investigators in applied as well as basic experimental psychology in Britain. It is also true for prominent younger investigators such as Schneider and Wickens from Illinois and Gopher from Haifa. Many psychologists-ergonomists are researchers in the field of experimental psychology. This is usually not the case for industrial psychologists who are faremost practitioners. And when industrial psychologists carry out research it is usually not connected to basic issues in personality and social psychology. Rather the aims are directed towards the construction of selection batteries and towards direct problems in social structures of the organisation. I may add that the ergonomist is found much more frequently in the laboratory than the industrial psychologist. Usually he is employed by research departments and not by direct consulting sections. Within the same organisation the industrial psychologist and the ergonomist are found at very different spots.

This general state of affairs led a prominent industrial psychologist, upon hearing about my appointment as professor in industrial psychology to remark that "he is not an industrial psychologist but an experimental psychologist who has also carried out some applied projects." And she was right!

Let me summarize the contexts issue before turning to the conflicts. The differences concern issues like general vs differential psychology and individual skills vs social relations. Further on there are differences in the extent of interdisciplinary interaction, interest in basic research, and, finally, there is a difference in emphasis with respect to either laboratory or field orientation. All these issues are sources for differences and conflicts.

It could be argued that they are sufficiently large to set ergonomics and industrial psychology altogether apart. Yet, this should not be recommended. Instead it should be realised that despite the differences in background and point of view, ergonomists and industrial psychologists have a lot of common interests that deserve contact rather than conflict - What are possible sources of conflict?

A first possible source of conflict concerns the analysis of actual tasks and skills. The ergonomist attempts to shape the task demands so that they are well within human limits and so that, at least ideally, selection and training are minimal. The industrial psychologist, on the other hand, is primarily interested in selecting the successful from the unsuccessful. There are additional interests, of course, relating to organisational structure, work satisfaction etc. where ergonomists and industrial psychologists have strong common interests and complementary know-how. And with regard to the problem of human factoring vs selection the conflict could also easily turn into cooperation. A good example of the issue concerns the developments in air-traffic control. In the pre-radar days this was a most difficult task, with many elements of bad human factoring. In fact, air traffic control consisted of a kind of three dimensional problem solving in order to avoid collisions between aircrafts. The only visual aid was a set of strips, listing which aircrafts were under control or about to come under control. The strip listed speed, direction, altitude, and destination. A major problem was the pronounced short-term retention demands in keeping track of the several flights at once. This could only be reduced by, literally, rote learning of flight patterns that recurred daily. Very many student controllers failed during the on-the-job-training in which elementary requirements like practising strategies and knowledge of results were absent. The best type of selection test, although not highly predictive, was some test of keeping track of multiple dynamic processes, as studied by Yntema (1967).

A first technological development concerned the introduction of raw radar and some forms of collision avoidance planning by computer. The enormous advantage of the computer over man with regard to short-term storage and updating of information was well realized at that time. Yet, raw radar and planning had not removed the memory problem altogether. There remained the problem that radar blips had to be identified and controlled for altitude by sheer memory. The reduction came much later when synthetic radar allowed representation of the major parameters on the screen. Since then, the controlling task is a visual search for conflicts but without a considerable memory load.

Thus the task has changed considerably and, if the traffic volume had remained the same, it would be a trivial one, well within the potential skills of very many. But the traffic volume has increased, so that there are still always bottlenecks. Yet they are of a nature that is very different from two decades ago. The example of the air-traffic control is described so far as a story of technology and improved man–machine communication. But there are many consequences for industrial psychologists. Thus the selection tests and training procedures have to be changed, since the nature of the task has become so different. And, of course, there is more to it. Problems of reluctance to accept change, to loose an existing skill, to start all over again, and to loose prestige, are all important to industrial psychologists and therefore industrial psychologists are badly needed. Hence a strong argument in favour of cooperation and contact with ergonomists. A common approach of ergonomists, psychologists, interested in selection and training, and organisational psychologists is required.

A second source of conflict and contact concerns the growing interest of industrial psychologists for experimental paradigms that have been investigated during the last decades in human performance theory. The question is whether versions of such paradigms are suitable for selection purposes. This is an obvious contact; the conflict is due to hesitation from ergonomists with regard to this type of application. On the one hand the hesitation is due to a lack of experience with individual differences; on the other hand to doubts about the extent that results obtained in simple paradigms can be generalized to real life skills (e.g. Sanders, 1984).

A good example of a profitable use of experimental paradigms for industrial psychology is the dichotic listening paradigm, originally designed by Broadbent (1954) to study selective attention in multi-channel listening of aircraft pilots. In a dichotic listening task two streams of data are simultaneously presented, one stream to the left and one stream to the right ear. There are numerous experimental variations with regard to the actual task but a common finding is that focussing attention to one ear seriously affects detection of targets at the other ear, in particular when a person is actually involved in acting and responding. Another common feature is that it takes a non-negligible time to shift attention from one to the other ear. That is to say that when a subject is signalled to shift focus optimum efficiency is not immediately attained.

Such results belong to the core data of emerging concepts about select-ive attention. In itself, this might not evoke direct interest of industrial psychologists. The dichotic listening task became interest-ing, however, when it turned out that individual differences in shifting efficiency proved to be a good predictor of pilot's success in training (North and Gopher, 1976). In the same way there has been ongoing work on continuing memory, namely on processes involved in updating dynamic processes in memory and keeping track of several variables at the same time. Again, a matter of academic interest in the study of the relations between memory and attention. It became relevant to industrial psycho-logy when recent studies showed a relation between final success and continuing memory proficiency during early practice in diving. That is to say, that when trainees in early diving trials had to combine the diving with continuing memory, their performance in continuous memory was a good predictor (Jorna, 1981).

These successful uses are presently the main impetus for developing testbatteries derived from experimental paradigms. Examples are the so called "ten tasks" plan that is currently developed at the Institute for Perception at Soesterberg and the "criterion task set" from Wright-Patterson in the USA.

The source of conflict between ergonomists and industrial psychologists with regard to this development was already briefly touched upon: it is the fear of premature generalisation from simple laboratory tests to complex real life settings. Industrial psychologists traditionally suffer less from such theoretical arguments. "Once a good predictor has been established, why bother about its background?" Although I think that not all industrial psychologists would subscribe this view, there remains a difference in theoretical emphasis.

As an applied experimental psychologist I will attempt to elaborate on the ergonomist's point of view, and try to conclude this address with some alternative lines of approach. Let me start by saying that, despite the positive examples of dichotic listening and continuing memory, there have been also very disappointing experiences in the attempts to generalize from simple laboratory studies to real life skills. I have discussed the problems underlying these disappointments in my keynote address to the 10th Attention and Performance Symposium (Sanders, 1984). In summary, it boils down to the problem of communality or, better, of the lack of communality in cue utilisation in the experiment and in real life. There are classical examples, even in sensory domains, where test and real life diverge to the extent that the test is a bad predictor. I may refer to two classical examples. First the hemianopic patient who nevertheless had an accident free record of many years. Yet his driver's license was suspended once th hemianopia was discovered in the laborato-ry. It is impossible to drive without proper peripheral vision, and yet it appears to be possible! (Vos, 1974). The other example is the one-eyed crane operator who was excluded from his job because of deficient depth perception. Yet he had been performing well so far.

I think I have made the issue clear: If even sensory tests can fail in predicting complex real life performance – and sensory functions seem to be conditio-sine-qua-non! – what can be expected from relations between much less well established tests concerning selective attention and choice reaction processes on the one hand and flying or busdriving at the other hand? This is the main fear underlying the opposition of ergonomists when invited to apply their paradigms to selection.

Summarizing so far, there are at least two areas of contact or conflict: The first was concerned with different views with respect to selection vs human factoring. The second was concerned with different views concerning the use of paradigms from applied experimental psychology. I think there is a third area of contact or conflict concerned with the ultimate aims: The final aim of the experimental ergonomist is to build and construct sufficiently detailed and general theories about human performance to abolish experiments altogether and to recommend from his knowledge rather than from empirical search. Let me give some examples, derived from the areas of psychophysics and memory: In the Netherlands a new 2 1/2 guilders coin was introduced that at first created great confusion with the 1 guilder coin. Although relative discrimination was easy, an absolute discrimination turned out to be quite hard. This is not surprising when considering Weber's law, and I am convinced that many errors are still always occuring. Psychologists were not consulted when the coin was designed. In this respect the British did better when designing their pence coins. The different shape of the 50 p coin makes it easy to discriminate. The important thing is that the recommendation does not need research, a demonstration sufficed.

A second example concerns the design of number plates on cars. I remember I wrote the recommendation in two days when a new system was needed in the Netherlands. What would your prefer? Six digits? Six letters? Alternating digits and letters? Two groups of three digits and letters? Two letters followed by two digits and, then, again by two letters? Empirically it turns out that the first three solutions are about equally bad and inferior to the last two. Why is this? It turns out that, at least for this type of problem, the internal representations of letters and digits can be considered as distinct coding systems with stronger mutual intra relations than inter relations. The consequence is that if there are too many intra relations mutual interference builds up quite rapidly. On the other hand if there are only inter relations all connections are weak. The best solution is a combination of intra and inter relations to avoid the weakness of both. That means: Three letters followed by three digits or, second best, a 2-2-2 system.

It may seem that this ideal to apply theory to practice is at odds with the earlier discussed hesitations to use experimental paradigms as selection aids. I think, indeed, that the ergonomist follows a double logic of trust and distrust in his own tools, that may easily confuse the industrial psychologist. The one side of the logic is that knowledge should be applied as long as there is reasonable certainty about the ecological validity. The other side of the logic is that knowledge should not be applied as long as artifacts are likely to prevail. More research – and that should be predominantly basic research – is needed to learn about which cues people develop in real life that are absent in tests. This seems to be the only means of penetrating more deeply into the analysis of work and performance.

In my opinion simulations of real life performance constitute excellent tools for such analyses and for breaking down the components of human skills in various types of tasks.

It is my feeling that the area of task analysis and simulation is again an area of common ground to ergonomists and industrial psychologists. An area, also, where the conflict can be solved and turned into contact. There are various related areas such as stress research, work motivation, and environmental conditions that are of interest to both the ergonomist and the industrial psychologist.

Let me end with a final summary and a prospect at the beginning of this meeting with sessions on human factors as well as on typical industrial psychology: There are considerable differences in context that may easily lead to conflicts. They relate to differences in basic interests as well as in the primary aims of research and goals. Yet, I think that the existing common grounds and contacts should be elaborated and lead to a better mutual understanding. The common ground is sufficiently large to require cooperation to the benefit of both areas of psychology. The greatest error to be made would be to leave the field altogether to engineering. This is a realistic danger, more so in continental Europe than in the Anglosaxon world. Leaving the field to engineering would, first, increase the communication problems between psychologists and ergonomists, and, secondly, would take away an essential dimension of human factors research. It is the dimension of understanding human behavior which is the heart of all psychology, whatever its difference in interest may be.

REFERENCES

(1) Broadbent, D.E. (1954). The role of auditory localisation in attention and memory span. Journal of Experimental Psychology, 47, 191-196.
(2) Conrad, R. and Hull, A.J. (1964). Information, acoustic confusion and memory span. British Journal of Psychology, 55, 429-432.
(3) Crowder, R. and Morton, J. (1969). Precategorical acoustic storage (PAS). Perception and Psychophysics, 5, 365-373.
(4) Jorna, P.G.A.M. (1981). Stress, information processing and diving. IZF-Report, 1981-4.
(5) McCormick, E. (1957). Human Engineering. Mc Graw-Hill, New York.
(6) North, R.A. and Gopher, D. (1976). Measures of attention as predictors of flight performance. Human Factors, 18, 1-14.
(7) Sanders, A.F. (1984). Ten symposia on Attention and Performance. In: H. Bouma & D. Bouwhuis: Attention and Performance X. Erlbaum, Hillsdale, N.J.
(8) Vos, J.J. (1974). Over het verkeersgedrag van een man met uitval van de rechterehelft van het gezichtsveld aan beide ogen. IZF rapport, 1974-3.
(9) Tiffin, J. (1952). Industrial Psychology. McGraw Hill, New York.
(10) Yntema, D. and Schulman, G.M. (1967). Response selection in keeping track of several things at once. Acta Psychologica, 27, 325-332.

THE PSYCHOLOGY OF WORK AND ORGANIZATION
G. Debus and H.-W. Schroiff (Editors)
© Elsevier Science Publishers B.V. (North-Holland), 1986

AT THE CROSSROADS: AN EXAMINATION OF CONTENT AND VALUES
OF ORGANIZATION PSYCHOLOGY

Frank HELLER

Tavistock Institute of Human Relations
The Tavistock Centre
Belsize Lane London NW3 5BA

I sense that this West European conference on the pychology of Work and
Organization seeks to establish an important break with the past and I
hope that what I will say may contribute to this objective.

The debate on values, content and methods of psychology has gone on for
a long time but I believe that we have now arrived at a watershed which
requires a reexamination of received wisdoms.

Organizational psychology has lost much ground -- compared with other
sciences -- during the last three decades and we must take some time off
to question why this has happened. I say that we have lost much ground,
I mean that our work has received much less attention among potential
users and particularly among policy makers that it deserves. Other
voices have been clearer and addressed themselves to more relevant
issues.

Secondly and independently of this, Western European Psychology has
opportunities which it has yet to grasp fully. For very understandable
reasons, we have since 1945 been very strongly influenced by American
organizational psychology even when -- as I will show -- European
problems are often different from those across the Atlantic.

To sustain such broad generalizations would require a very extensive
review of the whole field covered by our discipline, but I will content
myself with some examples and a few suggestions. Inevitably they will be
influenced by my own experience. The comments will relate to three
overlapping topics. Firstly, fields of work for psychologists. I will
suggest that we have concentrated on an unnecessarily restricted area.
Secondly, values. Partly because of the limited topics of investigation
which we have pursued, and because many psychologists are employed by
companies, value orientations have been somewhat one sided and this has
reduced its policy relevance for the wider community. Yet in spite of
having a strong company focus, our work is not always taken very
seriously even within organizations. Thirdly, our choice of methods is
as limited as the scope of subjects of investigation and not well
adapted to modern needs.

The overlap between these three topics can be illustrated by my first
example. Psychologists working on organizational problems have inherited
a legacy for micro-level preferences; there is a long tradition of
research on areas like selection, training, labour turnover, morale,
incentive schemes and performance assessment. These and similar topics
tend to be treated as self-contained issues, confined to certain levels
of organization. The usual stimulus for these areas of work comes form
managerial preoccupations and is embedded in managerial values. The
usual objective is to increase intra organizational efficiency and this

almost automatically selects our criterion variable. The methods used to attack these micro level problems, tend to be written instruments like tests, questionnaires and interview schedules administered cross sectionally. Of course there are exceptions; labour turnover research for instance may entail several cross sectional slices.
There is nothing whatsoever wrong with these fields of work unless they were to exert a dominant influence on our field in the 1980s and 1990s. Such a restricted perspective would severely limit the intellectual development of our discipline. It would also reduce our ability to influence the well being of organizations in Western Europe.

If we look at the programme of the present conference we see that the winds of change are already blowing strongly. Allow me to add a little more velocity in the same direction.

I will use labour turnover as my first example. Until quite recently a company-based micro level focus saw labour turnover as a cost and therefore asked psychologists to find ways of reducing it. Today, of course, many organizations pay large sums of money to get rid of people, though it seems that they don't need psychologists to help them do it. In the 1960s and 70s when unemployment was low and dynamic companies urgently needed more employees, traditional organizations did not want to lose their staff. This was quite understandable even if they could not provide the same financial and promotion opportunities as their competitors. Psychologists as researchers or consultants were asked to deal with this problem. At the same time however, economists and sociologists looking at the same phenomenon from a macro perspective called it "labour mobility" and said that this was a highly desirable feature for a healthy economic system. Who was right?

In spite of a frightening level of unemployment in Europe today, there are still large pockets of labour shortages. This suggests to me that issues like training, labour turnover and incentives require a macro as well as a micro theoretical framework. Such a dual framework would also benefit from considering environmental factors like the fluctuations of economic climate, and a longitudinal rather than a cross sectional methodology (Levy-Leboyer, 1982).

My second preoccupation concerns values. Over the last decades, psychologists have made great strides to rebut the frequent accusation of bias. We have been accused of operating within a managerial value stance and the micro level focus I mentioned earlier contributed to this criticism (Baritz, 1960). Western European psychologists have done better than our American colleagues in this respect but we still have some way to go. Of course other social science disciplines, notably sociology, have sometimes shown at least as much bias, and economics has suffered grievously by being split into two ideologically opposed camps, barely on speaking terms with each other. The problems of other disciplines, however, do not absolve us from the responibility of facing up to this issue.

Organizational psychology has shown little interest in trade union topics and indeed in the whole area of industrial relations. Again there are a few notable exceptions (for instance Stephenson & Brotherton (1979)) but most of the work in this area -- particularly in Britain -- has been left to specialists who tend to have labour economics or sociology as a starting discipline. This has had two consequences. Firstly, very little organizational research has operated in areas of special interest to trade unions. The Scandinavian countries are exceptions. Secondly, particularly in Britain the industrial relations discipline has taken as uncritical a position vis-a-vis trade unions as psychology has taken vis-a-vis management. This has been bad for both disciplines and has not helped the interested parties.

All academic disciplines are expected to take a critical look at the phenomenon under investigation, to have original ideas, to find intellectually satisfying solutions for old problems and to go beyond the mere description of the status quo. Industrial relations research has not done this very well. At least in Britain it has rarely questioned trade union philosophy and practices which have changed very little since the early part of the 19th century, even though the socio-economic environment has undergone radical restructuring. The basic institution for solving all problems and improving the conditions of workers is still thought to be collective bargaining and no alternative to this ancient practice has been seriously considered. Nor has there been any attempt to investigate the value of alternative structural arrangements for trade union representation. The fact that industrial relations academics have tended to adopt the value position of the trade unions and reserved their critical evaluation for governments and employers has not helped trade union members in Britain to improve their standard of living compared with other European countries like the Netherlands, Scandinavia or Germany.

This particular example of ineffective academic bias may have special relevance for Britain. However with the possible exception of the Oslo Work Research Institute and the more recently set up Stockholm Work Investigation Centre, trade union issues have not received a great deal of attention from psychologists in Western Europe -- and one could add that most of the staff working in these two institutions would not describe themselves as psychologists.

It is possible that in neglecting industrial relations as a field of activity we have followed the American academic tradition. It must be remembered however that while the number of union members in the US has now declined to less than 20%, in Western Europe it is at least twice as strong and in some countries reached over 80% of the work force. There are other differences between Western Europe and the United States which we should recognize. What can be called organizational democracy in Europe is strongly influenced by a long series of legislative measures dating back to 1950 which require organizations above a certain size to set up structures for communication and influence sharing, giving worker representatives specific rights and in some cases allowing codetermination up to board room level. The European Economic Community is struggling to achieve harmonization of these West European initiatives.

In the United States there are no equivalent provisions and no equivalent motivations. Instead there are a large variety of voluntary practices usually treated under headings like participation and leadership styles which require a different research approach. There are important differences of tradition which affect multinational as well as national companies in Europe. It is probably no accident that we have here no large body of research to compare with the extensive American literature on leadership. This came out very clearly in a recent cross national conference where Americans dissatisfied with their own progress in this field came to Europe to see what alternatives are pursued here (Hunt et al., 1984).

A brief word about methods may be relevant here. Psychologists can be justly proud of the quality of methodological training most degree courses give. But using appropriate methods does not always follow easily from this training. We still use predominantly parametric techniques on ordinal scales and curvilinear variables and we assume that cross sectional data can adequately represent complex processes like leadership, decision making, job design changes, and even our much beloved job satisfaction criterion variable.

Let us look at this outcome variable for a moment. In cross sectional research we often measure job satisfaction on a particular day of the week. Our standard reliability criterion requires that the day is irrelevant. To be reliable, a job satisfaction measurement on a Monday morning should be the same as on Friday afternoon. But is it? If it is not, does it destroy our measure or does it increase its face validity? If we really get more or less the same answer on a Monday and Friday with employees engaged on routine undemanding work, this may simply hide an insensitivity of our measure. It is no answer to point to some apparent validity correlation coefficient to support the retention of a measurement of satisfaction since such a relationship measure rarely accounts for more than 10% of the variance and we usually do not know what the error variance is due to. In recent cross national research we have found general satisfaction measures to be fairly meaningless (IDE, 1981) but in longitudinal research a measure of "satisfaction with the process of decision making" and a later measure of "satisfaction with the outcome" yielded interesting, interpretable results (DIO in press).

The future lies firmly with non parametric methods and longitudinal research designs. My own experience over the years also suggests that we will do much better with appropriate in depth assessments whether qualitative or quantitative; and why not both at the same time?

There is much room for imaginative new ideas here. Apart from increasing the validity of our conclusions, there is evidence from research to suggest that traditional methods do not lead to policy applications while other methods do (Van der Vall, 1977, 1980).

I now return to the delicate issue of values. The socio-political climate in Western Europe shows great diversity and changes over time. Nevertheless, its experiences during two world wars, its emphasis on welfare and legislative provision as well as the growing importance of the European Economic Community influence values. The so-called work ethic which is said to have begun in Europe in the 15th and 16th century (Weber, 1930, Tawney, 1926) accompanied by changes in religious doctrines, is now much stronger in the United States than in Europe and it is stronger still in Japan (Mow, 1985 in press).

These value differences which have been well documented in cross national studies (Inglehart, 1977, Verba, 19XX) are very important for organizational psychology but it is easy to draw false conclusions from them. There is a current trend, particularly strong in the United States, to admire the Japanese work ethic and accompanying organization practices and build them up as ideal types to be emulated whenever possible. Psychologists have led the way with a considerable literature on "work commitment", "corporate loyalty" and "attachment to work" (Dubin, 1976; Steers, 1977, Russell, 1980, Rowan, 1981, Morrow, 1983; Salancik, 1983).

I do not believe that this recent trend in work commitment and loyalty research is congruent with West European values. Paternalism was well established in central Europe before 1939, but has been severely criti- cised and has now largely disappeared. Work commitment comes easily and naturally in some types of work, particularly in the professions which are characterized by substantial amounts of autonomy but it is unnatural to expect it in routine mass production work with a cycle of 30 seconds repeated throughout an 8 hour day and a 39 hour week. Even modern white collar work on desk top computers staring at green video screens unin- terruptedly for a full working day, processing material of no great interest to the operator is unlikely to induce loyalty.

In any case as scientists we should differentiate between legitimately different types of commitment. One can be committed to a skill or craft and to the work itself; a surgeon or a carpenter might have this kind of commitment. Secondly one could be committed to the users of ones work; teachers for instance can be committed to their pupils. And a garage mechanic repairing a fractured dual breaking system on a car may be committed to producing a safe product for his client. Finally, a person may be committed to the organization he works in. It is this organiza- tional commitment which takes up the bulk of the literature today -- and in the world's best selling book on organization: "In Search of Excellence: Lessons from America's Best Run Companies" (Peters & Water- man, 1982), commitment fostered by good old fashioned human relations techniques, shines through as the normative prescription.

In the almost religious fervour with which these values are pursued, nobody seems to notice that the three types of commitment I have men- tioned may be in serious conflict with each other. Should we take sides on which commitment orientation is better? Better for whom we might well ask? But this raises the controversial question of the criterion variable. Whose benefits are we trying to maximize?

Let us look at the case of a surgeon. He may consider that his primary responsibility is to improve the techniques of transplant operations. To achieve this objective he may have to use up much more scarce resour- ces than the employing hospital can afford. If he is loyal to his hospital he will give up his pioneering work. If he is attached to his discipline, he will change hospitals. Which outcome well benefit the wider community? Or take the case of the motor mechanic. He is highly skilled and can repair a faulty gear box by using only a small number of new parts. Alternatively he can ask his assistant to draw from the store a complete new gear box which can be installed without using much skill. The garage wants him to use new parts yielding a substantially higher return. At least three values or loyalties are now involved. Loyalty towards his professional skill versus loyalty towards his employing company. But there is also the question of the customer who may get a better deal from the repair than the replacement. If the spare part is imported from abroad, there is also the issue of loyalty to your own economic system. Although it is true that our sphere of operation is work and organizations, it does not follow that we must exclude the wider polity within which organizations function. We must not be tempted to oversimplify a complex multivalued phenomenon by the beguilingly simple term "attachment to work". The authors of "In Search of Excellence" and its sister volume "The Art of Japanese Management" (Pascale und Athos, 1981) are not psychologists but they are the product of major business schools which teach our subject and my recent teaching experience in the States leads me to believe that the undeniable Japanese business success is making its impact on psychology on both sides of the Atlantic. We are not paying enough attention to research which suggests that many highly praised Japanese practices do not travel well across large cultural distances and like some vines do not bear fruit in foreign soils (see Cole, 1979, Durlabhji, 1983; Seth, 1984).

It is also a little ironical and maybe sad to see that the recent Quality Circle movement is associated with Japan when, I believe, its origin can be traced back to work in the British Midlands in the late 1940s (Scott & Lynton, 1952) and to later theoretical and applied work on semi-autonomous groups in Norway and Sweden (Herbst, 1962). It has of course been adapted and improved in Japan but it is a pity that these psychological approaches to organizational effectiveness were not further developed in Europe either by our discipline or by management. The gap of over 30 years has been a loss for organizational effectiveness. If it is true that Japanese market penetration is in fact due to group decision methods like "quality circles" then this tardiness may have had an impact -- however small -- on European competitiveness.

We should not miss other opportunities. The codetermination movement which started in both Germany and Yugoslavia in the early 1950s received very little attention from psychologists for two decades. The problems raised by immigrant labour was often left to sociologists. The identification by economists of a dual labour market in the late 1960s has not been pursued by psychologists although our skills in this field of analysis were relevant (Piore, 1972, Bosanquet & Doeringer, 1973). The insidious growth of unemployment in Western Europe has only recently interested a handful of psychologists in Europe (for instance Warr, 1984) although important pioneering work in this field was done in Austria by a group including a psychologist in the 1930s (Jahoda, 1972). The related field of work creation research is not strongly pursued (Jackson & Hanby, 1979) and the fascinating problem of the black economy and its socio-psychological repercurssions is left to Economists (for instance Feige, 1981).

The impact of new technologies on the nature of work is another somewhat neglected field (but see Mumford, 1981, 1983) and very little work, apart from advertising psychology, has been done on the important relationship between producers and consumers. I am sure that there are many other new or relatively new areas for organizational psychologists to explore. One urgent topic is the impact of "distant working". Some organizations like Rank Xerox in my country have encouraged a few of their highly skilled and motivated staff to give up normal full time relations with their employers in exchange for a part-time contract to carry out quite similar work on a project basis from their homes or from some other regional office (Heller, 1984, Holt & Stern, 1984). If distant working were to spread it could have a significant -- but as yet unknown impact -- on the individual, the local community as well as the family. It is a form of decentralization which modern computer and communication technology could facilitate. But at what psychological costs?

Looking through the topics offered by the scientific programme of this conference, one realizes that organizational psychology is on the point of breaking out into exciting new fields. Western European psychologists have -- it seems to me -- special opportunities and special responsibilities. We live in a part of the world in which pluralism of values is much more in evidence than elsewhere. As a consequence, we can engage with the many-faceted reality of our social environment.

I started out by saying that organizational psychology has lost much ground over the last three decades and I gave some reasons why this happened. Of course, I am aware that the relative position of our discipline vis-a-vis other social sciences has not been established scientifically. Even so; that is to say if this part of my argument is not acceptable to some of you, the main thrust of my proposition can stand on its own.

There are, I believe, very substantial untapped opportunities for psychologists interested in organizations, industrial relations and the increasingly complex issues surrounding work, unemployment, the impact of new technologies and the challenge of multinational companies operating in distinctly different cultures, political systems and ethical climates.

Some of these issues have special significance for Europe and I hope that this conference of Western Psychologists will explore very carefully which issues now require our urgent attention. There is no denying that within Europe too there are interesting legal and historical differences and this requires cross national comparisons and therefore collaboration between European scientific institutions. Cross national comparisons provide very worth-while personal learning opportunities and they are also very relevant for policy making.
While unemployment remains a major challenge for Europe there should be no shortage of work opportunity in our field, as long as we make our skills relevant for the period in which we live.

REFERENCES

(1) Baritz, L.: Servants of Power, Weslyan Connecticut, University Press, 1960.
(2) Bonsanquet, N. & Doehringer, P.B.: Is There a Dual Labour Market in Britain, Economic Journal, June 1973.
(3) Cole, R.: Work, Mobility and Participation: A Comparative Study of American and Japanese Industry, Berkeley, University of California Press, 1979.
(4) D.I.O.: Decisions in Organizations, Journal of Occupational Psychology, 1983, 56, 1-18.
(5) Dubin, R. Hedley, A. & Traveggia, Th.: Attachment to Work, In: Dubin R. (Ed.), Handbook of Work Organization & Society, Rand Mc Nally, 1976.
(6) Durlabhji, S.: Japanese-Style American Management: Primary Relations and Social Organization, Human Relations, 1983, 36, 827-840.
(7) Feige, E.: The UK's Unobserved Economy: A Preliminary Assessment, Journal of Economic Affairs, 1981, Vol. 1, No. 4, 205-212.
(8) Herbst, P.G.: Autonomous Group Functioning, London, Tavistock Publications, 1962.
(9) Heller, F., Karapin, R. & Acuna, E.: How Technology Affects the

Quality of Employment, Part 2 Position Paper for Work and Society, Case Study Evidence and Example, Institute of Manpower Studies, University of Sussex, 1984.

(10) Holti, R. & Stern, E.: Social Aspects of New Information Technology in the UK, Tavistock Institute of Human Relations, August 1984.

(11) Hunt, J., Hosking, D., Schriesheim, Ch. & Stewart, R. (Eds.): Leaders and Managers, International Perspectives on Managerial Behaviour and Leadership, Pergamon Press, New York, 1984.

(12) IDE: Industrial Democracy in Europe International Group, Industrial Democracy in Europe, Oxford, Clarendon Press, 1981.

(13) Inglehart, R.: The Silent Revolution, Princeton, New Jersey, Prentice-Hall, 1977.

(14) Jackson, M.P. & Hanby, V. J.B.: Work Creation: International Experience, Gower Press, 1979.

(15) Jahoda, M., Lazarsfeld, P. & Zeisal, H.: Marienthal: The Sociography of an Unemployed Community, London, Tavistock, 1972.

(16) Levy-Leboyer, C.: Psychology and Environment, Beverly Hills, Sage Publications, 1982 (original French 1979).

(17) Morrow, P.C.: Concept of Redundancy in Organizational Research: The Case of Work Commitment, Academy of Management Journal, 1983, 8, 486-500.

(18) Mumford, E.: Participative System Design: Structure and Method, In: Systems, Objectives and Solutions, Amsterdam, North Holland, 1981.

(19) Mumford, E.: Participative Systems Design: Practice and Theory, Journal of Occupational Behaviour, 1983, 4, 47-57.

(20) Pascale, R. & Athos, A.: The Art of Japanese Management, London, Allen Lane, 1982.

(21) Peters, Th. & Waterman, R.Jr.: In Search of Excellence: Lessons from America's Best Run Companies, New York, Harper & Row, 1982.

(22) Piore, M.S.: Notes for a Theory of Labour Market Stratification, Working Paper 95, Department of Economics, Cambridge Mass, MIT Press, 1972.

(23) Rowan, R.: Rekindling Corporate Loyalty, Fortune, Feb. 9, 1981, pp. 54-58.

(24) Russell, K.: The Orientation to Work Controversy and the Social Construction of Work Value Systems, Journal of Management Studies, 1980, 17, 164-184.

(25) Salancik, G.: Commitment and the Control of Organizational Behavior, In: Barry Straw (Ed.), Psychological Foundations of Organizational Behavior, (2nd edition), Scott Foresman & Co., 1983.

(26) Scott, J. & Lynton, R.P.: Three Studies in Management, London, Routledge and Kegan Paul, 1952.

(27) Seth, P., Namiki, N. & Swanson, C.: The False Promise of the Japanese Miracle, Boston, Pitman, 1984.

(28) Steer, R.M.: Antecednets and Outcomes of Organizational Commitment, Administrative Science Quaterly, Vol. 22, 46-56, 1977.

(29) Tawney, R.: Religion and the Rise of Capitalism, Mass. Peter Smith, 1926.

(30) Van de Vall, M. & Bolas, Ch.: Policy Research as an Agent of Planned Social Intervention: An Evaluation of Methods, Standards, Data and Analytic Techniques, Sociological Practice, 2, 77-95, 1977.

(31) Van de Vall, M. & Bolas, Ch.: Applied Social Discipline Research or Social Policy Research: the Emergence of a Professional Paradigm in Sociological Research, American Sociologist, 15, 128-137. 1980.

(32) Weber, M.: The Protestant Ethic and the Spirit of Capitalism, London, George Allen & Unwin, 1930.

THE PSYCHOLOGY OF WORK AND ORGANIZATION
G. Debus and H.-W. Schroiff (Editors)
© *Elsevier Science Publishers B.V. (North-Holland), 1986*

COMPLETE VS. INCOMPLETE WORKING TASKS
- A CONCEPT AND ITS VERIFICATION -

Winfried HACKER

Technische Universität Dresden
Sektion Arbeitswissenschaften
Mommsenstr. 13
DDR-8027 Dresden, German Democratic Republic

1. FLEXIBLE AUTOMATION - A NEW CHALLENGE TO PSYCHOLOGY

For several reasons, the modern flexible computer-aided production techniques constitute also a challenge to psychology. One important resaon concerns the most favourable margins offered by them for the designing of work activities which are efficient as well as conducive to health and personality-promoting. This is possible due to the higher flexibility with smaller series of products having high quotas of renewal and due to the dependence of these technical systems on highly skilled workers who are able to learn and know how to utilize the plants in an optimum way. Flexible automation is connected with highly qualified work.

Job design more and more means the designing of information-processing cognitive processes and of social processes and less and less only the reduction of the expenditure of physical energy and motion rationaliz-ation. Therefore, job design becomes increasingly a psychological problem. Where psychology does not take up this challenge, there cogni-tive ergonomics or software-ergonomics try to close the gap originating.

Psychology requires unambiguous goal conceptions for the timely and purposive using of the new margins of design. What should be achieved when computer-aided working processes are designed for production, pre-paration of production, administration or service sectors? The psycholo-gical conceptions of goals must relate to the desired work activities, especially to their mental regulation and its interrelations with per-sonality features. Psychological contributions to the designing of machines or implements and of the programmes pertinent to them have effects on human beings via the resulting work activities and their demands. Psychological contributions to the development of organization are effective via the resulting work activities; work activities are taught by new training methods, the qualification for work activities is examined by ability tests - provided that the respective activities will be worthy of human beings to such a degree that for them a training or a selection is justified. To put it briefly: the common denominator of the most important psychological tasks is the analysis, evaluation and designing of work activities and of the conditions for executing them. Thus, the question arises about the desired properties of the work activities of individuals, groups and organizational units.

2.   PSYCHOLOGICAL GOALS GUIDING THE DESIGN OF WORKING PROCESSES

Working processes always have a double result: They generate products or
services and thereby they change the working man. They may motivate him,
may stimulate him to learn, may impart transferable abilities to him,
may stabilize his emotionality and mental health or they may de-
motivate, de-skill and impair well-being and health.

For us the most general aim consists in the designing of work activities
and the working conditions in such a way that they will be at the same
time as efficient as possible _and_ contribute to the stabilization of
health _and_ to the development of personality. This threefold aim has to
be differentiated and to be rendered more concrete by valid methods of
investigation, criteria of evaluation and aids for design in order to
make it useful for practice.

We use a system of four hierarchically ordered levels of evaluation, to
which sublevels and evaluation methods and partly also rules of evaluation can be assigned.

Evaluation begins with the question concerning the _feasibility_ of a job.
There is tested whether the required activity can be performed at all
for a long period of time in accordance with the demands. Not infrequently, however, jobs are designed which are too demanding for the
human senses or the cognitive capacity. Moreover, work activities have
to be _innocuous_. With a sufficient degree of probability there have to
be excluded accidents and occupational diseases as well as an increased
general sickness rate of a physical and psychosomatic type.

In addition to that, work activities have to be _free_ _from_ _impairments_.
This demand implies that the work activities and the conditions of their
execution do not cause any disturbances for the worker which - though
not yet having the character of a disease - would impair the worker's
physical and mental well-being and thus the efficiency of work. There
should be ruled out any level of stress due to work in the sense of a
fearful experience of threat, of mental satiation and of the experiencing of monotony as well as unreasonable degrees of mental fatigue. This
alone does not suffice, however: Moreover, activities which are free
from impairments should stabilize mental health and provide opportunities for _personality_ _promotion_. In this context, personality promotion
is understood as the acquisition of personality-central abilities and
attitudes. Therefore, the work activities should not only rule out any
de-skilling but should provide a learning potential for the whole
professional life.

What do these aims of the designing of - as we call them - progressive
work activities have to do with efficiency? By efficiency we designate
an efficiency/yield ratio which integrates also - inter alia - yields
from high quality and flexibility and expenditures or losses due to
diseases, required new engagements at turnover of labour or even losses
caused by poor motivation. We think we are able to prove that due to
computer-aided production techniques a high level of efficiency can be
ensured in the best way just by the designing of work activities which
are feasible, free from risks for health and impairments as well as
conducive to health and personality-promoting. A high efficiency can be
achieved not in spite of, but with the aid of progressively designed
work activities.

The margin of design for the activity features which are desired from the viewpoint of psychology is the wider, the earlier psychological targets are introduced into designing. When all technological stipulations have been made, the machines have been installed, the programmes have been fixed and the workplaces have been prepared and equipped, then it is too late for many proposals concerning desired features of activities. This subsequent, correcting job design will be less effective than the projecting job design for the future performed during the planning of new working processes. The novel feature in this is that not – as having been done for a long time – machines, tools and programmes are designed from which work activities result almost as a by-product whose properties were not aimed at in a purposive way. Rather, together with the technological solutions there are designed equivalent work activities having desired features for which – if necessary – the required organizational solutions or means of work have to be created. Thus, the straight-forward design procedure governed by a mis-guiding technological determinism should be replaced by an iterative and participative design procedure following socio-technological objectives.

For the greater co-operation of psychologists in the projecting of future work activities with desired features, two requirements have to be met in advance: It should be made clear to engineers that by many apparently purely technical decisions in reality they decide on the features of future work activities of human beings. Occupational diseases, boredom, pressure of time or, on the other hand, opportunities for learning and intrinsic work motivation are constructed and organized to a decisive degree. The engineer should be offered examples, fundamentals of design and aids by the psychologists. For example, such an aid is the operationalization of the outlined targets of design in concrete, engineer-adequate designable features of future work activities. We will return to that.

The psychologists themselves, however, must have means allowing them to co-operate actively in the projecting of future working systems.

3. JOB DESIGN AS THE DESIGNING OF GOAL-ORIENTED ACTIVITIES WHICH ARE REGULATED COGNITIVELY AND MOTIVATIONALLY

Today it is regarded a matter-of-course that work activities cannot be characterized satisfactorily as reactions to stimuli or as chains of motions. What else, however, is a satisfactory characterization?

Due to the societal division of labour, work activities have fundamental motivational and cognitive peculiarities compared with different activities: The needs can be met only mediated via the wage; because of economic demands the result and its consequences have to be anticipated and one has to proceed in a rational way.

Work activities are intentionally, cognitively and motivationally or volitionally regulated activities. The main chain-link of this mental regulation is represented by the workers' goals, in which the cognitive and motivational as well as volitional aspects of regulation are combined:
- The activities are guided by goals as an anticipation of the aspired future result.

- The activity is induced by goals as an intention to
  achieve the anticipated result by own efforts.
- Goals as representations of the planned result stored in
  the memory are underlying the comparison with the desired
  values and feed-back.
- Goals are starting-points for specific activity-guiding
  emotions and for the experiencing of success, failure or
  flow.
- The achieving or missing of self-set goals has a decisive
  influence on self-esteem as a personality trait.

For the regulating of complex activities it does not suffice to
establish chains of subgoals which have to be realized one after the
other. Because of the limitation of the mental capacity it is indispens-
able to combine several partial goals into one goal and to combine
several goals into one supreme goal or motive-goal. Thus, work activities are mentally regulated on several levels. Whereas for the setting
and realizing of superior goals the full, conscious devotion and controlled cognitive achievements are required, subordinate partial goals
can be treated at the periphery of consciousness and realized by
routinized or automated schemata. This hierarchy or heterarchy of goals
which are subordinate to each other together with the programmes of the
goal realization pertinent to them, however, can be implemented only
successively. Realization is possible only sequentially. Frequently,
operations serving different targets have to be nested. To put it briefly: The mental regulation of work activities is organized hierarchically
or heterarchically and sequentially; they are "nested multi-level multi-
goal" processes.

Therefore, the mental regulation of work activities may be guided by
systems of goals with different extents, may lie on different levels of
consciousness and may be realized by means of different mental processes
- from the automated recall of procedures to the solving or setting of
problems.

It is obvious that these different demands of mental regulation might
result also in different perceptions and assessments of the jobs, in
different states of well-being and amounts of intrinsic motivation as
well as - in the last analysis - in the development of different personality features. "Personality-forming forces which are inherent in the
comprehensive job tasks are not given with the less comprehensive ones,
which therefore are more lacking in wit, in the general sense of the
phrase. ... In the place of the normal self-confidence accruing from
work during which he has to bring into action all his thinking and his
total personality anew again and again gets the self-contentment - being
satisfied by a perfectly developed partial capability -, which fails to
notice the general incompleteness, since it notices only the individual
skill." (A. Schweitzer, 1971, pp. 36 - 37).

By the discrimination between mentally complete and incomplete or frag-
mented activities the attempt is made to make a differentiation concerning just this connection (proceeding from Volpert, 1976).

4. COMPLETE VS. INCOMPLETE WORKING TASKS

We have seen that work activities are organized sequentially and hierarchically.
A complete work activity is <u>cyclically</u> complete in a sequential respect.
In addition to mere execution, it comprises also
- preparatory steps (the establishing of goals, development
  of procedures, selection of expedient variants),
- steps of organization (co-ordinating with other workers)
  and
- steps of checking as a feed-back - involving comparison
  with the goals and, if necessary, corrections.

In the <u>hierarchical</u> respect, a complete activity makes demands on
different, alternating levels of mental regulation. Thus, it is confined
neither only to sensorimotor processes nor to cognitive ones. During
preparing and organizing, as a rule non-algorithmic "controlled" cognitive demands are given more freuquently than during the more routinized
or automated executing. A faulty job design produces mentally incomplete, almost partialized activities (Volpert, 1976). This is due to an
inadequate division of functions between man and machine or computer as
well as to an inefficient division of labour between workers.

Often machine operators still carry out residual functions with low
demands - as, e.g., the loading of machines - which have not been automatized, whereas potentially highly stimulating demands are transferred
to the machine or its software. For instance, many data processing
operations are executed by computers, whereas the narrow and monotonous
data input, which is only perceptively and mnestically demanding, has
remained with man.

Or: many workers perform operations which are prepared and organized -
i.e. thought over, planned, co-ordinated, decided - as well as checked
by others.

For incomplete activities there are lacking more or less the opportunities for independent goal-setting and deciding, for developing individual procedures or for sufficiently differentiated feed-backs. In particular, work activities may be incomplete with respect to one or several
of the following aspects:

1. Lack of activity
The opportunities for a sufficient autonomous activity may be reduced by
incomplete activities. The prevalence of passive monitoring is one
example of this.

2. Lack of goal-setting and deciding as well as, consequently, lack
of responsibility
Frequently there are given only restricted opportunities for independent
and therefore motivating self-set goals and thereby also for decisions
on the own approach. "If-then" connections (production rules) do not
constitute any decisions.
Therefore, also the opportunities for taking over responsibility are
insufficient: What cannot be influenced (in the sense of the concept of
control: not be "controlled"), cannot be answered for.
The independent goal-setting may be impaired also by insufficient possibilities of checking the own results of work: Without feed-back there is

no motivated pursuing of a goal.

3. Lack of demands concerning thinking
Incomplete activities offer insufficient opportunities for the cognitive preparation of work or for execution with non-algorithmic and sometimes creative demands on thinking.

4. Lack of co-operation
Co-operation is more than social interaction or communication. Incomplete activities reduce the opportunities for co-operation as a basis of social support in the working process as well as of the socially determined development of personality features.

5. Lack of demands concerning disponsibility or of learning potential
Incomplete activities provide only insufficient opportunties for the use and therfore the maintenance of the existing qualifications and for additional learning at least occasionally. The abilities and attitudes which can be learned on the job should be transferable to changing tasks within and also outside the position stipulated by the employment contract. With the flexible automation there increases the importance of technological knowledge and abilities as well as of flexibility, thus of the ability to learn.

Formulated summarily, incomplete activities as an expression of inadequate job design may restrict or eliminate the objective motivation and learning potentials of working processes.

The approach of complete or incomplete work activity allows rough predictions to be made of the effects of work tasks on well-being and on aspects of psychosomatic health, on the satisfactions with aspects of the working process, on motivation as well as on the promotion, especially of cognitive abilities. With the extent of the lacking of the features of cyclically and hierarchically complete activities there grows the probability of impairments of the working persons and of productivity.

Therefore, the concept provides some initial foundations for the designing of future tasks with desired features, as it was demanded at the outset.

5.   SOME EFFECTS OF ACTIVITIES WITH DIFFERENT DEGREES OF COMPLETENESS,
     ESPECIALLY WITHIN COMPUTER-AIDED TECHNOLOGIES

Let us start the sequence of the exemplary proofs with the requirement of a sufficient autonomous activity: With increasing periods of inactivity, e.g. passive vigilance periods in the supervising of automated chemical plants, a pronounced degree of mental satiation occurs. With a decreasing requirement of checking operations the extent of stress symptoms grows.

---

* All the statements concerning fatigue, experiencing of monotony, mental satiation and experiencing of stress were obtained by means of the interval-scaled BMS-method, which allowes a discrimination and measurement of these states (Plath and Richter, 1985).

The psychology of old-age shows, by the way, that here more comprehensive connections exist. The long-time active intellectual treatment of demanding tasks retards the degradation of intelligence even during the seventh or eighth decade of life when the required physical conditions are given.

With the restriction of the cyclic completeness, especially with the restriction of the steps of preparation and checking, there grow the mental satiation and the frequency of perceived complaints, e.g., troubles in the gastro-intestinal tract. These findings were obtained for computer-aided office work. They were investigated with a supplement of the "Task Diagnosis Survey" (TDS), an instrument designed for the objective task analysis (Hacker, Iwanowa and Richter, 1983). This instrument for the objective analysis of mental work activities, the method "TDS-mental work", is outlined by Hacker and Schönfelder (1985).

With the restriction of the margins of contents for self-set goals and autonomous variants of working procedures, the extent of phobic complaints grows even into critical domains under unfavourable conditions. If the margins of time or the autonomy of temporal disposition are restricted, the experiencing of underload grows; moreover thereby increases the blood pressure even into critical ranges. These data come from investigations into industrial work activities, especially assembling and machine-operating (see figure 1, next page)

Restricted degrees of autonomy for goal-setting are accompanied with restricted mental demands, especially cognitive demands, as well with a restricted learning potential of the work activity. Activities with demands on further learning at least every one or twp years show a diversity of demands by which the experiencing of monotony, mental satiation and also fatigue are excluded (see figure 2, next but one page).

From this we can derive: The features of incomplete activities do not occur in isolation, but they form configurations. The following example comes from a sample of assembling and machine-operating jobs, which is representative of the electrical industry. In the case of configurations of features which include sub-average degrees of autonomy, low possibilities for deciding and planning as well as low cognitive demands, the general job satisfaction is lower and the average duration of illness is longer. Between the most important activity features there are no additive relations, but interactions (see figure 3).

The approach of complete vs. partialized tasks proves itelf also in the psychological analysis and evaluation of the effects of different design variants for new production techniques:

We compared, e.g., different levels of automation and types of work organization when robots are employed. As an indicator of the effects on the workers a summary scale of the TDS was used by which the hierarchical completeness, i.e. the quality of the mental job demands, is recorded. Two variants of the coupling of NC-lathes with feeding robots are compared with two variants of conventional turning. The cognitive job demands are considerably higher in the case of the linkage of NC-lathes with feeding robots. This is caused to a decisive degree by the organization of manufacture, and not by the employment of robots alone. The highest cognitive demands are given in the case of a flexible manu-

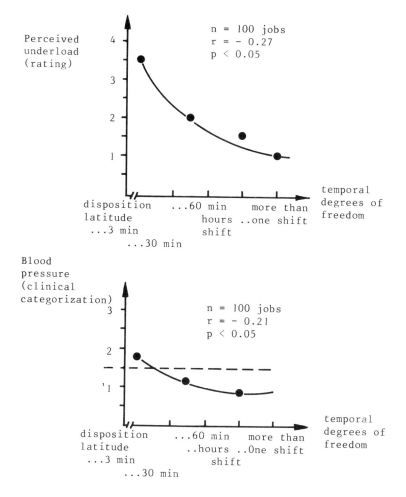

<u>Fig 1</u>:   (HACKER, IWANOWA & RICHTER, 1983): Relationship between temporal
         degrees of freedom and subjective and objective task effects.
         Assembling and machine operating tasks.

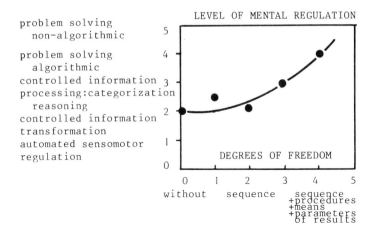

problem solving
  non-algorithmic

problem solving
  algorithmic

controlled information
processing:categorization
  reasoning
controlled information
transformation
automated sensomotor
regulation

LEVEL OF MENTAL REGULATION

DEGREES OF FREEDOM

without   sequence   sequence
                       +procedures
                       +means
                       +parameters
                        of results

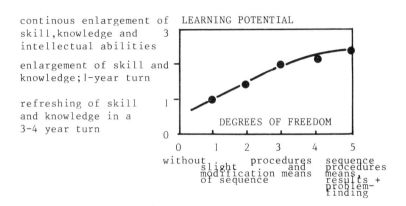

continous enlargement of
skill,knowledge and
intellectual abilities

enlargement of skill and
knowledge;1-year turn

refreshing of skill
and knowledge in a
3-4 year turn

LEARNING POTENTIAL

DEGREES OF FREEDOM

without   procedures   sequence
  slight   and   procedures
modification   means   means,
of sequence   results +
                          problem-
                          finding

Fig. 2: Relationships between task discretion, other task dimensions and
        mental task demands (99 assembling and machine-operating tasks).

criteria type of configuration	degrees of freedom	subtasks with different demands	level of information processing	decision making/ planning	learning demands	number of jobs
1	+	+	+	+	+	20
2	+	–	–	–	–	8
3	–	+	–	–	–	6
4	–	–	–	–	–	14

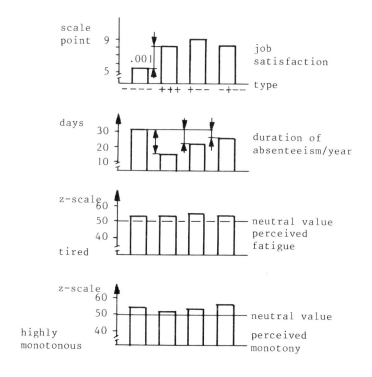

Fig. 3: (S. WOLFF, 1981) Relationship between job characteristic configurations and effects on employees (averaged over groups, electronic industries

facturing cell with two NC-lathes fed by a robot and two additionally available machine tools on which single parts are produced by the turner.

This principle holds for other industrial technologies, too: For welding we compared two organizational variants of the employment of welding robots with the conventional manual welding. Also here, the improvement of the cognitive job demands depends to a decisive degree on the organizational solution for the employment of the welding robots.

Even different solutions of the automation of text processing may be successfully analysed with the approach of complete vs. partialized tasks. We compared two variants of the computer-aided type setting with an identical devision of functions between the persons involved. One group of type setters sets belletristic German texts, a second group sets scientific texts in the German and foreign languages and, in addition, carries out all corrections. The work of the second group comprises a greater variety of diversified partial tasks. In contrast to the work of the first group, it is cyclically complete, since it includes activities of preparation, organization, checking and correction. It offers more degrees of freedom for autonomous goal-setting, decisions and the planning of a type setter's own work. The resulting cognitive demands are diversified and include even problem solving. In contrast to the first activity, this one is also hierarchically complete. Since both groups of type setters have the same qualification, one can expect undesired effects on the first group. This expectation can be confirmed: For the cyclically and hierarchically incomplete activity the job satisfaction is lower, and also the autonomy, the diversity of tasks, the transparency of the job situation and the requirements of co-operation are experienced as being significantly lower. Fatigue, satiation and psychosomatic troubles are more pronounced.

6.   MINIMUM DESIRED VALUES OF TASK CHARACTERISTICS

Can the most important task characteristics be stated and can their minimum desired values for preventing detrimental effects on the working persons be specified? The following statements are based on correlation- or regression-analytical investigations into the short- and medium-term effects of some hundred work activities in industry and administration on the working people, and they have their origin in comparisons with the basic ideas of experienced industrial psychologists concerning the minimum desired values of desired task characteristics for fully trained, healthy skilled workers (cf. Hacker and Iwanowa, 1984; Hacker, Iwanowa and Richter, 1983; Schönfelder, 1985).

The greatest importance for a potential personality development is due to the autonomy and the learning potential of work activities. Autonomy or "degrees of freedom" designate independent possibilities for deciding on the individual strategy and on adequate goals to be set. The learning potential designates the offer of permanent, long-term possibilities of learning in the work activity itself.

Very important are also some task characteristics which are closely connected with the two factors mentioned. These are the demands made on planning by the establishing of a sequence of subgoals and programmes pertinent to them. Moreover, very important are the cognitive demands, the reconstruction of knowledge and the opportunities for utilizing available abilities.

If one asks about those minimum steps of these dimensions of features which, on an average, rather are able to stabilize mental health and to induce processes of promotion than to impair them, there seems to be valid: The degrees of freedom should allow the working persons at least to take decisions on the sequence of their subtasks. These decisions should concern alternatives with a considerable influence on the own efficiency. Self-set goals and independent planning should be possible at least with respect to aspects of time, and rather with respect to the contents of the activity.

The cognitive demands resulting from that should – going beyond mere perceiving and classifying – include cognitive performances. At least at times they should demand algorithmically cognitive processing and occasionally also non-algorithmic thinking.

The available knowledge and abilities should be utilized by the activity at least approximately. The highly important opportunity for further learning while working should include an increase of knowledge and skill at least every two years and offer occasionally also opportunities for developing mental abilities further.

Further investigations, especially longitudinal studies, are required. For all that, the outlined task characteristics should be used for the present as the operationalization of the "personlity-forming forces of comprehensive job tasks" in job design in the interest of the working people – to refer to the formulation by Albert Schweitzer.

7.   STARTING POINTS FOR THE DESIGNING OF THE DESIRED FEATURES OF WORK
      ACTIVITIES

At the outset we stressed the greater possibilities of the early "projecting" design of tasks for the future compared with the only subsequently correcting of a bad one. There was left unanswered, however, what starting points will exist at all in the preparation of production for this "projecting" of tasks for the future.

The designing of job tasks begins with the development of the product or the service. There can be developed not only products which provide good conditions of operation, but also products with suitable manufactoring conditions. It is often possible to avoid not only the health-endangering, hard physical or monotonous activities, but also activities making too low mental demands by modifications at the product. These possibilities may be utilized with the aid of CAD. Models providing good assembly conditions in car production are examples which have been cited frequently.

The second starting point is the choosing of the production techniques and the division of functions between man and machine, inclusive of its software. We should not stare at the supposed or real technical impera-tive conditions as hypnotized, but we should place the question into the foreground whether the production techniques (e.g., the casting or turning of parts) and the means of work (e.g., NC- or CNC-machines) could be selected in such a way that they contribute to producing jobs with the desired progressive characteristics. In the centre of our interest should stand less the computer-aided manufacturing systems, but more the human specialist assisted by the computer als an aiding tool. In the choosing of the level of automation of the means of work, the technologically possible level of automation is not necessarily also the optimum one for the efficiency of the man-machine system. To utilize the abilities of man within the tasks of operating and monitoring which are still left to him there have to be still available to him sufficient physical and mental demands including decision requirements. As it was repeatedly demonstrated, efficiency and well-being are the worse the less activity, autonomy and flexibility are made available to man by the dialogue structure (Matern and Popowa, 1983; Spinas et al. 1983).

The third starting point concerns the division and combination of labour. It is the most efficient one with respect to high efficiency, optimum mental load and chances of learning. Here it is decisive that by no means an as high as possible degree of the division of labour is aimed at, but that an optimum ratio of the division and combination of tasks is aspired to. It has been proved unambiguously for blue- and white-collar jobs that the efficiency, well-being and psychosomatic health of well-trained and engaged employees improve in dependence on the increasing horizontal and vertical combination of tasks.

It is well-known: Increased cycle times during assembling or an increased complexity of intellectual routine activities due to the combination of several operations to be executed in the direction towards a sequential completeness of the activity result in the improving of productivity and the lowering of fatigue and monotony. As a rule, the combination of executing and dispositive operations leads to even more pronounced improvements of the quality of work, of subjective well-being and of motivation, since it contributes also to the hierarchical completeness of the activity. The problem proper consists in the determining of that condition- and development-dependent domain in which the advantages of the combination of work become lower than that of the division of labour.

A fourth starting point is the degree of the autonomy for individual or collective developing of own working procedures in adaptation to the employees' subjective prerequisites, e.g., their cognitive styles or pecularities due to their age. The offer of such opportunities for the development of individualized working procedures by themselves is used by most workers expediently for developing efficient working methods. This was shown, e.g., for selectable modes of the information offered in man-computer dialogue (e.g. Raum, 1983).

The working conditions are mentioned only as the last starting point for the designing of job tasks, not because their effects on achievement and load are low; the reason is rather that they are hardly able to change the contents of work and, thus, the most important demands.

Therefore we come to realize the following: The order of these starting points for the designing of work activities has not been selected arbitrarily. For instance, differently distributed or combined can be only those tasks which have not been eliminated by automation. The rank sequence begins at the starting point with the broadest and most effective possibilities of design and is concluded with that bringing about the lowest effects.

Without doubt, we – the psychologists – have been least oriented to just
the most effective starting points for job design. For us, they seem to
lie too far outside psychology, to have too much to do with engineering
or informatics. Perhaps, however, the following recommendation by one
of the great representatives of our discipline does apply to this
problem: "To give psychology a way – give psychology away?"

References

(1) Hacker, W., Iwanowa, A. & Richter, P.: Verfahren zur objektiven
     Tätigkeitsanalyse (TBS). Psychodiagnostisches Zentrum der Humboldt-
     Univerität, Berlin, 1983.
(2) Hacker, W. & Iwanowa, A.: Zur psychologischen Bewertung von Tätig-
     keitsmerkmalen. Zeitschrift für Psychologie, 1984, No. 2, 192, 103-
     121.
(3) Hacker, W. & Schönfelder, E.: Analyse und Bewertung der Arbeitstei-
     lung und –kombination sowie der Mensch-Rechner-Funktionsteilung bei
     Arbeitstätigkeiten mit Bildschirmtechnik. Wiss. Zeitschrift der TU
     Dresden, 1985, No. 5/6, 34, 79-81.
(4) Matern, B. & Popowa, A.: Aspekte der Gestaltung von Dialogarbeits-
     plätzen. Zeitschrift für Psychologie (Supplement 5), 1983, 73-83.
(5) Plath, H.-E. & Richter, P.: Ermüdung - Monotonie – Sättigung –
     Streß. Verfahren zur Erfassung erlebter Beanspruchungsfolgen.
     Psychodiagnostisches Zentrum der Humboldt-Universität, Berlin,
     1985.
(6) Raum, H.: Informationsgestaltung und Bildschirmarbeit. Zeitschrift
     für Psychologie (Supplement 5), 1983, 56-73.
(7) Schönfelder, E.: Entwicklung und Ersterprobung eines Verfahrens zur
     Analyse der Persönlichkeitsförderlichkeit von Arbeitstätigkeiten
     mit vorwiegend geistigen Anforderungen. Doctoral dissertation,
     Technische Universität Dresden, Faculty of natural sciences and
     mathematics, 1985.
(8) Schweitzer, A.: Verfall und Wiederaufbau der Kultur. Gesammelte
     Werke, Vol. 2, 17-94. Berlin, 1971.
(9) Spinas, N., Troy, N. & Ulich, E.: Leitfaden zur Einführung und
     Gestaltung von Arbeit mit Bildschirmsystemen. CW-Publikationen.
     Zürich, 1983.
(10) Volpert, W.: Überlegungen zum Vorgang der Planerzeugung. Probleme
     und Ergebnisse der Psychologie, 1976, No. 59, 19-24.

THE PSYCHOLOGY OF WORK AND ORGANIZATION
G. Debus and H.-W. Schroiff (Editors)
© Elsevier Science Publishers B.V. (North-Holland), 1986

ERGONOMICS AND ORGANIZATIONAL CONSULTING:
ACCENTUATION OR NEGLECT OF PSYCHOLOGY?

Pierre GOGUELIN

Psychologie du Travail,
Conservatoire National des Arts et des Metiers,
41, rue Gay Lussac,
F-75005 Paris, France

In an older workshop, a worker sits on a chest in order to work; on this chest he has put two cushions... they are dirty, disorderly, but always in the same position. Now the new wind of ergonomics blows through this old-fashioned setting. Postures, movements, and effort are investigated. The sitting position is found to be uncomfortable, there is no back-rest, etc. One day the old chest is replaced by a completely adjustable ergonomic chair. The seat is adjusted to the worker's body. Is he now happy, not having his chest and his cushions any more? Let us leave them in a corner and return a few days later. Now the chair stands in the corner, and the worker sits again on his chest and his cushions. Why? A psychological problem.

In another workshop, everybody complains about the noise, particularly the young ones. The ergonomic test results in 85 - 90 decibels. With great effort and expensive installations, the noise level is reduced. After leaving the factory, everyone jumps on his motor-bike or moped, and the noise is sheer pleasure. And on Saturdays and Sundays, in the disco, there are between 110 and 120 decibels, and they ask for more. Why? A psychological problem.

In a commercial office, there are video displays. Every five minutes, informations for the clients are shown screen. Screens are said to be straining for the eyes. Therefore, technical improvements are made here and there, expensive but often ineffective. Whenever an improvement has been made to avoid a nuisance, the complaints diminish or disappear, say for one week or month. But then the same complaints, or others, arise. In certain firms, screen work is reduced to half-day. But in the evenings, on Saturdays and Sundays, people easily consume up to 30 hours of television - to recreate themselves. This does not do them any harm and does not tire them... Why? A psychological problem.

In an airport, people have worked for years in airconditioned rooms without windows. The personnel are completely used to it, there are no complaints. But then, a new and more modern airport with more luxury is built - also without windows. Soon the personnel complain about disturbances of equilibrium when they leave the offices in the evening, women say they lose their hair, and plants perish. This happens in all offices but one: that of a plant hobbyist. A gorgeous philodendron flourishes there... Why? A psychological problem.

In an agency, everyone complains about the circulation of unclear, difficult, and incoherent documents. The organization consultant controls the whole work. Objectively seen, the personnel have less to do now, the printed matter is precise, less numerous, easy to fill in, and well coordinated. Two or three month later, the personnel complain they cannot manage it any more because everything is more complicated than before. Objectively seen, the work is not done in time any more. Why? A psychological problem.

I shall not quote any more examples. Of course, comfort should be improved, noise and visual fatigue should be reduced, work in windowless rooms should be avoided - even though our ancestors in the Stone Age lived in dark caves. And also disorder should naturally be counteracted.

But we observe that things still do not always function as they should. By solving one set of problems that people have complained about, a new set of problems arise, harder to solve and harder to recognize: psychological problems.

The following questions are put at once: Have we treated the true problems? Have we grasped them from the correct psychological view? And are the solutions good from that angle?

Have we really treated the true problems? If the personnel complain about too long and fatiguing workdays, does that mean that working time is too long - or too much energy was invested into the performance?

Or does this not rather mean that this work is uninteresting, and there is no other motivation to do it but the financial one? In that case, a reduction of the working time would be ineffective because the unmotivating contents of the work would remain the same. Also a development of procedures to reduce physical or mental stress would not solve the problem. Perhaps it is even possible that an uninteresting job becomes more unbearable the easier it can be done. Such a job may be done by anyone without special skill or great strength. Such work is devaluated and devaluating.

But if we do have treated the real problem, did we handle it properly? Did we impose our solutions because we are the experts, or do we admit that the social partners concerned participate to find the best solutions?

Are the solutions correct from a psychological point of view? Or did they create fears, actual or potential frustrating situations for the persons involved which may result in their opposition against these changes?

So the problem is clearly described: Should the consulting organizer and the ergonomic expert during their investigations always keep an eye on any psychological precautions, or should they, as is usually done, impose their expert authority to carry their point of view with the people concerned, hoping those will finally put up with it?

The answer is clear for me: any experts in organization and ergonomics without established psychological knowledge, or who do not implement it in practice, may lead to disastrous results.

A large part of ergonomists have come to ergonomics via a technical, medical, or physiological training. The majority of the organizers come from the fields of technical engineering, economics, or informatics. In order to find out where a neglect of psychology is most harmful, we have to run through a general intervention process in several stages.

Let us first keep in mind that only larger enterprises have ergonomic or organizational consultants in firm employments. A competent psychological training of those experts should be warmly recommended to their management. The experts start their work on the ground of a request, this request may come from the following sources: management, industrial medicine, security control, head of the department, a foreman, personnel, or works council.

Firms of smaller or medium size usually resort to independent experts, or, more rarely, to institutions specializing in this field. Notwithstanding the source of the request, it is the manager of the works who consults the expert.

In every ergonomic or organizational intervention, there are the following elements:

1. A problem causing a situation experienced as dissatisfactory, leading to an implicit demand.
2. A lack of efforts of the concerned to solve the problem themselves. This points out that they consider the problem to be beyond their sphere of influence.
3. A request or application for help, established on a number of defined arguments.
4. The acceptance of such a request, as it is, by the responsible authorities.
5. The request is passed on to the expert, and an agreement is made with him on the scope and performance of the intervention and its costs.
6. The intervention of the expert, and his attitude during the intervention.
7. The conclusions in his final report.
8. The acceptance or refusal of these conclusions by the competent authority, either the one who has called on the expert, or one of his superiors.
9. In case the proposals were accepted, their practical implementation.
10. The evaluation of the results.

On each of these ten stages, the psychological dimension can be either considered or neglected. We shall now go through these ten stages in order to find out the respective weak points:

1. The situation experienced as dissatisfactory: such a situation points to a neglected human need. With reference to the hierarchy of human needs in organzations as published by Maslow, Herzberg or Hughes, we may quote a few examples: A superior shows distinctly how little he respects his subordinates. The co-workers know exactly that any demands to the behaviour of the superior would not be considered, and also that the superior will not make any effort to change his behaviour. The demand will therefore deal with a certain objective point which has two advantages for the workers: firstly, there is a concrete request, mostly with a pragmatic character and little danger of psychologisation – secondly, the fulfilment of the demand would mean, more or less unconsciously, that workers have asserted themselves and gained respect from the superior.

Behind simple requests or demands, different and more profound requests are hidden in this way.

Let us presume that, in such an example, an ergonomist would investigate any such drawbacks without further interrogations, and would actually bring help, or an organizer would develop new and more flexible working procedures, considering some of the staff's demands. In principle, the problems should then be solved. After a certain period of satisfaction ("our demand has been fulfilled"), the superior's attitude would again be felt as being humiliating. Now the workers will make demands that were formerly considered to be secondary. Since the "primary" demands had been fulfilled, the "secondary" ones move to the foreground. These demands concerning working conditions, organization procedures, or management methods, may again be solved by consulting an expert. The fundamental problem, however, will resurge again and again like Phenix from the ashes, because it is the behaviour of the superior. The psychological problem has not been considered, only the symptom.

2. The lack of efforts of the concerned to solve the problem themselves. Let us pick up the same example: since a door does not close well, there is a draught in the workshop. At home, each one of the workers would have solved this problem by himself. Also the superior would have helped himself in his home, most probably. But there in the workshop, this is a symbol for the workers: it proves the ill will and disrespect of the superior. For the latter, it is a means to demonstrate his power and authority.
    If a nuisance or a problem is delayed too long, not the problem by itself is of importance, but a more profound problem which is not outspoken. The proposed problem has the function of a "scapegoat". Here it makes no sense to bring help, because a new, similar problem will come up soon. Perhaps it will be brought about on purpose.

3. An explicit demand for help, mostly on the ground of rational arguments. In our example, the demand might be backed by the following arguments: Danger of sickness for the workers, higher heating costs, etc. These demands will be fulfilled if a worker suffers a damage – at the latest.
    We may further state: Rational arguments frequently conceal irrational reasons. The psychologist knows these mechanisms: projection, compensation, rationalisation, etc. For non-psychologists, these phenomena remain in the dark or sound incredible.

4. The acceptance of such a request, as it is. The questions and demands are accepted by the deciding authority merely on a rational basis and are investigated no further, even if it is supposed that the problem is more profound. One remains on the simple but wrong level of definition on which solutions are perceived: The demands of the personnel will be fulfilled as they are, and that must be enough.

5. The request is passed on to the expert. In France, the majority of ergonomic experts at present come from medicine (more exactly: working medicine), physiology, or engineering technology. Scarcely 20 % have a basic psychological training.
    Complaints about the working conditions, comfort etc. are viewed from the respective expert's point of view. The physician looks at

the health problems, the physiologist at the degree of strain, physical or mental. The technician will try to improve the appliances according to the demands of physician and physiologist. Only some psychologists ask for problems of motivation and fulfilment of human needs, i.e. for "affective ergonomics", or one might speak of "social ergonomics".
In case of complaints about the work flow – often concealing profound communication problems – the organizer will modify the structures and communication channels; in reality, the problem may be elsewhere: Information is withheld for fear of losing power or scope of tasks, i.e. a zone of potential freedom.
So the problem must be tackled on the right level: The flow of information is not stopped for lack of channels, but the communication channels do not exist because information is not transmitted.
Since the expert for ergonomics or organization lacks the necessary training, he will solve the problem according to the definitions he has received. Thereby the psychological dimension is neglected.

6. The intervention of the expert in itself is psychologically deficient. As the solutions frequently only come from the experts, it is already a progress that some of them ask themselves critical questions on their work. The really concerned people only supply initial information and are not integrated in the solution of the problem. This results in a usually very poor acceptance of the solutions: as the management stands behind the expert, everybody simply waits for the end of the investigation. When the expert has left, they resume their work "as usual".
Here in the face of psychologists, I do not want to discuss the difference between a steady development and sudden changes, between slowly acquired, and imposed knowledge.

The items 7-8-9- (Conclusions of the experts, acceptance or refusal by the competent authority, and practical implementation) are only continuations of the stages described. With regard to item 10, "Evaluation of results", we may discern two periods: during the first period, a moderate satisfaction with people saying: "Our demands have been fulfilled, but our opinion still was not asked for." Then follows a second period with criticism on the new methods. Now there are two possibilities: either the old system is resumed, or people put up with the new system. But very soon they will find other reasons for potential requests.

If I had to come to a conclusion here, I should be very pessimistic: In ergonomic investigation and organizational consulting, the true problems are frequently omitted by neglect of the psychological dimension. The particular language of the French Trade Unions speaks of "recuperation" in any amelioration of working conditions or work flow!

What does "recuperation" of a movement mean in the motor sense of the word? It means to turn round a movement that was directed against us, in order to help us – without changing anything else. This is what actually happens: In order to avoid an investigation of the profound causes of dissatisfaction, superficial demands are fulfilled.

What are the conclusion to be drawn here? Defeatism is not appropriate! Fundamentally, there are two approaches that would help the workers as well as the management of an enterprise:

- the first approach: Ergonomic and organizational consultants should be
  trained to possess a solid knowledge of psychology. This is one of
  the goals we pursue at the "Conservatoire National des Arts et
  Metiers". My colleague, Prof. Wisner, who leads the Institute for
  Ergonomics and Working Physiology is trained both in medicine and psychology, and I am the leader of the Institute for Working Medicine. We
  try to organize the education towards an integration of these two
  guidelines.
- the second approach: To develop multi-disciplinary working groups. I
  believe that we, the psychologists, should seize the initiative and
  promote the formation and work of any such groups as often as
  possible.

All this would mean an immense progress.

PART II

SELECTED TOPICS

II.1. New Technologies, Automation, Organization and Job Design

THE PSYCHOLOGY OF WORK AND ORGANIZATION
G. Debus and H.-W. Schroiff (Editors)
© *Elsevier Science Publishers B.V. (North-Holland), 1986*

CURRENT BRITISH PRACTICE IN THE EVALUATION OF THE NEW INFORMATION
TECHNOLOGIES

Frank BLACKLER and Colin BROWN

Department of Behaviour in Organisations,
University of Lancaster,
Lancaster LA1 4YX, United Kingdom.

The results of a study of current practices in the evaluation of
new technologies being introduced into British work organisations
are presented. Systematic post-event evaluation is uncommon,
excepting some attempts to assess relative costings of the old and
new work systems. Interest in the technical capabilities of the
new equipments is not matched by an interest in the organisational
possibilities they may create. An analysis is presented of how
current assumptions of best practice in this area compare with an
approach developed from the social sciences. The present standard
of management of the new technologies is not high and it is
concluded that there is an important need for a wider appreciation
of psychological approaches.

1. RESEARCH OBJECTIVES AND METHODOLOGY

There has been much talk in the U.K. about the urgent need to introduce
information technologies if organisations are to remain competitive, with
stress being put on the possible technical opportunities that are provided
by the new systems. By way of contrast however, there has been little
public debate about the social and organisational options associated with
the new work systems. Yet in many cases employee attitudes are crucial for
a full utilisation of work systems built around the new technologies. It
is also often the case that the technologies offer considerable scope for
reorganising current working practices, either to expand or to reduce the
significance of employee contributions in decision making. In a research
project funded by the Economic and Social Research Council we set out to
study current practices in the evaluation of the new technologies being
introduced into work organisations in the United Kingdom at the present
time. Particular attention was paid in the research to the social and
organisational consequences of the new systems in the light of the
importance of the organisational choices being made.

The main sectors of the economy where the new technologies are being
introduced were identified and important applications considered. This
included, in manufacturing, CADCAM, CNC, process control and robotic
systems. In the service sectors people were interviewed from banking and
insurance organisations, central government agencies, local government,
health, education, large retailing organisations, telecommunications and
transport. Representatives of the main interest groups in each of the
sectors were interviewed. Over fifty semi-structured interviews were held
with managers, consultants, manufacturers, and trades union officials.

2. OVERVIEW OF THE RESULTS

In addition to efforts to assess the technical adequacy of new work systems based on the information technologies four approaches to evaluation can be distinguished. These are: cost substitution (where the relative costs of the old and new systems are compared); value added (where qualitative comparisons are made on such issues as service to customer, quality of product etc.); evaluation of the organisational effects of the new systems (including the attitudes of end-users); and evaluation of the processes themselves through which the new systems are designed and introduced (including the adequacy of project management and of support provided for end-users of the systems).

2.1. Prior-Event Evaluation

Strong emphasis is, typically, placed on prior-event evaluation. The research indicated:
  a) In manufacturing the demand for cost substitution type approaches is often emphasised. For example, one interviewee suggested that expenditure on production and cost control equipment was justifiable in these terms over about two years, CAD in three or four, and robotics over eight or ten. Such calculations are often thought to be unproblematical and 'can be done on the back of an envelope'. On the other hand, some applications in manufacturing industry (including CADMAT systems and some CADCAM) are increasingly regarded as essential equipment and a detailed case for justifying the equipment in cost or return on investment terms may not be required. Flexible manufacturing systems may be impossible to cost justify as the pay-back period can be as long as between ten to fifteen years.
  b) In office applications tight controls are often kept on cost reductions in certain areas where clerical work study is used (especially in banking and retailing). Staff savings are often sought elsewhere too, for example with word processing systems. On the other hand the relative cheapness of many new office technologies can ease the need for cost benefit justification and some applications (advanced management information systems for example) are notoriously difficult to justify in short term cost reduction terms.

Many of the people interviewed were highly critical of the emphasis that they reported is placed on prior justification through short term cost benefit calculations. It was argued that, in many instances, the principal benefits of the new technologies lie in the 'value added' benefits they can provide or, in the novel business opportunities that they can facilitate. It was emphasised to us that good task/systems analysis is necessary for the optimum use of the new systems but the mere automation of existing practices can amount to a misuse of the technology. In this vein certain interviewees suggested that the technologies require 'an act of faith', 'vision', or a 'guiding philosophy' for their justification.

2.2. Post-Event Evaluation

In contrast to the emphasis placed on prior-event evaluation, post-event evaluations are uncommon. Evaluations of the technical effectiveness of a new system may take place, especially if problems occur. Otherwise (excepting certain government funded demonstration projects) examples of attempts to undertake systematic post-event evaluation were difficult to find. This is despite persistent recommendations in the management literature that planning reviews should play an integral part in the introduction of the technologies. It emerged that:

a) Excepting technical assessments, if systematic post-event evaluation is undertaken at all it is likely to be concerned with cost benefit analysis.

b) 'Value added' evaluation is often recognised as important by the people involved, although its systematic assessment appears uncommon.

c) The ergonomic acceptability of equipment and user reactions to the software is often given some attention, but it is unusual for other psychological or organisational consequences to be carefully assessed.

d) We came across no examples of a prime concern in systematic evaluation with the manner in which the new systems have been designed and introduced.

Systematic assessments of value added benefits, organisational effects and of the processes themselves through which the systems were designed and introduced appear hampered by a perceived lack of accessible methodologies. Moreover, the strong pressures that people feel to justify their interest in the technologies before they are introduced seldom exist after their installation.

2.3. The Quality of the Management of the Introduction of the Technologies

Several factors suggested that, although there are differences across sectors, at the present time a poor standard of project management is typically characteristic of the introduction of the technologies. On the one hand this was indicated by accounts of the tactics people find it necessary to adopt to try and persuade management to release money to invest in the new technologies in the first place. Tactics reported to us include overexaggerated claims that substantial manpower savings will result from the new systems, claims that orders had already been lost because the new equipment was not already in place, and that competitors are already using it. On the other hand are the explanations people gave of why evaluations of the new systems are rarely systematically undertaken post-event. In explaining this references were sometimes made by the interviewees to the technical problems of accurate pre- and post-introduction measures. But it was the internal 'political' difficulties of evaluation reviews that dominated their explanations. Amongst the comments we heard were suggestions that in many organisations if a new system works tolerably well then detailed evaluation is not felt to be needed, that vested interests tend to prevent systematic reviews, and that the idea of an audit of end-user reactions was unfamiliar to many managers.

Most important in this connection was the apparently common failure for usage of the new technologies to be integrated into long term business objectives. This was especially true of the uses of the new office technologies, where there was something approaching general agreement that a lack of a strategy for utilising the technologies was common and that purchasers often only appeared to be looking for 'a better mousetrap'. It would seem that people often only look for the technologies 'to do what we were doing yesterday, only better'. Good examples of policies designed to maximise other potential benefits of the technologies, such as their ability to make information widely available, to decentralise decision making, involve staff and motivate staff, and to facilitate greater organisational integration in a way which effectively supports corporate objectives, were not in strong supply.

Major exceptions to the general failure to integrate uses of the technology into business objectives were in manufacturing, where a strong tradition of work rationalisation can be found, and in organisations with a strong tradition of clerical work study. One example from manufacturing industry involved a shift from a conventionally arranged design and production organisation, towards a system built around a small flexible central staff team supported by machine operators employed on a contract basis. An example from the service sector was of a system being designed to improve central management control, involving the automation of much routine clerical work, the increased employment of part-time staff, and a small flexibly structured central team.

3. DISCUSSION: STYLES OF PLANNING AND THE ASSUMPTIONS OF PLANNERS

To help interpret major findings of the survey and to help understand alternative possible approaches to the present poor management of the technologies an analysis of the cycles of innovation associated with the management of the new technologies seemed to be required. To do this we drew from a number of sources, incorporating these within the general thrust of our research findings. Our aims were to throw light on the perceived importance of prior-event and the relative neglect of post-event evaluation and, in addition to an analysis of the prevailing orthodoxy, we wished to explore the characteristics of an approach to the design and evaluation of the new systems that would give priority to possible organisational and behavioural outcomes associated with them.

In our analysis the cycle of innovation associated with the introduction of the technologies was divided into four stages: phase 1 includes the initial recognition that use of the technologies might be advantageous; in phase 2 a detailed feasibility review is undertaken leading to discussions, recommendations and decisions; phase 3 is when the accepted solution is further developed or the choice of an 'off the shelf' system is made; in phase 4 the system is installed and brought into service. The essence of the analysis is the specification of alternative guiding premises that may operate at each phase, indicating how different premises lead to different approaches to the organisation of the change process and to different priorities regarding work organisation issues. The alternative Models, slightly simplified for clarity of presentation, are shown on the following page: Model 1 is titled the 'Task and Technology Centred Approach' and Model 2 the 'Organisation and End User Centred Approach'.

For an analysis of the premises guiding phase 1 the labour process literature e.g. Child [1], proved helpful. On Models 1 and 2 the alternative organisational strategies that management may adopt to reduce costs, increase flexibility, improve quality and so on are shown as: either the attitude that people are a costly resource to be replaced or to be controlled by applications of the new technologies, or, the belief that people are a costly resource to the organisation whose contributions can be improved by appropriate technological development.

At phase 2, when a detailed exploration and prior justification of possibilities is undertaken, Herbst's [2] analysis of alternative approaches to planning helps distinguish alternative approaches. Herbst points out that while objectives for technological changes can be expressed through a detailed specification of required end-states, social

	Model 1: TASK AND TECHNOLOGY CENTRED APPROACH	**Model 2:** ORGANISATION AND END- USER CENTRED APPROACH
Phases:	**Guiding Premises and Key Actors**	**Guiding Premises and Key Actors**
1: INITIAL REVIEW initial recognition of possible opportunity	a) Operating conditions b) People are a costly resource to be reduced if possible c) Key actors: top and senior managers	a) Operating conditions b) People are a costly resource to be more fully utilised c) Key actors: initially from any part of org. then top management
2: EXPLORATION & PRIOR JUSTIFI- CATION analysis, discussions, feasibility review, recommend- ations	a) Tightly prescribed planning objectives b) Central co-ordination and control c) Expert driven d) "Most modern" syndrome e) Key actors: man- agerial project team including technical and financial experts	a) General policy formulation b) Decentralisation, staff involvement c) Concern for end users d) System development potential rather than machine capability e) Key actors: a diverse and representative group, or a consulting project group, or a management plus shadow group. Trades union involvement
3: DESIGN OF SYSTEM: design opera- tionalisation and detail or "off the shelf" choice	a) Machines over people b) Task fragmentation c) "Clean design" d) "Final design" e) Key actors: design engineers and tech- nical consultant	a) People to use machines b) Job enrichment, teams c) Operator and mainten- ance needs d) Incremental and educ- ative design approach e) Key actors: design engineers, technical consultants, behavior- al advisors, within consultative procedure
4: IMPLEMENTATION construction or install- ation, trial, operation	a) Machine capability b) Only minor modifi- cations expected c) "Once off" skill training d) Responsibility to line management e) Key actors: as stage 3, also line manag- ers and end users. Trades union negot- iations on conditions	a) User support b) Pilot projects used where possible c) Continuing staff and org. development d) Continuing reviews of operation and needs e) Key actors: as stage 3 also line managers and end users. Trade union negotiations on cond- itions, training, grading, etc.

planning may not best be undertaken in this way. Peoples' knowledge, skills and attitudes can be expected to develop as a result of the experiences that they have in a change programme. An alternative approach to the early formulation of specific organisational requirements is the specification therefore, not of the details of end states required, but of general principles which it is hoped will guide the directions that changes will take. As shown also on Models 1 and 2 a number of related assumptions can be identified at this stage of the innovation cycle. These include the assumption that the feasibility review process should be managed exclusively by a team of experts, or, the assumption that it is important that potential end-users should be involved at an early stage also. An important characteristic of many applications of the new technologies is the differences in interest that they may expose in organisations (Kling [3]). Unitary approaches to organisation may need to be replaced by an appreciation of the relevance of pluralist analysis.

The alternative approaches to phase 3 of the innovation cycle, when general plans are operationalised in design detail or an 'off the shelf' system is chosen, have been well discussed within the psychological literature on job design. On Models 1 and 2 these are summarily presented as, either the assumption that the new technologies should be used to take over from people where possible, or, the assumption that they should be developed to support peoples' endeavours. Task fragmentation and Tayloristic approaches to job simplification are contrasted to the principles underlying job enrichment, autonomous working groups, and organic structures. Related to these approaches are the contrasting orientations that Perrow [4] refers to as 'the logic of design' or the 'logic of operation', in that attention at this stage may either be focussed on the interests of designers or be directed towards the concerns of operators and maintenance staff.

Finally at phase 4, when the new system is installed and and bought on line, the end results of the two contrasting approaches become plain. Within a Model 1 approach only minor modifications are now anticipated to be required and, after a trial period, it is anticipated that responsibility for the system will pass from the design team to the line management. A Model 2 orientation is more gradualistic in its orientation, emphasizing the importance of ongoing reviews of the design and operation of the system, through prototyping, and pilot projects and incremental approaches to systems change. Training and end-user needs are accorded a higher priority in this case than in a Model 1 system.

Important consequences of these assumptions are presented on the Models. Regarding the key actors involved at each phase, a 'Task and Technology' orientation is characterised by a 'top down' approach to change: senior management initiates the activity then delegate the detail to functional specialists. An 'Organisation and End-User' orientation on the other hand is both participative and pluralist. Following Opperman [5], three approaches to the arrangement of end-user participation are shown: a project steering group including representatives of management, technical specialists and end-users; a project group that consults in detail with different interested parties; or separate working groups of management and workers who each explore possible solutions then negotiate together. Trade union negotiations also follow a different pattern in a Model 2 situation compared to a Model 1, with negotiations typically beginning earlier and covering a broader range of issues.

There are a number of points to be emphasised about these Models:

a) Within Model 1 systems we have encountered individuals who are sympathetic to Model 2 approaches. In particular, we have heard of cases where ergonomists have been engaged quite late in Phase 3 as it has become appreciated that the needs of end-users need to be recognised and of cases where organisational development consultants have become involved at a rather late stage in an effort to smooth the introduction of a system designed by a remote expert group. The essentially Model 1 nature of these systems was unaffected though.

b) While Model 2 is intended to incorporate the advantages of a number of behavioural science approaches (e.g. the notion of 'evolutionary systems design', the advantages of a participative approach to work systems redesign, a recognition of the pluralist nature of organisations, and of the value of adequately resourcing the end users of the new systems) it is less tidy and predictable and more difficult to manage than Model 1. Superficial attempts to gauge end-users views of the acceptability to them of certain proposals (e.g. through cursory briefing sessions or brief chats over coffee) should not be understood as indicative of a Model 2 approach.

c) Despite the potential advantages of a Model 2 orientation Model 1 approaches are effective in certain situations (e.g. McLoughlin et al, [6]). This is true where a straightforward automation of existing practices is a realistic aim for the new work system, i.e. where cost substitution techniques are perfectly sufficient for its evaluation.

We commented earlier on the generally poor standard of project management that is a common feature of many new technology projects in work organisations. It is important to note that the Models presented here outline alternative ideal types that can be adopted as an ideal to be aimed for. Current approaches to the introduction of the technologies quite frequently cannot be classified as following either a Model 1 or a Model 2 approach. The Models we have presented assume a certain purposiveness in the utilisation of the technologies. But the apparent 'muddling through' of many projects at the present time may be better understood as following no such logic. At their worst, current approaches to the technologies can be characterised as: phase 1 consisting of a vague awareness that some interesting hardware is now available; phase 2 a fascination with the novelty of the systems available; phase 3 a strong reliance on the promises of suppliers; and phase 4 by systems debugging, demarcation disputes, and a failure to train or resource end-users satisfactorily. The label 'Model 0' seems a suitable slogan for such approaches.

Nonetheless the interviews that we held during the research and in subsequent feedback discussions with those who had participated in it has led us to conclude that many people unquestioningly assume that a Model 1 approach is the ideal to which they should aspire. Few people appear to be aware that there is an alternative. Certainly the advice presented in popular introductory books is often very simplistic, but even some quite prestigious writings unquestioningly assume that a 'Task and Technology' orientation is the only realistic option available. (For example, the well publicised 1984 report by the Institute of Administrative Management and the Government Department of Trade and Industry into 'The Barriers and Opportunities of Information Technology' [7], distinguishes between firms who are 'lagging' or 'leading' in this area very much in 'Model 0' versus Model 1 terms). The problem is not that this belief is necessarily wrong; in some situations a 'Task and Technology Approach' can be highly

effective. Rather, to the extent that people remain unaware that there is
an alternative to a Model 1 orientation, the idea that there are
significant 'organisational choices' being made in the utilisation of the
technologies is something of a myth. Social science prescriptions for the
introduction of the technologies into work organisations are, in the U.K.
at the present time, largely being rejected by default.

4. CONCLUSIONS

The standard of management of the introduction of information technologies
into British work organisations is not high. Evaluation practices are
frequently neglected and the role the technologies can play in improving
an organisation's competitiveness is often only poorly understood.
Assumptions commonly held about appropriate ways of managing the
introduction of the technologies display only a very limited appreciation
of social scientific factors.

There is an important need for social scientists to present their
approaches with greater effect in this area. Important barriers to a more
effective utilisation of the technologies include the low level of
awareness that exists about the organisational potential of the
technologies, and the conventional approaches of systems designers and
accountants. The analysis presented here indicates that 'Organisation and
End-User' centred approaches will be most readily accepted in
organisations where a premium is placed on human resources, where end-user
attitudes are crucial to an effective utilisation of the technologies, or
where major changes in traditional organisational groupings are required.
A strong interest in ways in which industrial competitiveness may be
improved (e.g. Wheelwright and Hayes [8]) now exists in managerial
circles. The most effective way of stimulating an interest in the use of
'Organisation and End-User' centred approaches to the technology may, in
the first place, be to stress the differences that exist between them and
conventional approaches and, in the second, to emphasize their relevance
to attempts to organise for competitive advantage.

REFERENCES

[1] Child, J., Managerial Strategies, New Technology and the Labour
    Process, in: Knights, D., Willmott, H. and Collinson, D. (eds.), Job
    Redesign (Gower, Farnborough, 1985) pp. 107-141.
[2] Herbst, P.G., Socio-technical Design (Tavistock, London, 1974).
[3] Kling, R., Computerisation as an Ongoing Social and Political
    Process. Proceedings of the Conference on the Development of
    Computer-Based Systems and Tools (Aarhus University, Aarhus, 1985).
[4] Perrow, C., The Organisational Context of Human Factors Engineering.
    Administrative Science Quarterly (1983) 28, pp. 521-524.
[5] Opperman, R., User Participation: Some Experiences and
    Recommendations. Systems, Objectives, Solutions, in print.
[6] McLoughlin, I.P., Smith, J.H. and Dawson, P., The introduction of a
    Computerised Freight Information System in British Rail (University
    of Southampton, Mimeo, 1983)
[7] Bevington, T. and Hand, M., The Barriers and Opportunities of
    Information Technology (IAM/DTI, London, 1984)
[8] Wheelwright S., Hayes, R. Restoring our Competitive Edge (Wiley 1984)

THE PSYCHOLOGY OF WORK AND ORGANIZATION
G. Debus and H.-W. Schroiff (Editors)
© *Elsevier Science Publishers B.V. (North-Holland), 1986*

MANAGEMENT OF AUTOMATION PROJECTS

Herry P.J. Vijlbrief, Jen A. Algera & Paul L. Koopman*

Some preliminary results concerning decision-making processes in automation projects based on 9 cases in two organizations are presented. Management commitment and control, user involvement and the position of computer experts are discussed, as well as contingency factors that influence the relationship between decision-making and system success.

1. INTRODUCTION

The design and implementation of computer-based information systems may be regarded as a complex decision-making process. The number of people involved is often considerable, the material is complicated and largely very technical. The costs can be very high. In addition, at the start of the project it is not always clear whether automation is the best solution to the organization's problem (Algera and Koopman [1]). These characteristics make the control and management of automation projects difficult. Therefore "blueprints", manuals for automation, are generally used to divide up the process into separate phases; see for example PRODOSTA (PROject control and DOcumentation STAndards) used by the Dutch multinational Philips (figure 1).

PHASES	CENTRAL ISSUES
Preliminary survey	What is the organization's problem?
Application analysis	What is the optimal solution for the problem?
System specification	What are the system requirements, what is the logical design of the system?
System definition	What is the technical design of the system?
System development	Construction and implementation
Operational phase	Evaluation: have goals been achieved? Production and maintenance.

FIGURE 1. PRODOSTA - Phases and central issues (PRODOSTA [2]).

* Department of Industrial and Organizational Psychology, Free University, Amsterdam.

Management of automation projects as described here makes a logical and rational impression. Research however reveals that there are considerable discrepancies between blueprints and actual practice (Argelo [3]). The complexity of the information, the lack of essential (technical) knowledge and the conflicts of interests between the groups involved often make the process less orderly. Decision-making is not only a logical but also a political problem. Both quality and acceptance of the decision-making will influence the result. One of the central issues regarding the political character of decision-making is who is (or should be) involved. Generally three main categories of participants can be distinguished: management, computer experts (or system designers) and future users or their representatives. They have different roles and responsibilities in the design process.

User involvement usually is enthusiastically endorsed in the literature on the design of computer-based information systems (e.g. de Brabander and Edström [4]). Often it is assumed to be the key to successful implementation. A recent literature review however shows that the benefits of user involvement have not yet been convincingly demonstrated (Ives and Olson [5]). Experiences with other forms of consultation show the same results: participation only works under certain conditions (Koopman and Wierdsma [6]. We therefore agree with Ives and Olson that a link must be established between research on participative decision-making and organizational change.

The purpose of this paper is to present some preliminary results of a current research program concerning the decision-making processes in (administrative) automation projects. We will concentrate on: the structure of the decision-making process and the difficulties and opportunities for management to control the process; the possibilities of and limitations to user involvement; the position of the computer experts.

2. RESEARCH DESIGN AND METHODOLOGY

This research program concerning decision-making in automation projects is connected to earlier research regarding to Decision-making In Organizations (DIO [7]). In this research program we use a contingency approach. The central research question is: "What is the effect of different decision-making strategies on dependent variables such as effectiveness of the project, acceptance of the system, task content and centralization/ decentralization taking into account contingency variables like conflict between participants, external influences and nature of automation". Figure 2 shows our research model.

We plan to study 30 to 40 projects in different organizations in detail. The choice of organizations and projects is aimed at variety in the independent and the contingency variables. Far most of the variables are measured by "tracing"-interviews: after the decision-making process is finished or nearly so, the process is traced on a number of aspects by semi-structured interviews with key persons. Document analysis gives additional information on some of the variables. Questionnaires are used for some of the dependent variables. On the information thus obtained, using certain scoring and aggregation rules, a draft report of the process will be made. This report is presented to the key figures for a detailed assessment and discussed in a feedback session. Afterwards a final report is made.

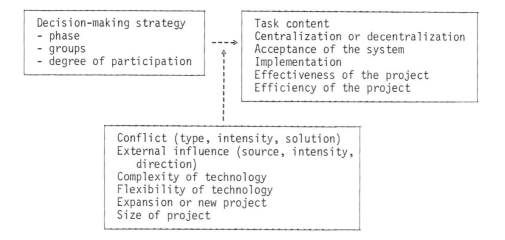

FIGURE 2. Research model

3. DATA COLLECTION

The preliminary results we report on are based on 9 cases in two Dutch organizations, an industrial firm which is part of a larger concern and a public utility company. The information systems studied vary in size and complexity. They all concern applications in administration or logistics. Available company documents on the design and implementation of a system were analysed. A total amount of 105 semi-structured interviews were conducted with key figures amongst management, system designers and users. Only those persons who had actually been involved in the design process have been interviewed. Furthermore 39 actual users of the different systems have been interviewed and filled out a questionnaire on the influence of the information system on their tasks and responsibilities.

4. RESULTS

4.1. Management control of the decision-making process

According to the blueprint the ideal situation is:
a. Management formulates goals for the information system based on a proper analysis of the company problem and the alternative solutions for this problem;
b. Management designs an adequate decision-making structure (which steps have to be taken, who is to participate, costs, turnaround time, information and training);
c. Management controls the process and evaluates each phase.
Actual practice however differs from this ideal situation on several points.

Preliminary survey and application analysis are usually given a very limited amount of time. In two cases this resulted in ignoring departments that should have been involved in the design process. They were confronted with a system that did not fit their working methods. The system had to be

changed substantially after the actual implementation. In two other cases
management did not formulate any clear goals for the information system.
In the analysis of the company's problem conflicts of interest occurred.
The problems were not faced, a kind of "muddling through" process took
place. Participants were frustrated because they saw no advance. In 3 out
of these 4 cases there were serious troubles at the end of the system specification phase. System designers were confronted with an inadequate
logical design and specifications that were too vague. Delays and feed-
back-loops to earlier phases resulted out of these problems.

The organizations we studied belonged to a larger network. Management had
to respect certain rules in planning an information system and was limited
in the choices it could make. In some cases we studied a problem occurred
that seems to be a logical consequence of this situation. A software
package that was already available seemed to be the logical choice for a
stock control system. Not enough attention had been given to the differences between the warehouses involved. Later on in the design process
serious adaptations had to be made to make the system function. In the
other organization the design of one of the more complex systems was a
joint operation with other public utility companies. Conflicts of interest
between the different companies finally resulted in breaking up the cooperation and starting a design process only for the company itself. One of
our conclusions for our research design is that external influences (or
metapower) and conflicts are relevant contingency variables indeed.

Prelimi- nary survey	Applica- tion analysis	System specifi- cation	System defini- tion	System develop- ment	Opera- tional phase

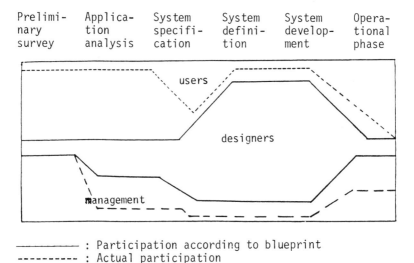

——————— : Participation according to blueprint
- - - - - - - - - : Actual participation

FIGURE 3. Participation of different groups in decision-making.

The role of management turns out to be more modest than the blueprint would
indicate (see figure 3). Although research reports that management support
is one of the factors that influences system success considerably our
findings indicate that management's commitment to the design and implementation of information systems is minimal. In 3 cases where the responsible
manager from the department concerned played an active role in the design
process system success was relatively high. This suggests that management

commitment really pays off. In both organizations it was quite difficult to discover who was responsible for certain project-management tasks. The structure of responsibilities was very complicated. Informally a different decision-making structure existed where system designers played an important role, mainly because of the lack of knowledge and commitment managers and users were showing.

Planning and control of budget and turnaround time is a problem. Regarding to turnaround time we found discrepancies between planning and reality from +15% up to +230%. Regarding to costs we found differences from +40% up to +125%. The most striking result however was that in 4 out of 9 cases there was no time planning and in 2 out of 9 cases there was no cost planning at all. In 5 cases there was no idea about the real costs of that particular project. There seem to be two factors that make costs exceed budgets most of all: an underestimation of implementation problems and insufficient attention to preliminary survey and application analysis.

Education and training to increase the users proficiency in utilizing the information system was a weak point in both organizations. In 7 out of 8 cases (in 1 case there were no data available) there was criticism on the amount of instruction and training afforded to the user. In 5 cases training was insufficient or completely lacking, in 2 cases the timing of the instruction was inaccurate. Problems in one of the projects caused such a delay that training occurred more than a year before working with the system actually started.

From figure 3 it will be clear that management control is less substantial than the blueprint indicates. Even quite formal controls on costs and turnaround time slip away during the design process. Lack of a certain amount of (technical) knowledge seems to be one of the main reasons for a "laissez-faire" management-style that is quite common in the management of automation projects.

4.2. Possibilities of and limitations to user involvement

From experiences with several forms of consultation Koopman and Wierdsma [6] conclude that participation in decision-making only "works" if the persons involved see the usefulness of it and if there is enough latitude for participation. We will discuss these factors in detail.
a. Users involved must see the usefulness of participation.

In every case we studied users were involved in the design process, most of all because their information about the departments that were involved was essential to the design process. Nevertheless user's influence on the decision-making process was less than the blueprint indicates (see figure 3). Two problems were often mentioned by users who actually participated in the design process:
1. Users lacked essential knowledge about the design of information systems. They could not comprehend the different possibilities the computer experts mentioned. They spoke different languages, communication problems were often mentioned, although the relationship between users and designers was generally rather good. Training and education of users that participated was often insufficient.
2. Users mentioned severe problems with the kind of abstract reasoning that was necessary to participate in an efficient way. They had to imagine what a future system would to for them, what kind of changes in task content and work organization would be caused by it, what kind of requirements

the system had to fulfill etc. "Selection" of participants seldomly takes
conceptual ability into account as an important factor. Users can easily
get caught in a hostage or indoctrination situation (Hedberg [8]).
Examples of both problems were often reported to us. There is no easy way
out of this trap. The most promising way is to present some basic knowledge of computer use and the design of an information system not only to
users that actually participate but also to the users they represent.
b. Users must have some latitude to influence the decision-making.

There were several factors that affected participation in a negative way
from this point of view.
1. When organizations have several departments that have the same function
they tend to stress uniformity. In designing an information system some
part of the organization is used to experiment with the system. This generally means a severe restriction to participation from other similar parts
of the organization. In one of our cases users from plant A had participated in the design process. The implementation of the system caused some
troubles, but eventually it was successful. The same system was implemented in the plant B. Implementation was very difficult and not really
successful.
2. When there are serious conflicts of interest between different user
departments or users and management the possibilities for participation
are restricted as well. Some consensus on goals has to exist. Participation tends to stress tendencies that already exist. This implies that
conflicts would tend to increase.
3. Organizations must have enough autonomy in decision-making. If the
larger network limits goals, alternative solutions and specifications,
participation is a rather frustrating activity. A clear example of this
was found in one of the more complex systems in the public utility company.
4. One of the factors that limits participation is the time users have to
play an active role in the design process. In 3 projects we found that
users had a very restricted amount of time for this, they had to do the
job next to their usual work.

In some situations, for example when the process is very complex, when
there are a lot of conflicts or when a substantial loss of jobs is expected, direct user participation may not be enough or may even be unattain-
able.

4.3. The role of the computer experts

The role of the computer experts, the system designers, is much more predominant than the blueprint would lead us to believe, as figure 3 shows
clearly. This applies especially to the first three phases of the design
process in which important choices have to be made. Designers have a great
advantage in knowledge over users and management. Expertise therefore
becomes the most important influence system. Managers tend to see automation as a technical problem, that must be solved by an expert. In our
interviews with system designers a lot of problems that have been described before reappeared (e.g. Algera and Koopman [1]). One point in particular attracted our attention. System designers often were not too happy
about their predominant role. But they were often confronted with a forced-choice situation. Management and users lacked the essential knowledge
to fulfill their roles in a proper way. They told the only expert available to behave as an expert. Neither management nor the users did commit
theirselves too much. In this position the designers were quite vulnerable.

They had to spend a lot of time in explaining their terminology to management and users to keep them informed at least. Even so there was a possibility that they were told during the implementation phase they had missed the point and had only been inspired by their own technical considerations. We don't mean to idealize the behavior or motivation of the system designers. But often some "scapegoating" is found when their role in design processes is described. We think that some of the problems that do occur in the design process are consequences of the forced-choice position designers are in.

5. CONCLUSION

The results of this study show that often there is a discrepancy between blueprint and actual practice in the design and implementation of computer-based information systems. Management commitment and control are less than would be expected. The effect of management and user involvement seems to be contingent upon a number of conditions. The predominant role system designers often have is partly explained by not fulfilling this conditions.

REFERENCES

[1] Algera, J.A. and Koopman, P.L., Automation: Design process and implementation, in: Drenth, P.J.D., Thierry, Hk., Willems, P.J. and Wolff, Ch.J. de, (eds.), Handbook of Work and Organizational Psychology (Wiley & Sons, Chichester, 1984).

[2] PROject control and DOcumentation STAndards (PRODOSTA) (Philips/CSD-ISA, 1977).

[3] Argelo, S.M., Valkuilen bij automatieprojecten. Informatie (1982) 24, 133-140.

[4] Brabander, B. de and Estrőm, A., Successful information systems development projects. Management Science (1977) 24, 2, 191-199.

[5] Ives, B. and Olson, M.H., User involvement and MIS success: A review of research. Management Science (1984) 30, 586-603.

[6] Koopman, P.L. and Wierdsma, A.F.M., Work consultation as a channel of communication and as a consultative framework, in: Drenth, P.J.D., Thierry, Hk., Willems, P.J. and Wolff, Ch.J. de, (eds.), Handbook of Work and Organizational Psychology (Wiley & Sons, Chichester, 1984).

[7] DIO-International Research Team, A contingency model of participative decision making: An analysis of 56 decisions in three Dutch organisations. Journal of Occupational Psychology (1983) 56, 1-18.

[8] Hedberg, B., Computer systems to support industrial democracy, in: Mumford, E. and Sackman, H., (eds.), Human Choice and Computers (Norht-Holland, Amsterdam, 1975).

THE PSYCHOLOGY OF WORK AND ORGANIZATION
G. Debus and H.-W. Schroiff (Editors)
© Elsevier Science Publishers B.V. (North-Holland), 1986

INTEGRATED SOFTWARE-DESIGN

A work-oriented approach to the
humanization of computerized clerical tasks

Lothar P. SCHARDT

German Trade Unions Federation - Federal Executive -
AWA Task Force "Ergonomics for Employees"
Tersteegenstraße 77, P.O. Box 2601, Phone-Nr. 0211-450690/9
D-4000 Düsseldorf 30, Federal Republic of Germany

ABSTRACT

The enhancing use of computers is a very big challenge not only
for the respective sciences but for the trade unions too. The
question is, how they can control and codetermine this development maintaining their fundamental objectives which stresses the
humanization of working life as well as the promotion of social
progress by the use of new technologies, especially EDP-systems.
This paper contains a very brief survey of the work oriented
approach to job design and EDP-system development in current
office automation promoted by the German Trade Unions Federation.
This presentation is focussed on the conception for the design of
the technical equipment, especially some remarkable attributes of
the user-surface of the software, the so-called man-machine-in-
terfaces. Finally few indications are made to the complexity of
the social interests of employees involved in EDP-system development, the respective claims and measures for worker representation in the process of office automation, and the need of integrating the ergonomically software-design into this framework.

1. OVERVIEW

The following is not a presentation of latest findings of research in ergonomics and computer science but an approach to the transfer of scientific knowledge about the area of human-computer-interaction into the office. It is dedicated to employees and their shop stewards as a guideline
for the work-oriented (re-)design of EDP-Systems. Humanization of working
life is the fundamental objective emphasized as an trade unionistic coun-
terpart to the current office automation which is primarily under control
of economic criteria (e.g. return of investment). This framework should
be taken into account although the following presentation cannot mention
it further but must be focussed on the technical system.

With reference to the IFIP-model of human-computer-interaction (cf. [1]),
we pragmatically differentiate four user-interfaces:

o   Input-Output-Interface:
     - techniques for manipulating the data input, e.g. keyboard, touch-
        screen, speech-input;
     - presentation of the information output on the screen, that is the
        design of the screen-layout (e.g. in accordance with the psycholo-
        gical 'Gestalt'-rules).

o   Dialogue-Interface (cf. ch. 2)

o   Tool-Interface (cf. ch. 3)

o   Monitoring-Interface: summarizes all software properties or options,
     which can be used for monitoring employees performance and behavior,
     with regard to the civil right on 'informational self-determination'.

What does 'work-oriented design' of these user-interfaces mean? I will
try to give an answer only for the design of the dialogue and the tool
interface; the other two interfaces must remain undiscussed because of
the limitations of this paper (cf. [2],[3]). After that I will give some
comments on further conceptions needed for embedding the software-design
in a comprehensive approach for the configuration of EDP (ch. 4) as well
as for the whole organization of the respective working group (ch. 5).

2. DIALOGUE-INTERFACE

The state of the art regarding the ergonomical design of dialogue-in-
terfaces is still rather poor: Most of the rules formulated in the literature are purely theoretical and deductive, and sometimes apparently
'constructed' by common sense-psychology of EDP-people; serious empirical
investigations at laboratories or even in the office or on the shop floor
are very seldom up to now and most of them are still running [4].

Nevertheless the DIN (German Institute for Standardization) has edited a
first proposal "VDT-work stations. Fundamentals of dialogue-design. (Nr.
66 234 part 8)" (reprinted in[5]). It emphasizes five criteria: reliability, fault tolerance and transparency, ability for self-explanations,
task fitting and controllability by the user. Instead of giving detailed
comments on these I will try to summarize our evaluation:

If enterprises would be obliged to accomplish that standard, most of the
software in use now, would be ready for the scrap heap - or has to be
adapted put up with an enormous expense. Without detriment of this the
fundamental objectives as well as most of their operationalization by
these five criteria is getting our support. Especially the renunciation
of the criteria "ease of learn" or "ease of use", which are very widespread and apparently fully accepted without reserve in the U.S. compu-
ter-science, is one of the most favourable aspects of the DIN approach.

Designing the dialogue-interface the most fundamental prerequisite for a
ergonomical use of computers is to avoid negative workload (under- as
well as overload). Current computer-systems very often are lacking in reliability, response time, consistency of command-names etc. This is frequently an important source of stress which is to be eliminated. Apart
from that, three requirements are specific and very crucial for the design of the dialogue-interface:

1. The dialogue process must always be <u>under control of the user</u>. A variety of options should be given to the user including procedures, which are related to the task content as well as to the sequence of transactions. A strictly system-guided dialogue cannot fulfill this requirement. The implementation of an universal "undo"-command e.g. with which you can interrupt active procedures whenever you want, preserves the actual state of the system; it can be reactivated if it is needed. The psychological benefit expected by this requirement is the recovery of flexibility as it was usual in the conventional office.

2. Our second crucial requirement claims the <u>possibility for individualizing</u> the methods and styles of task performance. We do know by ergonomic findings that such individual styles of performance are more efficient than standardized (e.g. in the assembly of motors [6]). Still more important from our point of view is the relation between individualized task performance and the amount of self-realization in working life. We don't want only adjustable desks for the terminals – but we want adjustable software for the users too. One technical solution for example is the option of status switching, that enables you to alternate with a menue-driven dialogue if you are a novice in the respective application domain or software, and command language if you are a sophisticated user.

3. Contrary to the "ease of learn"-philosophy of system development we particularly emphasize the <u>promotion of learning</u>, our third crucial requirement. It is founded by the theory of action as formulated especially by HACKER [8]; this theorectical approach seems to be quite well known in current European work psychology, so that I can renounce further comments. Indeed it is very difficult to get an operational definition on the basis of our actual knowledge – we too have no recipes. But often it is possible to identify specific features of a specific software that are obviously contradictory to the promotion of learning und learnability. Menues as the only one type of dialogue processing or pure form filling for example would be incompatible with this criterion.

Furthermore we are claiming additional software requirements regarding the dialogue-interface – in detail:

o <u>transparency of the system state</u> (according to NIEVERGELTs sites-modes-trails-model [10])

o <u>optimal mental workload</u> (e.g. by variations in tasks and performance conditions)

o <u>task fitting</u> (e.g. the correspondence of screen output and hard copy according to the WYSWYG-rule: "<u>W</u>hat <u>y</u>ou <u>s</u>ee is <u>w</u>hat <u>y</u>ou'll <u>g</u>et")

o <u>fault tolerance</u> (e.g. it should be impossible to activate mighty commands - like erasing - only by an erroneous keystroke)

o <u>consistency</u> (compatibility with the expectancies of the users like the obligation of the algebraic rules in a spreadsheet)

o <u>privacy of personal data</u> ('informational self-determinantion').

3. TOOL-INTERFACE

The 'tool-interface' is a logical construct which summarizes all features
and options which can be used additional to the routine application procedures. Functionally it enables the user to solve special problems, to
recover or to prevent faults, to perform new tasks, or to realize individual performance styles as yet mentioned above. In other words, we would
like to encourage personal computing in the strict sense of the term.
Therefore the tool-interface should have four crucial features:

1. The user should be able to manage local data, e.g. individual custo-
    mer data sheets for counselling of a bank clerk. In order to render
    this, usually a data base system is needed as a technical option.

2. EDP-Systems should be programmable at the local workstation by the
    user. Of course this demands a lot of specific computer knowledge by
    the employees. Under this presumption programmability may include
    even the production of small individual application procedures, e.g.
    by use of a fourth generation language. In the domain of word proces-
    sing, the programming of a dictionary of paragraphs for standardized
    correspondence (e.g. insurance contracts or selling offers) can be
    mentionend as an example.
3. The third crucial feature may be labelled with modifiability of stan-
    dard application software, which is primarily important for the in-
    formation input, retrieval and output. A screen management utility
    for instance is a useful software tool supporting this requirement.

4. For all tasks which are not fully determined by a completely defined
    quantity of information input (as it is usually in e.g. counselling
    jobs), it may be useful having the authorization for free access to
    central or public data bases - under strict consideration of the
    privacy of personal related data of course. As a minimum criterion
    the access to information must not be worse than it was before in the
    noncomputerized work environment.

Technical realizations for a comfortable tool-interface for instance are
spreadsheet, report utility, data base query languages, devices for the
support of programming like makros, fourth generation language. Those
features obviously will cost a lot, and the necessary qualifications also
will challenge the users as well as the resources of the companies.

This conception of software tools for the average user (and not only for
the programmers) belongs to the postulate of getting at least all degrees
of freedom in task performance by the use of computers, which had been
given formerly in the conventional office. With respect to the theory of
action, this tool-conception is dedicated to the enhancement of competence und autonomy in action by supporting the development of the so-called planning strategy (cf. [8]).

4. THE DIVISION OF FUNCTIONS BETWEEN MAN AND COMPUTER

Usually the requirements specification for system development emphasizes
three types of criteria:

o   Functionality: What tasks should be computerized? Does the computer
    (the algorithm) perform the task correctly?

o   Financial and economic frame: Does the system development fit the in-
    vestment plan? Is the system efficient with respect to the cost-bene-
    fit-relation?

o   Software-quality criteria: Does the system development suffice the
    technological state of the art (e.g. structured and modularized pro-
    gramming)? Does the system fit criteria such as correctness, portabi-
    lity, disposability etc.?

That's all! But the fact that the EDP-system development always necessarily implies the development of work organization and task contents too
apparently doesn't worry. Contrasting this technological-economical based
methodology, our approach is focussed on a work-oriented set of criteria:

1. First of all psychosocial aspects are to be taken into account, that
    means primarily the prevention of stress: Avoidance of quantitative
    und qualitative over- and underload, sufficient decision latitude und
    ob- jective resources for coping are the main topics.

2. Secondly the task content related scientific findings and principles
    should be mentioned. The most important catchwords for these organi-
    zational criteria are job enlargement, job enrichment, job rotation
    and (autonomous) groupworking. In addition special attention should
    be called to the two principals of "differential" and "dynamic work
    design" as formulated by ULICH and coworkers [9],[10].

3. The third set of criteria contains requirements specific to the re-
    spective organizational unit. That embraces problem domains such as
    the specific structure of personel, possibilities concerning the
    staffs' vocational development, the integration of handicapped etc.
    This set of criteria very often is the most important one with re-
    spect to the real chance for organizational change.

4. The fourth and very crucial set of criteria claims so-called minimum
    task contents. This conception emphasizes five subcriteria in detail:

    o   A minimum of variety in the type and content of the task must be
        given (only word processing the whole day would not fulfill this
        criterion).

    o   Holistic tasks, which are psychologically complete; especially
        physical and mental skill requirements must be combined as well as
        the different components of a complete task, namely planning, dis-
        position, performance and controlling must be represented in the
        individual job.

    o   Autonomy in task performance must be ensured; a minimum of con-
        trol- and decision-latitude should be guarenteed.

    o   Each job, especially computerized work, should enclose incentives
        and possibilities for learning.

    o   Last not least a minimum of formal and informal social contacts
        are absolutely necessary, because of the technical communication
        personal relationships are getting still more important.

Let me now give a short comment on the <u>procedure of system development</u>:
Usually EDP-systems are selected or developed, and when tests have been
successful, work organization is 'made'. That means the latter is only a
residue or a derived parameter. But it is our objective to converse this
procedure:

The first step is to construct a preliminary draft of the work organization, that may be characterized as an ideal conception focussed on the
task contents. That implies a concrete suggestion of the division of work
functions between the employee and the planned EDP-system. In the second
step, software engineering continues with an investigation of the actual
technical opportunities for realizing this preliminary layout of the
workstations in order to sustain the task performance by EDP. The result
usually will be only few technical solutions.

In the third step you have to test the compatibility of the selected
system configurations with the organizational layout. Usually both components will not fit best.Therefore you have to adjust both bringing them
nearer, the fourth step. That means you have to test it against the requirements specification, that encloses not only functional and technological but ergonomical criteria, too: The latter two measures are used for
the stepwise approximation of work organisation and EDP-system configuration in a long running spiral procedure at which each cycle represents a
complete feed back circle. The result of this procedure will be a comprehensive conception for an integrated technical and organizational redesign, at which the starting point of <u>EDP-system development</u> must be a
preliminary draft of the division of functions between man and computer
conjointly with a tentative layout of the work organization focussing the
task contents.

5. ON THE PRACTICAL AND POLITICAL SIGNIFICANCE OF THE WORK-ORIENTED
    APPROACH TO THE ERGONOMICAL DESIGN OF COMPUTERIZED OFFICE WORK

With respect to specific historical background in the FRG, our comprehensive concept for the humanization of computerized clerical work (figure
1) is labelled with "<u>qualified mixed work</u>". It is embracing much more social interests of employees involved in office automation, than are covered by the psychological and socio-technical criteria for software design
and system development presented above. Accordingly, we are claiming some
more very important issues:

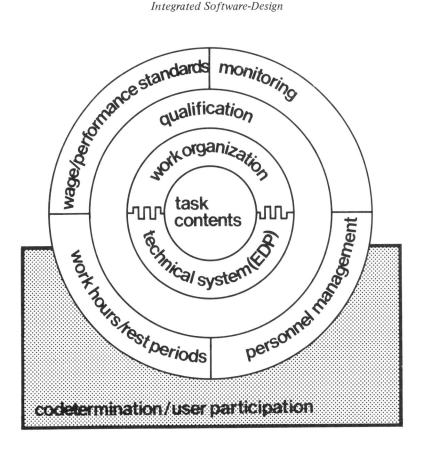

Fig. 1: The components of the "qualified mixed work"-conception

o   a programme for a comprehensive <u>EDP-training</u> of the users;

o   agreements about the <u>limitation of the rate of work</u> (performance
     standards), which usually in the area of white collars is to realize
     by ascertaining the quantity of the staff;

o   regulations about maximum <u>work hours</u> and <u>rest periods</u> at VDT-work-
     stations;

o   undertaking the privacy of personal data and the civil right on '<u>in-
     formational self-determination</u>' by sufficient regulations;

o   a systematically planned <u>development of personel</u> corresponding to the
     technical and organizational structure.

Last not least I will give some remarks on the political significance of
our approach in four theses:

1. We are asserting that such a work-oriented approach will only work,
   if there is additionally a serious and substantial involvement of and
   commitment by the users. This necessarily implies an active user participation guaranteed by collective union-management-agreements. For
   the German Trade Unions policy this is a question of the so-called
   co-determination at the workplace as it was adopted in 1984 by the
   Federal Committee of all affiliates (cf.[11]).

2. From our point of view the design of EDP-workstations doesn't matter
   at all if there is no sufficient solution for the avoidance or compensation of the generally occuring negative social impacts of the
   application of new technologies, especially the unemployment. Humanization by job design only will run if the most essential 'human' features of working life, namely employment and an adequate remuneration
   has been guaranteed.

Ensuring the latter was the main issue of German Unions policy in the
last three decades regarding mechanization and automation. Because this
is not sufficient today, the Unions have drawn two strategic consequences:

3. Shortening the amount of work hours; actually the introduction of
   35-work hours a week is claimed (for that reason in 1984 we have had
   a very big strike in the metal industry); respectively the most
   important objectives are securing and enhancing employment and
   decreasing workload.

4. Ergonomically and socially acceptable job and technology design is
   the second issue [12], [13]. This paper should have given a rough
   idea of what is meant herewith. The most crucial point of this policy
   is the objective to prevent negative individual and social impacts by
   intervening in system development and organizational change on the
   basis of an integrated and holistic work-oriented approach.

These short remarks should have made further evident the real complexity of the humanization framework and the necessity of embedding the particular measures, especially the ergonomically software-design, into a
comprehensive strategy of workers control.

REFERENCES

[1]   DZIDA, W.: Das IFIP-Modell für Benutzerschnittstellen. Office
        Management, Sonderheft 'Mensch-Maschine-Kommunikation', 1983, 6-8
[2]   SCHARDT, L.P.: Mischarbeit im Büro: Arbeitswissenschaftliche Kri-
        terien und Konzepte. In DGB-BUNDESVORSTAND (Ed.): Mischarbeit und
        Mitbestimmung. Düsseldorf: Selbstverlag, 1985, 30-40
[3]   CORNELIUS, D.: Arbeitsorientierte Softwaregestaltung. AWA-Arbeits-
        papier 122 (Ed.: DGB-Bundesvorstand, Projektgruppe AWA). Düssel-
        dorf: Selbstverlag, 1985
[4]   DZIDA, M.; LANGENHEDER, W.; CORNELIUS, D. & SCHARDT, L.P.: Auswir-
        kungen des EDV-Einsatzes auf die Arbeitssituation und Möglichkei-
        ten seiner arbeitsorientierten Gestaltung. Eine Dokumentation von
        Forschungs- und Entwicklungsprojekten in der Bundesrepublik
        Deutschland, Österreich und der Schweiz. GMD-Studien Nr. 82. St.
        Augustin: GMD, 1984
[5]   SCHARDT, L.P.: Integrierte Softwaregestaltung. Ein arbeitsorien-
        tiertes Konzept für Verwaltungstätigkeiten. AWA-Arbeitspapier 120
        (Ed.: DGB-Bundesvorstand, Projektgruppe AWA). Düsseldorf: Selbst-
        verlag, 1985
[6]   TRIEBE, J.K.: Untersuchungen zum Lernprozeß während des Erwerbs
        der Grundqualifikation. Zürich: Selbstverlag (Lehrstuhl für
        Arbeits- und Betriebspsychologie der ETH), 1978.
[7]   HACKER, W.: Allgemeine Arbeits- und Ingenieurspsychologie. Bern,
        Stuttgart, Wien: Huber, (2nd. ed.) 1978
[8]   NIEVERGELT, J.: Design of man-machine interfaces: Towards the
        integrated interactive system. Notizen zu interaktiven Systemen,
        1984, 13, 3-12
[9]   ULICH, E.: Über das Prinzip der differentiellen Arbeitsgestaltung.
        Industrielle Organisation, 1978, 47, 566-568
[10]   ULICH, E.; FREI, F. & BAISCH, C.: Zum Begriff der persönlichkeits-
        förderlichen Arbeitsgestaltung. Zeitschrift für Arbeitswissen-
        schaft, 1980, 34, 210-213
[11]   CORNELIUS, D. & SCHARDT, L.P.: Direkte Arbeitnehmerbeteiligung bei
        der betrieblichen EDV-Systementwicklung. Partizipative System-
        gestaltung - Mitbestimmung am Arbeitsplatz - Gewerkschaftliche
        Interessenvertretung. In Neue Medien und Technologien - Wie damit
        umgehen? Beiträge zu einer Strategiedebatte. Berlin: Die Arbeits-
        welt, 1984, 30-64
[12]   GERMAN TRADE UNIONS FEDERATION: Ergonomics for employees. The work
        of the DGB-Projektgruppe AWA. AWA-Arbeitspapier 128 (Ed.: DGB-Bun-
        desvorstand, Projektgruppe AWA). Düsseldorf: Selbstverlag, 1985
[13]   IG METALL: Das Aktionsprogramm: Arbeit und Technik - "Der Mensch
        muß bleiben!". Frankfurt/M.: Selbstverlag, 1984

THE PSYCHOLOGY OF WORK AND ORGANIZATION
G. Debus and H.-W. Schroiff (Editors)
© Elsevier Science Publishers B.V. (North-Holland), 1986

EVALUATION OF EXPERT SYSTEMS FOR DECISION SUPPORT

BERNHARD ZIMOLONG
Arbeits-und Organisationspsychologie
Ruhr Universität Bochum
4630 Bochum

1. INTRODUCTION

Advances in computer and communication technology are resulting in increasingly complex systems. This trend toward very complex and often very high risk systems has substantially increased the need for and interest in automatic operating systems and decision support systems (DSS).

DSS based on computer technology aid humans in operating nuclear or conventional power generation plants, supervising robots and manipulators, finding optimal courses for navigation systems, and improving troubleshooting in complex electronic equipment.

DSS try to match human cognitive behavior as closely as possible in order to communicate with users at their required knowledge level. Different approaches exist to model perception, judgment and decision-making, and motor performance. Systems engineering models (SEM, ROUSE 1980), or better known as 'optimal control' models simulate the operator's overall performance by combining mathematical models with the system's dynamics. They can claim only limited success. For application purposes, computational formulas are often not feasible, more important, however, they use decision-making and problem-solving strategies totally different from those of human operators.

In one area of artificial intelligence, however, that of expert systems, considerable progress has been made to model human cognitive behavior such as planning and scheduling, diagnosis, and problem-solving.

To understand the psychological requirements in aiding humans who are performing complex tasks, I will focus on dynamic process control, e.g., to navigate a vessel or to control a chemical plant.

The operator's task in dynamic process control mainly has shifted from direct manual control to a supervisor of semiautomated subsystems (SHERIDAN 1981). Consequently, the skills required shifted from perceptual and motor skills to planning and scheduling of tasks and actions, decision - making in multiple task situations, and problem solving in abnormal or emergency situations. The combination of task and situational demand determines the operators skill level.

2. PROCESSING REQUIREMENTS OF SKILL LEVELS

All tasks require a certain skill level. The required level is a function of the situational demands and the experience of the operator. In Fig. 1, the endpoints of the skill dimension are denoted as routine and knowledge level, respectively. The human processing characteristics refer to three basic information stages: perceptual, cognitive, and motor behavior. Experienced and inexperienced operators may be distinguished according to the required skill level and the information processing characteristics involved in accomplishing a task under given situational constraints. In Fig. 1, the shaded area (task block) indicates a failure detection task to be accomplished in an emergency case; perceptual-motor and cognitive activities are required at different skill levels (shaded areas of operator block).

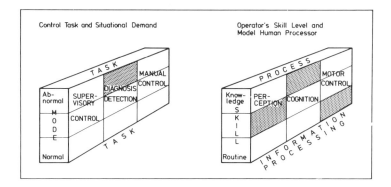

FIGURE 1
Process control tasks and human information processing at different skill levels.

Performance at a given skill level determines information input and cognitive processing. RASMUSSEN (1983) describes three levels of skilled performance, denoted as: skill (routine), rule, and knowledge based level performance (Fig. 2).

The skill based behavior represents highly automated sensory-motor and cognitive performance, and takes place without conscious control as smooth, highly integrated patterns of behavior. It maps stimuli to responses in a fairly rapid low-level cognition mode. Information or signals from the environment have no meaning or significance except as cues triggering the appropriate actions.

At the rule based level, an action is selected by activating in working memory a hierachy of rules. After mentally scanning those rules, the human will implement the appropriate rule or set of rules. Sequencing of automated subroutines in a familiar work situation is typically controlled by some external schedules, diagrams, menus, or decision rules. Signs are used to select or modify rules controlling the sequencing of skilled subroutines.

Knowledge based level behavior is evoked when entirely new, unstructured, or complex problems are encountered. In solving problems, identification of the current state is crucial; the user/operator searches for the target state and then employs a set of operators or methods to change the current state into the target state. The internal structure of the system to be controlled often is represented by a mental model. Information is perceived as symbols. They refer to meaningful concepts tied to functional or physical properties.

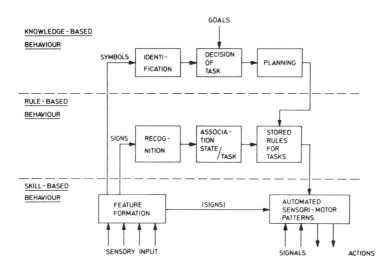

FIGURE 2
Performance levels of skilled human operators. From Rasmussen, 1983.

As might be expected, operators approach familiar and unfamiliar situations quite differently (Rasmussen 1983, Rouse 1984). Familiar situations call upon the human's pattern recognition abilities. Signals and signs are mapped directly to appropriate courses of action. For example, colorgraphic piecharts of economic information for a business, or circular profiles of physical variables for an engineering system are oriented toward pattern recognition.

In contrast, unfamiliar situations require that the system state be displayed as disaggregated elements. This is due to the fact that particular variables, e.g. temperatures, inflation rates, employee turnover rates, are usually needed to trace through causal or functional relationships.

Familiar and unfamiliar characteristics of situations are likely to be dependent on the particular individual who is to be aided by a DSS. As a result, strategies, and hence appropriate forms of information, are likely to vary with individuals. Ideally, therefore, the nature of the decision support as well as the human computer interface should be adapted to individual users. Rouse and Rouse (1983) presented a framework for characterizing adaptive decision aids.

To serve as a candidate for a DSS in dynamic process control, the following requirements seem to be important:

(1) FUNCTIONALITY: Overall performance of DSS
(2) FACTUAL KNOWLEDGE: Similarity of DSS factual or declarative know-
                            ledge base with operator's domain-specific
                            knowledge, hypotheses, and beliefs.
(3) PROCEDURAL KNOWLEDGE: Equivalence of DSS inference procedures with
                            operator's reasoning and inference strategies.
(4) ADAPTABILITY: Adapting DSS procedures and factual knowledge to
                            operator's skill level and situational require-
                            ments.

3. EXPERT COMPUTER SYSTEMS

Artificial intelligence (AI) is the branch of computer science that attempts to have machines emulate human intelligent behavior. Since the DENDRAL project began in the mid 60s at Stanford University, some of the most productive work in AI has been performed in the subdiscipline known as expert systems. The main goal is producing expert level performance in programs (see table 1).

Table 1   Expert Systems Applications Domain

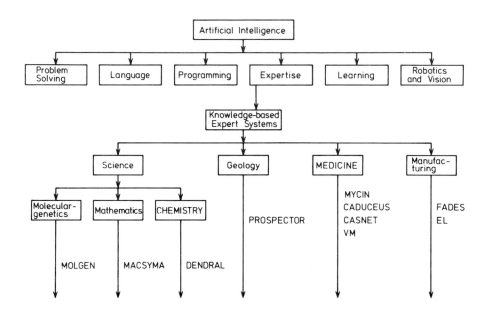

These systems have attained expert levels in several domains: mineral prospecting, computer configuration, chemical structure elucidation, symbolic mathematics, medical diagnosis and therapy, and electronic circuit analysis.

What distinguishes such a system from an ordinary applications program is that in most expert systems, the model of problem solving in the application domain is explicitly in view as a separate entity or knowledge base rather than appearing only implicitly as part of the coding program.

Ordinary computer programs organize knowledge on two levels: data and program. Most expert systems, however, organize knowledge on three levels: (1) declarative or data knowledge, (2) procedural or knowledge base, and (3) control level or inference machine.

In addition to these three components, an ideal architecture of an expert system would include the following components:

o an interface program which aids input/output understandability by the user,
o an explanation system ("Justifier") which accepts and replies to natural language queries from the user about the dynamic line of reasoning, or about the static knowledge base,
o a knowledge base editor to aid in constructing, debugging, and updating knowledge bases,
o a blackboard which allows for intermediate analysis of alternatives, and
o a scheduler for controlling which relevant "set" of knowledge is to be applied at any particular time.

(1) On the data level is declarative knowledge (facts) about the particular problem being solved and the current state of affairs in the attempt to solve the problem. Most of the knowledge is represented in a static collection of facts accompanied by a small set of general procedures for manipulating them. There are several ways to represent declarative knowledge:

o Rule based, representing knowledge as production rules,
o Logic based, representing knowledge as logic procedures,
o Frame based, employing semantic nets to organize and associate knowledge about each object in terms of various slots and slot values within logical frames.

One or more representation schemes can be selected for a particular expert system. NAU (1983) describes various represention implementations in expert systems.

(2) Domain specific problem solving knowledge is usually procedural in the sense that it tells how the knowledge for a problem can be manipulated in order to go about solving the problem. The bulk of this knowledge may be represented as procedures or operators for using it.

Two common forms to represent domain specific, problem-solving knowledge are logical representations and production rules. Production rules are of the form:

IF (premise) THEN (action).

The premise is a combination of predicates, which, when evaluated by the program as true, lead to the specified action. AI systems in which knowledge is represented by production rules are called production systems.

Table 2   MYCIN Production Rule (from Barr & Feigenbaum 1982).

A MYCIN PRODUCTION RULE RULE 050

PREMISE: (AND (SAME CNTXT INFECT PRIMARY-BACTEREMIA)
            (MEMBF CNTXT SITE STERILESITES)
            (SAME CNTXT PORTAL GI)
 	
ACTION: (CONCLUDE CNTXT IDENT BACTEROIDES TALLY .7)
 	
MYCINS English translation:
 	
IF   1. the infection is primary-bacteremia, and
      2. the site of the culture is one of the
         sterile sites, and
      3. the suspected portal of entry of the
         organism is the gastrointestinal tract,
 	
THEN there is suggestive evidence (.7) that the identity
      of the organism is bacteroides.

Production rules tend to better handle plausible reasoning, while logical procedures are very useful with logical, deductive inferences. PROLOG is an example of an AI language that relies on logic procedures.

(3)   The control and search strategy or inference engine governs the manner in which the problem-solving rules are applied. An inference engine can have an inherent control and search strategy, or the user can also have access to selecting the appropriate strategy to fit a particular need. NAU (1983) describes particular control strategies from the AI domain.

An application example of a production system in dynamic process control is KARL (Knowledgeable Application of Rule Based Logic, Knaeupper and Rouse 1983). It models human problem solving when controlling a dynamic process such as operating an aircraft or supervising a power plant. KARL consists of a set of production rules, i.e., it has a knowledge base and a control structure. A simplified flow chart is given in the following figure.

The model accomplishes four tasks:
  o Failure diagnosis and correction,
  o Transition tasks such as start-up, shutdown, takeoff, landing,
  o Steady state tuning involves actions oriented toward optimizing
     performance,
  o Procedures contain standard sequences of rules, each of which
     is applicable to particular operating situations.

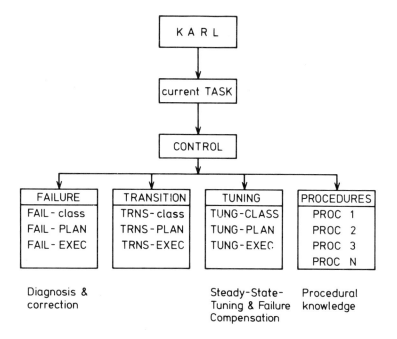

FIGURE 3
Flow chart of KARL (from Knaeupper & Rouse 1983).

Each module, except for procedures, is divided into three levels of human problem-solving: recognition and classification, planning, and execution and monitoring.
The control structure consists of two modules:

        o identification of current task
        o identification of knowledge base to perform the task.

KARL was tested in a process control simulation task. An overall evaluation of the model was performed by comparing the total production achieved by 32 subjects of 4 different groups and by the computer programm. The production system succeeded quite well in matching the average or typical behavior for all 4 groups. An action-by-action comparison between the model and a subset of subjects, however, produced a match of only 25% to 55% of actions. Subjects employed a variety of strategies to solve the problems, which neither corresponded very well with the strategies of the production system, nor with the strategies of other subjects.

4. EVALUATION OF EXPERTS SYSTEMS FOR DSS

As previously outlined, basic requirements for DSS are overall functionality, similarity of declarative and procedural knowledge, and adaptability of DSS to the user's skill level and situational requirements.

Expert systems match human behavior in terms of decision-making and problem-solving better than any other known models. They employ similar reasoning and inference strategies as compared to humans. Little, however, is known with respect to the factual knowledge base of operators in various process systems as well as procedural knowledge dependent on the operator's skill level. As compared to "mature" systems such as DENDRAL or MYCIN, the implementation of the human operator's knowledge should be straightforward, as far as factual knowledge is concerned.

Knowledge engineering is the process of acquiring knowledge and building an expert system (Feigenbaum 1977). Analysis of human repertory grids based on interviewing methods is an example of a knowledge elicitation technique (BOOSE 1984). The information is analysed and organized into knowledge bases, which may be directly read with expert system tools such as OPS (FORGY & McDermott, 1977).

Adapting an expert system to individual skill levels requires more knowledge about human information constraints and cognitive processing at different skill levels. KARL was not adjusted to individual strategies and factual knowledge bases of subjects. Presumedly, this would have improved the match between the actions of the human operators and the production system.

Methods of adaptation become the central issue. Via simulation studies it was found (ROUSE & ROUSE 1983) that DSS would be most effective if the system knew the human's current state of knowledge, current allocation of attention, and intended allocation of attention. The design of DSS, therefore, should allow for transitionality such that, after a time the user finds himself in an experienced mode of interaction simply by having practiced as a novice. BADRE (1984) describes some conditions a system should meet to provide transitionality by specifying a menu-driven interactive strategy. Other approaches (ROUSE 1984) consider direct but unobtrusive observation (e.g., eye tracking) inference via physiological measures and inference via model matching.

5. REFERENCES

Badre, A.N., Designing Transitionality into the User-Computer Interface. In G. Salvendy (Ed.), Human-Computer Interaction, Proc., First USA-Japan Conference on Human Computer Interaction. Amsterdam, Elsevier, 1984, 27-34.

Barr, A. & Feigenbaum, F.A., The Handbook of Artificial Intelligence, Vol. I, II . Los Altos, CA., William Kaufman, 1982.

Boose, J., A Framework for Transferring Human Expertise. In G. Salvendy (Ed.), Human Computer Interaction, Proc. First USA-Japan Conference on Human Computer Interaction. Amsterdam, Elsevier, 1984, 247-254.

Feigenbaum, E.A., The Art of Artificial Intelligence: Themes and Case Studies of Knowledge Engineering. Proc. IJCAI-77, 5, 1977, 1014-1029.

Forgy, C., and McDermott, J., OPS, A Domain Independent Production System Language. Proc. IJCAI-77, 5, 1977, 933-939.

Hayes-Roth, F., Waterman, D.A., and Lenat, D.B. Building Expert Systems. Reading, M.A., Addison-Wesley, 1983.

Knaeupper, A., and Rouse, W.B., A model of human problem solving in dynamic environments. Proc. Human Factors Society, 1983, 695-699.

Nau, D.S., Expert Computer Systems. In: IEEE Computer, 1983, 2, 63-85.

Rasmussen, J., Skills, Rules and Knowledge, Signals, Signs, and Symbols and other Distinctions in Human Performance Models. IEEE Transactions on Systems, Man, and Cybernetics, SMC-13, 1983, 3, 257-266.

Rouse, W.B., Systems Engineering Models of Human-Machine Interaction. New York, North Holland Inc., 1980.

Rouse, W.B., Design and Evaluation of Computerbased Decision Support Systems. In G. Salvendy (Ed.), Human-Computer Interaction, Proc., First USA-Japan Conference. Amsterdam, Elsevier, 1984, 229-246.

Rouse, W.B., and Rouse, S.H., A Framework for Research on Adaptive Decision Aids. In Aerospace Med.Research Lab., Wright-Patterson Air Force Base (Ed.), Report No. AFAMRL-TR-83-082. Ohio, 1983.

Sheridan, T., Supervisory Control: Problems, Theory and Experiment in Application to Undersea Remote Control Systems. In MIT Man Machine Systems Laboratory Report, February. Boston, MA., 1981.

THE PSYCHOLOGY OF WORK AND ORGANIZATION
G. Debus and H.-W. Schroiff (Editors)
© *Elsevier Science Publishers B.V. (North-Holland), 1986*

COGNITIVE ERGONOMICS and HUMAN-COMPUTER INTERACTION

Report of the chairman

Norbert A. Streitz

Institute of Psychology, Technical University Aachen
Jägerstr. 17 -19, D - 5100 Aachen, F.R. Germany

Contributors: Bevan (GB), Gaussin (B), Gerhardt (F), Hudson (NL), Pavard (F), Rohr (D), Streitz (D), Tauber (D)

1. INTRODUCTION

This workshop centered around the role psychologists might play in the design, evaluation, and improvement of information technologies, especially in work situations. The uprise of interactive computer systems for various facets of work and society within the last years has not been paralleled by an equal weighting within psychological research. Although there is some body of research on hardware ergonomics the above statement is especially true for what is called "software ergonomics" or "cognitive ergonomics". The workshop addressed this topic from different points of view. Although the researchers came from different backgrounds and institutions, they shared the opinion of a great need for more basic and cognitive oriented research on the psychology of human-computer interaction.

Following the introductory paper by the organizer and chairman, the workshop was divided into two parts. The first part consisted of three papers dealing with the notion of "mental models" and its principal relevance for designing interfaces of interactive systems. The three papers of the second part focussed on applied questions in rather different domains.

2. OVERVIEW ON TOPICS, CONTRIBUTORS AND THEIR AFFILIATIONS

- The notion of models in human-computer interaction and their role in the design of interactive systems
  Norbert Streitz (Institute of Psychology, Technical University Aachen)

- Cognitive models: A bridge between computer science and psychology
  Nigel Bevan (Division of Information Technology and Computing, National Physical Laboratory, Teddington, England)

- Mental models and the structure of displays
  Patrick Hudson (Institute of Perception, TNO, Soesterberg, Netherlands)

- Building up mental models in human-computer interaction:
  Some empirical results
  Gabriele Rohr & Michael J. Tauber
  (IBM Germany, Science Center, Heidelberg, F.R. Germany)

- Compatibility between cognitive processes and automatic assistance
  systems for collision avoidance procedures
  Detlef Gerhardt (OPEFORM, Malakoff, France)

- How to develop model constraints by task objectives, capacities of the
  human cognitive system, and hardware
  Bernard Pavard (Laboratoire d'Ergonomie, C.N.A.M., Paris, France)

- Mental workload and human-computer interaction
  Jose Gaussin (Centre de Psychologie du Travail et des Organisations,
                 Universite Catholique de Louvain, Belgium)

3. SUMMARY OF THE PRESENTED PAPERS

The report on the workshop is mainly based on additional descriptions re-
quested from the contributors subsequent to the conference. Unfortunately, not all of the contributors provided them. In these cases, initially
submitted abstracts and our own memory were the basis for the summary.

3.1 The notion of models in human-computer interaction
       and their role in the design of interactive systems

Norbert A. Streitz

The objective of the introductory paper was: to focus attention on research questions connected with cognitive aspects of using interactive
computer systems (ICS), to present a brief overview over existing notions
of the "model" - concept in human-computer interaction, and finally, to
propose a framework for studying the structure and relevance of different
kinds of models in cognitive ergonomics.

The uprise of information technology will result in a situation where
computers are becoming an integral aspect of life for almost anybody.
This implies two things: First, the increasing possibility to delegate
mental work to a machine. Second, this is paralled by a shift in who uses
computers, i.e., from the specialist to the "naive" user. It has to be
stated that society, in general, and decison makers in funding agencies,
in particular, are only beginning to acknowledge the consequences of
this development. Where human factors research in the past concentrated
on the design of keyboards, screens, and office furniture, there is now a
new challenge in the area of software ergonomics. The design of user-
oriented computer systems demands investigations of the fundamental principles of interaction (or "communication") between humans and computers.
Especially the increasing number of nonspecialists requires a detailed
analysis of the cognitive processes involved in using an ICS. The demand
of more user-orientation of an ICS might be formulated in terms of a
request of more "cognitive compatibility" between the way to represent
task domains and problem-solving strategies in the computer and the
"mental model" the user has of these components (Streitz, 1986). But what
is a mental model, how can we investigate its structure, and how can we
make use of the results in designing user-oriented systems?

Reading articles on human-computer interaction, one finds a variety of
usages of the word "model" and almost everybody has something different

in mind. A widely used notion has been introduced by Norman (1983). He proposed to distinguish between the target system, the user's mental model of the target system, the designer's conceptual model of the target system, and a scientist's conceptualization of the mental model (of the system). Norman focusses especially on the mental model and lists a number of characteristic properties. They are incomplete, unstable, parsimonious, and have no firm boundaries, i.e. similar devices get confused with one another. In addition, people's ability to "run" their models, in order to make predictions, are limited. Although we basically agree with these distinctions, there is still a need of extending this approach.

Due to limited space, we can only sketch our approach (for more details see Streitz, 1985, 1986). One basic aspect is to distinguish between the function (e.g., writing, drawing) and the system's implemention of this function. This corresponds with another differentiation we find useful. It results from viewing the use of an ICS as a problem-solving situation. Within this framework, we distinguish between the (original) content problem and an (additional) interaction problem. The content problem is determined by the user's objective to solve a problem in a given domain (e.g. an engineer constructing a piece of equipment). In order to achieve this goal, the engineer makes use of a CAD-system. Assuming that the user is no computer specialist, he is faced with an additional problem: mastering the interaction with the computer system.

Our discussion of the notion of "models" leads to a classification schema of the various models constructed, e.g., by the designer who implements the functions and by the psychologist who studies the mental models of the user. In cases where the system is supposed to be adaptive, it monitors the user's behavior and then constructs a model of the mental model. Thus, we arrive at – what we call – "higher order" models. Our approach allows to specify all (formally derived) models. The number of models of the order n is 4^n and, so far, we considered models up to the order 3 and 4. The approach provides also information on the relevance of each of them for the design of user-oriented systems. It turns out that not all of them are of practical or theoretical relevance.
In addition, we commented on techniques to diagnose the structure of mental models and how to make use of this knowledge about existing user's models. This is connected with the idea of providing metaphors and the principle of direct manipulation. But it can be demonstrated that this reliance on metaphors and analogical thinking is not without substantial problems , especially in cases of mismatches between the metaphor domain and the structure of the actual ICS.

3.2 Cognitive models: A bridge between computer science and psychology

Nigel Bevan

The professional priorities of computer scientists emphasize the functional efficiency of computers as stand alone systems, while the psychologist measures the combined efficiency of integrated human-computer systems. Cognitive modelling provides for objective measurement of user requirements based on established IKBS techniques, thus providing a formal link between computer science and psychology. The paper provided a taxonomy of approaches to the implementation of cognitive models, and indicated the role of cognitive modelling research within the Alvey programme in Great Britain.

3.3 Mental models and the structure of displays

Patrick T.W. Hudson

How we should organize visual displays is a major question which is usually answered in an ad hoc way in most applications. What is proposed is an attempt to answer the question "What makes a good display?". It is generally agreed that a good system will be one which reflects the user's model of the task and of the machine with which that user is interacting. The problem, however, is how to define such models and, then, how to translate such insights into effective displays for those tasks. A formal model, originally based upon an attempt to justify the use of colour in displays (Hudson, 1984) is presented. This model defines the task space into a structure of task predicates. A similar, independent analysis can be made of display capabilities. It is shown how a good display can be made (algorithmically) by the mapping of the display and task structures. A good display will be defined as one which has a homomorphic mapping between task and display.

The general notion of the approach used is that there are tasks which can be either discrete (a word is or is not a keyword) or continuous (e.g. height of an airplane). Discrete values can be two or multi-valued (e.g. status as Own-side, Friendly, Neutral and Hostile is 4 valued). Display predicates can also be two or multi-valued (e.g. Size, To-The-Left-of and Colour (Red, Blue, Yellow)). The initial proposal of Hudson (1984) had task predicates mapped onto the same sort of display predicates (i.e. colour mapping onto status because both take one argument and can have multiple but discrete values). This relationship cannot, however, be a mere list. The structure of predicates is given by the **‹Combination›** and **‹Distinction›** rules developed in Hudson (1985). These rules define how structures can be built up and, almost more importantly, how they can be reduced. What this means is that they define what it is possible to 'ignore' on a display. These rules explain why for instance, one can selectively attend to the whole left side, or the bottom part of a display, but not the top left and bottom right quadrants. The Combination and Distinction rules turn out to define the nature of the mental models a user has of the task he is performing as well as offering a way of structuring the display to suport this model optimally. The formal approach developed can serve as the basis for an algorithm which, given a task description, could define appropriate displays or, alternatively, provide a metric for measuring the quality of displays in terms of tasks.

3.4 Building up mental models: Some empirical results

Gabriele Rohr & Michael J. Tauber

Investigating mental models users build up about a software system means to analyse which information of a system is taken into account. Primarily, we have to distinguish the underlying deep structure of a system (system entities like objects, functions, and their interconnections) and its symbolic representation at the surface (i.e., command words, icons, visual spatial arrangements, manipulation devices like mouse input for direct manipulation, etc.). Furthermore, we have to analyse the meaning the pictures (icons) or the (command) words impart.

Our main hypothesis was that it is more important to represent real structure entities as operations on objects with properties and defined on places than hiding functional components by representing the system's structure by means of function names driven from an original task environment (e.g., desk-top environment for editing and file organisation tasks).

Two different command sets were chosen to represent the same system structure of a file organisation and editing system. The one set, an icon set, expressed system entities as objects on places (e.g., file on (to) storage, etc.) and objects with properties (attributes). The other set, a command word set, expressed only the system's functions with words driven from an original task environment (e.g., "replace" for changing a word into another one, "select" for taking a special file from the storage).

10 subjects performing tasks either with the one or the other command set editor system had to group those commands together which apparently belonged together before and after working with the editor. According to our hypotheses, the subjects in the icon condition grouped those commands together which expressed operations on the same objects and places (semantic grouping of system concepts), while the subjects under the command word condition grouped those commands together which expressed command steps of a subtask (sequential grouping). In addition, there was a high positive significant correlation (1% level) between semantic grouping and performance (i.e., the more the subjects grouped semantically with respect to system components the faster they performed the editing tasks), and a high significant negative correlation (the higher the worse) between sequential grouping and performance (1% level).

These results confirmed our hypotheses postulated above and got an additional confirmation in another experiment. 40 subjects were asked how they build up commands from elementary components. The analysis concentrated on: object vs. function centered and task vs. procedural orientation in composing commands. Subjects who composed commands object-centered and procedural-oriented showed the highest performance on editor tasks.
Summarizing, we can say that for building up an adequate mental model about a system's structure, system entities have to be expressed as procedures executed on objects and places.

3.5 Compatibility between cognitive processes and automatic
     assistance systems for collision avoidance procedures *

     Detlef Gerhardt

Various automatic systems are currently proposed by industry to assist operators in the execution of their tasks. These systems are typically controlled by computer – based information processing systems. However the use of certain systems can present various problems in different tasks. The particular task to be discussed here is collision avoidance procedure at sea.

─────────

*) This research has been carried out within a research contract between
   the Research Department of the Ministry of Transports and OPEFORM.

This task requires the application of various cognitive processes by the
operator. The radar screen constitutes the principal means of acquiring
information in this task (especially in foggy conditions). Supplementary
and supposedly pertinent graphic or numerical information is presented on
the screen by automatic aid systems.

In order to study the contribution of these aids we were interested in
the integration of the information within the set of processes used by
the operator. For the purpose of analysis we have distinguished two main
phases in collision avoidance procedure: the detection of the conflict
and its solution. The operator has an information set which is used as a
basis for setting up the operative representation of the situation to
find the solutions. In order to select one among a number of possible
solutions the operator has to anticipate the development of the situation. The greater the complexity of the conflict, the higher the level
of anticipation of its development will be required. Analysis of the
anticipation level attained and, in particular, the information used with
each of the different automatic systems will, in our opinion, provide
valuable criteria for assessing the compatibility of the information
presented with the cognitive processes used by the operators.

We described an experiment conducted on a micro-computer programmed as a
radar simulator. On this simulator we introduced two modes of representing the information for use in automatic aids for collision avoidance
procedures. We showed the influence of these two modes of presentation on
the processes applied and the performances attained by the operators with
particular emphasis on the question of anticipation.

3.6 How to develop model constraints by task objectives,
     capacities of the human cognitive system, and hardware

     Bernard Pavard

In this study, we attempted to demonstrate that the cognitive activities
in word processing are determined by three types of constraints:

  - task objectives
  - capacities of the human cognitive system
  - editing functions of the equipment used

It can be demonstrated that these three constraints can be related to
psycholinguistic strategies in editing. The object of this study was
initially to analyze the effects of these constraints on both the
writer's strategies for text conception and the structure of the resulting text. To do this, the work of professional journalists was analysed
using two different word processing systems (type-writer and visual
display). This analysis enabled identification of the main constraints
for each task in the hardware concerned with editing strategies. Subsequently, the problem of conception in word processing was investigated.
Our methodological approach consists in the definition of the editing
functions in the word processing system using a model for human operator
behaviour integrating the three types of constraints previously discussed. The model treats the writer as a "manager" of constraints. The
writer can be considered as being in a situation of "overload", unable to
satisfy all the constraints simultaneously imposed by language structure

(syntax, semantics, etc.), discourse objectives (informing, convincing, etc.) and characteristics of the editing material (erasing, insertion, etc.). Hence, strategies are adopted with respect to cognitive system limits (memorization, linguistic competence, etc.) which allow step-by-step attainment of redactional objectives.

Thus, our method for system's conception involved identification of the cognitive operations necessary for task achievement. This was followed by selection of editing commands for the word processor system according to the constraints on the cognitive operations. Our concern was not on commands which "facilitate" any given operation (such as entry or word removal) but on editing commands which authorize text planning and coherence operations on the text, given that they are both necessary for task achievement. As can be seen, this method results also in recommendations for hardware related to editing tasks.

3.7 Mental workload and human-computer interaction

     Jose Gaussin

The evaluation of the global mental workload is a problem which has been faced for many years, and yet is not completely elucidated. However, following other authors (e.g. Sperandio, 1984; Leplat, 1985), we think it would be helpful to bring some light about (1) the concept itself, and (2) the evaluation methods.

Regarding the concept, we should know <u>what</u> we want to evaluate. Is it a stress deriving from the task, or a strain representing the subjective effects of the external demands? Is it a mental load attendant to the work situation or a nervous fatigue consecutive (or previous) to the job carried out? Are we interested in the quantitative aspect of it, expressed as a number of conscious decisions per unit of time, or in the qualitative one, referring to the level of thinking involved in the task? And finally, are we concerned with the mental load strictly resulting from the job contents itself, or with the much wider psychic load arising from the human operators' specific states, from the environment, or from anything else than the job activities?

As concerns the methods, <u>how</u> should mental workload be evaluated? Should we use physiological or psychological indicators, or further subjective evaluations? Among the methods centered on the operators' performances, mention should be made of the possibility of a self-evaluation of the quantitive mental load using a binary-choices scale as reference, based on the well-known human decisional capacity. The conclusive thesis is that mental workload can be an operational concept if restricted to the contents of the job, both in its quantitive and qualitative aspects, to the strain, and to the on-line effects of the work. Furthermore, to be reliable, the evaluation methods of mental workload have to be based on well-defined conditions of use.

4. DISCUSSION

The contributions presented by the invited workshop members served as a starting point for discussions between them and the participants in the audience. With respect to the "mental model" - part of the workshop, it was argued that the "mental model"-notion needs a stronger basis and, especially, much more experimental work in order to have a real impact on system's design. Up to now and in most cases, research in this field is largely theoretically and sometimes even intuitively oriented. There was agreement on this point and several proposals on how to proceed were put forward because of the great potential which was attributed to this approach. In addition, there seemed to be a neccessity for providing theoretical frameworks for cognitive ergonomics to build on for subsequent experiments. Those papers concentrating more on applied questions were found to provide quite interesting points of view with respect to actual system design or evaluating mental load of existing systems.

References

Hudson, P.T.W. (1984) Encoding information in displays: colour vs. non-coloured methods and their uses, or, what can you do extra with a colour display? In C.P. Gibson (Ed.), Nato Symposium on Colour vs. Monochrome Displays. Farnborough, R.A.E.

Hudson, P.T.W. (1985) What can you do with a Colour Display you can't do with a Black and White one? In Colour in Information Technology and Visual Displays. I.E.R.E. Publication No. 61. Institute of Electronic and Radio Engineers, London.

Leplat, J. (1985) Erreur humaine, fiabilite humaine dans le travail. Paris: A. Colin.

Norman, D. A. (1983) Some observations on mental models. In D. Gentner & A.L. Stevens (Eds.), Mental models (p. 7 - 14). Hillsdale: Erlbaum.

Sperandio, J.C. (1984) L'ergonomie du travail mental. Paris: Masson.

Streitz, N.A. (1985) Die Rolle von mentalen und konzeptuellen Modellen in der Mensch-Computer-Interaktion: Konsequenzen für die Software-Ergonomie? In H. Bullinger (Hrsg.), Software-Ergonomie '85: Mensch-Computer Interaktion. Berichte des German Chapter of the ACM (p.280-292). Stuttgart: Teubner.

Streitz, N.A. (1986) Cognitive Ergonomics: An approach for the design of user-oriented interactive systems. In F. Klix (Ed.), MACINTER I (Man-Computer Interaction Research). Amsterdam: North-Holland.

Additional information about the authors and their contributions to the workshop can be obtained from: Dr. Norbert A. Streitz (The address is given at the beginning of this report.)

THE PSYCHOLOGY OF WORK AND ORGANIZATION
G. Debus and H.-W. Schroiff (Editors)
© *Elsevier Science Publishers B.V. (North-Holland), 1986*

AUTOMATION IN PUBLIC LIBRARIES

Effects on the organization, quality of working life, and quality
of services

L.A. TEN HORN and R.A. ROE

Delft University of Technology, Department of Philosophy and
Social Sciences, Kanaalweg 2B
2628 EB Delft, The Netherlands

1. INTRODUCTION

The purpose of this study has been to investigate the effects that automation in public libraries has on the organization of work, the quality of
working life of the employees, and the quality of the services rendered to
the library users. In recent years public libraries have rapidly automated
their administrative procedures, particularly those around their lending
activities. Lending is the most central of all library activities, it constitutes almost two third of the time that employees spend on their job,
and it is the most important service to the users. A drastic change in
lending technology may therefore have a great impact on the organization,
the workers and the clients.

The conceptual basis of this study lies in interactionism (Endler and
Magnusson, 1976; Magnusson, 1981). It is assumed that work outcomes are
the product of an interaction between individuals, and a certain organizational environment which includes tasks, technology, social structure,
etc. Several types of outcomes may be distinguished: (1) organizational
outcomes, such as productivity, efficiency, product quality, (2) personal
outcomes, like job involvement, stress, work load, health, and (3) client
outcomes, like speed and quality of service, client satisfaction, etc.
Figure 1 gives an overview.

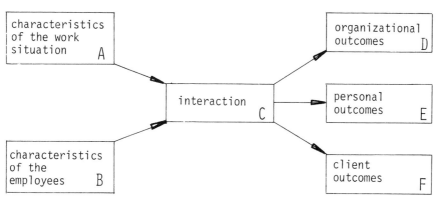

FIGURE 1
The interactional model of work and outcomes

The present study deals with all five blocks of variables. We assume that the introduction of an automated system leads to changes in the work situation, and thus affects work behaviors (interaction) and work outcomes. Employee characteristics will not show any direct change. However, they may co-determine the type of interaction and hence affect the outcomes as well. This paper focuses mainly on the blocks A, D, E and F, as they are influenced by automation. The other parts of our research model will be dealt with only briefly.

It should be noted that the relationships of situational characteristics to personal outcomes, which depend on the type of interaction that develops in the presence of given employees' characteristics, constitute the empirical component of quality of working life, as it is conceived of in this study (Roe, 1982). The evaluative component, which addresses the (un)desirability of personal outcomes and the degree to which they are accounted for by situational factors, is not explicitly considered here. Apart from the actual effects of automation, we are also interested in aspects of management. Specific points of interest are the organization's strategic as well as operational management with regard to automation in relation to organizational and personnel policies.

The research reported in this paper has not yet been finished completely. Particularly the last aspects mentioned are still being researched. Here we focus mainly on the effects, but these will force us to give some preliminary comments on the subjects of policy, and organizational control.

2. FIELD OF STUDY

The study was done in two large public library organizations in the Netherlands, covering the provinces of North and South Holland respectively. Both organizations provide library facilities to small towns (up to 30.000 inhabitants) and villages throughout their province. The organizational structure includes a central office and a large number of relatively independent local libraries. The central office takes care of functions like administration, finance and personnel, and provides support facilities like a central book collection. Some 40-50 libraries are being served by each organization. The local libraries employ 5-15 persons under the direction of a chief-librarian. Most employees are women in part-time jobs. The total number of employees is some 600 in each organization. There are four hierarchical levels covering the range between the managing director in the central office and the lowest personnel in the libraries. The organizations are characterized by a lack of formalized control systems. They seem to be bound together mainly by strong cultural values and norms, stemming from a common educational background of management and staff and a policy of internal promotions.

Both organizations are in the process of automating the local lending administrations. At the moment of study (1984-1985) four lending systems were in use:

- Detroit, the usual manual system with physical cards;
- Karto, a system using photographic means for recording data, that are consequently fed into a centrally located computer;
- ALS (Automated Library System).

ALS is a centralized system with a computer placed in the head-office, and registration devices in the libraries. There are an off-line and an on-line version. In the off-line one data are recorded on tape or disk to be processed later. In the on-line version data are fed into the computer directly and processed at once. The on-line system has several advantages over the off-line one.

The South-Holland organization used the Detroit system and both ALS systems. It has had its own automation department as well as computer, right from the start. ALS off-line is seen as an intermediate phase and the organization is changing over to on-line in all its libraries, except for the very small ones. The on-line system is the largest in Europe with 307.000 readers, more than two million volumes and 25 million transactions a year.

The North-Holland organization used Detroit, Karto and ALS off-line at the moment of study. While it made use of a computer service bureau before, it was changing over to ALS on-line with its own computer.

3.   RESEARCH DESIGN

In order to get a good view of the automation process and its consequences, it was decided to use three different approaches.

1. A comparison between libraries at a different stage of automation, in North and South-Holland separately.
2. A longitudinal study of one library in each province using a before-after design.
3. A comparative analysis of organization and automation policies, strategy of implementation, and operational and cultural characteristics of the organizations.

There were two independent variables: stage of automation, and library-size. Size was operationalized by the number of people living in the area served by the library. This number correlates strongly with the total number of books, the number of employees, and the number of library users.
A 3 x 3 design (automation x size) with 1 or 2 libraries per cell was used for both organizations. Libraries were chosen at random, but some adjustments had to be made to suit the interests of the organizations. Three of the 18 cells remained empty because those combinations did not exist. The total number of participating libraries was 25.

4.   INSTRUMENTS

The instruments used in gathering the data were: semi-structured interviews with key-informants in the central offices and with the 25 library heads, analysis of documents, group interviews with the employees in each of the libraries studied, analysis of tasks, observation of the work process, an employee questionnaire measuring job characteristics, worker characteristics and personal work outcomes, and a client questionnaire measuring aspects of the quality of service to the public.

The semi-structured interviews were in part based on Forslin et al. (1979) and covered aspects like organization structure and strategy, communication, participation and automation policy. The group interviews focussed on expectations towards automation, the introduction process and the consequences.

The employee questionnaire consists of a selection of instruments taken from the Delft Measurement Kit for the Quality of Working Life (Ten Horn & Roe, 1984) and two instruments developed by Dijkstra et al. (1981) and Van Wezel (1972). The questionnaire was distributed to all employees in the libraries studied (N = 195; average response rate 91%, varying slightly accross libraries, lending systems and sizes).

The service questionnaire was developed especially for the purpose and contained some 60 questions concerning the book collection, the catalogue, lending and reservation, waiting time, attitudes of personnel etc. It was distributed to users in the libraries. 1380 forms were returned by mail to the researchers. The response rate was 58%, with little variance between libraries, systems and size-categories.

5. ANALYSIS

The data from the interviews were partly used in their own right and partly as a way of validating findings from the questionnaires. The data from the questionnaires were analysed using one-way and two-way analyses of variance to establish primary and interaction effects of the major independent variables (automation-level and size). Variances were checked for homogeneity by way of Cochran's test. Additional analyses were made for categories of personnel (e.g. with or without library education) and for separate libraries. The data were also compared to data from non-library organizations in order to gain insight in the specificity of library work and work-situation.

6. RESULTS

In this paper we only select the most conspicuous results. Details may be found in Aders and De Bruin (1985), Van Dijk and De Veer (1985), Van Beugen and Van Schendel (1985).

To start with the *work situation*, it appears that there is an influence of automation on *task division* between personnel with and without library education. Shifts were noticed in activities regarding the collection, information giving and book promotion. Management tasks, however, remained the exclusive responsibility of the chief librarian. The changes in task content resulted in enriching the jobs of the lower level employees in some libraries, while de-enrichment was noticed in others.
Regarding *job characteristics*, and *organizational climate* several observations may be made. First of all, there is little evidence for the view that the lending systems form a continuum ranging from Detroit via Karto and ALS-off-line to ALS-on-line. There may be ground for it from a technological perspective, but from the point of view of this study there is not. Job characteristics did not differ systematically with lending system. Secondly, although some differences between the two organizations were found, the similarities stand out. Library work in both organizations has much in common, compared to reference data based on large and varied samples from Ten Horn (1983) and Dijkstra et al. (1981). Library work has less task identity, skill variety, task specialization, autonomy and opportunity for informal contacts; it is more standardized and there are more deviations from the normal course of events. Organizational climate is somewhat more person-oriented and reflects more McGregor's theory Y (McGregor, 1960).
Regarding the specific lending systems, the following conclusions may be drawn. The *Karto* system, as compared to Detroit, gives more task variety and less opportunity for informal contacts. *ALS off-line* shows more task variation as well, the workers experience more positive sanctions for doing a good job, and they perceive better career opportunities. However there are considerable differences between the two organizations here. *ALS on-line* compared to Detroit provides more specialization and less feedback from the work. Deviations from the normal course of events are

much more common. The number of disturbances is also striking compared to
the off-line situation.
Clear impacts of automation on organizational climate have not been found.
This is especially noteworthy, since climate showed strong relationships
with many variables in the present study and seems to be of particular
importance in determining the attitudes of library personnel.

An important aspect of the *interaction* between the employees and the work
situation is the utilization of aptitudes and skills. Generally speaking,
automation in all three forms obviates much tedious card-filing, making
more time available for non-lending activities. This means that the work
is somewhat upgraded, generally. Higher demands are found to be made on
intelligence, planning, decision making, attentiveness, physical effort,
verbal skills and knowledge of the english language (ALS being a system
imported from Great Britain).

With respect to *personal outcomes* the same general comment can be given as
when discussing job characteristics and climate. There is no clear association with the degree of automation. Job satisfaction, job involvement,
and tendency to leave were about the same across situations. Only minor
variations were found. Feelings of control over the work, job involvement,
and the work load were somewhat higher, and health problems were less in
the Karto system as compared to the Detroit method. Differences between
the other lending systems were negligible. In some libraries a high work
pressure was observed, either as a temporary result of data conversion
activities, or as a general reaction to a high work load.
In evaluating these results, it should be noted that the library sample
as a whole compares favorably to the other samples, mentioned above. Both
the level of job satisfaction, and the level of involvement are extremely
high. The tendency to leave is definitely lower. This is remarkable, since
the job characteristics were found to be clearly less favorable, as mentioned.

An increase in productivity is the most striking of the *organizational
outcomes*. Generally speaking, productivity is positively associated with
degree of automation. In Detroit libraries more time is spent on lending
activities than in Karto or ALS libraries. The on-line system tends to
give best results. Gains, however, are not spectacular and differ considerably between libraries. Because no personnel has been laid off in
automated libraries more time is available for non-lending activities
like promotion of books and reading, attention to special groups of
readers, and making book and other collections more easily accessible.
In most libraries a shift in emphasis to such activities is noticed, but
not in all. Two out of four on-line libraries did not differ much from
the Detroit pattern of operation.

Regarding quality *of service*, the data show much more uniformity. Automation affects several aspects of service, almost regardless of the system
previously in use. We already mentioned the shift towards non-lending
activities. This is also noticed and appreciated by the public. Readers
of automated libraries report more special activities like exhibitions,
specific service to the elderly, etc. Employees are observed to be less
hurrying, but in some automated libraries behavior of personnel tends to
be perceived as somewhat less friendly, attentive and helpful. This may
be due to the shortening of contacts during the registration of books.
The automated systems give rise to more waiting by clients. Customers of
Detroit libraries report almost no waiting at all. Some discomfort exists

regarding expiration dates that are no longer recorded in the book itself
and tend to be forgotten. Customers also complain that the way overdue
charges are computed, is less clear and that rules are more strictly observed. Clients of the on-line system report more problems with the
reliability of service. This corresponds to the observation by the employees that more deviations from normal operations occur. It is also a
reflection of the functioning of the system at the time.
Finally, clients of automated libraries show more positive attitudes toward automation than those of Detroit ones. They agree more often to
statements that automation is inevitable and will benefit library work.

7. DISCUSSION

Automation of the lending administration of public libraries is an
operation of great potential impact. In the organizations studied, however, only relatively small changes were observed. No fundamental reorganization of tasks, only little change in job characteristics, hardly
any change in organizational climate and personal outcomes. All in all,
the quality of the work situation has somewhat improved, but only slightly
so.
How was this relatively positive result brought about? First of all, the
results do not seem to have been caused by explicit policy. Quality of
work was not a central issue, and little attention was payed to it during
the process. Neither has there been direct participation in decision
making by lower level personnel.
In our view, however, the results could be attributed to a set of strong
organizational values, that permeates thought and action on all levels of
the organization. Most employees share the same ideas on service, the
essence of library work, the way an organization should be run, and how
employees should relate to one another. Informality in relationships and
good cooperation are stressed, and the work situation does not normally
obstruct the expression of opinions and feelings. This common culture
makes it possible to have a good and intimate understanding of issues,
problems and perspectives on all levels without much need to be very
explicit about it.
A second factor, as we see it, is the fact that local libraries are
free to   choose the work organization they prefer. Moreover, most have
some form of work consultation, providing a platform for discussing
problems, voicing discontent and finding solutions. So local libraries
seem to have ways to cope creatively with new situations like automation.
The common values also make it easy to pass ideas and feelings to those
higher up in the hierarchy.

Although quality of the work situation may not have been a central issue
in management thinking, quality of service certainly was. An explicit
objective of automation was to reduce the time spent on administration in
favor of other aspects of service. Here the libraries were allowed freedom
as well. It was hoped that the intended shift in emphasis would be brought
about simply because the new systems made it possible to do so. High identification of the employees with the goals of library work was expected
to do the job. We got the impression that this assumption was fundamentally right, although we found some cases where the change did not occur.

Generally speaking, the organizations studied were able to introduce a
major change in a most central part of operations. They did this in an
effective way without much trouble and without severe operational or

human consequences. As this seems to be due to a pervasive system of organizational values, rather than an explicit system of organizational control, our study suggests that organizational values deserve more attention than is usually given in the study of automation impacts. It would be worthwhile to focus on the way organizations are integrated, bound together and directed towards their goals: either by formalized control mechanisms, organization structure and bureaucratic means, or by organizational values, informal and mutually accepted ways of control and informal communication.

A remarkable finding of this study was that the relatively unfavorable task characteristics, especially for lower personnel, were associated with very positive personal outcomes and job satisfaction. This result might be explained by considering the fact that most of the employees involved are women with part-time jobs, showing a strong motivation to be engaged in the well-visible, high-status activity that library work is within the local community. The part-time nature of their job may prevent these workers from developing negative reactions to their routine-like tasks. Such an explanation would underline the fruitfulness of the interactionist approach followed in this study.

ACKNOWLEDGEMENTS

We wish to acknowledge the contribution of the students E. Aders, E. de Bruin, H. van Beugen, R. van Dijk, R. van Schendel and J. de Veer. They carried the daily burden of the research in doing the fieldwork, in analyzing the data and trying to structure the findings in a comprehensive way.

REFERENCES

Aders, E., and Bruin, E. de, *Automatisering bij openbare bibliotheken*; gevolgen van automatisering voor de kwaliteit van arbeid en dienstverlening bij de PBC Zuid-Holland. Delft: Delft University of Technology, Department of Philosophy and Social Sciences, Research report, 1985.

Beugen, H. van, and Schendel, R. van, *Automatisering bij openbare bibliotheken*; een longitudinale studie naar effecten voor kwaliteit van arbeid en dienstverlening. Delft: Delft University of Technology, Department of Philosophy and Social Sciences. Research report, 1985.

Dijk, R. van, and Veer, J. de, *Automatisering bij openbare bibliotheken*; gevolgen van automatisering voor de kwaliteit van arbeid en dienstverlening bij de PBC Noord-Holland. Delft: University of Technology, Department Philosophy and Social Sciences. Research report, 1985.

Dijkstra, A., Grinten, M.P. van der, Schlatman, M.J.Th., and Winter, C.R. de, *Funktioneren in de arbeidssituatie*; uitgangspunten, ontwerp en handleiding voor onderzoek onder werknemers naar gezondheid, werk en werkomstandigheden. Leiden: Nederlands Instituut voor Praeventieve Gezondheidszorg, TNO, 1981.

Endler, N.S., and Magnusson, D., Toward an interactional psychology of personality. *Psychological Bulletin*, 1976, 83, 956-974.

Forslin, J., Garapata, A., and Withehill, A.M., *Automation and industrial workers*; a fifteen nation study. Volume I, part 1, Oxford, 1979.

Horn, L.A. ten, *Behoeften, werksituatie en arbeidsbeleving* (diss.). Pijnacker, 1983.

Horn, L.A. ten, and Roe, R.A., *De Delftse Meetdoos voor Kwaliteit van Arbeid*; oriëntatie voor gebruikers. Delft: Delft University of Technology, Department of Philosophy and Social Sciences, 1984.
Magnusson, D., *Toward a psychology of situations*; an interactional perspective. Hillsdale, N.J., 1981.
McGregor, D., *The human side of enterprise*. New York, 1960.
Roe, R.A., *Kwaliteit van arbeid en het onderzoek van arbeid en gevolgen*. Delft: Delft University of Technology, Department of Philosophy and Social Sciences, 1982.
Wezel, J.A.M. van, *Herintreding in het arbeidsproces* (diss.). Tilburg, 1972.

THE PSYCHOLOGY OF WORK AND ORGANIZATION
G. Debus and H.-W. Schroiff (Editors)
© Elsevier Science Publishers B.V. (North-Holland), 1986

THE ALGORITHMIC APPROACH IN ERGONOMICS : THE CASE OF OPTIMAL
COLOURS AND AMBIENTS FOR DISPLAY WORK

W. DE CORTE

Laboratory of Applied Psychology, Ghent University,
L. Pasteurlaan 2, B-9000 GHENT BELGIUM

Most man-machine interfaces (MMI) are implemented by means of a
CRT (i.e., a Cathode Ray Tube) terminal. Color is one of the
most important coding vehicles which can be used to support the
MMI. For an adequate use, the generated colors should be
optimal from an ergonomical point of view. This implies the
specification of high contrast sets of colors which satisfy a
number of constraints. The basic problem can be solved
approximately by an algorithm which integrates the results from
both vision and human factors research.
The algorithm computes optimal values for two sets of
parameters. The first set is related to the chromaticity of a
surrounding ambient. The phosphor luminances for the RGB
phosphors constitute the second set. The computations aim at
the determination of colors which 1) are as far as possible away
from each other within the 1976 CIEL*u*v* uniform color space ;
and 2) respect several restrictions which translate luminance
and saturation conditions. The latter conditions aim at
diminishing visual fatigue. They also intend to remediate
certain perceptual artifacts that may interfere with color
coding on visual displays. A pilot application illustrates the
usefulness of the algorithm. Furthermore, it is shown how the
approach can be extended to the computation of colors for CRT
operators with color vision defects. Throughout the paper the
complementarity is stressed between the present algorithmic, and
the more usual experimental approach.

1. INTRODUCTION

Ergonomics cherishes its latest born : the leading review journal,
Ergonomics Abstract, added a special section on human-computer
interaction. Up till now, the human-computer interface is dominated by
the use of CRT (Cathode Ray Tube) displays. A lot of the ergonomic
research on the hardware components of the interface is of the
experimental type. The designs typically compare, in a controlled
environment, such aspects as keyboard lay-outs, letter types, coding
devices, etc. These studies primarily aim to develop new knowledge in
the field. They are not essentially targetted at the integration of
existing knowledge ; whether that knowledge stems from psychology,
psychophysics, human physiology, or the engineering sciences. For many
questions on hardware ergonomic issues, this type of synthetic approach
is not yet feasible. However, there are exceptions. Some relatively
simple, and well posed questions already allow for a synthesis. This
paper presents one such case. The example addresses the problem : "If

colour CRTs are used, <u>which</u> set of colours should be used ?". The answer is based on facts, proposals and theories from human factors research, colour vision, psychonomics, colorimetry and photometry. These bits of knowledge are all integrated into a working algorithm which specifies an ergonomically optimal set of high contrasting colours. The algorithm, implemented by a (set of) computer program(s) called COLSET, is thereby an instance of what we labeled the "algorithmic" approach. While the experimental approach is knowledge oriented, the algorithmic approach systematizes the knowledge into a model which is further simulated in an algorithm. Thus the algorithmic approach is essentially application oriented.

The next section deals with the notion of an ergonomically optimal set of high contrasting colours. Then the basic COLSET algorithm is exposed and several extensions are commented upon. This is followed by an illustrative application. In the final section the practical relevance of the algorithm is discussed.

2. ERGONOMICALLY OPTIMAL SETS OF HIGH CONTRAST COLOURS

Obviously, the running head of this section is the answer to the simple question that was formulated in the introduction. What then constitutes an ergonomically optimal set of high contrast colours ? First of all, it is a set of colours that are as discriminable as possible, given the nature of the application situation and the physical limits of the CRT device. The notion DMIN is introduced to capture the requirement. DMIN refers to the minimal perceived distance between any pair of colours from the set. Perceived colour distances will be quantified using the familiar CIELUV system. The CIELUV system is one of the uniform colour spaces agreed upon by the CIE (Commission International d'Eclairage). CIELUV is chosen because it incorporates the additive feature shared by the colour rendering device. It was Carter and Carter (1982) who first devised an algorithm based on the CIELUV colour difference formulae. They also clarified the usage of the formulae for self-luminous displays (Carter and Carter, 1983). Some recent research on colour contrast (Post, Constanza and Lippert, 1982 ; Silverstein and Merrifield, 1981) and on colour conspicuousness (Carter and Carter, 1981) confirmed CIELUV to be a fairly adequate choice to translate perceived colour distances. Galves and Brun (1975) developed another metric for perceived colour differences. The metric seems particularly well suited for the evaluation of colour perceptions on airborne displays (Laycock, 1985). Their proposal is commented upon in the next section.

So a set of colours will be highly discriminable if DMIN is maximized. As reported above, the maximization depends on both the nature of the application and the physical characteristics of the CRT device. The subsequent proposals by De Corte (1985a, and 1985b) precisely aim, among others, at gearing the solution of the colour identification problem towards the application setting. The specification of the setting is no longer restricted to the number of colours that is to be determined. The strenght and type (i.e., the chromaticity as measured in the CIE 1931 x,y diagram) of the ambient conditions are also taken into account.

In order to be of any practical relevance, the maximization of DMIN should ultimately relate to the CRT characteristics. The formulae, presented by Robertson (1977), Carter and Carter (1982, 1983), and De Corte (1985 e), show that d_{ij} (i.e., the distance between the colours i and j in the 1976 CIELUV space) depends on the luminances L_{ik} with which the three phosphors k (k = 1 to 3, with k = 1 the red ; k = 2 the green ; and k = 3 the blue phosphor) combine in the formation of a CRT colour. Maximization of DMIN thus implies finding optimal values for the set (L_{ik}).

Apart from being highly discriminable, the colour set should also be ergonomically optimal. The latter notion is captured by the ERGQ index. ERGQ is a compound index which translates several requirements on the use of CRT colours. The requirements are derived from vision and human factors research. They are discussed by Laycock (1984) and Walraven (1984). De Corte (1985d) indicates how these requirements can be translated into a set of inequality constraints. The translation implies that the more a set of colours is ergonomically optimal, the lower will be the value of ERGQ.

3. THE BASIC COLSET ALGORITHM

According to the above analysis, the determination of an ergonomically optimal colour set implies the maximization, over the set of possible luminances L_{ik}, of DMIN. Furthermore the optimization is a constrained one : the constraints are expressed by the inequalities which constitute ERGQ. However, maximizing DMIN means maximizing the minimum of a series of between colour distances. The Carter and Carter (1982) algorithm provided a heuristic solution to the unconstrained problem. De Corte (1985a, 1985b) developed a totally different approach which allowed the solution of the constrained problem. The new approach relies on current numerical techniques for function minimization. The latter techniques can be applied by virtue of a reformulation of the basic problem. Instead of maximizing the minimum of the d_{ij} series, an equivalent, smooth function is minimized. The translation is documented in De Corte (1985b, 1985e). The basic algorithm results in a computer program called COLSET.

The basic scheme can be extended in several ways. The following extensions are briefly discussed : a) estimating the best ambient chromaticity ; b) optimal colour sets for colour defective CRT operators; c) optimal colours for non-fixed ambient conditions ; d) the addition of the DBAK criterion (see further) ; and e) the introduction of a new colour difference metric.

The set of optimal L_{ik} values depends upon the chromaticity of the surrounding ambient A. This chromaticity is indicated by the corresponding CIE 1931 x_A and y_A coordinates. It is also true that, given a fixed set of colours, the minimal between colour distance varies as a function of x_A and y_A (see De Corte, 1985d). For the human factors specialist it is of great practical importance to be able to suggest optimal ambient conditions. The basic COLSET algorithm can be extended to estimate both the set (L_{ik}) and the set (x_A, y_A), given the intensity E_A (in lux) of the illuminant. The modifications are discussed in De Corte (1985b).

The calculations on which COLSET is based are no longer valid when the

CRT operator is not a normal trichromat. However, it remains possible
to locate confusion areas in the 1931 CIE and the 1976 UCS diagrams when
the operator belongs to either one of the three dichromat types. The
loci of the confusion points are given by Wyszecki and Stiles
(1967).These data enable to modify the distance calculations such that
the corrected d_{ij} estimates agree substantially with the colour
perceptions of the dichromat. Apart from these modifications, De Corte
(1985c) indicates another two corrections in order to estimate a set of
optimal contrast colours for the dichromats. The first correction
involves the determination of the maximum phosphor luminances, L_{kmax},
for each of the three phosphors. The L_{kmax} values must now be computed
on the basis of the luminous efficiency functions, $V(\lambda)$ (with the
wavelength), which typify the specified dichromat. The second
correction concerns the quantification of the constraints : the
luminance ratio between colours, and the saturation level of colours are
both perceived differently by a dichromat. For more details on the
former, as well as on the latter correction, we refer to De Corte
(1985c).

The practical advantage that COLSET takes account of the surrounding
ambient may also turn into a disadvantage. Most CRT displays are used
in multiple settings. These settings often have varying illumination
characteristics. The illumination intensity and the ambient
chromaticity are generally non-fixed. What then is the ergonomically
optimal colour set the CRT manufacturer should implement ? At least two
answers are possible within the COLSET framework. The first solution
determines the optimal colour set as the one which is optimal for the
worst ambient condition. The second solution optimizes the colours with
regard to a weighted combination of the ambient conditions the display
is likely to be used in. The weighting of the conditions can be based
on several principles. Market tracking may indicate the most common
types of illuminants. Also the weighting may agree with certain task
specific requirements, etc. The two alternative solutions are fully
documented by De Corte (1985f), who also provides an illustrative
application.

The washing-out of CRT colours by the surrounding ambient becomes a
serious problem for airborne displays. There, the colours, generated on
the screen, should not only be discriminable one from the other ; they
must also be detectable against the background reflection. To ensure
the latter condition, De Corte (1985e) introduced a third notion, DBAK,
besides the DMIN and the ERGQ criteria. The notion expresses the
minimal perceived colour difference between any colour from a given set
and the background colour. The simultaneous maximization of DMIN and
DBAK, given the ERGQ constraints, results in two proposals. The first
solution concentrates on maximizing either the minimal between colour
distance or the minimal distance between a colour and the background,
whichever is smallest. The second proposal minimizes a suitable
weighted combination of DMIN and DBAK. Again, the choice between the
two proposals is guided by substantial concerns. If the surrounding
ambient is really strong (e.g., about or over 10000 lux), and the
consequences of negating a (colour-coded) signal are dramatic, the first
proposal should be implemented. If failure to discriminate between
signals is to be avoided, and the ambient is not all too strong, the
second proposal seems more appropriate.

The fifth, and last extension is related to the former one in that the field of its application is also primarily aimed at the use of airborne displays. After extensive experimentation, Galves and Brun (1975) proposed a new metric for evaluating differences in colour perception. The overall colour difference is decomposed into a luminance difference and into a chromaticity difference. Although the 1976 CIELUV colour coordinates serve as a start, the estimation of the perceived differences is related to units which express either just noticable, or comfortable discriminable colour differences. Having compared both metrics on the basis of a sample application, De Corte (1985e) concludes that the two sytems essentially differ in the calculation of the perceived difference between the colours and the background.

All five extensions, discussed above, are presently being integrated into a single computer program, thus resulting into a generalized version of COLSET : COLSET-G. Due to space limitations, we present only one of the possible COLSET-G applications. The example illustrates the difference of ergonomically optimal high contrast sets of colours, depending on whether the set is calculated for normal trichromats or for tritanopes.

4. APPLICATION EXAMPLE

COLSET-G is used to determine two ergonomically optimal sets of 6 colours ; one in case the CRT operator is a normal trichromat ; a second for the case where the operator is a tritanope. Apart from estimating the optimal (L_{ik}) values, the algorithm also determines the chromaticities x_A and y_A of the best ambient A. The initial conditions concerning the surrounding and the CRT hardware are the same for both applications. The CRT display is equipped with red phosphors, R (x_R = .643 ; y_R = .339) ; green phosphors, G (x_G = .302 ; y_G = .566) ; and blue phosphors, B (x_B = .149 ; y_B = .073) ; while its (supposedly uniform) reflection and transmission coefficients are set at .2 and 1 respectively. Besides the ambient A (E_A = 700 lux), which is to be optimized, a fixed ambient D is also present. The fixed ambient D is characterized by x_D = .317 ; y_D = .329 ; and E_D = 300 lux. The maximum luminances for the three phosphors are 60 nit for the red, 150 nit for the green, and 20 nit for the blue phosphors. These maxima correspond to the trichromat luminous efficiency curve. For the sake of comparability, we will keep the same maximum luminances for the tritanope condition.

The two sets are estimated under an equal set of constraints. One set of constraints prevents colours from being too different in terms of luminance,while the other requires the colours to be neither too saturated nor too desaturated. Finally, the distance (in the 1931 CIE x, y plane) of the additional illuminant A to the fixed ambient D must not exceed .21. The results of COLSET-G are summarized in Table 1. The table indicates for the two conditions (i.e., the normal trichromat and the tritanope case) the set of optimal L_{ik} values (Parameter set 1), and the chromaticity coordinates x_A, y_A of the additional ambient (Parameter set 2). For each condition, the smallest between colour distance (DMIN) is given after, and before the maximization process. The two sets of CRT colours are also characterized : their name (based on a proposal by Kelly (1943)) and their tristimulus values X, Y, Z are summarized.

A. Case 1 : normal trichromat
Parameter set 1 : Phosphor luminances L_{ik}

		Phosphors				
Colour	(i)	Red	(k=1)	Green (k=2)	Blue	(k=3)
1		60.0		0.0	13.3	
2		60.0		10.1	0.0	
3		0.0		124.0	16.3	
4		0.0		138.0	0.0	
5		46.8		87.6	5.8	
6		19.7		30.4	20.0	

Parameter set 2 : chromaticity (x_A, y_A) additional ambient
$x_A = .522$ $y_A = .385$
Smallest between colours distance (CIELUV) : 80.04
Initial smallest distance (CIELUV) : 29.88
CRT colours specification

	Name	X	Y	Z
1.	Purplish pink	74.8	46.6	60.0
2.	Orange pink	67.4	45.6	12.5
3.	Blue green	60.6	69.3	79.6
4.	Yellowish green	51.8	68.5	21.6
5.	Yellowish orange	77.0	69.4	39.4
6.	Bluish purple	59.0	45.6	86.0

B. Case 2 : Tritanope
Parameter set 1 : phosphor luminances L_{ik}

		Phosphors		
Colour (i)	Red (k=1)	Green (k=2)	Blue (k=3)
1	15.5	45.1	0.0
2	60.0	0.6	0.0
3	12.0	109.0	0.0
4	43.9	16.8	0.0
5	48.3	73.1	0.0
6	0.0	101.0	20.0

Parameter set 2 : chromaticity (x_A, y_A) additional ambient
$x_A = .451$ $y_A = .491$
Smallest between colours distance (CIELUV) : 35.87
Initial smallest distance (CIELUV) : 14.04
CRT colours specification

	Name	X	Y	Z
1.	Greenish yellow	38.4	42.3	12.7
2.	Orange pink	59.1	42.3	9.9
3.	Yellow green	47.8	63.0	17.7
4.	Orange pink	51.6	42.4	10.9
5.	Yellow	64.7	63.0	15.5
6.	Greenish blue	52.5	63.0	89.4

Table 1. COLSET-G solutions for an ergonomically optimal high contrast
set of 6 colours. First condition : normal trichromats ;
second condition : tritanopes.

5. DISCUSSION

The COLSET-G program, presented above, is a typical example of the algorithmic approach to ergonomic problems. As such, it is the result of knowledge gathered by many experiments in the field of vision and human factors research. However, the algorithm is not an end-point in itself. Instead, it is to be conceived as the starting point for a new experimental program. Indeed, COLSET-G can be used to make all sorts of predictions. Some of these pertain to the CRT colours that can be best discriminated. Others point to desired ambient chromaticities. Whether or not these predictions reveal true can only be decided by new experiments. In this way, the algorithmic endeavour corresponds to the intermediate step of prediction specification within the classical empirical cycle of knowledge building. Without the earlier experimental results, the algorithms could never have been built ; without the algorithms, the new experimental program cannot be realized. This reflects the ultimate interdependence between the experimental and the algorithmic approach in ergonomics.

Of course, the COLSET-G algorithm is still to be perfected. One of the major aspects of the perception of CRT colours is not dealt with. The calculations make no explicit provisions for chromatic induction (i.e., the fact that a colour field, surrounded by a field of a different colour, is perceived differently). This shortcoming is particularly relevant in certain database applications. Another problem with the current approach relates to the difference between the perceived brightness of a CRT colour and its measured luminance. Kinney (1982) summarizes the progress that was recently made in this area.

Still other imperfections could be added to the list. The choice of the CIELUV metric to measure large colour differences is one of them. Nevertheless, for the time being, COLSET-G is the only computational technique which integrates the current knowledge to generate ergonomically optimal high contrast sets of CRT colours.

REFERENCES

Carter, E.C., and Carter, R.C. Color and conspiciousness. Journal of the Optical Society of America, 1981, 71, 723-729.

Carter, R.C., and Carter, E.C. High contrast sets of color. Applied Optics, (1982), 21, 2936-2939.

Carter, R.C., and Carter, E.C. CIELUV color-difference equations for self-luminous displays. Color Research and Application, 1983,8, 252-253.

De Corte, W. Finding appropriate colors for color displays. Color Research and Application, 1985a (in press).

De Corte, W. Optimal colors, phosphors and illuminant characteristics for CRT displays : the algorithmic approach. Human Factors, 1985b (in press).

De Corte, W. Ergonomically optimal colours for colour defective CRT operators. In G. Verriest (Ed.). Proceedings of the Eight International Research Group for Colour Vision Deficiencies, 1985c (in press).

De Corte, W. The effect of various ambients on the contrast and ergonomic quality of CRT colours. Applied Ergonomics, 1985d (submitted).

De Corte, W. The determination of ergonomically optimal multiple contrast colours for airborne displays. Paper prepared for the conference on 'Work with display units', Stockholm, 1985e.

De Corte, W. Ergonomically optimal CRT colours for non-fixed ambient illumination conditions. Ergonomics, 1985f (submitted).

Galves, J., and Brun, J. Colour and brightness requirements for cockpit displays : proposals to evaluate their characteristics. Thomson CSF Electron Tube Group, Lecture n°6, AGARD Avionics Panel Technical Meeting on Electronic Displays, Paris, 1975.

Kelly, K.L. Color designations for lights. Journal of the Optical Society of America, 1943, 33, 627.

Kinney, J.A. Brightness of colored self-luminous displays. Color Research and Application, 1982, 7, 82–89.

Laycock, J. Selected colours for use on colour cathode ray tubes. Displays, 1984, 5, 3–14.

Laycock, J. Colour contrast calculations for displays viewed in illumination. Unpublished paper, 1985.

Post, D.L., Constanza, E.B., and Lippert, T.M. Expressions of color contrast as equivalent achromatic contrast. Proceedings of the Human Factors 26th Annual Meeting, 1982, 26, 581–585.

Robertson, A.R. The CIE 1976 color-difference formulae. Color Research and Application, 1977, 2, 7–11.

Siverstein, L.D., and Merrifield, R.M. Color selection and verification testing for airborne color CRT displays. Proceedings of the fifth Advanced Aircrew Display Symposium, Naval Air Test Center, Patuxent River, MD, September, 1981.

Walraven, J. Perceptual artifacts that may interfere with color coding on visual displays. Proceedings of the NATO Workshop on 'Colour coded vs monochrome electronic displays', Farnborough, UK, 1984.

Wyszecki, G.W., and Stiles, W.S. Color Science, New York : Wiley, 1967.

II.2. Employment and Unemployment Problems

THE PSYCHOLOGY OF WORK AND ORGANIZATION
G. Debus and H.-W. Schroiff (Editors)
© *Elsevier Science Publishers B.V. (North-Holland), 1986*

WORK EXPERIENCES OF FEMALE ENGINEERS IN THE UK

Tony KEENAN & Tim NEWTON

Dept. of Business Organisation,
Heriot-Watt University,
31-35 Grassmarket,
Edinburgh, EH1 2HT, United Kingdom

1.   INTRODUCTION

Keenan and Newton (1) recently reported the results of a series of in depth interviews with a small group of female engineers. Their findings indicated that young graduate female engineers are treated differently at work form their male counterparts in a number of ways. The investigation reported here followed up that pilot study. The objective was to survey a larger group of people in order to establish whether or not the findings of the pilot study were generally applicable.

The original investigation suggested that women were often treated differently at the recruitment phase from men. While this differential treatment often appeared to have an adverse impact on them, this was not always so and in some instances women felt themselves to be at an advantage because of their sex. The investigation reported here considered this issue in more depth. There was evidence from the pilot study that women at work were treated differently from men, both in their everyday interactions with them, and in terms of the policies of organisations towards them. Both of these processes were therefore investigated. Once again, while there was evidence in the previous study of adverse impact there were also indications that in some respects women received more favourable treatment compared to male colleagues.

If women are treated differently from men in the workplace, it seems possible that this kind of sex role stereotyping had adverse psychological consequences. The present investigation attempted to identify psychological effects of sex stereotyping. One obvious possibility is that such attitudes would be associated with low job satisfaction. Also, if sex role stereotyping leads to a view that women are less capable than their male counterparts of performing effectively, even partial acceptance of these attitudes by women themselves is likely to be ego threatening and could consequently lead to feelings of anxiety. The study investigated the association between sex stereotyping and job satisfaction and feelings of anxiety.

Sex stereotyping is unlikely to be the only factor which affects psychological responses at work. Consequently, it seemed appropriate to include another set of predictors of psychological reactions in order to give some approximate indication of the relative importance of stereotyped attitudes compared with other variables. In a previous study, Keenan and Newton (2) found that psychological need fulfilment was quite a strong correlate of job satisfaction. This measure was therefore included in the study for purposes of comparison.

2.   METHOD

The data were collected in the form of responses to a postal questionnaire which was distributed through the Women's Engineering Society
of Great Britain. Out of a total of 400 questionnaires, 150 women
returned them completed. However, some were not in full time employment
and others returned incomplete questionnaires. As a result, the final
usable sample consisted of 94 respondents.

3.   RESULTS

3.1. Recruitment

Respondents were asked "were you ever treated differently at interviews
from male applicants?". Thirty-five per cent of respondents answered
yes, either "very often" or "often". A further 30 per cent said this
happend "sometimes" and the remaining 35 per cent replied that this
happened "seldom" or "never".

Respondents were then asked an open ended question asking for information about how they had been treated differently at interviews. Content
analysis of this data produced four main categories of response. The
first related to issues connected with marriage and children. One common
type of complaint concerned excessive questioning about current and
planned family, marriage plans etc, accounting for 34 per cent of
responses. Some women even said that they had been explicitly told that
they would only obtain employment if they agreed not to marry or have
children. The second category as labelled "the condescending approach"
and consisted of 36 per cent of all answers. The unifying theme of the
responses in this category was an unwillingness on the part of interviewers to accept that women have the skills and motivation to handle a
professional engineer's job successfully. The women reported scepticism
on the part of interviews about both their technical and managerial
competence and about their motivation to be an engineer. The third
response category was labelled "the considerate approach". Ten per cent
of responses fell into this category. These women implied they had been
placed in an advantageous position because they were female. The general
view was that interviewers were more considerate and helpful towards
them because they were female. Ten per cent of women mentioned the
novelty factor when describing how they had been treated differently at
interviews. Typical comments here referred to being treated as an oddity
or a curiosity. However, while it is not clear how these attitudes
influenced the actual outcomes of the interviews, it seems likely that
some women benefited from this rarity factor whereas others found it a
disadvantage.

3.2. Sex role stereotyping and everyday work experiences

To assess negative experiences at work, respondents were asked to say
how much they agreed with each of a series of statements on a five point
scale ranging from "strongly agree" to "strongly disagree". The twelve
statements covered both interpersonal interactions at the workplace and
issues relating to organisational policies. A second part of the questionnaire attempted to identify more positive experiences at work. In
this case an open ended response format was used and the women were
asked "Are there any ways in which your job as an engineer is made

easier because you are a female?". These responses were subjected to content analysis.

Adverse treatment of women engineers. Table 1 shows the 12 items dealing with negative experiences at work and summarises the results obtained. For clarity of presentation, the responses in the "strong agree" and "agree" categories are combined. It is apparent from Table 1 that differential treatment of women was more prevalent in the interpersonal domain than in areas of organisational policy. It seems that both technical and non-technical colleagues were sceptical about female engineers' technical abilitites. However, it is noticeable that colleagues at the same level were felt to be less likely to treat women differently than were superiors or subordinates. Perhaps this is because same level colleagues had more opportunity to observe their abilities at first hand.

Turning to the question of organisational practices, roughly one-third of people suggested that their company took the view that certain jobs were not appropriate for females. Responses to an open ended question on this issue indicated that areas where the women felt they were restricted included construction work, site work, and production. It is interesting however that only eight per cent of respondents felt that they were offered less challenging work than men. Given the strong evidence that women's chances of advancement at work are generally less than those of men, it is encouraging that only one in five female engineers agreed this was the case within their company. Similarly, only seven per cent felt that they were less well paid than their male counterparts.

Favourable treatment of women engineers. Fifty six per cent of the sample replied in the affirmative when asked if there were any ways in which their job was made easier because they were female. Roughly half of these women suggested that, because they were female, others were more co-operative when it came to getting the job done. One reason for this, in the view of some women, was that men saw them as less threatening and felt less need to compete with them. Another frequent suggestion was that women are less conscious of position than male engineers and this allows them to concentrate more on the task in hand. Yet others suggested that men use less aggressive and abusive behaviour towards females than towards other men. One quarter of those who answered this question highlighted the advantages of being very much in a minority at work. Rarities are more easily remembered and recognised. They stand out and are often singled out for special treatment.

Table   1:   Respondents who agreed with 12 statements relating to the experiences of female engineers at work

	percentage saying "strongly agree" or "somewhat agree"
Interpersonal relationships	
It is often the case that male engineers are sceptical about a female engineer's technical competence	63
It is often the case that male non-engineering colleagues of female engineers are sceptical about their competence	57
Female engineers are treated differently from male engineers by:	
(i) lower-level colleagues	54
(ii) superiors	48
(iii) same-level colleagues	33
Organisational practices	
In this organisation there are some jobs considered to be more appropriate for male engineers than for female engineers	36
Female engineers are discouraged from doing certain kinds of work in this company	21
It is mainly the female engineers who are given the less challenging jobs in this organisation	8
Female engineers are given the same range of work to do as male engineers	87
Female engineers in this organisation have less chance of advancement than their male counterparts	20
Female engineers have less status than male engineers in this organisation	11
Female engineers in this organisation are not paid as well as their male colleagues for the same job	7

3.3 Sex role stereotyping, higher order need fulfilment, and affective
     responses

The 12 items referring to differential treatment of women at work shown
in Table 1 constituted the sex role stereotyping items. The items used
to measure higher order need fulfilment have been described in detail
elsewhere by Keenan and Newton (2). Briefly, they consist of a set of
eight Likert type scales. These ask the respondent the extent to which
their job provides the opportunity to fulfil a series of needs such as,
for example, being able to influence decisions about work or being able
to make friends at work. Other examples include having a job which
extends abilities, and having the opportunity of applying knowledge
gained in higher education. In addition to the eight items on higher
order needs, there were also two items designed to measure satisfaction
of economic needs. One of these was gross salary. The other was intended
to assess equity of pay. Respondents were asked the question "Compared
to most people how fair do you feel your pay is?". Anxiety was measured
using a tension at work scale developed by Keenan and McBain (3). This
asks respondents to describe their feelings at the end of a typical day
at work using eight Likert-type items. Three Likert items were used to
measure job satisfaction. Respondents were asked whether they would take
the same job again given the opportunity. Second, they were asked how
satisfied they were with their present job. Third, they were asked how
strongly they would recommend their job to a friend who was an engineer.
All three used five point scales and they were summed to form a measure
of overall satisfaction.

The 10 items relating to fulfilment of work needs and the 12 items
relating to stereotyped attitudes were entered together into two
separate regressions as predictors of job satisfaction and anxiety. For
job satisfaction, the multiple regression explained just over half the
variance (R^2 = .53). For anxiety, 30 per cent of the variance was
accounted for by the multiple regression. Inspection of the regressions
suggested that fulfilment of work needs was more strongly related to job
satisfaction than stereotyped attitudes, while the reverse was true for
the tension at work variable. In order to test this more directly, four
further regressions were carried out. Fulfilment of work needs was
entered into two separate regressions against job stereotyped attitudes
as the predictor. Taking fulfilment of work needs first, the multiple R
against job satisfaction was 0.60 and that against tension was 0.34. For
stereotyped attitudes, the multiple R against job satisfaction was 0.37
and that against tension was 0.45. Thus the suggestion that stereotyped
attitudes were more strongly related to anxiety while fulfilment of work
needs was more strongly associated with job satisfaction was confirmed
by these further regression analysis.

4.   DISCUSSION

These results suggest that many of the women in this sample had received
unfavourable treatment at the hands of interviewers both in the form of
excessive questioning about marriage and children and in the form of a
sceptical attitude about their abilities as engineers and motivations
for entering the profession. The evidence indicated that the kind of
sceptical attitudes encountered at interview were also quite prevalent
in the workplace.

Clearly, any kind of organisational practice which has an adverse impact on women cannot be condoned. However, one encouraging feature of the results was the finding that at least some of the organisational practices which put women at a disadvantage (such as restrictions on career advancement or low pay) were only reported in a minority of cases.

These results suggest that it would be a mistake to assume that differential treatment of women only has adverse consequences. A number of women reported that there were ways in which they were more favourably treated than their male counterparts, both in terms of recruitment, and in terms of treatment at the everyday level at work. For example, some felt that they were at an advantage in the interview situation because of their relative rarity and others felt they were in a favourable position because men tended to treat them in a more helpful and considerate manner. It is of interest that when it came to describing ways in which their job was made easier because they were female, most of the comments focused on social interactions in the workplace. It appeared that the presence of a woman encouraged more co-operation and less conflict. This state of affairs is somewhat ironic if one considers that the fields of engineering which probably have the highest potential for interpersonal conflict (such as construction and production) are the very areas where the women reported that organisations were reluctant to employ them.

The results suggest that the adverse impact of stereotyped attitudes is mainly on affective reactions such as anxiety rather than on job satisfaction. The future investigation of the effects of sex stereotyping should therefore go beyond attitudinal measures such as job satisfaction and employ scales which assess both affective responses and psychological strain.

References

(1) Keenan, A. & Newton, T.J.: Women as engineers; Wise or folly? Chartered Mechanical Engineer, 1984.
(2) Keenan, A. & Newton, T.J.: Work aspirations and experiences of young graduate engineers, In Print.
(3) Keenan, A. & McBain, G.D.M.: Effects of Type A behaviour, intolerance of ambiguity, and locus of control on the relationships between role stress and work-related outcomes. Journal of Occupational Psychology, 1979, 52, 277-285.

THE PSYCHOLOGY OF WORK AND ORGANIZATION
G. Debus and H.-W. Schroiff (Editors)
© Elsevier Science Publishers B.V. (North-Holland), 1986

WORKTIME REDUCTION IN THE NETHERLANDS

M. Demenint and K. Disselen

Department of Social and Organizational Psychology,
Leiden State University, Hooigracht 15,
2312 KM Leiden, The Netherlands.

One of the major organizational problems in 1985 in the Netherlands concerns the introduction of a general worktime reduction.
Organization psychologists occupied in solving the technical and
psychological problems in the organizations involved, tend to
forget, however, that the practical solutions on the organization
level have important social consequences as well.

1. INTRODUCTION

In this article the current discussion concerning a general worktime reduction in The Netherlands is reviewed. The topics of redistribution of
work, part-time work and women's emancipation are taken into account.
In paragraph 2 the point of departure is stated: paid work as a central
value in our society.
In paragraph 3 the labour market position of women is discussed, especially in reference to part-time work and a general worktime reduction.
The "history" of worktime reduction as a political issue in The Netherlands
is reported in paragraph 4.
In paragraph 5 the conclusion is drawn, that it is not possible to discuss
worktime reduction in general terms, as "the best way to organize" - and
even means and stated goal of a worktime reduction - always reflect the
point of view (e.g. the government, unions, employers, organizations, wom-
en) of the participants in the discussion. On balance the article is concluded with the notion that organization psychologists should at least be
aware of the different points of view on this topic.

2. PAID WORK AS A CENTRAL VALUE IN OUR SOCIETY

In the special issue on worktime reduction of the "Tijdschrift voor Arbeid en Bewustzijn" (1984, 5) the following imaginary case-example of
Bertrand Russell (1935) is quoted.
> Suppose that a certain time a certain number of people is producing
> pins. Working for eight hours a day, they produce as much pins as the
> world needs. Now someone invents a pin-producing machine and the same
> number of people, working in this trade as before, is able to produce
> twice as much pins. But ..... the world does not need twice as much
> pins. In a reasonable world everyone in the pin-producing-trade would
> from there on work for four hours a day. But in our world we think
> that working for only half a day is "demoralizing". So we keep up the
> eight-hour working day. As a result, there are too many pins (that the
> world does not need or buy) and half of the workers is discharged.

Now half of the people is working full time, producing pins, and the
other half is without job: the inevitable "leisure time" sure to create misery everywhere, in stead of being the universal source of
happiness. Can we imagine anything more insane?
In 1985, fifty years later, Russell's case-example is incredibly timely.
The mentioned relation between the introduction of advanced technological
equipment and the workers' discharge of course being an oversimplification
of reality (but we *do* have these problems on our hands), the quintessence
is that Russell, observing that work is a central value in our society,
expects people to have an inflexible mind in this kind of employment problems.
In this respect hardly anything has changed in fifty years. Work is still
a central value in our western society. Paid work functions as a distributive principle of status and income. We even can define paid work as a
concrete resource of power (power as a relational concept, Lukes, 1974).
It provides the opportunity to live your own life in the way you choose
and the possibility to be or become influential. Money, status and power
depend largely on employment. People holding a job thus might be inclined
to "defend the premises".

3. WOMEN AND THE (RE)DISTRIBUTION OF WORK

In The Netherlands originally the concept of redistribution of work was introduced by a noticeable group of women, headed by Joke Smit. In 1978 Joke
Smit defined redistribution of work as the redistribution of all work (including household work) over all people of both sexes. She introduced the
idea of a five-hour working day as a means to a fair distribution of work.
This idea was not well received. The five-hour working day was generally
thought impossible and discussion centered on the redistribution of work
over the sexes. Looking at it from the power perspective: these women started to redefine economical and social relationships from their own perspective and no longer accepted the "common" interpretation of reality, that
is, the traditional division of labour. Asking for a redistribution of all
work and a general worktime reduction produced a conflict of interest with
establishment and as a result, probably, the topic did not get too much
attention throughout the country.
In The Netherlands traditionally less women are professionally employed,
compared with the European Community countries. In 1960 in The Netherlands 22% of the women was employed. In 1980 30% of the Dutch women had a
paid job, as the average for the EEC reached 50% (Oudijk, 1983).
But in 1985 (despite the economic recession, so probably it could have
been even more) already 35% of the Dutch women between 15 and 65 years of
age is professionally employed and over one third of the labourforce consists of women.
The Central Planning Office (CPB, 1985) assumes that the labourmarket participation of women will continue: it predicts a growth to 38% by 1995.
As the number of women working is rapidly rising, in qualitative sense the
labourmarket position of women has hardly changed since 1960 (Oudijk, 1983).
Siegers (1980) showed that women are overrepresented in the lowest prestige class. In 1982 50% of the Dutch working women were employed in only
twenty-two out of 293 classified professions. As far as there is a tendency
of breaking through this professional segregation, it is because the men
start entering women's jobs in stead of the reverse (Ott, 1985). In 1980
only 2% of the women was working in a management function, compared to 10%
of the men.

One might expect that the labourmarket position depends for a large part on the education level. This does not, however, explain the relatively low labourmarket position of the Dutch women. Although in The Netherlands men are generally higher educated than women, from 1975 onwards, the women in the labourforce have, in average, a higher education level than their male colleagues (Meyer, 1977).

The main factors that account for the relatively low working level of the Dutch women probably are the following.

First, the fact that 95% of the working women has household responsibility, which influences their ability to accept a primary labourmarket function.

Secondly, the statistical discrimination (ascribing group characteristics to an individual woman) and probably discrimination in general as well (but this is hardly discussable, let alone demonstrable).

And third, the fact that approximately 50% of the Dutch working women have part-time jobs.

Research shows that part-time workers hardly ever rise to functions of importance and usually work in dead-end-jobs. Conditions of employment in general are much better for full-time workers (Oudijk, 1983; Demenint et al., 1982).

As part-time work became popular in the seventies, it was expected to contribute to women's emancipation, as it increased the possibilities for labourmarket participation. And part-time work was implicitly thought to contribute to some redistribution of the unpaid and household work as well. But the men kept a preference for full-time jobs. (In the Netherlands only very few part-timers are men: income, status, power?). Even in an organization with a relatively high average function level (Leiden University) part-time work increased only among the women. Between 1976 and 1982 the number of women with a full-time position even decreased. Considering the total amount of work done at the university, "women's share" had not grown at all: the women simply divided up the jobs among themselves into more and smaller part-time functions. The few men with a part-time job at Leiden University usually were employed somewhere else as well (Demenint et al., 1985). From this research the conclusion was drawn "that women's position will be improved only when the current dominating work ethic is changed and when the standard forty-hour workweek is drastically shortened".

4. WORKTIME REDUCTION AS A POLITICAL ISSUE

In 1978 part-time work had become the central action issue in the government's emancipation policy. "Equal treatment" for part-timers was proclaimed and support funds for the introduction of part-time work in higher functions was set up.

As this was not a success (see e.g. the research findings reported in the previous paragraph) and the rate of unemployment became more and more pressing, in 1981 part-time work became a part of the governmental employment policy, in which women's emancipation was less important.

In 1983, when unemployment figures in The Netherlands were still rising with astonishing speed (over 15% unemployment) a general worktime reduction was politically taken into consideration for the first time.

As goal was stated the redistribution of the paid work between the employed and the unemployed. Redistribution of the unpaid work and redistribution of work over the sexes is not taken into account in this new discussion.

Momentarily government, employers and the unions in The Netherlands are discussing the 38- or 36-hour workweek. At least, that is what it is called.

In reality this worktime reduction takes the form of several free days in
a monthly or yearly schedule: the 40-hour workweek stays unaffected. Despite the creation of + 40.000 new jobs (which is not too much, compared
to a 5% worktime reduction and a labourforce of over 4.5 million people),
the total number of the unemployed in The Netherlands in 1984 still rose
with approximately 10.000. [1]
In some cases the worktime reduction averted a number of planned discharges
(Rapportage Arbeidsmarkt, 1984).
At the moment, there are several groups, that are hardly able to gain access to the labourmarket anymore: newcomers to the market (schoolleavers)
and reentering women. The Dutch government is aware of this problem. Although political attention is primarily focussed on youth unemployment, in
1984 35 million guilders, 10% of the total budget of the employment
bureau, was "earmarked" to be used for the labour market (re)entering of
women. Evaluating the use of this budget, it appears that the money often
is used for different purposes or not yet spent at all (Stichting Ombudsvrouw, 1985).

5. DISCUSSION: WORKTIME REDUCTION, A QUESTION OF "WHOSE POINT OF VIEW"?

In paragraph 3 Joke Smit's idea of a five-hour working day in order to facilitate a fair distribution of all work (paid and unpaid) over all people
(male and female) was introduced. In 1978 only women were interested in
this scheme; politically it was ignored. Since the government in 1983 stated a general worktime reduction as a means to fight unemployment (see paragraph 4) several politicians have been engaged in the design of a twenty-
five-hour working week (De Populier, 1985). It is important to discern
that these two forms of worktime reduction are not necessarily alike, nor
are their consequences. A five-hour working day basically guarantees that
every adult person daily will have time enough to attend to both professional and household work. A twenty-five-hour working week could take any
form, from 3 workdays a week of approximately 8 hours to a 3 weeks on - 2
weeks off schedule in which the forty-hour week stays unaffected.
The differences in the form of the worktime reduction are the result of
different stated goals: women's emancipation versus the advancement of
general employment.
In any case the twenty-five-hour working week is utopian, but in the actual
worktime reduction of 5% in the Netherlands a similar case can be pointed
out. Some organizations already introduced the seven-hour workday and are
preparing for a further worktime reduction per day, as others scheduled
the worktime reduction of 5% in eleven free days on a yearly basis.
Organizations/employers, who take the latter action usually complain that
it is impossible to organize a worktime reduction in any other way. As the
unions are traditionally more interested in reducing the numbers of the
unemployed (and less in women's emancipation), they accept the statement
that a shorter working week cannot be organized and gladly accept a worktime reduction in any offered form.
It is rather an interesting question, whether the 36- or 38-hour working
week really is a threat to organizational effectiveness. Relying on prior
research on the organization of part-time work (Schoemaker et al., 1981;
Demenint et al., 1982) and worktime reduction (Weeda et al., 1985) the
authors are inclined to doubt this. The main problem probably is that
there are no "general instructions on the best strategies" for the introduction of a worktime reduction. The quoted research reports showed that
in each case the circumstances differ and that "tailor-made" solutions had

to be sought, depending on factors as organization structure and -culture, size, product and production time, technology involved and financial/economical position of the organization involved. This means that organizations must invest time (money) to solve their organization problems in relation to worktime reduction. An advice for a relatively simple but usually effective work strategy can be given: let the employees involved put in writing why a worktime reduction in specific functions or departments is thought not possible. Thus a very detailed list of "problems to be solved" can be collected.

Usually it turns out that solutions can be found. Of course there are also organizational problems that cannot be solved without considerable effort. Two examples of problematical situations that keep turning up will be named. First the problem that (in spite of the general level of unemployment) there is a shortage of qualified workers in some professions. Second, the fact that small organizations (up to approximately 10 employees) are far less flexible and have less means for finding alternatives, either financial or in (wo)manpower. In small organizations redistribution of tasks over the functions is not always easy and funds are usually limited. But why should these specific organizations prevent a general introduction of worktime reduction?

Why not make a temporary exception in these specific cases?

It is in contradiction with the research findings quoted above that most organizations should not be able to cope with the organizational problems of a shorter working week.

Summarizing: whether organizations will be able to cope with a worktime reduction per day or per week probably depends largely on their willingness to do so.

Also it will have been made obvious that in matters concerning worktime reduction the point of view that is or will be taken, depends on the party or parties involved (as mentioned above: the government, unions, employers, organizations, women).

And on balance: it is important that organization psychologists involved in the organizational problems of a worktime reduction, whether acting as personnel manager, researcher or organization consultant should be aware of these differences in viewpoint and as a consequence of the different implications of a chosen definition or a stated goal for any of the here mentioned parties.

NOTE

1) Note that in 1984 unemployed people over 56 years of age were not included in the statistics anymore, so the figure of 10.000 gives a flattered impression.

LITERATURE

Centraal Planbureau, Vooruitberekeningen van het trendmatig arbeidsaanbod tussen 1980 en 2010 ('s-Gravenhage, Staatsuitgeverij, 1983)

Demenint, M., S. Cohen Tervaert, J. Vollering, e.a., Deeltijdarbeid: een tovermiddel? (Leiden, Rijksuniversiteit, Werkgroep Arbeidsvraagstukken en Welzijn, 1982)

Lukes, S., Power, a radical view (London, MacMillan, 1974)

Meyer, J., Sociale Atlas van de Vrouw, (p. 173), SCP cahier no. 11, ('s-Gravenhage, Staatsuitgeverij, 1977)

Ott, M., Assepoesters en kroonprinsen; een onderzoek naar de minderheids-positie van agentes en verplegers, (Amsterdam, Sua, 1985)

Oudijk, C., Sociale Atlas van de Vrouw 1983, (chapter 5), Sociale en Cul-turele Studies 3, ('s-Gravenhage, Staatsuitgeverij, 1983)

Populier, Stichting de, Arbeidstijdverkorting: haalbaar en betaalbaar, (Amsterdam, de Populier, 1985)

Rapportage Arbeidsmarkt 1984 ('s-Gravenhage, Ministerie van Sociale Zaken en Werkgelegenheid, 1984)

Schoemaker, N., A. van Gageldonk, M. Demenint & A. van Vianen, Deeltijd-arbeid in het bedrijf (Alphen aan de Rijn, Samsom, 1981)

Siegers, J.J., Beroepssegregatie en sociale ongelijkheid tussen mannen en vrouwen op de Nederlandse arbeidsmarkt (Sociale Wetenschappen, 1980, p. 280-290)

Tijdschrift voor Arbeid en Bewustzijn, jaargang 8, no. 5, 1984 (themanum-mer Arbeidstijdverkorting)

Weeda, P., A.M. Pals, C.L. Steensma, M. Demenint, Organisatie en Arbeids-duur. Handleiding voor analyse en aanpak van organisatievraagstukken bij de verkorting van de arbeidsduur ('s-Gravenhage, Ministerie van Sociale Zaken en Werkgelegenheid, 1985)

Stichting Ombudsvrouw, Evaluatie van de 10% regeling ('s-Gravenhage, 1985)

THE PSYCHOLOGY OF WORK AND ORGANIZATION
G. Debus and H.-W. Schroiff (Editors)
© Elsevier Science Publishers B.V. (North-Holland), 1986

A SOCIO-COGNITIVE APPROACH TO THE
PSYCHOLOGY OF UNEMPLOYMENT

Marco DEPOLO & Guido SARCHIELLI

Dipartimento di Politica Sociale,
Universita di Trento, Via Verdi, 26,
38100 Trento, Italy

It is well known that a large number of people nowadays have to face the problem of finding work or of holding the job they have, and forecasts for the future only seem to confirm this tendency. Unemployment above 10% is no longer an exception, and this means millions of people are wrestling with the effects of being unemployed, for long or short-term periods and with different chances of escaping this situation. Public opinion seems to view this problem from, above all, an economic point of view: however, if it is true that a country's economic situation plays an important role in determining the quantity and quality of work available, "... the ultimate criterion by which economic strategies must be judged... is the quality of life people experience. Being employed or unemployed is a major component of this quality" (1).

Such an affirmation can be based on different arguments. In the first place, most people live on their work and welfare payments for the unemployed usually are not a sufficient economic substitute. But work activity has - from a psychosocial point of view - other important characteristics the lack of which due to unemployment would seem to pose important problems for those involved (1, 2, 3).

Work in fact helps to structure social identity; it is an important occasion for socialization; it structures the day; it permits the development of personal skills, requiring normally regular activity levels. It is clear that all these characteristics do not solely concern work; the latter is not in fact the only instance of the socialization process; it is not the only factor which helps building identity; people find themselves together in other situations, too, which require the activation of complex behaviour strategies. What is important however is that we find all these factors present in work activity.

It is the more recent research that has cast doubt on the interpretative model which we can describe as "catastrophe/deprivation". A lot of research data (3, 7) does not confirm the hypotheses that unemployment is, for everybody and in all situations, something which necessarily involves a drastic diminution in psychological well-being.

In effect, if work is not a quasi-biological necessity, but rather a socially determined activity, one could expect that its absence would have different effects depending on the many factors which determine the balance between costs and benefits that each subject can get out of it. It would not as yet appear satisfactory to say that unemployment is psychologically "expensive" simply because of the lack of work, which is psychologically so important. In saying this, one forgets that the people psychologically who have lost their jobs are not the same as before, minus simply their work: becoming unemployed is a major change, which may generate "... instability and unpredictability, an experienced

loss of personal control, a need to cope through the acquisition of new
perspectives and skills, and a requirement to resolve questions about
oneself which may otherwise never be raised" (8).

Abandoning   the   "catastrophe/deprivation" model means   underlining   the
importance of studying how individuals try to elaborate strategies of
response to a critical event such as the loss of work. Within this
perspective it becomes important to gather representational and attribu-
tional data which help understanding the socio-cognitive bases of such
strategies. One puts forward the question for example of how unemployed
people make some sense of this phenomenon, that is, what system of
opinions, beliefs and attitudes they possess; if such a system is
shared by larger groups or if there are remarkable differences; which
attributions of causality are given pride of place: what is the perception of the effects of unemployment on everyday life, etc..

It is therefore a question of investigating those psychosocial dimensions which emphasize the assumption of an active role by the subjects
in the processes of reconstruction and interpretation of the social
reality. Within this perspective, we have carried out two pilot studies
in Italy. In Italy, as in all the other countries of the European
Community, the job situation is difficult, especially for youngsters. As
well as the problem of those who are trying to get into the job market
there is also a larger number of people who find themselves without
work, without being exactly fired. This is due to the existence of a
juridical instrument called C.I.G. (Cassa Integrazione Guadagni) which
allows ailing companies to ask the government to declare them "in a
state of crisis" so that the surplus work force may be laid off
(continuing however to receive about 80% of their salaries) for periods
lasting anywhere from several days to many months.

The C.I.G. is not unemployment; the workers do not lose their jobs, but
are out of work all the same; the status of the worker is more uncertain
because he stays at home without working even though he continues to
receive a salary.

It is just such a fact which allows us to study a situation of absence
from work, keeping the variable "economic discomfort" under control
which in this case is limited to receiving 20% less in the pay picket.
This constitutes a sort of "minimal situation" for studying, for
example, the effects of lack of work on psychological well-being: if
such effects appear even when only temporarily out of work and without
any pressing economic discomfort, then the hypothesis that work activity
plays a very$_1$important role in the well-being of the individual may find
confirmation^1.

This article will present some research data concerning the representation of unemployment and, more especially, the attribution of causes for
this phenomenon. As stated previously, we believe it important to have a
greater understanding of the effects of job loss on psychological well-
being, and to have data on the concrete strategies adopted by people to
face up to this state of affairs. A part of these strategies is mediated
by unemployment representations in which the causality links adopted
play a role of prime importance.

Furnham (9) has studied this particular theme in Great Britain discover-
ing several factors which explain the modalities commonly used for

talking about unemployment, according to certain variables (political orientation, occupational status etc.). We confronted it by using the concept of social representation (10, 11) trying to find out how real groups can elaborate common ways of defining and of explaining the social object "unemployment". Both studies that we carried out used the same type of questionnaire in two different situations².

In the first we studied two groups of subjects with similar socio-anagraphical and occupational characteristics who were workers in an industrial area of northern Italy. One group (SG) had been on C.I.G. only for a short while (maximum 30 days), the other (LG) for much longer (up to five years). The two groups were made up of 50 and 48 subjects respectively.
We imagined that the two groups – replying to our list of items – would have been more in agreement with those items talking about socio-economic causes than those underlining the responsability of the un-employed. This is in effect what happened: agreement was highest in the two groups over items 2, 4, 5 and 8.

But what interested us most, however, was the structure of the replies, that is the combination of items to certain clusters. The question can be formulated in this way: in the replies of the two groups, beyond the frequencies, which items go with which and what is the field of representation which results? One of the techniques that can be used to this end is the similarity analysis (12, 13): its application leads to the spanning tree in Fig. 1, which was constructed from the data of SG (see next page).
One can discern a grouping of closely connected items (1, 3, 7, 9) concerning causes of a "personal" nature referring to the unemployed, while the other items are connected by branches of the tree which have lower similarity values.

Without going into details about the structure, it is enough to notice that the subjects of SG use the "personal" items as a structured whole (to declare their disagreement of course) while the remaining items are less "similar" among them; to accept (or refuse) one does not mean the subjects have to accept (or refuse) the others too.

The data concerning LG however, presented in Fig. 2, show certain differences (see next page).

As we can see, the two blocks ("general" and "personal" causes) both appear more clearly on the tree. Opinions on the main causes of unemployment are in the same direction as the other group, but here it is easier to identify a bi-polarized structure. One can say that the workers who have had a longer spell on C.I.G. adopt a system of repre-sentation of the causes of unemployment which more clearly distinguishes the two types of explanation.

In the second study, the same list of items was given to subjects coming from the same factory. When the owner decided to close it down, a group of workers tried an experiment with self-management by founding a co-operative: others, however, decided to look for another job on their own.

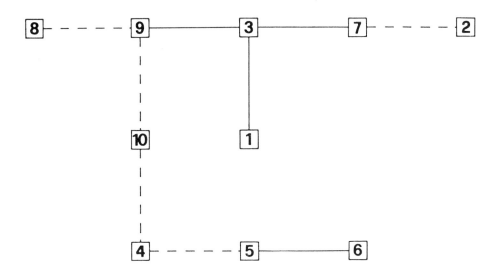

Figure 1: Spanning tree of items about unemployment (SG)

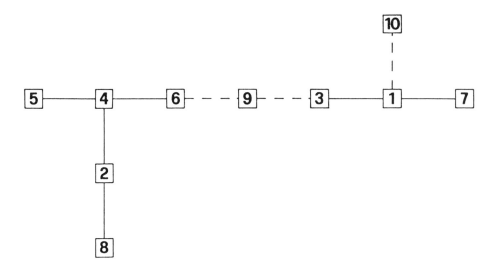

Figure 2: Spanning tree of items about unemployment (LG)

The two groups that we studied (30 subjects from those who formed the cooperative: CG; 28 subjects from those who tried to find a new job on their own: IG) could therefore be seen as representing two different strategies, one collective, the other individual, for facing the problem of job loss.

Data analysis was carried out in the same way as in the previous study. As far as frequency is concerned, we find "general" causes in the front ranks, such as items 2, 4 and 5, but it is important to note that the "personal" items (1, 3, 7, 9) are placed more clearly in the last positions by the CG group.

A similarity analysis was made on the data and the spanning tree which resulted for the CG group can be seen in Fig. 3.

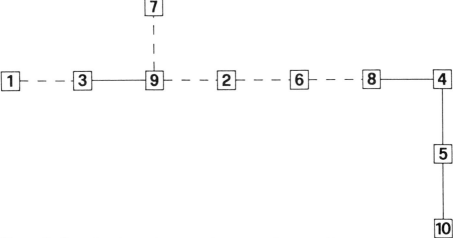

Figure 3: Spanning tree of items about unemployment (CG)

To synthesize, one can see that the strongest branches connect two groups of items: 3 and 9 on the one hand 4, 5, 8, 10 on the other, along a chain in which the "personal" and "general" causes tend to group themselves at the two extremities.

The result is different for the tree concerning IG (Fig. 4, see next page)

Three groupings appear here which are (following the decreasing order of similarity values): 2 and 4; 1, 3, 5 and 7; 6 and 9. These groupings do not exactly reproduce the division between "personal" and "general" causes: the two types of causes mingle more than in the other group so as to be able to affirm that two similar, though not equal, modalities for representing the system of the causes of unemployment correspond to the two strategies mentioned.

In conclusion, even though the data presented here is clearly not suffi- cient to be definitely evaluated, it does seem to us that it at least points to the fact that there are modalities of representation of a socio-cognitive nature that are shared by real groups regarding the social object "unemployment".

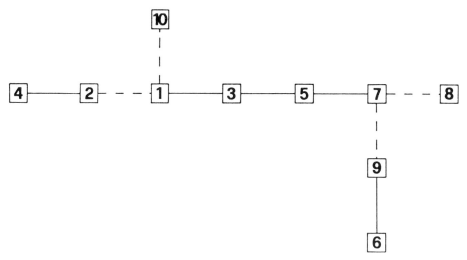

Figure 4: Spanning tree of items about unemployment (IG)

Such ways of thinking seem to be related to important characteristics of
the situation and can help explaining the behaviour of individuals and
groups coping with the problem of losing their jobs.

NOTES

[1] Even though one talks of "minimal situation", it should be remembered
that the National Health Service has signalled out a certain number of
cases of depression, alcoholism, psychotic crisis, and suicide attempts
among the FIAT workers on C.I.G. (for several months) in Turin. There
have also been cases of suicide though the direct cases have yet to be
proved.

[2] The list of items given to the subjects (on a 4-point "agree/disagree"
scale), under the heading "Unemployment is caused by...", is the following:
1) Lack of initiative of the unemployed; 2) Government policy; 3) The
unwillingness of the unemployed to change work; 4) World recession; 5)
Automation; 6) Italian industry's low competitivity; 7) The acceptance
by unemployed of the role of "assisted"; 8) The incompetence of the
managers; 9) The poor professional qualifications of the unemployed; 10)
Trade union weakness.

[3] The index of similarity used is the phi, which gives a measure of the
force of association between the ways of replying for each pair of
items.

REFERENCES

(1) Jahoda, M. (1982). Employment and unemployment. A social-psycholo-
     gical analysis. Cambridge: Cambridge Univ. Press.
(2) Jahoda, M. (1981). Employment and Unemployment. American Psycholo-
     gist, 2, 184-191.

(3) Warr, P.B. (1983). Work and Unemployment. In Handbook of Work and Organization Psychology, eds. P.J.D. Drent, H. Thierry, P.J. Willems, C.J. de Wolff (Wiley).
(4) Jahoda, M., Lazarsfeld, P.F., Zeisel, H. (1933). Marienthal: The Sociography of an Unemployed Community (engl. transl. 1972). London: Tavistock Publications.
(5) Bakke, E.W. (1933). The Unemployed Man. London: Nisbet.
(6) Zawadki, B., Lazarsfeld, P. (1935). The psychological consequences of unemployment. The Journal of Social Psychology, VI, 224-251.
(7) Hartley, J., Fryer, D. (1984). The Psychology of Unemployment: A Critical Appraisal. In Progress in Applied Social Psychology (vol. 2). eds. G.M. Stephenson, J.H. Davis (Wiley).
(8) Warr, P.B. (1983). Job Loss, Unemployment and Psychological Well-Being. In Role Transitions, eds. E. van de Vliert, V. Allen (Plenum).
(9) Furnham, A. (1982). Explanations for unemployment in Britain. European Journal of Social Psychology, 12, 335-352.
(10) Moscovici, S. (1981). On social representations. In Social Cognition, ed. J.P. Forgas (Academic Press).
(11) Jaspars, J.M.F., Fraser, C. (1984). Attitudes and social representations. In Social Representations, eds. S. Moscovici and R. Farr (Cambridge Univ. Press).
(12) Degenne, A., Vergès, P. (1973). Introduction à l'analyse de similitude. Révue Française de Sociologie, 14, 471-512.
(13) Flament, C. (1981). L'analyse de similitude: une technique pour les recherches sur les représentations sociales. Cahiers de Psychologie Cognitive, 1, 375-395.

INDIVIDUAL AND COLLECTIVE RESPONSES TO JOB INSECURITY

J.F. HARTLEY and P.G. KLANDERMANS

1. INTRODUCTION

1.1 The Prevalence of Job Insecurity

Job insecurity is a neglected topic in psychological research. For those
in employment, the high level of unemployment, redundancy, company deaths,
plant closure, automation and reorganization may have an unsettling effect
and create anxieties about the future of their own jobs. Few sectors of
the economy are immune from these developments. The recent recession has
created large redundancies and plant closures, especially in manufacturing. Even for those companies which are relatively more successful,
competitive pressures have resulted in restructuring, with less profitable
concerns closing, with introduction of new technology, and with extensive
transfer of capital to plants overseas.

It is expected that job insecurity will continue in the future. As well
as the recession and capital restructuring effects, there is the impact
of changes in employment contracts at an individual level. There has
been a significant increase in less-secure employment, for example,
fixed-term contracts, temporary workers, part-time working and home-
working (Rubery and Tarling, 1981). Some experts predict developments
towards Japanese employment relations: a small number of workers in
secure, longterm jobs and a larger number of workers in temporary, insecure employment (Brown, 1983). Unions are increasingly concerned with
developments in job insecurity (Edmonds, 1984). Employers urge governments to eliminate barriers to greater mobility (for example to make
dismissal and redundancy easier). These arguments legitimate the urgent
need for research on reactions to job insecurity.

At a psychological level, there are significant questions to ask about
the impact of insecure employment. What is it like to work in an organization or a job which has a pessimistic or uncertain future? What is it
like to work in an organization which has experienced cutbacks in staff-
ing? What is redundancy like, not for those who leave but those who
remain?

Psychologists have not yet developed the conceptual tools or theory to
understand job insecurity to any major extent. There is a vast literature on the psychological impact of unemployment (e.g. Jahoda, 1982;
Warr, 1983) but there has been a tendency to dichotomise employment and
unemployment. Some psychologists have criticised this simple division,
calling for an investigation of job insecurity rather than worklessness
(Hartley, 1980; Hartley and Fryer, 1984). There needs to be wider recognition of the point made by Townsend (1977):

'There are not two broad states of employment and
unemployment, but a hierarchy of states from whole-
time secure employment through discontinuous employment to continuous unemployment. It is a continuum.'
(p.10)

There is now some evidence that jobs at risk of redundancy cause stress
(Kasl, Gore and Cobb, 1975). More widely job insecurity has been found,
in stress research, to be a significant stressor in a number of studies
(Caplan et al, 1975; Dijkhuizen, 1980).

1.2 Defining the field of enquiry

In exploring a new field, it is important to define an area and limit it
from other, overlapping areas of research. Job insecurity is a concern
about the future existence of the job or sometimes a concern about a
significant deterioration in terms and conditions of employment. Job
insecurity may vary from person to person, both due to the individual's
vulnerability to job termination and also the individuals's own perceptions of his/her objective environment. In conducting research on felt
job insecurity, which is based on the worker's perceptions, one must seek
situations of objective uncertainty about the future, as an anchor point
for subjective experience. For Hartley, job insecurity may occur in the
objective conditions of a history of previous job loss and an uncertain
future facing the organization. For Jacobson, job insecurity may occur
in an organization in the period preceding formal notification of lay-off,
where the individual perceives certain signals in the organization's
internal and external environments which imply job terminations at some
stage in the future. A situation of job insecurity may suggest entirely
different behaviours than when redundancy has been announced.

We suggest that job insecurity has consequences in three distinguishable
areas: the individual, the organizational, and the industrial relations
areas.

In the individual area we may think about stress related phenomena like
mental health, psychological well-being, anxiety, self-esteem, job satisfaction and about different coping strategies like inertia, search for
change, and denial, and about changes in commitment to the union and in
willingness to participate in union action.

In the organizational area we may think of organizational effectiveness,
decision making, organizational change, organizational commitment, morale
and other organizational indicators.

In the industrial relations area, we may think of union behaviour, management behaviour toward unions, concepts like mutual trust between
management and workers, industrial relations climate, perceptions of
own and others bargaining power.

Research can be done in each of the three areas and the papers in our
workshop address one or more of them. Jacobson's and De Polo and
Sarchielli's papers discuss consequences of job insecurity at the individual level. Hartley's paper is about observations on union/management
relations.

It is also important to develop theory. That will necessarily be middle range theorising, addressing determinants and relations of some of the areas instead of altogether. Jacobson uses value-expectancy and decision-making theories to suggest differences in individual reactions to job insecurity. In research on job insecurity, psychological well-being and willingness to participate in collective action, which the second author is conducting, a similar framework is used (Klandermans, 1984). De Polo and Sarchielli lean on the social representations approach, pointing to collective processes of sharing definitions of the situation to explain reactions to lay-off. Hartley uses theories about inter-group relations and power to understand union/management relations. Of course theoretical possibilities are not exhausted with these approaches, and certainly others will prove fruitful.

2.　DETERMINANTS OF "JOB AT RISK" (JAR) BEHAVIOUR

This paper is by Dan Jacobson.

The paper develops a theoretical approach and model for understanding the set of role behaviours grouped under the label "job at risk" (JAR) behaviour. The JAR role relates to the period of uncertainty that precedes formal notification of job termination, (which may or may not come) that is, when workers perceive that something is amiss with their employing organization which poses a potential threat to their job security. Only a handful of studies have, in the past, focused directly on the ambiguous period when termination is perceived as a possibility or a potential threat though not formally announced. The paper suggests that job uncertainty may evoke a range of possible responses quite distinct from those generated by actual redundancy or unemployment. It suggests that a person's JAR state, in which he/she is clearly employed but knows that one or more risk factors are present which render him/her vulnerable to job loss does not fit the conceptual definition of the securely employed, nor of the unemployed, and thus constitutes a separate mental state. This paper addresses theoretically what variables determine what workers do and how they cope with job insecurity.

The model presented here is essentially derived from "value x expectancy" theory. As a model of decision-making under conditions of uncertainty it also borrows its outcome components from the Janis and Mann (1977) conflict-theory model of decision-making. In understanding felt job insecurity the model also makes use of, in adapted form, Greenhalgh and Rosenblatt's (1984) conceptualization of job insecurity.

The JAR model consists of the following major elements:

i)　the occurrence of potentially "threatening indications" in the workers organizational environment. These are signs that something is amiss in the organization and that job losses may be called for

ii)　the worker's felt job insecurity relative to the threatening indications as determined by his/her belief in the likelihood of own job termination (perceived susceptibility) and belief in the seriousness of the consequences that job termination would have for him/her (perceived severity)

iii) the existence of a relevant stimulus termed here as "cues to action" that would trigger the consideration of a specific course of action or courses of action by the affected worker

iv) the worker's evaluation of the feasibility and efficacy - "benefits" - weighed against the worker's estimates of social, psychological or other "barriers" or "costs" involved in the proposed action

v) alternative coping mechanisms, namely "inertia", "unconflicted change", "defensive avoidance" and "vigilance".

The model posits, in essence, that in the face of potentially threatening indications, the specific coping pattern adopted will be a function of the individual's felt job insecurity, the availability of cues to action (i.e. the belief that there are ways of reducing the danger of job termination or of making it less serious) and the perceived benefits of taking action minus the perceived costs of the action. The paper expands in detail on these elements and their relationships and especially considers coping patterns.

The model offers an abstract explanation of JAR behaviour. It assumes that the impact of organizational instability is not equal for sub-groups of individuals, suggesting differential vulnerability to felt job insecurity and variation in coping patterns. It is too early to pit the JAR model against some alternative formulation and express a scholarly preference for one or the other. Rather, the next step is to adequately operationalise the model's components and design a research strategy to test the model or perhaps more probably, a subset of its components. There is no presumption that the proposed model is the beginning of a JAR theory. Rather, it can perhaps be used as an analytical device to guide empirical research and to organise the data obtained from such investigations. It is hoped that this paper stimulates research, which will lead to refinements in the model and clarify the influence of personal, environmental and organizational factors on the coping behaviour of individuals in organizations facing difficulties that pose threats to the continuity of employment.

3   JOB INSECURITY, PSYCHOLOGICAL WELL-BEING AND SOCIAL REPRESENTATION: A CASE OF COST SHARING

This paper is by Marco Depolo and Guido Sarchielli.

Reactions to job insecurity are often considered in a somewhat over-simplified fashion as "automatic" reactions to frustrating events. However, in contrast, it is important to know how subjects perceive the idea of job loss, the categorizations and interpretations they make of it, and what causal attributions they are making. At the same time one has to evaluate how these cognitive processes can influence attempts to actively tackle the problems and obstacles that go to make up people's own actual experience. In this paper it is argued that a study of the effects of unemployment and of some of its implications on the importance of work and work practices can be usefully linked to the theoretical idea of "social representations" (Moscovici, 1981). Jaspars and Fraser (1984) underline just such a possibility and confirm the usefulness of a study of widespread shared attitudes or "social representations" or ideologies concerning unemployment and the unemployed. According to this method the way in which a subject approaches job insecurity or reacts to job loss should be analysed in relation to a much larger series of beliefs, values, concepts, and assumptions of unemployment shared and valued by the subject's own social group and accepted by the subject him/herself.

These ideas were tested empirically in research among workers from an Italian company. These workers decided to tackle the problem of redundancy by using the so-called Cassa Integrazione Guardagni (CIG). According to this regulation, the workers involved are paid by the state the equivalent of 80% of their wages. In this way, companies in a critical economic situation can lay off a part of their work force without firing them. Application of CIG creates two groups of workers - those on CIG and those who are still working.

A questionnaire was administered to a sample of 112 skilled manual workers (37 working, 75 on CIG). The questionnaire included the General Health Questionnaire (GHQ) and questions about CIG.

Results showed that the image of CIG among both groups of workers was rather similar. It is argued that this delineates a socially shared "universe of meanings", focussing the attention on   i) the limits of CIG as a mechanism (it doesn't create a final solution, it is socially expensive, it is worrying as far as future company performance is concerned) and ii) the changes it offers to avoid a worsening of living conditions. Such a common "cognitive mechanism" is useful for the whole group for understanding their actual condition of job insecurity, for talking it over amongst themselves, for working out an appropriate strategy to deal with it.

Scores on the GHQ of both groups were rather high, approximating the scores of unemployed men reported in other studies. A distinction was made between those workers on CIG for a second time compared with those who had never been on it before. GHQ-scores of subjects on CIG for the second time were much higher. It appears that the lack of psychological well-being as a consequence of job insecurity involved all the workers in the company, although more so if they were struck by it a second time. Considering the financial situation of the company this is not surprising. In fact the job insecurity involved the whole group, even those still working full-time. The negative psychological effects of job insecurity are not significantly reduced by arrangements like CIG, however important these arrangements are as financial support systems.

4.   JOB INSECURITY AND UNION-MANAGEMENT RELATIONS

This paper is by Jean Hartley.

This paper examines union-management relations in a situation where job insecurity is prevalent. It examines a single case study. Job insecurity can be caused by a number of factors (company merger, new technology, restructuring etc.) but here the focus is on job insecurity created by organizational decline i.e. where employment and production have decreased, and there is little sign of the trend changing.

Psychologists have tended to neglect the impact of job insecurity on individuals and groups but the industrial relations literature has examined
the impact of high unemployment and fear of unemployment on industrial
relations. It suggests that recession creates pressures on management:
to maintain markets in an increasingly competitive situation, to cut production costs and increase productivity, to reassert control over industrial relations. Pressures on unions caused by recession are to defend
workers' jobs and labour practices. There is widespread suggestion that
recession causes job insecurity which causes timidity in unions, and a
"new realism" in attitudes. Overall, however, in terms of the balance of
power, management is thought to have gained from the recession. The overall effect of the "recession literature", then, is increased managerial
power, reduction in shop steward organization and influence, intensifi-
cation of work and greater flexibility, and industrial relations climate
changes.

This literature generates a number of psychological questions, for example, what is job insecurity and how can it be conceptualised and measured?
How is the industrial relations climate changed by job insecurity? How is
inter-group relations (between unions and management) influenced by job
insecurity? How is the threat to jobs perceived? How is power between
unions and management affected by a situation of job insecurity?

In particular, the paper hypothesises that inter-group relations will be
crucially affected by attributions about the causation of company difficulties (and accompanying job insecurity). If explanations for company
difficulty are seen by workers to reside in factors internal to the company, then a co-operative relation with management in the face of threats
to company performance would not be anticipated, but rather would increase
hostility and tension in union-management relations. Also, it is suggested that power, as manifested in union-management relations, is not a
uni-dimensional variable, but consists of resources held by either party.
It is suggested that a situation of company difficulty may actually weaken
both unions and management, contrary to the industrial relations recession
literature which suggests that, largely, management alone gains from a
situation of job insecurity.

The case study is based on interviews, observation and documentary material from an engineering company experiencing difficulties in its markets.
The case study is used to illustrate concepts and processes, and especially, in the context of the conference workshop, to raise questions. The
paper uses illustrative material from the case study to indicate the following in relation to job insecurity, inter-group relations and power.

Job insecurity was widespread in the plant. There were fears for the
future and concern about living standards currently. Redundancies were
expected at some stage in the future. In terms of perceptions, the unions
saw the company as being in an on-going crisis which was largely due to
internal factors, especially the lack of competence of local management.
Given these perceptions, collaboration in the face of external threat
would not be expected from the unions. Management with its concern for
production was also not looking for collaboration. Company difficulties
intensified pressures on both sides. Unions were pressurised by low morale, increasing frustration and past redundancy. Management were pressurised by their vulnerability in the product market. The industrial relations climate deteriorated. Inter-group understanding was low. There

was little trust. There was no evidence of "new realism" attitudes and power did not shift unambiguously to management. Both sides were weakened by pressures created by organizational decline.

5. WORKSHOP DISCUSSION AND CONCLUSIONS

The papers generated considerable discussion, which principally developed around two themes. First, a concern with the precise nature of job security - how it could be conceptualised, how to identify it in particular contexts and how it could be measured. Second, practical and ethical questions about how a researcher could gain access to organizations which were in decline, or otherwise experiencing difficulties which might pose a threat to job security. Access was recognised to be difficult to obtain, and there were also, after entry, important moral considerations about confidentiality of data, being worthy of the trust organizational members placed in the researcher, and the sensitive industrial relations issues which have to be faced. Despite these difficulties, there was a general feeling that job insecurity was widespread and growing, and urgently required detailed psychological analysis.

In conclusion, the workshop contributors identified a number of themes and research problems which are important. This is not an exhaustive enumeration, but could form a starting point for further enquiry. For example i) what are the appropriate indicators of job insecurity (for example, objective and subjective indicators and how they relate)? ii) What indicators of psychological well-being can be used in this sensitive context? iii) What are the external circumstances which influence job insecurity? Should all circumstances of job insecurity be treated as similar? iv) What factors determine variations between individuals and work-groups in their feelings about job insecurity? v) What features of the organization and the industrial relations system influence reactions to job insecurity? vi) How can effective longitudinal research take place? vii) What methodologies and research designs are appropriate? viii) What theories can be developed on reactions to job insecurity at individual, organizational and industrial relations levels? ix) How can cross-cultural comparisons be achieved?

Although there are considerable questions still to be researched in the area of job insecurity, there was an optimistic sense that a start was being made.

6. REFERENCES

Brown, W. (1983) The Emergence of Enterprise Unionism. Personnel Management, October.

Caplan, R.D., Cobb, S., French, J.R.P., Harrison, R. van, and Pinneau, S.R. (1975) Job demands and worker health. Washington: NIOSH.

Edmonds, J. (1984) Decline of the Big Battalions. Personnel Management, March.

Greenhalgh, L. and Rosenblatt, Z. (1984) Job insecurity: toward conceptual clarity, Academy of Management Review 9, 438-448.

Hartley, J.F. (1980) Psychological approaches to unemployment. Bulletin of The British Psychological Society, 33, 412-414.

Hartley, J.F., and Fryer, D. (1984) The Psychology of Unemployment: A Critical Appraisal in Stephenson, G.and Davis, J.H. (eds). Progress in Applied Social Psychology, 2, 3-30.

Jahoda, M. (1982) Employment and Unemployment. Cambridge: Cambridge University Press.

Janis, I. and Mann, L. (1977) Decision-making. New York: Free Press.

Jaspars, J. and Fraser, C. (1984) Attitudes and social representations in Moscovici, S. and Farr, R. (eds). Social representations. Cambridge: Cambridge University Press.

Kasl, S., Gore, S., and Cobb, S. (1975) The experience of losing a job: reported changes in health, symptoms and illness behaviour. Psychosomatic Medicine, 37, 106-122.

Klandermans, P.G. (1984) Psychological well-being, willingness to participate in collective action and job insecurity. ZWO-Research proposal. Amsterdam: Vakgroep Sociale Psychologie, Vrije Universiteit.

Moscovici, S. (1981) On social representations in Forgas, J.P. (ed). Social cognition. London: Academic Press.

Rubery, J., and Tarling, R. (1982) Women in the Recession. Socialist Economic Review.

Townsend, P. (1977) The Neglect of Mass Unemployment. New Statesman, 7th October.

Van Dijkhuizen, M. (1980) From stressors to strains: Research into their interrelationships. Lisse: Swets and Zeitlinger.

Warr, P. (1983) Work and unemployment. In Drenth, P.J.D., Thierry, H., Willens, P.J., and de Wolff, C.J. (eds). Handbook of Work and Organizational Psychology. Chichester: Wiley.

THE PSYCHOLOGY OF WORK AND ORGANIZATION
G. Debus and H.-W. Schroiff (Editors)
© Elsevier Science Publishers B.V. (North-Holland), 1986

WORKER RESPONSES TO JOB INSECURITY:
A QUASI-EXPERIMENTAL FIELD INVESTIGATION

ANDRE BüSSING

Department of Medical Psychology, RWTH Aachen
Pauwelsstraße (Neuklinikum)
5100 Aachen, Federal Republic of Germany

A quasi-experimental field investigation was conducted with the
cooperation of blast furnace workers from two steel companies.
105 workers came from a company offering only highly insecure
employment and 75 from a company with no job insecurity.
Statistical comparisons show no increase in psychosomatic
complaints or job strain but for workers with high job insecurity
diminished job satisfaction, hope for control, perceived
alternatives on the labour market and perceived collective
control. Aspects of controllability/predictability at work as
regards job insecurity as well as the difference between job
insecurity and anticipation of job loss are discussed.

1. INTRODUCTION

For more than 10 years we have had a high rate of unemployment both in the
FRG and most other industrial countries; it is distributed inhomogenously,
particulary as regards its regional basis and specific branches of
activity.   In recent years the psychosocial consequences of the present
unemployment situation have increasingly been the subject of research
(e.g.   Hartley & Fryer, 1984; Kieselbach & Wacker, 1985; Mackay & Haines,
1982; Warr, 1984). Up till now little scientific attention has been paid
to possible psychosocial consequences of job insecurity, although in times
of economic crisis it comes to concern increasing sections of the
population. Only a few studies have empirically considered job insecurity
as an independent variable (e.g. Brenner, 1985; Brenner et al., 1983;
Büssing, 1985a; Büssing & Jochum, 1985; Depolo & Sarchielli, 1985). Job
insecurity has to be distinguished from anticipation of certain
forthcoming unemployment. Büssing (1985a) concludes that results obtained
from studies on the anticipation of unemployment cannot be readily carried
over to the situation of job insecurity.   Whereas job insecurity is
characterized by the ambiguity of the situation, which the experience of
insecurity with regard to the interpretation of the situation can elicit
(Folkman et al., 1979), the phase of anticipation of unemployment in times
of economic crisis is typified by an extensive uncontrollability as
regards retaining the present or gaining new employment. In the phase of
anticipation of unemployment an employee increasingly runs the danger of

experiencing symptoms of helplessness and psychological stress. In contrast, up till now, virtually nothing could be said about the effects of job insecurity on psychological stress and the feeling of helplessness. As long as job insecurity does not develop into the certainty of impending unemployment, the question remains, as to whether job insecurity leads to symptoms of psychological stress and helplessness comparable to those experienced during anticipation of unemployment or rather, whether in the run-up to such stress symptoms it contributes for example to negative changes in the perceived controllability or job satisfaction. Here I wish to investigate the following question: *Does prolonged job insecurity have a negative influence on psychosomatic complaints, on strain/irritability, on job satisfaction or on different aspects of perceived controllability with regard to the work?*

2. METHODS

2.1. Subjects

In the FRG, as in other western countries, the steel industry is one of the problem branches in terms of the labour market. The crisis in the steel industry implies at the same time depression of whole regions, because as a key-industry, it largely determines economic life (Judith, 1980). For this investigation of the effects of job insecurity, blast furnace workers from two steel companies in the Saarland were interviewed. Whereas one of the two steel companies in question has been fighting for its economic existence for years and has already cut back half of its work force by early retirement, the second steel company has no economic difficulties. Blast furnace workers in the "crisis company" ("experimental group": EG) know that the old blast furnace will be closed in the middle of 1986. Only a small group of workers in the EG can be transferred to a new blast furnace plant; the majority will be retired early under a social plan or will be moved to other parts of the company. Up till now the workers have not been informed as to who will be taken over to the new blast furnace plant, nor do they know whether the promises of early retirement and transference to other parts of the company will actually be fulfilled. It is these ambiguities of the work situation which determine the insecurity experience of the workers in the EG.

Out of 105 blast furnace workers with insecure employment who took part in the study, only those 48 working directly on the blast furnace (excluding coking plant and sintering plant) were selected to ensure the necessary comparability of the EG and the "control group" (CG). These 48 workers in the EG were compared with 75 workers from the direct blast furnace plant of the prospering steel company. The work activities in the direct blast furnace plants of the two companies are basically comparable, though the machinery in the prospering steel company is on the whole more advanced. The personal data differ only slightly between the two samples with respect to age, length of service, net family income and level of vocational training (for details see Büssing, 1985a; Büssing & Jochum, 1985). About 90% of the workers in both companies and in both samples are members of the union. The two companies are situated near each other and are subject to similar regional conditions. In particular the alternatives on the labour market for the workers of both steel companies are equally adverse owing to the very poor regional and steel-specific employment situation.

2.2. Measures

The instruments used were developed in studies in the German metal and steel industries (Greif et al., 1983), except for the two scales of psychosomatic complaints and job satisfaction; some of these instruments were revised by the author in another study (e.g. Büssing, 1985b). The internal consistency (Cronbach's alpha) of the scales was calculated on the basis of the total sample (N=180). The following variables will be analyzed in this paper.

Perceived job security: A single item.

Psychosomatic complaints: Items were derived from the Freiburger Beschwerdeliste (Fahrenberg, 1975); (12 items; alpha=0,84).

Strain/irritability: Includes not sporadically, but permanently occurring states of strain, exhaustion and anger (8 items; alpha=0,91).

Job satisfaction: Includes in part specific aspects of blast furnace work and was especially developed for this study (17 items; alpha=0,87).

Action control: Includes action and decision latitudes in an individual's work activity regardless of its complexity (6 Items; alpha=0,89).

Individual control: Comprises possibilities of exerting influence, which an individual can exercise on his own in the areas of work place, plant, works council and union (4 items; alpha=0,68).

Collective control: Consists of the same items as the scale of "individual control", but relates to possibilities of exerting influence in collaboration with colleagues (4 Items; alpha=0,80).

Hope for control: Includes again the same items, but relates to future control (4 Items; alpha=0,95).

Perceived alternatives on the labour market: Comprises the expectation of being able to give notice at any time and to find an equivalent job somewhere else (4 Items; alpha=0,85).

Responses had to be given on five-point rating scales with 1=low to 5=strong agreement. For "psychosomatic complaints" a rating scale with scale points: 1=never, 2=every few months, 3=every few weeks, 4= every few days, 5=almost daily was used. The data were collected in February 1985.

3. RESULTS

In accordance with the objective insecurity of their work places the members of the EG rated their job security very low and considerably lower than the CG (see Table 1). The non-"significant"[1] differences between the EG and the CG in the variables psychosomatic complaints and strain/irritability on the one hand and the significantly lower job satisfaction of the EG on the other confirmed the view that job insecurity, in contrast to the anticipation of certain unemployment, does not altogether lead to a deterioration in psychophysical health, but is already accompanied by a reduction in job satisfaction. There is no statistical difference between the EG and CG in their work-specific action control. But collective control of decisions affecting both the immediate work place as well as the plant which for industrial workers is an important means of influence is rated significantly less effective by the EG than by the workers of the CG, even though both groups are almost identical in their degree of unionism and both companies underly the Montan participation.[2] The hope that possibilities for exerting influence on the work place will arise in the future is considered less likely by the EG (Hope for control in Table 1). There is no significant difference in the assessment of the extent of individual control on the work place and at plant level which is regarded as being low, both by the EG and by the CG. The alternatives on the labour market were also rated very unfavorably by both groups of workers, an assessment reflecting the real labour market situation; for this reason the small difference between the two groups, which is just above chance (at a level of .05), cannot be adequately interpreted in terms of content.

Table 1: Comparisons between responses of blast furnace workers
at *insecure work places (EG)* and *secure work places (CG)*

Variable	EG (n=48)		CG (n=75)		EG v CG
	Mean	SD	Mean	SD	p-value*
Perceived job security	2.00	0.94	3.18	0.81	<0.0001
Psychosomatic complaints	3.00	1.03	2.81	0.82	0.29**
Strain/irritability	2.67	1.06	2.50	0.70	0.34
Job satisfaction	2.55	0.59	2.87	0.47	0.003
Action control	2.55	1.05	2.33	0.71	0.20
Individual control	1.98	0.73	2.07	0.54	0.49
Collective control	2.19	0.59	2.79	0.76	<0.0001
Hope for control	2.61	1.14	3.38	0.73	0.0001
Perceived alternatives on the labour market	1.63	0.70	1.37	0.63	0.048

* p-value for t-test. If homogeneity of variances is violated
    (Levene-test: p-value < 0.15) a modified t-statistic with separate
    variances is used.
** p-value for Mann-Whitney-Wilcoxon U-test. Applied, as variable shows
    large departure from normality.

4. CONCLUSION AND DISCUSSION

The results show that the workers in the EG consider their jobs to be very insecure in accordance with the objective job insecurity. Despite the high job insecurity experienced over several years blast furnace workers in the EG report neither higher psychosomatic complaints nor higher strain/irritability than workers in the CG. In contrast to the anticipation of forthcoming unemployment (e.g. Cobb et al., 1966; Kasl et al., 1972, 1975), on average job insecurity per se does not lead to impaired psychophysical health in this study. This result is supported by an investigation carried out by Depolo & Sarchielli (1985). Among other things they compared workers in secure jobs with full-time workers, who had just experienced a period of short-time work. Employing the General Health Questionnaire (GHQ 12; Banks et al., 1980) they found no statistical difference between the workers in secure jobs and the ex-short-time-workers, who were re-employed and whose jobs were rated insecure. However, one of the few other studies, namely the project currently being run by Brenner et al. (1983), that takes job insecurity to be an independent variable and includes a control group, does find an increased psychophysical strain for workers in insecure jobs. Just how far these results present an opposite view to the results described here, will only be seen when Brenner et al. (1983, 1985) publish detailed information about their study.

From the results of our study, job insecurity appears to exert a negative influence on variables that can be found in the run-up to psychophysical stress reactions and psychosomatic complaints. Apart from job satisfaction this is especially true for two very important aspects of controllability at the work place, namely for collective control and hope for control, both of which were judged by the EG to be significantly lower compared to the CG. In meeting the threat of job insecurity, there are only slight possibilities for an individual to exert any influence at the work place. The possible means of action that workers can use as a control, such as negotiation of social plans, are usually only successful if a collective procedure is chosen. Here the union membership is an important requirement for increasing the individual participation in collective control (e.g. Neal & Seeman, 1964). In spite of a high degree of unionism, the workers in the EG see only small collective possibilities of control. And thereby an important resource for protection against threats is reduced, which job insecurity not only has in relation to a possible loss of the job, but also with respect to undesired moves, declines, dequalifications, and loss of income etc.. Reasons for the relatively low assessment of collective control by the EG are probably arise because apart from some successes, persistent efforts by the workers, the works council and the union over the previous few years have increasingly made clear the confines of collective control in such a economic situation of the steel company undergoing a crisis (Gruber & Sörgel, 1984).

A further particular aspect of job insecurity is the considerably lower hope for control by the EG. The hope for control — similar to the personal control (Averill, 1973) — is determined by both the controllability and the predictability. Monat et al. (1972)

differentiate between time uncertainty, event uncertainty and general unpredictability. The ambiguity of job insecurity presented above is especially reflected in experiencing uncertainty as to when (time uncertainty), and which (event uncertainty) changes and decisions to what extent will take place in concerning personal decisions. The lower hope for control in the EG is in my opinion critically determined by the low predictability of events with respect to the work place.

Finally, I should comment on the overview, which is all that could be presented in this paper, in order to avoid possible misunderstandings. Firstly, I could not go into details as to what determines the perception of objective job insecurity (e.g. Büssing, 1985a; Greenhalgh & Rosenblatt, 1984; Jacobson, 1985) and which moderating function the percepted job insecurity has, for example on psychological stress due to objective job insecurity. Secondly, although psychosomatic complaints and strain/irritability of the EG compared to the CG are not significantly increased, it should not be understood that such an increase can be excluded for each individual worker. In coping with job insecurity individual differences between the workers, such as economic resources, work commitment, desire for control, social support etc., have an important function (e.g. Büssing, 1985c). Thirdly, the not significantly increased psychosomatic complaints of workers in the EG compared to workers in the CG cannot be interpreted to mean that there is an acceptable state of well-being, as shown well for example by the low job satisfaction of the EG. Finally, in further analyses the social network of members of the families and friends should be taken into account since they too are indirectly affected by the job insecurity and thus also take part in the process of coping.

FOOTNOTES

1.) In the following we have analyzed explorative formulations of questions. Hypotheses to be tested statistically cannot be sufficiently postulated, because up till now so few theoretical and empirical facts are known about the effects of job insecurity. The p-values therefore will be interpreted in terms of explorative data analysis only descriptively as information on the "distance" between "hypotheses" and "alternative hypotheses" and thus only as "strength of significance". Where I use the term "significant", I will refer to these considerations.

2.) The Montan participation is valid for the Montan industries, to which the mining, iron and steel industries belong. In particular it provides for a board of trustees (Aufsichtsrat) consisting of employees and employers represented equally. Its members elect one further neutral member.

REFERENCES

AVERILL, J.R.: Personal control over aversive stimuli and its relation to stress. Psychological Bulletin, 1973, 80, 286-303

BANKS, M.H. & CLEGG, C.W. & JACKSON, P.R. & KEMP, N.J. & STAFFORD, E.M. & WALL, T.D.: The use of the General Health Questionnaire as an indicator of mental health in occupational studies. Journal of Occupational Psychology, 1980, 53, 187-194

BRENNER, S.-O. & ARNETZ, B. & LEVI, L. & HALL, E. & HJELM, R. & PETTERSON, I.-L. & SALOVAARA, H. & SÖRBOM, D. & TELLENBACK, S. & AKERSTEDT, T.: The effects of insecurity at work, job loss and unemployment: An investigation of the psychological, social, and biochemical impacts of unemployment. Project description and preliminary findings. Paper presented at the WHO conference on unemployment and health. Stockholm, December 5.-7., 1983

BRENNER, S.-O.: Arbeitsplatzunsicherheit, Arbeitslosigkeit und Morbidität - Bericht über eine interdisziplinäre Interventionsstudie des Forschungszentrums "Psychosoziale Faktoren und Gesundheit" (Stockholm). In: Kieselbach, T. & Wacker, A. (Eds.): Individuelle und gesellschaftliche Kosten der Massenarbeitslosigkeit. Psychologische Theorie und Praxis. Weinheim: Beltz, 1985, 42-54

BÜSSING, A.: Job insecurity: An investigation of its psychological and psychosomatic consequences. Working paper, Department of Medical Psychology, RWTH Aachen, 1985a

BÜSSING, A.: Gemeinde- und traditionelle Krankenhauspsychiatrie. Eine arbeitspsychologische Untersuchung der Auswirkungen unterschiedlicher Organisationsstrukturen auf die Arbeitstätigkeit und das Belastungserleben des Pflegepersonals. In: Keupp, H. & Kleiber, D. & Scholten, B. (Eds.): Im Schatten der Wende. Tübingen: DGVT, 1985b, 33-45

BÜSSING, A.: Work commitment as a moderator of job insecurity. Working paper, Department of Medical Psychology, RWTH Aachen, 1985c

BÜSSING, A. & JOCHUM, I.: Arbeitsplatzunsicherheit, Belastungserleben und Kontrollwahrnehmung. Ergebnisse einer quasi-experimentellen Untersuchung in der Stahlindustrie. In print, 1985

COBB, S. & BROOKS, G.W. & KASL, S.V. & CONALLY, W.E.: The health of people changing jobs: A description of a longitudinal study. American Journal of Public Health, 1966, 56, 1476-1481

DEPOLO, M. & SARCHIELLI, G.: Job insecurity, psychological well-being, and social representation: A case of cost sharing in industrial relations. Paper presented at the "West European Congress on the Psychology of Work and Organization", Aachen, 1.-3. April, 1985

FAHRENBERG, J.: Die Freiburger Beschwerdenliste FBL. Zeitschrift für Klinische Psychologie, 1975, 4, 79-100

FOLKMAN, S. & SCHAEFER , C. & LAZARUS, R.S.: Cognitive processes as mediators of stress and coping. In: Hamilton, V. & Warburton, D.M. (Eds.): Human stress and cognition. Chichester: Wiley, 1979, 265-298

GREIF, S. & BAMBERG, E. & DUNCKEL, H. & FRESE, M. & MOHR, G. & RÜCKERT, D. & RUMMEL, M. & SEMMER, N. & ZAPF, D.: Abschlußbericht des Forschungsprojektes "Psychischer Stress am Arbeitsplatz - Hemmende und fördernde Bedingungen für humanere Arbeitsplätze". Unveröffentlichter Bericht an den Projektträger "Humanisierung des Arbeitslebens", Universität Osnabrück,

Fachbereich Psychologie, 1983

GREENHALGH, L. & ROSENBLATT, Z.: Job insecurity: Toward conceptual clarity. Academy of Management Review, 1984, 9, 438-448

GRUBER, W. & SÖRGEL, P. (Eds.): Stahl ohne Zukunft? Hamburg: VSA, 1984

HARTLEY, J. & FRYER, D.: The psychology of unemployment: A critical appraisal. In: Stephenson, G. & Davis, J. (Eds.): Progress in applied social psychology, Vol. 2. Chichester: Wiley, 1984, 3-30

JACOBSON, D.: Determinants of "JOB AT RISK" (JAR) behavior. Paper presented at the "West European Congress of the Psychology of Work and Organization", Aachen, 1.-3. April, 1985

JUDITH, R. (Ed.): Die Krise der Stahlindustrie - Krise einer Region. Das Beispiel Saarland. Köln: Bund-Verlag, 1980

KASL, S.V. & COBB, S. & GORE, S.: Changes in reported illness behaviour related to termination of employment. A preliminary report. International Journal of Epidemiology, 1972, 1, 111-118

KASL, S.V. & GORE, S. & COBB, S.: The experience of losing a job: Reported changes in health, symptomes and illness behaviour. Psychosomatic Medicine, 1975, 37, 106-122

KIESELBACH, T. & WACKER, A. (Eds.): Individuelle und gesellschaftliche Kosten der Massenarbeitslosigkeit. Psychologische Theorie und Praxis. Weinheim: Beltz, 1985

MACKAY, K. & HAINES, H.: The psychological effects of unemployment: A review of the literature. New Zealand Journal of Industrial Relations, 1982, 7, 123-135

MONAT, A. & AVERILL, J.R. & LAZARUS, R.S.: Anticipatory stress and coping reactions under various conditions of uncertainty. Journal of Personality and Social Psychology, 1972, 24, 237-253

NEAL, A.G. & SEEMAN, M.: Organization and powerlessness. American Sociological Review, 1964, 29, 216-226

WARR, P.: Work and unemployment. In: Drenth, P.J.D. & Thierry, H. & Willems, P.J. & de Wolff, C.J. (Eds.): Handbook of work and organizational psychology. Chichester: Wiley, 1984, 413-443

THE PSYCHOLOGY OF WORK AND ORGANIZATION
G. Debus and H.-W. Schroiff (Editors)
© Elsevier Science Publishers B.V. (North-Holland), 1986   145

WORK ENTRY PROBLEMS OF YOUNG ADULTS

RITA CLAES

Laboratory for Sociopsychology of Work and Organization, State
University of Ghent*

Workshop organized and chaired by R. Claes (B.). Contributions
from G. Sarchielli (I.), J.A. Feij (Nl.) and R. Claes (B.).

1. INTRODUCTION

Life changes by beginning work (i.e. paid employment). A number of
changes in the young person take place in and because of working. For
instance : acquiring new knowledge and skills (technical and social);
learning work related behaviours; adapting attitudes; perceiving the
world of work; growing self-confidence, self-worth, self-concept;
developing roles and values; experiencing to earn money. The totality
of these learning processes through work is called 'work socialization'.

The workshop presents several aspects of work socialization of youth :
Guido Sarchielli (University of Trento, Italy) comments on his research
on occupational socialization; Jan Feij (Free University of Amsterdam)
introduces a starting longitudinal study on social integration of youth;
Rita Claes (State University of Ghent) presents the results of a study
on work entry problems.

From the three contributions it becomes clear that work socialization of
youth is a complex topic. Not only is work socialization a process with
a life span character, but also a great number of actors are involved in
it : youth, school, family, broader society, social partners, government
etc. No wonder research on work socialization uses a wide variety of
social science methods.

In the following summary of the workshop the focus is first on the
definition of work socialization. Then the work entry as one phase in
the work socialization process is discussed. Finally some conditions
for and consequences of a successful work entry are presented.

2. WORK SOCIALIZATION DEFINED

The concept of work socialization as rigidly predetermined learning
processes leaves the individual – the socializee – very few opportunities for autonomous action. He is only influenced by the work situation
and reacts automatically to its pressures.
However, the idea of reciprocity in the 'socializee/work situation'

---
*Louis Pasteurlaan 2, B-9000 Gent

relationship, sees the person as an actor capable of active negotiation in his own work destiny. Here the assumption is that the individual is able to take into account the situation; to interpret it; to act upon it according to his own interests and objectives. Work socialization is then a negotiation process in which the actors (individual, organization, other socializing agents) play an active part capable of influencing one another. For the individual, work socialization results in cognitive, affective and behavioural changes.

The process of work socialization is function of more or less stable characteristics of the individual in interaction with elements from the environment (both broader society and direct work settings). It comprises three phases : pre work; the actual work entry and subsequent work experiences. Work socialization is considered a life span development.

3. THE WORK ENTRY PHASE

The phase of beginning work is crucial in the work socialization process.
First of all the work entry can be conflictuous because of different objectives of the individual and of the organization.
Second, beginning work includes a change in membership groups which requires an adequate cognitive reorganization.
Finally the work entry assumes confrontations within the individual : clarification of his identity; evaluations by others; possible penalizations from others.

It would be useful to have a better understanding of the characteristics of this initiation phase — the work entry — : its duration; the factors that most deeply affect the youngster; to what extent and in what way the individual can maintain the projects and the expectations he elaborated in the pre-work phase; whether there are expectations or representations regarding his social and work future which are modified selectively in relation to his entry work and so on.

4. RELEVANT CONDITIONS FOR THE WORK ENTRY

In the analysis of the way young adults take part in working life or how they integrate in an organization, two broad categories of promoting or hindering variables are theoretically considered as important.

On the one hand there are a number of personal characteristics of the individual; on the other hand there is the environment (macro and micro). The former include e.g. : interests; personal and interpersonal values; capacities; temperamental characteristics; self-concept; attitudes and values concerning school, work, interpersonal relationships; future orientations; expectations; life events; coping styles; psychological and physical health depression.

The latter comprises in the macro sense : socio-economic and cultural evolutions; labour market situation; educational and training systems; legislation concerning employment of youth; career guidance systems; employment centres a.s.o.
The micro environment deals with socio - economical status; characteris-

tics of parental home; forms and ways of living; work reference; organizational characteristics etc.

One study reported upon in the workshop uses questionnaires and in-depth interviews with a limited sample of young male adults with specialized training for industry. The youngsters are interviewed during a period of 3 to 6 months after school leaving. The criterion for successful work entry is working (as paid employee in an organization) at the moment of the interview. Comparison of working versus non working subsamples of young adults, result in some – preliminary and tentative – relations between background (micro environment), personal characteristics and successful work entry.

A favourable background for work entry is characterized by : the absence of unemployment in family and friends; the 'good example' of a stable career of one or both parents; the presence and pressures of a working partner; the near distance of an industrial region.
Some other background elements, however not showing a consistent direction of relation to a successful work entry yet, seem relevant to be studied in the future,too. They concern: the parents' occupational level; the educational level of the family (parents, brothers, sisters); the socio-economical status of the family.

Favourable personal characteristics for work entry are : high degree of work centrality; high evaluation of income, contacts and work itself as results of working; self–concept (competent, good, sportive, hard, courageous, responsible, autonomous); high life satisfaction, positive opinion on own labour market value; parallel trainings; optimistic future views; intellectual leisure activities.

From the in-depth interviews in which the youngsters tell the story of their work entry, additional favourable elements for a smooth work entry emerge : free of military service; union membership; active community life; schools' connections and attitudes towards organizations; application behaviour; mobility; work experiences during school training.

These preliminary findings include implications for the role, the policy and the concrete action of socializing agents such as schools, social partners, career guidance centres, employment centres and government.

5. EFFECTS OF THE WORK ENTRY

Another study commented upon in the workshop deals with the future time perspective (content and extension) in employed versus unemployed youth. The hypothesis is that – assuming the work entry influences the individual's hopes, expectations and goals – in planning their future professional career, employed have a greater concern for working conditions than for social relations and personal development. In the used research technique, the youngsters spontaneously express facts and events that they believe could turn up in their future working career and arrange these within a predetermined temporal scheme. These events are classified by judges in four categories and a density index is calculated which allows comparisons between the employed and unemployed subsamples.

The employed subsample concentrates on well defined job performance and job security; while contents of personal and social type are of secondary importance. The unemployed subsample puts more emphasis on contents of personal type. The extension of the future time perspective is very reduced : there is a marked utilization of short times for both subsamples.

In short, the brief period of work experience appears to be capable of shifting the attention of the subjects from personal demands to characteristics that define the work setting and of inducing a strong "reality orientation" in identifying events located in narrow temporal perspective.

6 DISCUSSION TOPICS

The colleagues attending the workshop mainly asked clarifications on the three presented papers. However following topics were discussed with the audience : the broader societal impact of successful or failed work entry; the role of the unions in work socializations; the importance of a positive work reference (no unemployment in family, support from family, good example in parents' career); the selection of target groups of youngsters versus representative samples of a certain age; the measurement of outcomes of work socialization; the development of a scale of work socialization.
Finally some of the workshop participants communicated their own experiences on and approaches towards work socialization of youth.

THE PSYCHOLOGY OF WORK AND ORGANIZATION
G. Debus and H.-W. Schroiff (Editors)
© *Elsevier Science Publishers B.V. (North-Holland), 1986*

THE SIMONA PROJECT: The Introduction of Information Processing
in Labour Market Administration

K. BAECK & Y. BOSTYN

Rijksdienst voor Arbeidsvoorziening
Keizerslaan 7, B-1000 Brussels, Belgium

The following text gives a short introduction to the contents of
the SIMONA project. The project was realized within the R V A.
At the end of 1981, a test project was started and by the end of
1984 it was fully operational in the whole of Flanders. This
system, operated in over 75 regional branch offices, is consulted
by approx. 600 labour mediation officers. The system is used
daily for reference by members of the administrative   and
technical departments as well. They include people from a wide
variety of services: the B T K and D A C files administration,
medical and psychological services, the vocational training
centres.   Of course, the executive and managerial staff members
constitute a third group that makes regular use of   SIMONA.

1. THE ISSUE

Although the labour market has changed considerably since 1973 **, the
staff of the Labour Mediation Service has never been adjusted. Due to
the alarming increase in the number of unemployed, the average labour mediation officer was forced to spend more time dealing with the administrative aspects of his job, often at the expense of actual labour mediation.

The development of computerized information systems has provided the
means to rearrange working procedures and job contents. So time for more
essential tasks was again available and the National Employment Service
became man-centred again.

Being responsible for employment policy, the Flemish Federal Administration thought it desirable to equip the Labour Mediation Services with an
up-to-date information system (SIMONA), fitting in with the information
plan for Flanders.

In cooperation with C O I, the R V A started a test project in Vilvoorde
at the end of October 1981. With the approval of the Management Board of
the R V A, all subregional mediation branches were later on connected to
the network.

** National Labour Conference. Since then the number of unemployed has
   increased more than 5 times. The number of labour mediation officers
   however, has not changed.

2. OBJECTIVES

"The development of a system providing policy information with a view to dynamic labour mediation" :

2.1.1. Supporting the labour mediation function through decreasing paperflow and offering automatic computer functions (control function, automatic compilation of statistics, automatic updating of various databanks, ...).

2.1.2. Revaluating the mediation function. The computer cannot replace the labour mediation officer. On the contrary : he will be playing a prominent part in the selection of persons seeking employment, in the search for appropriate jobs and in job-counseling in general.

2.1.3. Providing a complete set of central databanks to the geographically decentralized offices (75 of them are permanent), offering the persons interested a complete range of services :

- in collaboration with the mediator, persons seeking employment can look for the appropriate vacancy, wherever it is.

- employers will be stimulated to announce vacancies more often because of the advantages they can benefit from. As a result, the Labour Mediation Service will increase its share in filling up vacancies.

2.2. Supplying information needed by management and administration which will enable a dynamic policy on the basis of a sounder judgement of the labour market. This concerns the subregional offices as well as the Flemish Community. To this end all information on applicants and vacancies should be processed into statistics for ease of reference.

3. DESCRIPTION OF THE SYSTEM

3.1. Hardware

C O I has an I B M computer 3083-BX at its disposal for the daily use of data-processing and for the pre-selection system. An I B M 3031-AP is used for statistics and graphics. 341 terminals and 92 printers are connected to the network.

The present operating expenses amount to 201 million BF per annum. This includes the cost of development, the network, the infrastructure (modems, terminals, printers), computer time. The costs of greater efficiency are compensated by fewer expenses for printed matter, postage, telephone, office furniture and by more productive labour time.

3.2. Software

In its present form, the SIMONA project consists of a triptych of
mutually connected information systems :

              - data control system : - 3 functional databanks
                                        = applicants bank
                                        = vacancy bank
                                        = employers bank

                                      - electronic mail

              - preselection system : the search for the right applicant
                                      the search for the right vacancy

              - statistical and graphic system.

At the moment, the **applicants bank** already contains 630,000 files *. For
each applicant about 150 items are stored. An innovation is surely the
input of the professional aspirations and the possibility to subscribe
for 8 different professions.

Now, the **vacancy bank** contains permanently about 5,500 * vacancies. For
each vacancy the skills, working conditions and wages, as well as the
recruiting procedure are mentioned.

The **employers bank** - which is still in evolution - contains the
identification of the employer as well as information about the number of
employees, the industrial sector and so on. Each vacancy description
automatically includes the identification data about the firm.

The different databanks have built-in automatic quality control systems.
The software automatically generates the daily statistics required on the
national level.

The **electronic mail** provides the labour mediation officers with a simple
means of communication via their terminal, and this without any
additional costs.

The **preselection system** allows for preselection of possible applicants
for a vacancy, taking into account the criteria for success. In the same
way, the labour mediation officer can look up the vacancies which seem
the most suitable, taking into account the professional know-how and the
motivation of the persons seeking employment. The officer occupies a
central position in this preselection, because he is the link between
employer and unemployed. So, we are talking about an open system : man
is making the decisions, not the computer. The officer puts in the
preselection criteria, the system reads its databanks and puts out the
selected files. Actual mediation is done only after reading and control
of the data.

---

* Situation on 2nd May 1985

The **statistical and graphic system** enables the user to answer questions which are important, not only for policy, but also for the applied scientific research.   A study concerning the employment situation of young graduates with different backgrounds is a very good example.

The system has recently proved its value in giving information to meet the needs of policy on the level of employment (see Figure 2)   and vocational training (see Figure 1).

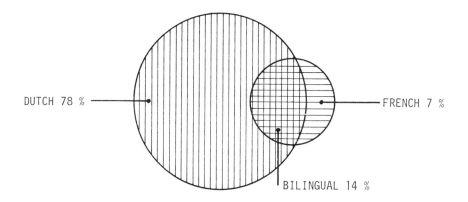

SUBREGIONAL EMPLOYMENT AGENCIES AROUND BRUSSELS

Figure 1: Sufficient job-aimed knowledge of language(s) by applicants

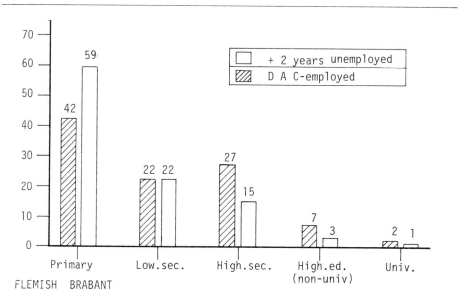

Figure 2: Educational level of D A C-employed and unemployed (1st March 1985)

Examples of other problems that can be solved :

- distribution of the applicants according to their aspirations and motivations for: e.g. = jobs abroad
                    = part-time work
                    = salary and labour regulations

- distribution of vacancies according to the type of job, the necessary
  certificates, the required knowledge of languages, etc.

- analysis of unfilled vacancies.

4. PRESENT RESULTS AND PROSPECTS

By introducing information processing, the outlook of the labour exchange
offices has changed significantly. Administrative documents have disappeared for about 95 % and the labour mediation officer can by now spend
his whole day communicating with employers and unemployed and mediating
between the two. Moreover, his job-organisation has become clear-cut.
There is more teamwork (even beyond the borders of the labour exchange
office) and the staff have more time to follow up and organise activities. The confidence the users (employers, unemployed) have in the system is shown by the number of vacancies dealt with within the normal economic circuit :

- For 1985 a target-number of "vacancies to be filled in" was given to
  each subregional employment office. The main objective was to enlarge
  the market share thanks to SIMONA. Figure 3 shows a comparison on
  the level of the Flemish Region between :
        - the number of vacancies dealt with in 1984;
        - the target-number for 1985;
        - the number of vacancies dealt with in 1985.

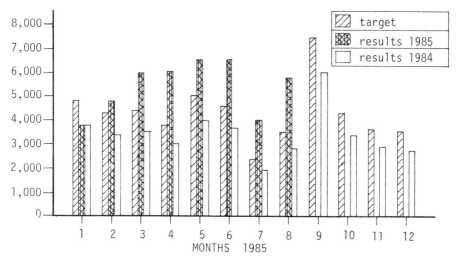

Figure 3: FLANDERS -- VACANCIES RECEIVED IN 1985

(Omitting special employment frameworks)

Besides the fact that SIMONA helped to enlarge the market share of vacancies the R V A is entrusted with, a very favourable qualitative evolution in the vacancies themselves could be noticed.

SIMONA is not a static system. For example, it is used in expanding the network of R V A-run interim bureaus. A jobservice was created : new vacancies are published daily in some important newspapers.

In the near future, the following SIMONA-linked prospects are to be realized :

- to use teletex to replace typed instructions. This will enable all users both to receive their instructions more promptly and to gain access to new information databanks (e.g. C A O, ...)

- to enhance the efficiency of R V A-centres for vocational training. This will include : - administration of applicants;
                                 - administration of trainees;
                                 - means-management.

II.3. The Effects of Work Characteristics

THE PSYCHOLOGY OF WORK AND ORGANIZATION
G. Debus and H.-W. Schroiff (Editors)
© *Elsevier Science Publishers B.V. (North-Holland), 1986*

A VITAMIN MODEL OF JOBS AND MENTAL HEALTH

Peter Warr

MRC/ESRC Social and Applied Psychology Unit, University
of Sheffield, Sheffield S10 2TN, United Kingdom

1. INTRODUCTION

This paper has two main purposes. First, I will outline some ideas about
the notion of mental health, and aspects of this which deserve greater
attention by work and occupational psychologists. Second, I will
introduce a model under development which aims to account for the impact
of jobs on mental health. This is based upon an analogy with the
importance of vitamins to physical health.

In considering the impact of jobs on mental health we can make two rather
different comparisons. First, we can compare having a job against not
having a job, being employed versus being unemployed. And second we can
compare one job against another job, examining differences in the mental
health of people in different jobs. When we make these comparisons we
find that in general mental health during unemployment tends to be
significantly lower than when in a job [1, 2, 3]. But there are also
wide differences between people in different jobs, and wide differences
between people who are unemployed.

The vitamin model seeks to explain variations in mental health both
between unemployment and employment, and also within unemployment and
within employment, in the same terms. My current thinking argues for
nine features of the environment, the same ones in each case. I will
introduce these later, and this paper will concentrate on their
importance within jobs. A fuller account, extending to the processes
influencing the impact of unemployment, will be presented later in book
form [4].

2. MENTAL HEALTH

We can think in terms of five principal components of mental health:
affective well-being, competence, aspiration, autonomy, and integrated
functioning. The first of these, affective well-being, seems to be the
central component, providing a key indicator to the level of someone's
mental health. Well-being is often viewed in overall terms along a
single dimension, roughly from feeling bad to feeling good. However, it
is preferable to identify two separate dimensions, "pleasure" and
"arousal", which may be treated as orthogonal to each other.

We can view any affective state in terms of its location on the two
separate dimensions, so that the specific quality of a particular affect
derives from both of them. For example, depressed feelings are
characterized by low scores on each dimension, and anxiety may be

described in terms of a low score on pleasure and a high score on arousal.

Within the framework of two orthogonal dimensions, pleasure and arousal, three principal axes of measurement deserve special consideration. These are as follows:

Pleasure	Arousal	Measurement Axis	Pleasure	Arousal
Low	Medium	"Discontented" to "Contented"	High	Medium
Low	High	"Anxious" to "Comfortable"	High	Low
Low	Low	"Depressed" to "Actively pleased"	High	High

I take these three axes to be the main ones we need to measure in respect of affective well-being. And we can study well-being at two different levels. First, we can measure it in general, without confining it to a particular setting; let us call that "context-free" well-being. Or we can measure "context-specific" well-being, in one limited setting. We might do that, for example, in relation specifically to the family environment, or in respect of jobs. In that case it is job-related affective well-being which is of research concern.

Studies of context-free affective well-being (concerned with life in general) have made quite good progress in measuring the three principal axes. There are several established inventories of distress, life satisfaction, anxiety, depression and so on, which can tap these three forms of affective well-being in an overall, context-free sense. But job-related well-being has almost always been measured along the first axis shown above, usually in terms of scales of job satisfaction. Those can vary in several ways, but they all fail to consider the arousal axis.

The second main dimension (from "anxious" to "comfortable") has been studied in occupational settings through measures of job-related tension, anxiety or strain. There are several measures which cover high arousal and low pleasure, but the opposite pole appears to have been largely ignored by occupational psychologists. That is a pity, since that sector seems to be particularly important in respect of low-arousal, resigned job satisfaction: workers in that quadrant are not complaining about their job, but they are apathetic and uninvolved.

The third axis includes (to the left) job-related depression in the low-low category. Also concepts like job-related exhaustion, burnout, and boredom. All these have been measured fairly successfully, but once again we have done less well at the opposite pole: high arousal and high pleasure. Here we might include "job involvement", which seems rather like high-arousal job satisfaction, and also "morale", which covers feelings of active involvement as well as a pleasure in working. In general, I think that occupational psychologists should be more concerned with tapping job-related feelings of high pleasure at each of the three levels of arousal indicated above.

Turning to the other components of mental health, competence, has been emphasized by many writers. Terms used have included effective coping, environmental mastery, self-efficacy, effectance motivation, and so on. It is widely held that a key feature of mental health is an ability to handle life's problems and in some ways successfully to act upon the environment. However, it would be wrong to view all types of low competence as evidence of low mental health; everyone is incompetent in some respects. The key factor seems to be a link with affective well-being, in that low competence which is not associated with negative affect would normally be viewed as having no bearing on mental health.

We also need to include within any model of mental health both "subjective" and "objective" perspectives. The former are as experienced by the person, the latter as viewed by an independent observer. Thus, for example, we can look separately at "subjective competence", how well a person believes he or she is able to deal with the environment, and also at "objective competence", how successful the person is seen to be in practice.

Next, aspiration. The mentally healthy person is often viewed as someone who establishes realistic goals and makes active efforts to attain them. Such people show an interest in the environment, they engage in motivated activity, and seek to extend themselves in ways that are personally significant. The converse is apathy and acceptance of the status quo, no matter how unsatisfactory. This dimension is sometimes thought to be of greater concern in Western societies than in the East or in less developed countries, where alternative models of mental health might be more appropriate.

Autonomy has also been emphasized more by Western than by Eastern writers. It is widely held that mentally healthy people are able to resist environmental influences and determine their own opinions and actions. They feel and are autonomous and personally responsible for what they do. However, a curvilinear pattern is usually assumed. It is interdependence that is considered healthy rather than extreme independence or extreme dependence.

Finally, we should include integrated functioning as an overall feature, which is qualitatively different from the others. This concerns the person as a whole and the relationships between other components. People who are mentally healthy exhibit several forms of balance, harmony and inner relatedness. Different writers have their own notions of integrated functioning, usually within their preferred theoretical structure, and needless to say this is a concept which is particularly difficult to operationalize.

3.   ENVIRONMENTAL FEATURES

I have found it helpful to consider nine aspects of the environment, which together act to determine a person's mental health. These are:

1. Opportunity for control
2. Opportunity for skill use
3. Externally generated goals
4. Variety
5. Environmental clarity
6. Availability of money
7. Physical security
8. Opportunity for interpersonal contact
9. Valued social position

I believe that it is the level of these nine features which primarily
determines a person's mental health, both in a "context-free" sense and
in "job-related" terms. But this is not a question of a simple linear
relationship between an environmental feature and an aspect of mental
health. Such a linear pattern is quite implausible, and instead I prefer
to think in terms of an analogy. For this purpose I have found it useful
to consider the influence of vitamins on physiological effectiveness.

The intake of vitamins is important for physical health up to but not
beyond a certain level: their absence gives rise to an impairment in
health, but their presence beyond a required level does not further
enhance health. In addition, several vitamins become harmful in very
large doses, so that the association between increased vitamin intake and
physical health becomes negative after a broad range of moderate amounts.
I believe that this is also the case for several job features and their
impact upon mental health. This is summarized in the diagram below.

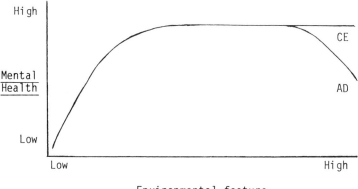

Environmental feature

Among the vitamins which are toxic in very large quantities are vitamins
A and D. I have illustrated that on the right-hand side of the diagram,
and find it helpful to think of "AD" as short-hand for "additional
decrement". Other vitamins appear to have no ill effects, even in large
doses. These include vitamins C and E, which can conveniently be taken
as standing for "constant effect".

We may thus think in terms of a general model, which covers vitamins of
both the AD and the CE kind. Next we have to apply this part of the
analogy to the nine job features, to decide which fall into the
categories of "constant effect" and which give rise to an "additional
decrement".

My current thinking is that features 1, 2, 3, 4, 5 and 8 (see above) fit
the AD model, whereas features 6, 7 and 9 parallel the CE vitamins. I
will have to leave out the reasoning in respect of each one, but I might
mention that I view an "opportunity" (for example, in features 1 and 2)
as taking on a quite different character at extremely high levels. There
it turns from a feature which promotes or facilitates, into one which
demands or coerces. It is that switch which causes the additional
decrement at extremely high levels.

But of course these nine terms are very general ones. We need to look at specific aspects of each feature within a job to get closer to understanding how they can affect mental health. For example, within the first feature we can distinguish between intrinsic and extrinsic control, and measure those separately. And we might include aspects of machine-pacing versus self-pacing. In respect of opportunity for skill use (feature number 2) we would need to include ideas by Kornhauser, and measures of skill "under-utilization" by Caplan and colleagues.

Within feature number 3 (externally generated goals), we would first be concerned with the intrinsic demands which a job makes, especially noting the value of external targets and the problems of very low and very high workload. The notion of "traction", being drawn along by a job, would also be of interest here [5]. Conflicts between demands are themselves a form of high load, as are extrinsic demands in terms of time. Here we are concerned with both amount of time required for a job and the pattern of that time, across a day or week for example.

In terms of variety (feature number 4), we would again look separately at intrinsic and extrinsic aspects. And we might include cycle time as one component which can be independently measured. Within environmental clarity (number 5), three groups of elements need consideration. A clear environment, in a job or elsewhere, is one which provides three principal kinds of information. These are about the consequences of behaviour, about the future, and about the kinds of behaviours which are considered appropriate or inappropriate.

Feature number 6 is availability of money. Here we are concerned with both adequacy and fairness. Within feature number 7 (physical security) are included traditional ergonomic criteria. These are likely to be widely associated with job-related and context-free mental health through the pattern suggested by the vitamin model. Finally, opportunity for interpersonal contact and valued social position also need to be viewed in several specific terms. Amount and quality of interaction fall within the first of these features; and social esteem and individuals' feelings of job meaningfulness and significance are included within the second.

There is no space here to pursue all these components in greater detail. My purpose is to emphasize how a comprehensive assessment of any job environment should include specific elements within the nine features. Furthermore, research is increasingly supporting the argument that each characteristic has a substantial impact upon employees' mental health [4]. The data are particularly strong in respect of job-related mental health, but there is a growing body of evidence that each of these job features can also influence mental health widely beyond the work-place. That is not merely a question of presence or absence of transient strain, but is also exhibited in context-free mental health which is chronically poor or indeed chronically good. And the evidence extends beyond merely affective well-being into aspects of context-free competence, aspiration and autonomy.

Individual differences must of course be accommodated within the vitamin model. The key feature is what might be referred to as "baseline mental health" [4]. In effect we need to learn how far job features bring about deviations from each person's baseline. For example, some people have higher levels of affective well-being in almost any environment. Since they start from a higher baseline, we ideally need to take that into account in studying the way they are affected by job characteristics. In practical terms that is often difficult, within any model of environmental influence.

What of the shape of the relationships between job factors and mental health? Does the pattern of the vitamin model find support in the empirical data? Almost all investigators have merely used linear correlation procedures, thus excluding the possibility of finding either AD or CE relationships. Two authors have published sub-group analyses, which broadly support the model [6, 7]. In practice, however, there are limitations in the evidence currently available, and we certainly cannot describe the model as empirically validated.

4.   IMPLICATIONS

Nevertheless, as a set of working assumptions, the model contains some important features. For example, it proposes that across a broad range of middle values changes in job content have no impact upon mental health. On the other hand, the steeply rising curve to the left-hand side of the diagram indicates that small changes to jobs in that section have substantial psychological consequences.

The model also provides a comprehensive framework for viewing together the environments of jobs and unemployment. In general, unemployed people are located to the left of the horizontal axis in respect of all nine features. But that is not necessarily the case, and it appears possible to start to explain differences between the mental health of individual unemployed people in these nine terms.

This is important for both theoretical and practical reasons. There is a shortage of good theories about why unemployment is in general so harmful. Research has tended to focus primarily on outcomes rather than processes. The present approach can be extended to account for the mental health impact of unemployment through nine different types of process [4]. Furthermore, concrete applications of the general framework may yield practical ways forward to help the unemployed. For example, it might be possible for local communities to develop institutions and processes which provide increased opportunities for personal control and for skill use.

The model also has some value in respect of transitions, actual or potential. For instance, the psychological impact of a move between jobs is likely to be a function of magnitude and direction of changes in the nine characteristics, especially after allowing for non-linear influences of the vitamin kind. And there may be applications in counselling and in individual decision-making. For example, in assessing whether to move back into the labour market, a married woman with children might compare her domestic environment with the combined environment of home-plus-job. In terms of the nine features, there would be some gains and some losses, but in many cases the plateau of the middle of the figure may indicate no substantial overall effect one way or the other.

However, concentrating upon people in jobs, several other aspects of the vitamin model appear to deserve attention. First is a suggested shift in terminology and emphasis. We must move away from the conventional narrow focus upon "job satisfaction". This orthodoxy and its associated forms of measurement have greatly hampered the development of occupational psychology. We must of course work to understand job-related well-being and the factors influencing it, but we need a shift in perspective away from job satisfaction. As argued earlier, it now seems desirable to focus upon three dimensions of measurement, including arousal as well as pleasure in our theories and measuring instruments.

In addition, I would like to urge that we think hard once again about the utility of the notion of job "stress". There are several well-known difficulties with that term, but I am particularly concerned in this context that it often leads to a focus upon very short-term episodes. Most healthy people in effect move about in the space comprising pleasure and arousal dimensions of affective well-being. Periods experiencing high arousal and low pleasure may often be necessary, within longer sequences of events which as a whole promote rather than impair health.

The comprehensiveness of the framework also deserves special emphasis. At a practical level it can provide a detailed check-list of features, all of which need examination. Too often we focus upon one feature to the exclusion of important others.

Pressing the vitamin analogy a little further, organizations might be urged to carry out a "vitamin count" on their employees. Are they all receiving the "minimum recommended dose" within the nine categories? Because of the plateau I have suggested for the middle range of the environmental features, such investigations would almost certainly indicate that for most groups no further action was needed. However, employees at the extremes of the nine features would stand out as warranting attention and intervention.

But why should organizations be concerned with job characteristics in this way? First, I would press the moral argument. Given that there are significant causal effects of these nine factors on mental health in general, outside as well as inside the work-place, we have a moral responsibility to act upon that knowledge.

However, busy managers might respond that their first responsibility is to the continued effectiveness of their organization. That may be true, but in all except the most difficult of economic circumstances high employee mental health of the kind I have described is likely to be associated with effective work performance. It is one of several factors giving rise to effective work performance, and changes are well within management's power and capability.

Research into the association between job-related well-being and job performance has almost always focused upon measures of satisfaction. Within this tradition, it has become clear that there is a significant correlation between intrinsic work satisfaction and employee performance [8]. Of course that correlation is likely to be circular in causal terms, rather than being merely unidirectional.

I take job satisfaction to be a set of feelings along the first axis of well-being identified above; no consideration is taken of level of arousal. If we were also to measure the other two dimensions described above, I believe that the impact of job-related well-being on performance would be particularly clear.

Some evidence is accumulating in respect of the dimension from anxious to comfortable. Job-related tension is typically found to be significantly correlated with lower ratings of performance [9]. That is of course to be expected if high levels of tension are linked with an inability to cope with job demands. The third dimension, from depressed to actively pleased, seems to be of particular importance here. Employees whose positive job feelings are accompanied by high levels of arousal are likely to be particularly high performers. As suggested earlier, this type of well-being is similar to what is often referred to as high "morale". Unfortunately, there do not appear to be any published studies examining job performance as a function of scores on this third dimension.

It seems clear that other mental health components are also likely to be associated with more effective performance. Low job-related competence is associated with a limited ability to cope; low job-related aspiration is seen in apathy and non-involvement; and low job-related autonomy is reflected in a sense of external control and inability to determine your own future.

This pattern of relationships between mental health and performance seems to be implied by the concept of mental health that I have been using. Research has not yet proceeded in these terms, so that I cannot cite supportive empirical findings. I hope that these will not be long delayed.

5.   REFERENCES

[1]   Warr, P.B., Work and Unemployment, in: Drenth, P.J.D., Thierry, H., and de Wolff, C.J. (eds.), Handbook of Work and Organizational Psychology (Wiley, Chichester, 1984) pp. 413-443.
[2]   Warr, P.B., Twelve Questions about Unemployment and Health, in: Roberts, B., Finnegan, R., and Gallie, D. (eds.), New Approaches to Economic Life (Manchester University Press, Manchester, 1985). pp. 302-318.
[3]   Fryer, D.M. and Payne, R.L., Being Unemployed, in Cooper, C.L., and Robertson, I. (eds.), Review of Industrial and Organizational Psychology (Wiley, Chichester, in press).
[4]   Warr, P.B., Work, Unemployment and Mental Health (Oxford University Press, Oxford, in press).
[5]   Baldamus, W., Efficiency and Effort (Tavistock, London, 1961).
[6]   Karasek, R.A., Administrative Science Quarterly (1979) pp. 285-308.
[7]   Dijkhuizen, N. van, From Stressors to Strains (Swets and Zeitlinger, Lisse, 1980).
[8]   Iaffaldano, M.T. and Muchinsky, P.M., Psychological Bulletin (1985) pp. 251-273.
[9]   Jamal, M., Human Relations (1985) pp. 409-424.

THE PSYCHOLOGY OF WORK AND ORGANIZATION
G. Debus and H.-W. Schroiff (Editors)
© *Elsevier Science Publishers B.V. (North-Holland), 1986*

METHODOLOGICAL PROBLEMS IN STRESS STUDIES

Charles J. de Wolff

Katholieke Universiteit Nijmegen
Vakgroep Arbeids- en Organisatiepsychologie
Montessorilaan 3
6525 HR Nijmegen

There are some psychologists who like to relate the story about the
drunk and the lamppost. At 2 a.m. one night, a drunken man is searching
for something under a lamppost when a police officer approaches him and
asks him what he's doing. He says he's lost his car keys and the police
officer assists him in his search. Neither finds the keys. Asked by the
police officer where he lost them, the drunk replies he doesn't know.
So why is he looking under the lamppost? Because that's where the light
is.

When psychologists tell this story they do so to illustrate the restriction of their methodology. It implies that we may use a given research
design just because it is easy to do so, while the design may actually
be inadequate in providing the answers to our problems. Although we show
our willingness to conduct empirical research, the method is not always
appropriate for a given problem.

The story is not really an amusing one and triggers a number of questions.
Do psychologists concentrate too much on ritual, for instance? Do they
go along with perceived norms among their colleagues? Are they perhaps not
being critical enough about how to approach the problems?

In this chapter I will examine stress research in an effort to determine
to what extent research methods are appropriate in investigating a given
problem. It is not an exercise aimed at demonstrating that psychologists
act in a foolish way but an effort to identify a number of methodological
issues and to examine the consequences for research designs.

The Relationship between Stressors and Illness

An important issue over the past decade has been the relationship between
stressors and illness. It was in 1973 that French and Kaplan, two researchers from Ann Arbor, proposed a model (figure 1) based on research
conducted previously in their Institute of Social Research, particularly
research done by Kahn in the early sixties (Kahn, 1964) and on subsequent
research findings, summarized by Kahn in his books of 1978 and 1981
(Katz and Kahn, 1978, and Kahn, 1981). The basic idea of their model concerns the relationship between what is happening in the world and the way
people react physiologically and psychologically. The objective environment is perceived in a certain way, which leads to individuals' responses
and eventually to health or illness. These relations are influenced by
both individual and organizational properties.

Ch.J. de Wolff

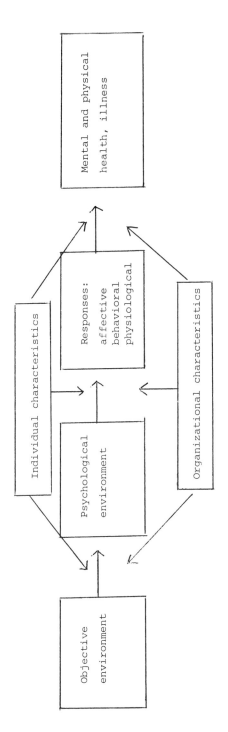

Fig. 1. The ISR model: relationship between environment and health.

The psychological variables in the ISR stress model can be measured with questionnaires. The Institute of Social Research (ISR) Questionnaire was used in the NIOSH-studies, a book published in 1975 by Caplan and his associates. VOS, a Dutch questionnaire based on the ISR questionnaire has been researched extensively in the Netherlands and has been demonstrated to have good psychometric properties (Van Bastelaer & Van Beers, 1983). In addition there is the Dutch Copih-program, designed by Dutch health officers to measure the physiological relations which are presented in figure 2, a more detailed model (Van Vucht Tijssen, 1976).

The Nijmegen Research Group has used this model in its research, primarily in field studies, to explore what stressful conditions exist in certain occupations. Different samples were used, including among others, middle managers (Van Vucht Tijssen, et al., 1978), head nurses (Van de Bergh-Braam, 1981), personnel officers (Van Bastelaer & Van Beers, 1981), as well as their roleset members, including their superiors and subordinates. These studies explore tasks but also relationships between job incumbents and their rolesenders. Most of these studies are field studies, using questionnaires and interviews.

The ISR- model has also been used by other researchers. It has, in fact, served as the basis for many work psychological studies. There have been many attempts to validate it, i.e. to find out if stressors lead to illness. However, in utilizing the model, and in computing the correlations between the given variables, the results are somewhat disappointing. There are reasonable correlations (as high as .50 and .60 occasionally) between stressors and psychological strains, but correlations between stressors and physiological strains are usually insignificant. One may wonder why this is the case and whether or not it is because the model is invalid. The answer to this is: "not likely", for a number of reasons. For one, other field research strongly suggests this type of relationship. Secondly, experimental research demonstrates a relationship between psychological stressors and physiological strains.

Concerning the first line of research, it must be noted that many studies have shown substantial differences between mean scores for stressors and strains, both for occupations and for organizations. If the mean scores for a number of occupations are computed and compared, it will become evident that there are large differences. Some occupations show much higher scores for role conflict and role ambiguity than do others. For non-technical staff positions, for instance, there are much higher scores for role ambiguity (e.g. Van Vucht Tijssen et al., 1978). Furthermore, studies using analysis of variance indicate that a considerable part of the variance of stressors and strains, including physiological strains, can largely be attributed to differences between organizations and departments (Van Bastelaer, 1980). There are substantial differences in mean scores between organizations and departments. However, studies have concentrated more on differences between occupations than on differences between organizations. Finally, a number of studies have indicated that stressful life events are related to illness. In these studies it is consistently found that stressful life events (i.e. death of a partner, move to another city, etc.) are related to increased levels of illness (Dohrenwend & Dohrenwend, 1974; Kleber, 1982).

The second line of research consists of the experimental studies, particularly those conducted by physiologists, relating the psychological sti-

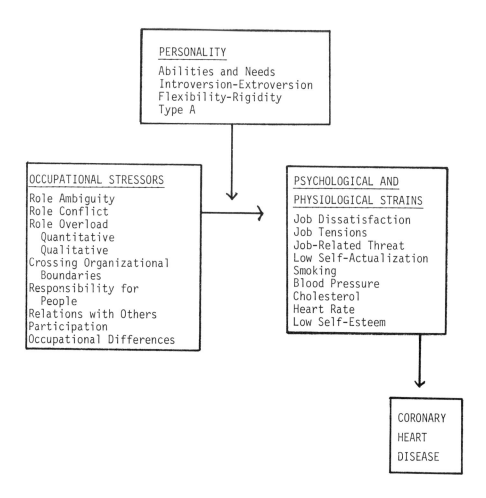

Figure 2: Stressors and strains

muli to physiological responses. These studies indicate that many of these psychological stimuli evoke the General Adaptation Syndrome (e.g. Elliot & Eisdorfer, 1982). By utilizing such stimuli as electric shock and sleep deprivation, a large number of physiological responses may be measured. In addition, such stimuli as social crowding, social isolation and competitive social interaction also lead to physiological responses. Thus, a number of studies indicate a clear relationship between psychological stimuli and such physiological responses as increased heart rate, blood pressure, and cathecholamine production.

In line with the above, several interesting studies have been conducted by Mary Frankenhaueser and her co-workers (Frankenhaueser et al., 1980). She examined the relationship between stressors and physiological responses. As a result, she was able to demonstrate that subjective estimates of stress by the individual are substantially related to his or her physiological responses. Particularly interesting are the stressors she has studied, e.g. defending a dissertation, working overtime, using the subway in a crowded area, having to deal with noisy conditions and machine-paced and monotonous work. Through her experiments she has convincingly demonstrated that stressors evoke immediate physiological and endocrine responses, firmly establishing one link in the long chain between stressors and eventual illness.

Although the experimental studies demonstrate that stress leads to immediate physiological responses, and thus at least demonstrates short term effects, it still has not been ascertained what causes long term effects.

Intervention studies indicate that psychological programs can lead to the reduction of blood pressure. A number of studies by Chandra Patel (in Gentry et al., 1985), who primarily focuses upon relaxation and particular forms of psychotherapy, utilize a type of relaxation therapy with people suffering from hypertension. She demonstrates that, after a couple of months, the hypertension has been reduced. In some of her studies the mean reduction is as high as 15 points (reference).

In conclusion, it thus makes sense to continue to search for relationships between organizational variables and strains. Then the question is, in the cases where we do not find a high correlation between psychological stimuli and physiological responses, should this be attributed to research designs or to the variables used?

We, referring to the Nijmegen Stress Research Group, identified several weaknesses in our designs. Among them are the linearity of relationships between variables, the time factor involved, the impact of moderator variables, the interaction between stressors and the composition of samples.

Concerning the possibility of nonlinear relationships between variables, theory suggests that load is critical when it exceeds certain levels. And if that is the case, one should not calculate linear correlations but nonlinear ones. Research on thresholds indicates the possibility of nonlinear relationships. In a study by Van Dijkhuizen (1980), linear and nonlinear correlations were computed and tested with regard to significant differences between the two. The results were that many relationships as indicated in the ISR model are indeed nonlinear.
However, taking such relationships into account by using eta's instead of

Pearson r's does not dramatically improve the prediction of physiological responses.

Several moderator variables have been used in studies, both individual and organizational characteristics. The most important individual characteristic is the A-type, whereas support is most important in terms of organizational characteristics. A study by Reiche (1981) indicates that the use of moderators can improve the correlations.

Concerning the time factor problem, it seems likely that significant physiological and behavioral changes will only take place after individuals have been exposed to stressors for a considerable period of time. Thus, if someone is working under stressful conditions, it will take some time before his or her behavior begins to change and before his or her blood pressure and cholestrol level increases. If that is the case, cross sectional studies, whereby variables are measured only once, within a relatively short time span, might not be adequate in showing relationships between stressors and strains. Therefore a need exists for longitudinal studies, despite the organizational and methodological problems these studies pose to researchers. Back in 1978, Kasl stated: "Longitudinal studies will get us away from the plethora of hopeless cross sectional studies, which attack extremely complex issues with the weakest of research designs. They are found to yield uninterpretable findings in spite of the extensive effort that may go into collecting the data."

We did set up some longitudinal studies in Nijmegen during the late seventies. The first was by Van Bastelaer and Van Beers (1982), the second by Winnubst et al. (1982, 1983). Although not yet completed, there is indication of improvement. Support, particularly in Winnubst's study, turns out to be an important variable in reducing the stressfulness of conditions. Individuals experiencing support also tend to suffer less from strains. In organizations, the support of one's superior and colleagues is particularly important. Leadership studies have given much attention to support and consideration. Many of the findings can be applied towards organizations, e.g. in the structuring of management training programs. Examples include the behavior-modeling programs developed by AT&T and General Electric (Goldstein & Sorcher, 1974; Burnaska, 1976; Moses & Ritchie, 1976).

As for the interaction between stressors, it is likely that there are cumulative effects. The consequences of being exposed to stressful conditions can hardly be attributed to a single stressful condition but are the result of complex processes in which stressors play a more or less important role. If you experience more than one stressor at a time, the effect may be much greater than if experienced separately. This is particularly the case with stressful life events. Scales for stressful life events give a summation of these events, which are used to predict illness.

Thus many methodological issues are involved, requiring careful reflection both upon what one wants to accomplish as well as the adequate design of the study necessary in completing this goal.

There are also theoretical developments which lead to similar questions. Stress is commonly defined as a situation where the demands upon the individual exceed adjustive resources. This raises two questions: What are demands? What are adjustive resources?

One is tempted to prove that stressors cause illness and physiological changes and to find significant correlations to prove causality. But this is probably not the most adequate approach for psychologists.

Work and organizational psychology has always been involved in problem-oriented research. Some interesting studies on stress date back to World War II (Stoufer, The American Soldier, 1949), when research was done into problems with motivation, breakdown and psychosomatic complaints suffered by bomber pilots and combat soldiers. And early pioneering work on the problem of organizational stress took place in the early sixties (Kahn et al., 1964; Kornhauser, 1965).

It has gradually become apparent that health problems, and problems related to behavior change attributed to organizational stress, are of an enormous magnitude. Subsequent inability to cope has surfaced in dropping out, absenteeism, illness, lack of motivation as well as dissatisfaction, turnover and emotional problems.

Research has to lead to adequate theories but also to the development of prevention and intervention methods. These must be done on an individual basis (i.e. what you can do to help the individual) and on an organizational basis (i.e. what can the organization do to lend assistance to the individual). It is therefore important to explore what the demands and adjustive resources are. Both demands and coping behavior seem to be highly specific, related to the type of organization and to the occupation.

It looks as though work and organizational psychologists would do better to concentrate on exploring demands and coping behavior in specific situations, leaving the problems of how physiological strains lead to illness to physiologists and medical researchers. A good question for work psychologists to explore is why certain individuals are successful in coping while others are not. Such explorative studies require homogeneous samples that also take organizational differences into account. By studying particular groups, one learns more about the ways in which people cope.

There is still room for correlational studies, but these should employ more detailed approaches, and be based on theoretical starting points, as can be seen from a study by Stor (1985) who reanalyzed the data from a study of personnel officers working in 42 organizations. He categorized the organizations on the basis of two dimensions of their task environment: simple-complex and stable-dynamic (c.f. Mintzberg, 1979). In reanalyzing the data, Stor found that personnel officers working in machine-run bureaucracies experience less stressors and strains, more support and a higher level of satisfaction. On the other hand, in professional bureaucracies the workload is high, as are the scores on stressors and strains. Stor's findings led to a marked improvement in predicting physiological strains. For example, in the total sample only 3% of high blood pressure could be predicted while in the four subsamples the figures were 19, 17, 13 and even 52%. Support variables turned out to be good predictors of physiological variables. He found similar data for cholestrol.

It is particularly important to develop methods of intervention and approaches for prevention. This will be easier with sound theories and detailed knowledge of the processes involved.

Stress is an interdisciplinary field. Scientists from different disciplines should not attempt to solve the same problems, but should ask themselves what specific contributions they have to make. It appears to me that workpsychologists can do most when they concentrate on the first part of the model, exploring stressful conditions in organizations and the ways to cope with these conditions. Others can do more about the second part, explaining why stressful conditions might lead to illness.

Thus, there exist some important questions about strategy and methodology. Based on our current knowledge, we can carry out more appropriate studies. In searching we do not have to restrict ourselves to a very limited lighted area; we should search there where we can expect the highest return on investments.

REFERENCES

Bastelaer, A. van and Beers, W. van. *Organisatiestress en personeelsfunctionaris.* Lisse: Swets & Zeitlinger, 1982.

Bastelaer, A. van and Beers, W. van. *Vragenlijst Organisatiestress, Testhandleiding deel 2: Konstruktie en normering.* Katholieke Universiteit Nijmegen, publ. 24, 1980.

Bastelaer, A. van and Beers, W. van. *Stress and some public background variables: an analysis of variances on replicated data.* Unpublished article. University of Nijmegen, 1980.

Bergh-Braam, A. van de. *De Hoofdverpleegkundigen.* Publ. 28, Stress Research Group Nijmegen, Katholieke Universiteit Nijmegen, 1981.

Burnaska, R.F. The effects of behavioral modeling training upon managers' behavior and employees' perceptions. *Personnel Psychology, 1976, 29,* 329-335.

Caplan, R.D., Cobb, S., French, J.R.P., Jr., Harrison, R.D. and Pinneau, S.R., Jr. *Job demands and worker health: main effects and occupational differences.* Washington, U.S. Government Printing Office, 1975.

Dijkhuizen, N. van. *From stressors to strains: research into their relationships.* Lisse: Swets & Zeitlinger, 1980.

Dohrenwend, B.S. & Dohrenwend, B.P. (eds.). *Stressful life events; their nature and effects.* New York: Wiley, 1974.

Elliot, G.R. & Eisdorfer, C. (eds.). *Stress and human Health.* New York: Springer, 1982.

French, J.R.P. and Caplan, R.D. Organizational stress and individual strain. In Marrow, A.J. (ed.). *The failure of success.* New York: AMACOM, 1973.

Gentry, D., Benson, H. & Wolff, Ch.J. de (eds.). *Work, Stress and Health.* Dordrecht: Martinus Nijhoff, 1985.

Goldstein, A.D. & Sorcher, M. *Changing supervisor behavior.* New York: Pergamon, 1979.

Kahn, R.L., Wolfe, D.M., Snoek, J.E. & Rosenthal, R.A. *Organizational stress: studies in role conflict and ambiguity.* New York: Wiley, 1964.

Kahn, R.L. *Work and Health.* New York: Wiley, 1981.

Katz, D. and Kahn, R.L. *The Social Psychology of Organizations.* New York: Wiley, 1978.

Kleber, R.J. *Stressbenaderingen in de psychologie.* Deventer: Van Loghum Slaterus, 1982.

Mintzberg, H. *The structuring of organizations.* Englewood Cliffs: Prentice Hall, 1979.

Moses, J.L. & Ritchie, R.J. Supervisory relationships training: a behavio-
  ral evaluation of a behavior modeling program. *Personnel Psychology,*
  1976, *29*, 337-344.
Reiche, H.M.J.K.I. *Stress aan het werk.* Lisse: Swets & Zeitlinger, 1981.
Stor, Th., *Spanningen bij personeelsfunktionarissen in verschillende*
  organisatie-typen. Nijmegen, doctoral thesis, 1985.
Stouffer, S.A. *The American soldier.* Wiley, 1949.
Vucht Tijssen, J. van,Broecke, A.A.J. van den. Dijkhuizen, N. van,
  Reiche, H.M.J.K.I. and Wolff, Ch.J. de. *Middenkader en stress.*
  Commissie Opvoering Productiviteit van de Sociaal Economische Raad,
  Den Haag, 1978.
Winnubst, J.A.M., Marcelissen, F.H.G. & Kleber, R.J. Effects of social
  support in the stressor-strain relationship: a Dutch sample.
  Social Science and Medicine, 1982, *16*, 475-482.
Winnubst, J.A.M., Marcelissen, F.H.G. & Kleber, R.J. Social support as a
  moderator of stressor-strain relationships in industrial organizations.
  In: M. Horvath & E. Frantic (eds.). *Psychophysiological risk factors*
  of cardiovascular diseases. Basel: Karger, 1983.
Winnubst, J.A.M., Marcelissen, F.H.G., Bastelaer, A.M.L. van, Wolff, Ch.J.
  de & Leufting, A.E. Type A behaviour pattern as a moderator in the
  stressor-strain relationship. In: A.M. Koopman-Iwema & R. Roe (eds.)
  Work and Organizational Psychology: European perspectives. Lisse:
  Swets & Zeitlinger, 1984.

THE PSYCHOLOGY OF WORK AND ORGANIZATION
G. Debus and H.-W. Schroiff (Editors)
© Elsevier Science Publishers B.V. (North-Holland), 1986

CAUSAL MODELING OF QUALITY OF WORK

Jen A. Algera*

Henk van der Flier[+]

Leo J.Th. van der Kamp[§]

In the task design literature several causal models have been proposed, e.g. job characteristics leading to personal and work outcomes via a class of intermediate variables. In the research reported in this paper five blocks of variables are distinguished:
- independent assessments of job characteristics
- task performers' assessments of job characteristics
- intermediate variables pertaining to experience of the work
- satisfaction
- psychic complaints.
Sequential causal links between the blocks of variables are tested by means of linear structural equation analyses (LISREL). Data from two samples are used for this model testing. The theoretical and practical implications of the results are discussed.

1. INTRODUCTION

In the measurement of the quality of work two basic aspects are involved: first, measurement of the (objective) characteristics of the job and second, workers' responses. The validity of instruments, measuring some job characteristics, intended to provide an indication of the quality of work is dependent on their power to predict workers' reactions. In the literature, several causal models have been proposed. The Job Characteristics Model, proposed by Hackman and Oldham [1], has led to much empirical research. This model proposes causal relationships among three classes of variables: core dimensions of jobs, intervening psychological states and work behavior, moderated by individual differences. The results of this empirical research for the total model are mixed.

Main problems with the model are the precise causal paths between variables in the model and the measurement of job characteristics (see e.g. Roberts and Glick [2]; Algera [3]). Reformulations of the model have been proposed. For example, Wall et al. [4] considered internal work motivation to be an intervening psychological state, rather than an outcome variable. Further, they suggested that absence and mental health might be better considered as a fourth stage dependent on job satisfaction or growth satisfaction. Roberts and Glick [2] state that a clear distinction

---

* Free University, De Boelelaan 1081, 1081 HV Amsterdam, The Netherlands
[+] Dutch Railways, Moreelsepark 1, 3500 HA Utrecht, The Netherlands
[§] Leyden University, Hooigracht 15, 2312 KM Leyden, The Netherlands

should be made between person-situation relations and within-person relations. The first refers to relations between independently assessed characteristics of jobs and workers' responses; the second refers to incumbents' perceptions of job characteristics and their responses.

In this paper we will report the results of causal modeling with four classes of variables: job characteristics, intermediate variables pertaining to the experience of the work, satisfaction and psychic complaints. As far as the job characteristics are concerned, both incumbents' perceptions of job characteristics and independent assessments of job characteristics were gathered.

2. METHOD

2.1. Samples

Two different samples are involved. One sample consists of 61 different jobs in the steel industry; far most of these 61 jobs can be described as blue-collar jobs specific to the steel industry. The other sample contains 46 jobs in the public transport sector; far most of these 46 jobs were blue-collar jobs too.

2.2. Job characteristics

For the assessment of job characteristics two types of judges were used: job incumbents and non-job incumbents, in general superiors. In both samples each job was assessed by three job incumbents, the independent assessments were made by three non-job incumbents in the steel industry sample and by two non-job incumbents in the public transport sample.

In this study 24 job characteristics are involved, defined at a level of abstraction comparable to the subscales in the classic study by Turner and Lawrence [5]. Much effort was invested in constructing measuring instruments for these 24 characteristics, that would be easily comprehended by the blue-collar workers involved in this research. Each characteristic was represented by a vertical graphic scale. The scales were also anchored, with professions or work situations as scale anchors (see Algera [3]). The position of each anchor on the scale was established empirically. Psychometric properties (e.g. reliability estimates by means of intra-class correlations) turned out to be satisfactory in general. On the basis of different clustering techniques a 6-cluster structure could be identified that was reasonably stable across the two different samples of jobs in this study. The definitions of these six job characteristics on a more abstract level, comparable to the core job dimensions of the Job Characteristics Model were:
1. significance (e.g. seriousness of potential errors or mistakes)
2. complexity (e.g. ambiguity in solving daily problems)
3. object variety (e.g. number of different tools, controls, etc., worked on)
4. interaction (e.g. interaction opportunities on the job)
5. autonomy (e.g. sequence choice)
6. motor variety (e.g. change in physical location).

Of special interest within the framework of this research are the correlations between job characteristics ratings by job incumbents and non-job incumbents. Correlations between mean ratings are presented in Table 1.

TABLE 1. Correlations between mean ratings of job incumbents and non-job
         incumbents in two samples.

Sample A* Job characteristic	r	Sample B+ Job characteristic	r
significance	.67	significance	.71
complexity	.86	complexity	.55
object variety	.59	object variety	.61
interaction	.68	interaction	.45
autonomy	.75	autonomy	.66
motor variety	.71	motor variety	.84

* 61 jobs from the steel industry
+ 46 jobs from the public transport sector

2.3. Workers' responses

Workers' responses were obtained by means of questionnaires. For each job,
the three job incumbents that assessed their job on the job characteristics scales also were respondents on the questionnaires. The variables
measured stem from the mediating and outcome variables in the Job Characteristics Model, and from other suggestions in the task design literature
(e.g. Wall et al. [4]). In general the coefficient alpha reliabilities for
these variables, determined on the steel industry sample (N = 183 respondents), were satisfactory.

3. ANALYSES

Different kinds of analyses have been used in the literature to test the
Job Characteristics Model, such as analysis by zero-order correlation of
the relationships amongst the variables in the model, analysis by multiple
regression of the mediating role of the critical psychological states and
path analysis of the model. This last mode of analysis is the most
stringent in the requirements it places upon the model. However, in the
path analysis studies to date path coefficients were estimated by performing a series of regression analyses. That means that the relations in the
model are not tested simultaneously. By means of the LISREL-program
however, a simultaneous test of the causal relations among the variables
in the model is possible.

Both multiple regression analysis and path analysis can be looked upon as
submodels of a more general structural model known as Jöreskog's LISREL
model (see Jöreskog and Sörbom [6]). The latter model is used for "causal
modeling", i.e. for hypothesis testing in the context of an entire system
of nonexperimental data. The word "modeling" refers to the fact that the
data analysis will have to be guided by theoretical specification, and the
word "causal" refers to the fact that such a specification is typically
intended to explain, rather than describe, the data.

The LISREL model consists of two parts: the *measurement* part and the *structural* or *theoretical* part. The measurement part specifies how the latent
variables or hypothetical constructs are measured in terms of the
observed variables. The structural part specifies the causal relationships

among the latent variables and is used to describe the causal effects and
the overall fit of the model. In other words, the measurement part
relates the latent dependent variables and latent independent variables
as measured in terms of the observed variables. The structural part describes the causal relationships between latent dependent variables on the
one hand and latent independent variables on the other.

3.1. Tests of the Job Characteristics Model by means of the LISREL-program

On the basis of the correlations among the variables as presented in the
literature, we first tested the Job Characteristics Model using the
LISREL-program with three outcome variables (general satisfaction, internal work motivation and growth satisfaction). The causal links between
variables are indicated in Figure 1. For a full specification of the
measurement part and the structural part of the LISREL-model for this
test, see Algera [7].

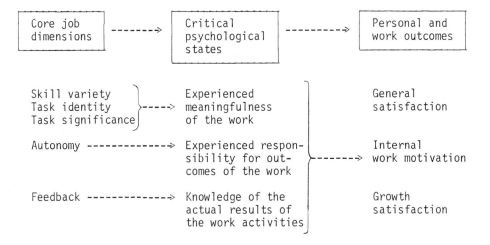

FIGURE 1. The Job Characteristics Model with three outcome variables.

Table 2 shows the resulting chi-square values for the studies of Hackman
and Oldham [1] and Wall et al. [4], implying a bad fit between the model
and the empirical data.

TABLE 2. LISREL-results of two studies.

Study	N	χ^2	df	p-value
Hackman and Oldham [1]	658	470.2	28	<.001
Wall et al. [4]	47	46.5	28	.016

In addition to these analyses we tested the model in the same way on our steel industry sample for both job incumbents and non-job incumbents as sources of task assessments. The unit of observation here is the job (N = 61) because only on that level of aggregation it is possible to connect the independent task assessments by non-job incumbents and workers' responses. The five job characteristics most closely to the five job dimensions from the model were selected from the original list of 24 job characteristics (see sub-section 2.2.).
Table 3 shows the results for both research situations.

TABLE 3. LISREL-results for the steel industry sample.

Research situation	N	χ^2	df	p-value
Job characteristics assessed by non-job incumbents	61	51.9	28	.004
Job characteristics assessed by job incumbents	61	73.6	28	<.001

Again the goodness-of-fit between the Job Characteristics Model and the data turns out to be bad. Including need for autonomy as a moderator did not improve the fit. Therefore, moderating variables will not be considered in the next analyses.

Although substantial correlations exist between the variables from the three classes of variables, the model as originally formulated is not consistent with empirical findings. Thus reformulations of the model is called for. These modifications were based on suggestions found in the literature on job design and quality of work and on inspection of the patterns of correlations in the steel industry sample.

3.2. Testing modifications of the Job Characteristics Model

An elaboration of the Job Characteristics Model described earlier is the one where four classes of variables are involved: job characteristics, intermediate variables pertaining to work experience (or, critical psychological states), satisfaction and psychic complaints. Figure 2 gives a representation of the Modified Job Characteristics Model with the four blocks of variables.

As mentioned before, data were gathered from a sample in the steel industry (N = 61) and one in the public transport sector (N = 46). As far as the job characteristics are concerned, incumbents' perceptions as well as independent assessments of job characteristics were collected. In all, this results in the following four possible combinations:

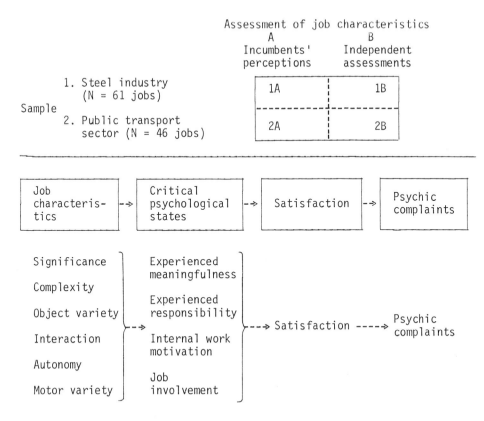

FIGURE 2. The Modified Job Characteristics Model.

For each of these four combinations the Modified Job Characteristics
Model was tested using the LISREL program with satisfaction and psychic
complaints as the dependent variables. The results are shown in Table 4.

TABLE 4. LISREL-results for the Modified Job Characteristics Model.

Sample	N	χ^2	df	p-value
1A	61	157.66	54	<.001
1B	61	143.73	54	<.001
2A	46	94.79	54	<.001
2B	46	117.68	54	<.001

Unfortunately, the Modified Job Characteristics Model turns out to fit
the empirical data unsatisfactorily. As can be seen from Table 4, each of
the four obtained chi-sqaure values is rather high and much larger than is
expected by chance in 95% of the cases. So, according to this procedure we
must conclude that the Modified Job Characteristics Model as given in
Figure 2 is uninformative for the causal modeling of quality of work.

It must be concluded that the Modified Job Characteristics Model must again be adjusted to satisfactorily account for the empirical data. Two kinds of adjustments can be suggested: elimination of a class of variables and elimination of single variables. Both are based on the inspection of the residual variances/covariances, as indicators of misfit between model and data. In this study only the first option has been explored yet. The main source of misfit of the model as a whole is located in (some of) the relationships between job characteristics and critical psychological states. Therefore, a simplified model (see figure 3) leaving out the whole class of critical psychological states was formulated and tested.

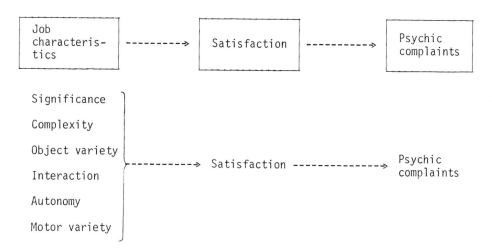

FIGURE 3. The simplified model.

The results are shown in Table 5.

TABLE 5. LISREL-results for a simplified model.

Sample	N	χ^2	df	p-value
1A	61	80.09	20	<.001
1B	61	101.54	20	<.001
2A	46	49.18	20	<.001
2B	46	51.70	20	<.001

Taking into account the lower number of degrees of freedom the decrease in the chi-square values does not really improve the fit. The second option, leaving out those job characteristics and critical psychological states for which residuals are consistently high for the relationships with other variables, will be explored in the near future.

4. CONCLUDING REMARKS

Looking at the zero-order correlations in both samples it appears that a number of the job characteristics do correlate higher with satisfaction than would be expected in terms of the causal model on the basis of the correlations between job characteristics and critical psychological states and between critical psychological states and satisfaction. In one of the four sub-samples the correlations between some of the job characteristics and satisfaction are even higher than those between job characteristics and critical psychological states.

On the other hand, the zero-order correlations between job characteristics, satisfaction and psychic complaints allow for a causal model where satisfaction mediates between job characteristics and psychic complaints. An extension of the model with absenteeism data as a dependent variable in the same stage as psychic complaints is planned. For one of the samples absenteeism indices on job level have been computed. In the other sample analysis of absenteeism data has not been completed yet. Again some of the job characteristics turn out to show higher correlations with these dependent variables than expected on the basis of the relationship with intervening variables in the model.

So, although it may be very difficult to model the precise causal relations between the many variables in this field of research, a more positive conclusion of the study is that individual job characteristics as measured by the 24 graphic scales have substantial correlations with both work satisfaction and absenteeism on job level. Therefore this study substantiates the practical relevance of this instrument for the measuring of quality of work.

REFERENCES

[1] Hackman, J.R. and Oldham, G.R., Motivation through the design of work: Test of a theory. Organizational Behavior and Human Performance (1976), 16, 250-279.
[2] Roberts, K.H. and Glick, W., The job characteristics approach to task design: A critical review. Journal of Applied Psychology (1981), 66, 193-217.
[3] Algera, J.A., 'Objective' and perceived task characteristics as a determinant of reactions by task performers. Journal of Occupational Psychology (1983), 56, 97-107.
[4] Wall, T.D., Clegg, C.W. and Jackson, P.R., An evaluation of the Job Characteristics Model. Journal of Occupational Psychology (1978), 51, 183-196.
[5] Turner, A.N. and Lawrence, P.R., Industrial jobs and the worker. An investigation of response to task attributes (Harvard University, Boston, MA, 1965).
[6] Jöreskog, K.G. and Sörbom, D., LISREL IV, A general computer program for estimation of linear structural equation systems by maximum likelihood methods (University of Uppsala, Uppsala, 1978).
[7] Algera, J.A., Kenmerken van werk [Characteristics of work] (Swets & Zeitlinger, Lisse, 1981).

THE PSYCHOLOGY OF WORK AND ORGANIZATION
G. Debus and H.-W. Schroiff (Editors)
© Elsevier Science Publishers B.V. (North-Holland), 1986

DEGREE AND QUALITY OF JOB SATISFACTION IN RELATION TO THE DEGREE
OF IDENTIFICATION WITH THE COMPANY

Diether GEBERT

Universität Bayreuth, Postfach 3008, 8580 Bayreuth

Abstract

The following investigation tries to predict degrees of identification with the company on the basis of the measurement of the
degree and quality of job satisfaction. In Western Germany within
one company we administered a standardized questionnaire to N =
343 employees. The result of an analysis of variance shows (1)
There are two main effects; the degree and quality of job satisfaction are significantly positively related to the degree of identification with the company (2) There is a significant interaction
effect too; the interaction between the degree and the quality of
job satisfaction explains more variance of the degree of identification with the company than one of these predictors alone. In
predicting degrees of identification with the company therefore
it is useful, to measure both, the degree and the quality of job
satisfaction.

1. THE PROBLEM

The empirical studies usually result in only slightly positive correlations
between the degrees of job satisfaction and some dependent variables, like
turnover, performance criteria etc. Thus the measurement of the degree of
satisfaction with certain aspects of the job seems to be insufficient for
a more accurate prediction of such criteria like the degree of identification with the company; an additional information in respect to the quality
of satisfaction seems to be necessary. For instance, it may happen that an
employee showing a low degree of satisfaction with the present work contents may still hope that future will improve the existing situation. In
this case, despite the low degree of satisfaction with the present work
quality, a strong identification with the company is possible. In the
opposite case when the hope for improvement is absent, the emigration in
a subjective way - recentering the life around private objectives (e.g.
family) - may be expected and thus may result in a low degree of identification with the company. Dependent on the quality of perceived future
(being one dimension of the quality of job satisfaction) identical degrees
of job satisfaction suppose to correlate differently with the measures of
identification with the company. The above will be the main subject of our
investigation. We intend to answer specifically to the following questions:
-what type of relation exists between the degree of satisfaction and the
  degree of identification?
-what type of relation exists between the quality of satisfaction and the
  degree of identification?
-can we explain more of the variance of the identification with the company, if we measure the degree and (in parallel) the quality of job satisfaction? Will (in statistical terms) the interaction between the degree

and quality of job satisfaction explain more variance than one of these
predictors alone?
-dependent on what qualities of job satisfaction the relation between identical degrees of job satisfaction and the degree of identification will
vary in what way?

2. THEORY AND METHOD

The investigation was carried out in a company located in a small town
within a rural area which produces small electronical elements and has
labour force of about 700 employees in Western Germany. All 700 employees
received the standardized questionnaire; a total amount of N = 343 (49 %)
of the questionnaires was returned. The sample can be described as follows:

professional position:

under apprenticeship	2,2 %	semi-skilled labour	19,4 %
fitters	24,4 %	skilled labour	16,1 %
gangmen	1,8 %	foremen	1,4 %
office clerks	29,7 %	executives	5,0 %
sex: male	44,0 %	female	56,0 %

The willingness to personally accept certain material and/or immaterial
costs was taken as a criterion of the identification with the company.
A questionnaire comprising 10 questions (see Hirsch, 1985) was administered, to measure the identification, out of which the following 4 questions illustrate how the above mentioned "costs" are defined.

I actively support improvements of the company even if it consumes a lot
of time and even if it can create additional annoyance to me.

very true   true   untrue   very untrue

If I am told that my company needs me, I am prepared to sacrifice a day
of my annual leave.

very true   true   untrue   very untrue

If I am told that my company needs me, I would go to work even if I was
on a sick leave.

very true   true   untrue   very untrue

Even if I have an offer of appointment which guarantees the same position
and salary at the time when my company is facing a crisis, within a limited time, I would still continue my service without being paid.

very true   true   untrue   very untrue

The sum of agreement scores to these statements reflect the degree of
identification with the company.
We realize that we defined and measured our construct "identification" in
an unusual way; but we think that our conceptual approach has the advantage of a clear dimensional structure and is important in practical terms,
too: Many entrepreneurs are interested in this criterion especially in
times of declining business chances.

In measuring the degree of job satisfaction we define job satisfaction as the attitude to the various aspects of the job. As a measurement tool we use the ABB (Arbeitsbeschreibungsbogen) of Neuberger et al. (1979), which is a German adaptation of the JDI (Job Description Index) of Smith et al. (1969). In the ABB (as in the JDI) the employee has to mark the degree to which he agrees to some short characteristics of his superior, his colleagues, his job contents, the kind of surrounding organization, his chances of making a career, his pay etc. The sum of all agreement scores reflects the degree of the overall job satisfaction of the employee.

In respect to the definition and measurement of the quality of job satisfaction we refer to the work of Bruggemann (1974), but we make some important theoretical differentiations. First, we do not think, that there are "the" dimensions of quality of job satisfaction. In order to predict or to explain different criteria we may need different dimensions of quality of job satisfaction. In order to decide on the type of dimension or to make a fruitful selection out of the range of possible dimensions, we first need a theoretical framework, in which we can integrate the structure of our criterion (identification) and the dimensions of the quality of job satisfaction. We believe to find this theoretical framework in the equity-theory of Adams (1965) or more fundamentally in the social exchange theories (for example Homans, 1960), in which the person relates the received material or immaterial returns to his own material or immaterial investments and tries to reach a proportion, which he can perceive as fair in the sense, that he perceives the distribution of the benefits and costs between the two interacting social systems (persons) as fair. In the model of Adams (1965) that means: If the employee perceives the inputs and outcomes in the social relation between himself and the (owner of the) company as well balanced in the past and the employee now gets some more benefits, he will - subjectively - reach a new state of equity and fairness in rising his investments; in our case this means he will rise his degree of identification (in the sense of acceptance of costs).

In this way we think that a person is not only satisfied to a certain degree in a specific area of his job (for example in the area of his job contents); in addition he evaluates and interprets his result (of a certain degree of satisfaction) in terms of a social exchange. In respect to this evaluation process we predict: If the expected and/or perceived input/outcomes relation exceeds his aspiration level or comparison level (learned during the socialization) his willingness will rise to accept additional costs in the future and vice versa.

From this background we differentiate mainly two dimensions in order to describe the quality of job satisfaction: First the expected relation between input and outcomes in the future and secondly the perceived relation between input and outcomes within the social exchange process in the past; the evaluation of those expected or perceived relations then may result in feelings of equity and fairness.

We arbitrarily differentiate three types of job satisfaction, which refer, despite a different theoretical context, to what Bruggemann (1974) called "progressive", "resignative", and "stabilized" quality of job satisfaction. The progressive form refers to progressive expectations. This quality of job satisfaction refers to the employee's future expectations in the sense that the conditions (in the area of work) will improve. In addition - and this may be one reason for his optimistic view - he perceives his working conditions at least to some extent as controllable and he has the experience that even a worker can expect something in his working life. Also in the past his expectations were fulfilled. This employee explicitly expects rising outcomes within the exchange process.

On the contrary the "resignative" and the "stabilized" quality of satisfaction do not imply these positive expectations. An employee with the
"resignative" quality agrees to the statement, that life in the work context is not controllable and that one cannot expect too much as a worker
and the employee with the "stabilized" satisfaction structure explicitly
agrees to the statement that there will be no major change in respect to
his working life.
Both measurements of satisfaction qualities do not imply any positive development in respect to the future and so we assume, that the employees
with the progressive expectations will show higher degrees of identification than the employees with the other qualities of satisfaction structure, because they differ in the exchange related evaluation of the future.
On the other side we can make a difference between the "stabilized" and
the "resignative" quality of satisfaction: The way in which they are
measured in the Bruggemann study and in our questionnaire, gives sense to
the hypothesis, that these qualities differ in the perception of the past:
The employee with the "stabilized" quality received, in his own perception,
in the past what he expected (and in this sense he is stabilized), but not
more; so he has a feeling of equity. The employee with the "resignative"
quality thought, that one cannot expect too much in the work life and he
often said to himself, "it could even be worse". So looking back into the
past he is surprised and in his perception he received more than he had
expected. Whereas the employee with the stabilized quality of satisfaction
in his perception so does not see any reason for rising the investment
within the exchange process (in the past he received only, what was entitled to him), the employee with the resignative quality of satisfaction
seems to have some feelings of thankfulness (he received in his perception
more than was entitled to him and so he has feelings of inequity) and because of this may rise his investment within the social interaction. In
sum, we assume, that the employee with the so-called resignative feelings
of satisfaction shows higher degrees of identification than the employee
with the so-called stabilized quality of satisfaction, because they differ
in the exchange related evaluation of the past.

3. RESULTS AND DISCUSSION

The next table shows the distribution of frequencies in respect to the
degree and quality of satisfaction and the degree of identification with
the company.

Table 1:

Frequency distributions

degree of job satisfaction	very satis- fied	satis- fied	less satis- fied	less unsatis- fied	unsatis- fied	very unsatis- fied
	13,7	49,3	31,0	6,0	0	0

quality of job satisfaction	progressive		resignative		stabilized	
	35,3		39,5		25,1	

degree of identi- fication with the company	very high	high	small	very small
	24,4	30,5	23,4	21,6

As in other studies, the proportion of employees who perceive themselves

as very satisfied is surprisingly high. In respect to the relation between
the degree of job satisfaction and the degree of identification with the
company we got the following results (see Fig. 1):

FIGURE 1: IDENTIFICATION AND DEGREE OF JOB-SATISFACTION

For the three groups of very satisfied, satisfied and less satisfied employees one can see the respective mean degree of identification, expressed as the overall sample mean value deviations. On the basis of an analysis of variance in respect to the relation between the degree of job satisfaction and the degree of identification with the company the result
is an eta = .37 which is highly significant. As supposed, the degree of
job satisfaction is significantly positively related to the degree of identification with the company.
It may be useful to report in addition, that the highest single correlation (Pearson) between a special area of the job and the identification
exists between the satisfaction with the job contents and the identification with the company (r = .31, p = .001). This result is in accordance
with all humanistic theories of job motivation (Maslow, Herzberg, etc.);
the job contents are a more important source for identification processes
than for example the relationship to the supervisor or colleagues.
Now to the second question: What is the relationship between the quality
of job satisfaction and the degree of identification with the company
(see Fig. 2)?
For the groups of employees with a stabilized, resignative or progressive
quality of satisfaction Figure 2 shows the respective mean degree of identification, expressed as the overall sample mean value deviations. As supposed, the progressive quality is correlated with higher degrees of identification than the resignative or stabilized quality of satisfaction;
also the other hypothesis is confirmed: The resignative quality is connected with a higher identification degree than the stabilized quality.
Within the analysis of variance as a result we get for the description

of the relationship between all three qualities of satisfaction and the
identification dimension an eta = .39, which is highly significant too.

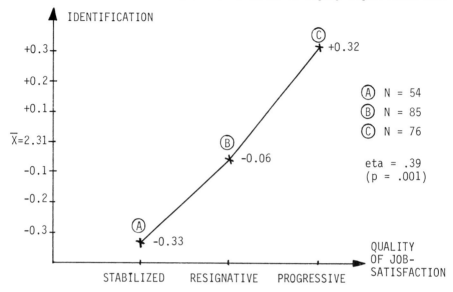

FIGURE 2: IDENTIFICATION AND QUALITY OF JOB-SATISFACTION

The quality of job satisfaction, here specified a) as the evaluated expected relation between input and outcomes in the future and the perceived
relation between input and outcomes in the past on the one side and b) as
the (with these evaluations) corresponding feeling of equity/inequity on
the other side, is a significant predictor of the identification degree
too. The quality of job satisfaction explains as much variance of the
identification dimension as the degree of job satisfaction. As a consequence it seems to be useful, to measure both, the degree and the quality
of job satisfaction, if there is interest in predicting degrees of identification with the company. This impression is stressed by the results
of the last analysis (see Fig. 3):
Figure 3 shows, that the employees, who reach the same degree of job satisfaction (in the case of the degree "satisfied": N = 147) realize different degrees of identification with the company, depending on the corresponding quality of job satisfaction. That means in the above example: Although all the 147 employees are satisfied to the same degree, N = 55 employees with the progressive qualities realize more identification than
the N = 53 resignative employees, who in turn show more identification
than the employees with the stabilized quality of job satisfaction. Thus
the picture also demonstrates, that the degree and the quality of job
satisfaction are at least partially independent one from another. So it
makes sense to measure both!
The important content of the below Figure 3 is the information, that the
analysis of variance does not only show (in statistical terms) two main
effects (see Fig. 1 and 2), but an interaction effect too (see Fig. 3):
The main effects and the interaction effect together are reflected in an

eta = .50, which is highly significant and higher than the eta of the main effects alone.

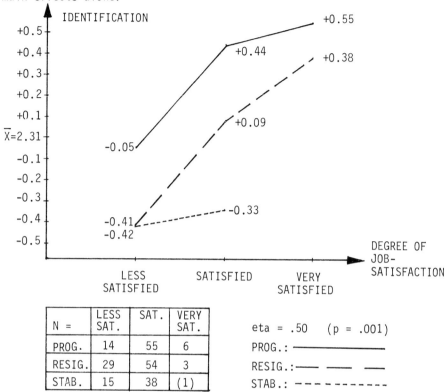

FIGURE 3: IDENTIFICATION AND INTERACTION BETWEEN DEGREE AND QUALITY
OF JOB-SATISFACTION

The interaction effect can be illustrated: If an employee is very satisfied and this at the same time in a progressive way, he realizes a higher degree of identification (0,55), compared with the case, when he is "only" very satisfied (0,29; see Fig. 1) or "only" in qualitative terms, progressively satisfied (0,32; see Fig. 2). So the interaction effect rises the identification degree, independent of the basic main effects. This fact once more stresses the fact, that it is useful to predict identification degrees on the basis of the measurement of the degree and the quality of job satisfaction.

Although our approach in defining the construct of "quality" of job satisfaction (see above) is only a first trial, we think the approach is in the right direction: We need additional information in respect to the question, how the employees organize their perceptions of the work situation in respect to the past and the future.

References

(1) Homans, G.C., Theorie der sozialen Gruppe. Köln, 1960
(2) Adams, S.J., Inequity in social exchange. in: Berkowitz, L. (ed.):
    Advances in experimental social psychology II, N.Y., 1965, 267-299
(3) Smith, P.C., Kendall, L.M., Hulin, C.L., The measurement of satis-
    faction in work and retirement: A strategy for the study of attitudes.
    Chicago, 1969
(4) Bruggemann, A., Zur Unterscheidung verschiedener Formen von Arbeits-
    zufriedenheit, Arbeit und Leistung, 1974, 28, 281-284
(5) Neuberger, O., Allerbeck, M., Messung und Analyse von Arbeitszufrie-
    denheit, Stuttgart, 1978
(6) Hirsch, H., Arbeitszufriedenheit und Engagement. Unveröffentlichte
    Diplomarbeit an der Universität Bayreuth, Bayreuth, 1985

THE PSYCHOLOGY OF WORK AND ORGANIZATION
G. Debus and H.-W. Schroiff (Editors)
© Elsevier Science Publishers B.V. (North-Holland), 1986

PSYCHOSOCIAL IMPAIRMENT OF DOUBLE-DAY WORKERS AND POSSIBLE CORRECTIVE MEASURES

Hanspeter BETSCHART[*]

Swiss Federal Institute of Technology,
Work and Organizational Psychology Unit,
Nelkenstr. 11, CH-8092 Zürich

The present study was concerned with the
frequency of specific impairments of
double-day, former double-day and non-shift
workers. A questionnaire was given to 1599
workers in four car-manufacturing plants.
Summarizing the results it is concluded
that double-day workers constitute a
population with an increased risk of
specific impairments. Two measures capable
of reducing some of the impairments are
discussed.

1. SET-UP OF THE RESEARCH PROJECT

A research project entitled "The Psychosocial Effects of Double-Day Work" was carried out between 1981 and 1984. The central question to be investigated was the relative frequency of specific impairments for double-day, former double-day and non-shift workers.

Empirical investigations took place in four German car-manufacturing plants. The shift system in question consisted of weekly changing discontinuous double-day work with an early shift from 6.00 a.m. to 2.30 p.m. and a late shift from 2.30 p.m. to 11.00 p.m. The sequential method of data gathering included interviews, group discussions and questionnaires. In the following, only results from the questionnaires will be presented.

For the selection of the persons to be given questionnaires, two samples were drawn of the total number of male workers in the four car-manufacturing plants. A representative German sample was formed out of all German double-day and non-shift workers by means of stratified random sampling. In view of the large number of foreign workers employed in the four manufacturing plants, a small foreign sample was also selected.

The workers sampled were given information on the project groupwise and asked about their willingness to participate in the survey. A participation quota of about 95% resulted. Sample distribution of the 1559 workers who were given questionnaires is shown in Table 1.

---
[*] Apart from the author, the following individuals participated in research work, which was under the supervision of Eberhard Ulich: Thomas Odersky, Monika Schefer, Peter Sprachve, Hans Wälti and Kitty Fischer.

Table 1: Sample composition for the survey (questionnaires)
        - absolute frequencies

Survey samples	non-shift and former double-day workers	double-day workers	total
German workers sample	664	802	1466
foreign workers sample	---	133	133
total	664	935	1599

Questionnaire surveys took place in November and December 1983 during working time in groups of 20 to 30 workers. Members of the research staff were present at all times.

Besides many standardized single items that had been specifically constructed, the questionnaire also contained items that had already been used in other surveys (e.g. "Subjective Work Analysis" by Alioth & Udris (1980) and the "Freiburg Inventory of Physical Complaints" by Fahrenberg (1975)). Most people included in the survey considered the items as well comprehensible, some, however, thought that the time required for filling out - about three hours on the average - was somewhat too long.

2.   COMPARISON OF SELECTED RESULTS: PRESENT DOUBLE-DAY, FORMER DOUBLE-
      DAY AND NON-SHIFT WORKERS

Only data concerning the statements of the 1466 German workers questioned will be reported here, thus neglecting the foreign workers sample. A problem in the comparison was the fact that there were highly significant differences in age (as reported by the workers) between the former double-day workers (drop-outs) and the other two groups. In order to avoid results biased by age effects, the drop-out group was corrected for age before data analysis reducing sample size by 134 subjects. For this reason, all the following results will be based on the reduced sample amounting to a total of 1332 subjects.

2.1   Health impairments

Various psychosomatic complaints were recorded by means of the "Freiburg Inventory of Physical Complaints" (Fahrenberg, 1975).

Double-day workers and also part of former double-day workers (drop-outs) clearly reported higher degrees of impairment in terms of lack of appetite, feelings of dizziness and heart troubles (Table 2).

Table 2: Comparison of selected psychosomatic complaints within the last
two years as reported by 1259 subjects surveyed – frequencies
in percent

Psychosomatic complaints	double-day workers (S) n = 783	drop-outs (D) n = 300	non-shift workers (N) n = 176	signi-ficance
lack of appetite	19.9	8.8	8.1	S/D:*** S/N:***
feelings of dizziness	20.3	21.9	7.6	S/N:** D/N:**
heart troubles	20.8	15.7	12.7	S/N:** D/N:***

Double-day workers also complainted markedly more often about increased
nervous strain (Table 3).

Table 3: Comparison of nervous strain as reported by 1270 subjects
surveyed – frequencies in percent

Nervous strain	double-day workers (S) n = 783	drop-outs (D) n = 308	non-shift workers (N) n = 179	signi-ficance
nervousness after work	55.1	43.8	43.6	S/D:* S/N:*
irritation	70.7	64.3	67.4	n.s.

With respect to reported doctors' diagnoses of illness within the last
two years, however, there were no significant differences between the
three groups – neither for stomach-intestine nor heart and circulation
problems.

In a wider sense sleep disturbances can be seen as health impairs, too.
Double-day workers and also drop-outs reported significantly more problems in going to sleep and in sleeping through than did non-shift
workers (Table 4).

---

* In Table 2 and the following Tables only those subjects are
considered that correctly answered the specific question; therefore
sample size is below the total age-corrected sample size of 1332
German subjects surveyed.

Table 4:   Comparison of reported impairments of sleep quality for   1262
           subjects surveyed – frequencies in percent

Disturbances of sleep quality	double-day workers (S) n = 784	drop-outs (D) n = 304	non-shift- workers (N) n = 174	signi- ficance
problems in going to sleep	59.8	44.1	27.4	S/D:*** S/N:*** D/N:***
problems in sleeping through	54.4	52.3	42.0	S/D:* S/N:**

The double-day workers concerned also reported higher intensitites of
sleep disturbances as compared to the other two groups. E.g., more than
half of the double-day workers in question indicated problems in going
to sleep occuring daily or several times a week.

2.2. Psychosocial impairments

Research based on role theory (e.g. Mott et. al., 1965) has pointed to
role conflicts that potentially can arise for shift workers as a consequence of their irregular rhythm of living. In the present study, such
role conflicts could, to a certain extent, be identified for the family
sphere. Significantly more often that the other two groups, double-day
workers especially reported having too little time for being with their
wife/partner and children (Table 5).

Table 5: Comparison of amount of time for being with the family as
           reported by 972 subjects surveyed – frequencies in percent

Amount of time for being with family	double-day workers (S)	drop-outs (D)	non-shift workers (N)	signi- ficance
too little time for wife/partner	34.0 (n=591)	16.3 (n=257)	16.9 (n=124)	S/D:*** S/N:***
too little time for children	58.2 (n=435)	50.9 (n=175)	44.0 (n=84)	S/N:*

About one out of ten double-day workers reported feelings of not really
being part of his family any more and fears of his partner being dissatisfied with the relationship. Astonishingly, for the extra-family
sphere no discrimination of the double-day workers was found in
comparison to the other two groups. This includes social contacts with
friends, political activities and participation in sport and cultural
clubs.

3.   RELATIONSHIP BETWEEN DOUBLE-DAY WORKERS' SCOPE OF WORK
      ACTIVITIES AND DEGREE OF IMPAIRMENTS

In some studies it was shown that risks associated with shift work
increase considerably if other job stressors are present (so-called
"multiple load", cf. Aanonsen, 1964). In our study this problem was
examined with respect to the multiple load arising from a restricted
scope of work activities. Based on data collected through "Subjective
Work Analysis" by Alioth & Udris (1980), the double-day workers surveyed
were either assigned to a group with a rather large scope of work activities (n = 298) or to another group with a rather narrow scope (n =
399). It turned out that especially the younger double-day workers
reported more limited scopes of work activities, and that a narrow scope
of activities often went hand in hand with a lot of further stressors
such as noise or time pressure.
A few rather distinct differences can be shown between some forms of
impairment for the double-day workers with a narrow scope of work activities and those with a large one. In the area of health, the group with
a small scope of work activities reported impairments especially for the
items "lack of appetite", "nervousness" and "going to sleep" (Table 6).

Table 6:   Comparison of health impairments as reported by 691 double-day
           workers surveyed – frequencies in percent

| Selected forms of health impairments | double-day workers | | signi-ficance |
	with a rather narrow scope of work activities n = 398	with a rather large scope of work activities n = 293	
lack of appetite	25.1	17.7	**
nervousness after work	76.2	63.7	**
irritation	59.0	50.9	*
disturbance of going to sleep	63.1	52.2	**

Concerning psychosocial impairments strikingly more double-day workers
with a narrow scope of work activities stated that they had too little
time for being with their families (Table 7).

Table 7: Comparison of time available for being with family as reported
          by 516 double-day workers surveyed – frequencies in percent

Time for being with family	double-day workers		signi-ficance
	with a rather narrow scope of work activities	with a rather large scope of work activities	
too little time for being with wife/partner	40.4 (n=275)	28.6 (n=241)	**
too little time for being with children	65.3 (n=196)	54.5 (n=178)	*

4.   POTENTIAL CORRECTIVE MEASURES

Nearly half of the double-day workers surveyed expressed their willingness to change to a comparable form of non-shift work and to accept a
possibly resulting cut in salary at the same time (Table 8).

Table 8: Distribution of answers concerning desires to change to
          comparable non-shift workers accepting a cut in salary as
          reported by 776 double-day workers surveyed – frequencies in
          percent

Desire to change to non-shift work accepting a cut in salary	n = 776
yes	47.4
no	46.3
I don't know	6.3

Interestingly especially those double-day workers wanted to switch to
non-shift work who stated that they had begun double-day work for
necessities caused by labor market conditions (Table 9).

Table 9: Comparison of main reason given for taking up double-day work and desire to change to non-shift work accepting a cut in salary, data from 689 double-day workers surveyed – frequencies in percent

	Main reason for taking up double-day work		
Desire to change to non-shift work accepting a cut in salary	labor market conditions n = 360	extra pay n = 255	other reasons n = 74
yes	63.6	28.6	7.8
no	36.4	71.4	92.2

Obviously, many of the subjects took up double-day work merely for necessities caused by labor market conditions. The desire to exchange double-day work with a comparable kind of non-shift work remains strong for these subjects – even after having been involved in double-day work for many years. In our opinion, at least this group of people should, after a certain number of years in double-day work, be given the opportunity to change working times. In part, this would imply the creation of more non-shift jobs in the four car-manufacturing plants investigated.

Because of the relationship between the scope of work activities and the degree of impairments, which we showed above, it also seems obvious to search for ways of enlarging the scope of work activities of double-day workers. In our questionnaire survey, two alternative forms of work were to be rated by the subjects. The majority of the double-day workers participating in the survey evaluated both job enrichment and the introduction of semi-autonomous work groups favorably and indicated to prefer these forms of work to their current one. Interestingly, double-day workers with a rather narrow scope of work activities seemed to prefer the alternative work forms more frequently (Table 10).

Table 10: Indicated preferences of alternative forms of work to actual work form as reported by 559 double-day workers surveyed – frequencies in percent

Preference of alternative forms of work	double day workers		
	with a rather narrow scope of work activities n = 293	with a rather large scope of work activities n = 208	all n = 559
job enrichment	73.5	52.5	64.9
semi-autonomous working groups	59.7	39.4	52.2

5.   CONCLUSIONS

According to the results of the present study double-day workers constitute a population with an increased risk of specific impairments. With regard to health lack of appetite, nervousness and disturbances of sleep seem to predominate, concerning psychosocial problems insufficient time for being with the family played an important role. These impairments were especially grave for double-day workers with a rather narrow scope of activities. Remarkably, degree of impairment was in part also significantly higher for former double-day workers (drop-outs) than for non-shift workers. It could be shown that there are some presumingly very effective measures capable of reducing some of these impairments. The facilitating of switching to a comparable form of non-shift work many constitute one such measure. Another may be seen in the reduction of multiple stressors through the introduction of alternative forms of work such as job enrichment or semi-autonomous groups.

REFERENCES

(1) Aanonsen, A., Shiftwork and health (Copenhagen, 1964).
(2) Alioth, A. & Udris, I., Fragebogen zur "Subjektiven Arbeitsanalyse" (SAA), in: Martin, E., Udris, I., Ackermann, U. & Oegerli, K., Monotonie in der Industrie (Huber, Bern, 1980) pp. 61-68.
(3) Betschart, H., Odersky, T., Schefer-Held, M., Sprave, P. & Ulich, E., Psychosoziale Auswirkungen der Arbeit im Zweischichtsystem, in: Sektion Arbeits- und Betriebspsychologie im Berufsverband Deutscher Psychologen (Hrsg.), Arbeit in moderner Technik (Duisburg, 1984) pp. 367-384.
(4) Betschart, H., Odersky, T., Schefer, M. & Ulich, E., Forschungsbericht "Die psychosozialen Auswirkungen der Arbeit im Zweischichtsystem" (Lehrstuhl für Arbeits- und Organisationspsychologie der ETHZ, Zürich, 1985).
(5) Fahrenberg, J., Die Freiburger Beschwerdenliste FBL, Zeitschrift für klinische Psychologie, 4, (1975) pp. 79-100.
(6) Mott, P.E., Mann, F.L., McLoughlin, Q. & Warwick, D.P., Shiftwork - the social, psychological and physical consequences (University of Michigan Press, Ann Arbor, 1965).
(7) Ulich, E. & Baitsch, C., Schicht- und Nachtarbeit im Betrieb, 2nd Ed. (gdi, Rüschlikon/Zürich, 1979).

THE PSYCHOLOGY OF WORK AND ORGANIZATION
G. Debus and H.-W. Schroiff (Editors)
© *Elsevier Science Publishers B.V. (North-Holland), 1986*

METHODOLOGICAL PROBLEMS OF FIELD-RESEARCH ON WORKPLACES IN OFFICES

Andreas KREUZIG and Reiner BORRETTY

Siemens AG   ZTP FWO 23, Otto-Hahn-Ring 6,
8000 München 83, Federal Republic of Germany

The necessity of field-research and its significance in the research process will be discussed. A discussion of validity based
on COOK and CAMPBELL leads to conclusions about the design of
field-studies. The selection of contents, methods, and samples
will be discussed. As an example for the outlined proceeding, a
field-study on workplaces in offices, centered around VDU-aided
workplaces, shows practical problems and ways to realize those
requirements.

1. INTRODUCTION

This paper is about a comprehensive study of workplaces in offices, especially workplaces equipped with VDU's. It is centered around methodological
problems. The study was motivated by heterogeneous and in part critical results and design recommendations against the background of a predicted rapid
increase of the number of VDU's. The body of knowledge about VDU workplaces
was not very comprehensive then [1]. Target of the study was to get an overview of design features of VDU-aided workplaces at Siemens and to develop
rules for proper design.

2. THE VALIDITY OF FIELD-RESEARCH

Since the real world is comprised of complex systems, solely linear-causal
models are not appropriate. BISCHOF [3] has pointed out the inadequacy of
the Physical paradigma for Psychology. You got to have an idea of structure and boundaries of the system in question to develop meaningful laboratory experiments. These considerations clearly lead to a field-study. On the
other hand, validity is not easy to manage.

In the following discussion, we draw from COOK and CAMPBELL [4]. They differentiate between four categories of validity, namely statistical conclusion validity, internal validity, construct validity, and external validity.

2.1. Statistical conclusion validity

Basic question: Is there a relationship between the two variables?
Conclusive statistics serve to detect covariations between assumed independent and dependent variables. A study as a whole should be sensitive enough
to render the detection of covariations possible. This is endangered among
other things by unreliable instruments and group-specific effects.

2.2. Internal validity

Basic question: Given that there is a relationship, is it plausibly causal from one operational variable to the other or would the effect have been obtained even without treatment?
That is, if there is covariation, can alternative potential explanations be excluded? This is a question of sampling, but also of the research design.

2.3. Construct validity of causes and effects

Basic question: Given that the relationship is plausibly causal and is reasonably known to be from one variable to another, what are the particular cause and effect constructs involved in the relationship?
In the research process, samples of causes, effects, measurements, subjects, settings, etc. are denominated in generalizable expressions. Statements about constructs thus always are conclusions from data. To secure construct validity, it is necessary to precisely describe constructs prior to the study, to include alternative constructs, and to use various methods of measurement.

2.4. External validity

Basic question: Given there is probably a causal relationship from construct A to construct B, how generalizable is this relationship across persons, settings, and times? Crucial is the adequate definition of populations and samples.
For both internal and external validity the following rules hold true:
- Selecting in advance and selective mortality should be low.
- Not only the selection of subjects, but also that of settings, sampling intervals, etc. should be unbiased. For instance, sampling for companies may be more useful than sampling for subjects if the company climate has a strong standardizing effect upon its members.
- Accidental samples render the identification of the target population more difficult. However, that kind of bias is frequent not only with field-research, but also with laboratory experiments using volunteering students.
- If homogeneity cannot be secured, the next best thing to do is the sampling for deliberate heterogeneity, e. g. extreme populations.

3. METHODS

3.1. Design

The study is to be characterized as a quasi-experiment, i. e. a field-study with ex-post-facto design and one time of measurement. The basic design is shown in fig. 1.

3.2. Field of research, sectors, and methods

The field of research was defined after a comprehensive overview had been achieved, its sectors were fixed guided partly by theory and prior research, partly by plausibility. There were several constructs taken into account, and features were collected by more than one method.

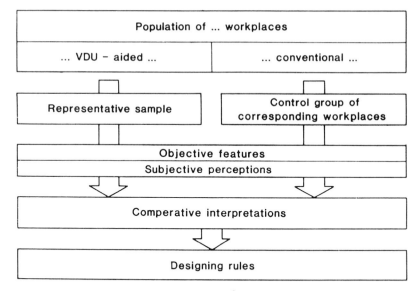

FIGURE 1
Basic design of the study

The research team consisted of an ergonomist and an occupational psychologist. The research task covered measurements and ergonomic judgements of
the workplaces and structured interviews with subjects. Judgements of software, organizational environment, and other sectors were based in part on
these interviews and used as quasi-objective data; from the FAA [8] and AET
[11] items were used in a modified form. A self-administering questionnaire
covered working conditions, occupational satisfaction, and indicators of
strain consisting in part of approved scales [5,7,10].

Some examples for theory-derived hypotheses are the following:
- Physical strain should refer to corresponding stress.
- Mental strain by information processing presumably depends on objective
  information load including factors like coding type, organization of dialogue, and failproofness; training may increase competences.
- Other stressors are time pressure, forced decisions, and other organizational conditions. Whether or not they produce strain, may depend on acceptance and motivation. Aspects of personality, like self-confidence, we
  did not ask for to avoid resistance.

3.3. Sampling and other issues

How is the sample to be characterized?
Target population are actual and potential users of VDU-aided workplaces.
Within reach for us were VDU-aided and corresponding conventional workplaces at Siemens, their representativity for - say - Germany remaining uncertain because of missing external statistical data.
Based on a survey classifying VDU workplaces roughly, experts choose representative sectors and departments considering hardware, location and organizational structure. The research sample consisted of 404 employees at VDU-
aided workplaces, the control group consisted of more than 50 subjects at
workplaces of similar activities without VDU's (fig. 2).

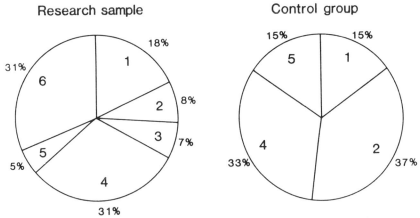

1   Entry of data
2   Text processing
3   Operating
4   Expert office work
5   Technical design
6   Programming

FIGURE 2
Types of workplaces

Operating and programming are found with VDU's exclusively but there is no hint the answering behaviour of the subjects would differ from other sub-groups. Thus, representativity and heterogeneity with regard to setting, type of workplace, and task is assured. No total correspondence could be achieved with demographic characteristics, e. g. age.

Small differences between research sample and controls make marked selection processes less probable. Thus the results of the study may be generalized to actual and future VDU users and settings.

There must not be any chance to identify individual employees or workplaces. Data are protected and will be destroyed afterwards. Information is given only in a more general form.

4. RESULTS AND DISCUSSION

4.1. VDU work duration

60 % of the VDU-users spend less than four hours a day at the VDU, about 1/4 more than six hours. Figure 3 shows unequal distributions of time spent at VDU's across types of workplaces. For long durations, an analysis of work sequences demonstrates visual contact with source documents to predominate contact with screen by far.

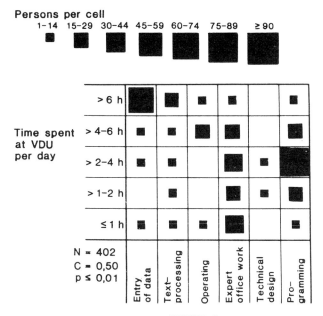

FIGURE 3
Time spent at VDU and type of workplace

4.2. Work design

Two examples for less favourable aspects: Reflections were intensive on one
third of the screens because of positioning. Only 24 % of the screens were
not dirty. Cleaning procedures in most cases are simple but unknown to
subjects.
At the time of the study, system bottlenecks and crashes were frequent. As
not fully satisfying the research team judged the participation of employees
in the implementation process.

In general, work design of VDU-aided workplaces was good and was better than
in the control group, VDU-typical problems unexistent there, naturally.

4.3. Subjective responses

Concerning general acceptance of modern office technology and VDU'S, answers were preponderantly clearly positive. Most subjects feel that VDU's
make work more easy. While experience with VDU's seems to lead to overwhelm-
ing acceptance, the control group, too, shows a clearly positive attitude.

Some design features were even judged more positive by the subjects than by
the research team. Criticism was made of reflections and dirty screens, i. e.
of objectively existing but removable disadvantages. Subjects feel that concentrated work is hindered by lacking chances to withdraw oneself.
Letting aside chances to participate in the design process, all other aspects of office design and work environment receive prevailingly positive
judgements.

The same is valid for performances and potentials of the VDU systems. Only
exceptions: System bottlenecks and crashes, response times, and participation
in designing the software.

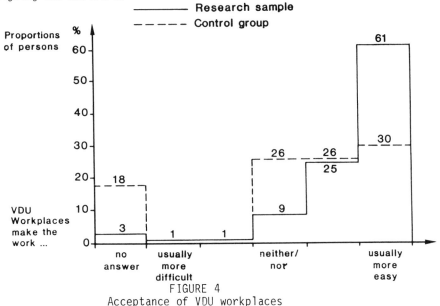

FIGURE 4
Acceptance of VDU workplaces

As usual, general work satisfaction shows a tendency skewed to the positive
end (fig. 5). VDU employees tend to be more satisfied than subjects at conventional workplaces. To check the hypothesis that this result is biased
by extreme satisfaction of a subsample, values of CAD subjects are drawn in
(N = 20). There is virtually no difference to the entire VDU sample.

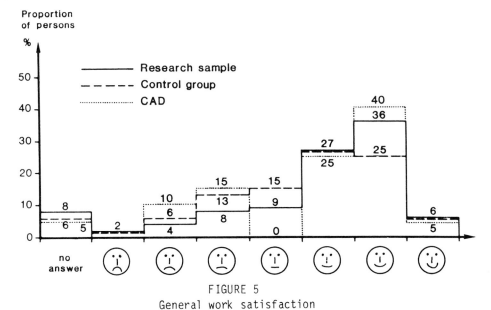

FIGURE 5
General work satisfaction

If VDU work was to lessen satisfaction, this effect should be stronger with longer durations of VDU work. However, the coefficient of contingency is not significant. Diverse items differentiating work satisfaction show this positive tendency, too. VDU employees in general tend to be slightly more satisfied.

Work satisfaction of the subjects in this study does not differ from other samples. For the SAZ-Kurzskala we found an average of 28.7 (N = 404), compared with FISCHER's [6] of 26.5 (N = 343), and for the KUNIN-scale our average is 4.76 while NEUBERGER and ALLERBECK [10] found 4.73 (N > 2000).

The subjective state of health for most aspects is quite good, a great majority of answers falling into the three favourable categories. We used a shortened version of the FBL [5] that asks for strain of eyes, muscular tension, and general psychosomatic symptoms like headache. Answering distributions of research sample and control group in most cases show a strong resemblance (e. g. fig. 6), with a slight tendency in favour of the VDU subjects. Complaints covary only slightly with time spent at the VDU.

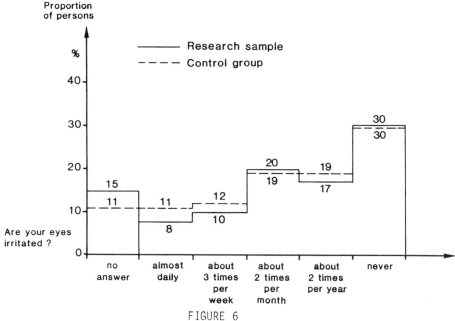

FIGURE 6
Irritation of eyes

These results should not be interpreted to the extent that VDU work causes negative effects. Those subjects who spend a long time at the VDU seldom look at the screen, their work sequences resembling that of conventional work, so distributions for this subsample and for controls should be expected to be similar.

FAHRENBERG [5] found an average of 167.37 for the sum of all items
(N = 330), in this study the average is 165.9 (adjusted for number of
items). Subjects at VDU-aided workplaces do not differ from other healthy
people in the their rating of health but differ from sick persons [9].

4.4. Summary

To sum up the results, no clearcut differences were found between employees
at VDU-aided workplaces and the control group or other standard populations.
If there are differences at all, they tend to be slightly in favour of the
research sample. There are no hints concerning special stresses resulting
from VDU work. Some weak points are found both by researchers and subjects
that require measures.

5. CONCLUSION

Methodically, heterogeneity has proved useful. While in most cases being
quite positive, responses to some items are slightly negative, proving the
potential of the questions to elicit sufficient variation. There is correspondence between objective and subjective features. Distributions of
subjective responses can be in part led back to objective features.

REFERENCES

[1]   Armbruster, A., Stand der Forschung zur Bildschirmarbeit, Humane
      Produktion 10 (1982) 14-16.
[2]   Benz, C., Grob, R., and Haubner, R., Gestaltung von Bildschirm-
      arbeitsplätzen (Köln, 1981).
[3]   Bischof, N., Aristoteles, Galilei, Kurt Lewin - und die Folgen,
      in: Michaelis, W. (ed.), Bericht über den 32. Kongreß der Deutschen
      Gesellschaft für Psychologie in Zürich 1980 (Göttingen, 1981).
[4]   Cook, T.D. and Campbell, D.T., Quasi-experimentation, design and
      analysis issues for field settings (Chicago, 1979).
[5]   Fahrenberg, J., Die Freiburger Beschwerdenliste, Zeitschrift für
      Klinische Psychologie 4 (1975).
[6]   Fischer, L., Normwerte der SAZ-Kurz (Universität Köln, Institut
      für Sozialpsychologie, 1982), not published.
[7]   Fischer, L., Lück, H.E., Entwicklung einer Skala zur Messung von
      Arbeitszufriedenheit, Psychologie und Praxis 16 (1972) 64-76.
[8]   Frieling, E. and Hoyos, C. Graf, Fragebogen zur Arbeitsanalyse
      (Bern, 1978).
[9]   Hampel, R. and Fahrenberg, J., Die Freiburger Beschwerdenliste FBL:
      Gruppenvergleiche und andere Studien zur Validität (Universität Frei-
      burg i. Br., Psychologisches Institut, 1982), not published.
[10] Neuberger, O. and Allerbeck, M., Messung und Analyse von Arbeits-
      zufriedenheit (Bern, 1978).
[11] Rohmert, W. and Landau, K., Das Arbeitswissenschaftliche Erhebungs-
      verfahren zur Tätigkeitsanalyse (Bern, 1979).

THE PSYCHOLOGY OF WORK AND ORGANIZATION
G. Debus and H.-W. Schroiff (Editors)
© Elsevier Science Publishers B.V. (North-Holland), 1986

ORGANIZATIONAL CLIMATE: ITS RELATIONSHIP WITH MANAGERIAL
ACTIVITIES AND COMMUNICATION STRUCTURES

Karel DE WITTE & Gaston DE COCK

Center for Organizational and Personnel Psychology,
University of Leuven/Louvain
102 Tiensestraat
B-3000 Leuven, Belgium

1. A HISTORICAL OVERVIEW OF THE RESEARCH ON ORGANIZATIONAL CLIMATE AT THE CENTER FOR ORGANIZATIONAL AND PERSONNEL PSYCHOLOGY

Since the start of the Center for Organizational and Personnel Psychology there has been a focus on organization development. French & Bell
define organization development as "a long-range effort to improve an
organization's problemsolving and renewal processes, particularly
through a more effective and collaborative management of organization
culture - with special emphasis on the culture of formal work team -
with the theory and technology of applied behavioral sciences, including
action-research" (1). It is in this research dirction that the research
on organizational climate started. We began with a translation and a
reconstruction of the Business Organizational Climate Index (BOCI) (2)
into Dutch. In a second phase we made an overview of all existing
questionnaires on organizational climate in order to construct a new
instrument. This instrument would serve to measure the organizational
climate in hospitals. Meanwhile in other research projects the correlation of organizational climate with other organizational variables was
studied. Furthermore, the developed instruments served in organization
development projects. Since the start of the project more than 15.000
questionnaires were administered, several seminars were organised and 15
reports on research projects are now available.

Notwithstanding this large and fruitful work, there remained some
serious problems in this research field. Guion stated that "the construct (or, perhaps, family of constructs) implied by the term organizational climate, may be one of the most important to enter the thinking
of industrial-organizational psychologists in many years" (3). The
reason herefore lies in the supposed relationship with other organizational variables. However if we take a look at the literature we see
that research on organizational climate is mostly limited to conceptual
clarification and measurement problems. Studies which go further
restrict themselves to the study of the relationship between organizational climate and performance/satisfaction. There is clearly a lack of
studies which make the link between organizational climate and other
studies on organizational theory, although this seems us to be the only
way organizational climate research could hold its promises. Another
problem connected with the first one has to do with the fact that we
have neglected to clarify our opinion about organizational effectiveness. Cameron's warning that "... the concept of effectiveness is
linked, at least implicitly, to almost all research on organizations"
(4) is not yet been heard. The research on organizational climate will
have to clarify what is meant by effectiveness to make real progress.
There are a lot of definitions about organizational climate in the
literature. But a clear description of how organizational climate fits

into organizational theories is seldom made. Because of this atheoreti-
cal research approach no real progress is made.

In the second paragraph we will give a definition of organizational
climate and describe its relationship with other organizational
variables.

2. DEFINITION OF ORGANIZATIONAL CLIMATE AND ITS RELATIONSHIP WITH OTHER ORGANIZATIONAL VARIABLES

2.1 Definition of organizational climate

Although we can find a lot of different definitions of organizational
climate, most of them share the same core items. We define organizational climate as "the synthetical perception of a relative stable set of
value-orientations of the organization as a whole, which influences the
behavior of the organizational members with respect to organizational
effectiveness and which are measured through a descriptive perception by
the members of the organization" (5). As in most definitions the content
of the characteristics or value-orientations is not specified. We will
come back to this point when we treat the measurement of organizational
climate.

2.2 Organizational climate and other organizational variables

The theoretical model mostly used to situate organizational climate is
that of Likert (6). Organizational climate is situated as an intervening
variable between causal variables as leadership, goal setting, decision
making, ... and end-result variables, performance and satisfaction
measures. This model implicitly refers to a linear way of reasoning.
This way of reasoning is also present in some definitions, where one
states that the organizational climate is mainly influenced by top level
management. In a research on top management (7) we couldn't find this
relationship. Moreover some top managers clearly stated that they follow
more the organizational climate they experience than that they influence
themselves the organizational climate in a certain direction. Most other
research projects are correlational studies which do not permit to make
causal statements. A more circular approach seems appropriate.

An elaboration of this formal description of the relationship of
organizational climate with other organizational variables is necessary.
This is the purpose of our research. Before reporting on this research
we need to explain how we measure organizational climate.

3. THE MEASUREMENT OF ORGANIZATIONAL CLIMATE

A questionnaire for profit organizations was developed as well as one
for hospitals. As said above we situate the organizational climate
research in the perspective of organization development. Porras & Berg
(8) state: "Up to this point, the primary technique for collecting
quantified data on organizational processes has been through the use of
questionnaires. We all know the biases in this method of data
collection, yet we continue using it for a wide variety of reasons:
questionnaires are relatively easy to administer; are economical; the
resulting data are less hassle to analyse; a large number of instruments

are available or new ones relatively easy to develop; ... ." The same reasons influenced us to choose a questionnaire. We wanted an instrument that not only could serve for research purposes, but that would also be useful for practitioners.

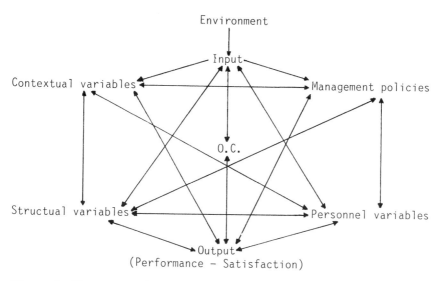

Figure 1: The proposed model of organizational climate

As our research took place in hospitals we will only explain the construction of the questionnaire for hospitals.

We started with an overview of all the existing questionnaires on organizational climate. From this overview we got 45 categories of possible subscales. As this number was too large, we reduced it to 18 categories. These were presented to practitioners in hospitals to test the relevance of those categories. Two new categories were added. For these 20 categories 96 existing or new items were formulated. This formed our preliminary questionnaire, which was tested in two phases. The result was a questionnaire of 27 items, split up into two subscales. The composition of the subscales is based on several factor analyses and on an overview of the literature concerning the core dimensions of organizational climate. We also tried to relate these dimensions to organizational theories. The two core dimensions which we found are at the one hand control and on the other hand organizational dynamism. Those two dimensions are basic discussion points within organizational theories.

On the basis of these two dimensions we get four categories (see figure 2, next page)

At this moment we took the option not to give a specific name to the four different quadrants. There were two reasons. First of all such names have a high level of abstraction so it may easily lead to misinterpretations. Secondly, it is very difficult to find neutral names. Most names that we could borrow from the literature have a positive or negative connotation. Therefore in this phase of the research working with the names of the subscales seemd more appropriate.

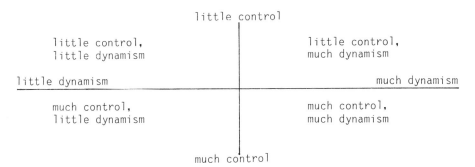

Figure 2: Preliminary framework for organizational climate

4. THE RESEARCH DESIGN

The purpose of the research was to investigate whether hospitals with a
different organizational climate would be characterised by different
organizational processes. We looked, in the line of action-research, for
variables which could be influenced by the organizational members. In
this article we will deal with the two main variables, namely the managerial activities and the communication structures.

4.1 Managerial activities

Our aim was to gather data on the management or leadership style and
activities. As Hunt & Osborn (9) remarked, leadership studies concentrated more at a group than at an organizational level and more on the
style (HOW) than on the activities (WHAT). Other researchers like
Stewart and Kotter (10) followed another approach. They carried out
their research starting from a lot of data about the activities of
managers. This approach seemed more promising for the organizational
climate research. In our study the whole management team was asked to
take note of the time consumed by their activities during fourteen days.
This was new since all other studies looked at the activities of individual managers.

The purpose of this part is to see if managers of hospitals with a
different organizational climate have different activities which are
related to organizational climate.

4.2 Communication structures

In hospitals coordination is one of the core problems. Coordination
takes place through communication patterns, which are partly formalized
in communication structures. We asked the hospitals to make an overview
of all the existing formal organizational communication and information
channels.
The purpose of this part is to investigate the relationship between the
organizational climate and the communication structures.

4.3 Organizational climate

For the measurement of the organizational climate we make use of our questionnaire. To avoid problems of representativeness we asked the hospitals to administer the questionnaire on a full scale basis. They agreed.

4.4 Selection of the hospitals

For this project, which is quite demanding, we solicited the cooperation of 15 hospitals which were already involved in earlier phases of this research program. Nine of them were willing to deliver the different data we asked for.

5. RESULTS

5.1 Data basis and evaluation

We received the following data:
- 2.302 questionnaires of organizational climate;
- a list of the activities of 36 managers during 14 days forming a total of 326 pages;
- 162 regular meetings and 51 information-channels were reported.

In a first phase we will situate the 9 hospitals within the four quadrants of our preliminary framework of organizational climate.

In the second phase a strategy of "direct" research as formulated by Mintzberg (11) was used. For such an inductional method there are two steps: a first one is an inspection of the data to discover patterns of similarity or dissimilarity and a second step is an effort towards the development of a model. Our ultimate goal is to formulate a provisional model about organizational effectiveness starting from the relationship between organizational climate and the other organizational variables.

Taking into account this research strategy, the data which we want to use for the development of our provisional model must meet the following criteria:
- there have to be differences between the hospitals for the managerial activities and the communication structures;
- those differences have to be parallel with the differences in organizational climate;
- those founded parallels must be possible to be explained in a meaningful way towards a model.

5.2 Organizational climate

On the basis of the results from the questionnaires we situate the 9 hospitals in the different quadrants of our preliminary framework. In all four quadrants there was at least one hospital.

In the quadrant of much dynamism, much control there is only one hospital. In the other quadrants we have three or two hospitals. Those results were presented to the different hospitals and they were asked if they could agree with our diagnosis. During those meetings many anecdotes were mentioned to illustrate their organizational climate. All hospitals agreed with our diagnosis.

5.3   Relationship between organizational climate and organizational
      processes

In the following scheme the main characteristics of the four types of
organizational climate are presented.

Table 1: Synthesis of the main results

Variable	Little dynamism, little control	much dynamism, little control	much dynamism, much control	little dynamism, much control
Managerial activities	informal, few meetings	wandering around	give directives	alone, own office
Communication form	oral	oral and written	oral, directives	written
direction	upwards	all directions	downwards	upwards and downwards
Structure	informal	network	unclear, dependent on status of persons	hierarchy
Leadership	relation-oriented	task + relation	task-oriented	procedure-oriented

6.   TOWARDS A MODEL OF ORGANIZATIONAL EFFECTIVENESS

Our research results lead to four types of organizational climate and
the relation with communication structures and managerial activities.
Other authors like Handy (12) and Harrison (13) also come up with four
types of organizational culture or organizational character. These typologies show resemblences with the four types we found. However there is
no research about these typologies. Nevertheless they may help for
developing a model.

We find more support for our results in the work done by Quinn (14). He
asked organizational theorists to order a list of effectiveness
criteria. On the basis of this research he proposed three basic dimensions of effectiveness. He summarised them in three dichotomies. The
first is concerned with the orientation towards people in the organization against the orientation towards the organization as a whole. The
second is related to flexibility against control. These two factors show
resemblance with our two factors, although ours are not bipolar. Further
research must demonstrate if our negative poles may be compared with the
positive name that Quinn is giving. A third dimension Quinn mentions is
the time horizon (nearby or distant). This dimension does not show up
from our research.

The four fields of the Quinn research are combined by himself with
organizational theories, namely the human relations model; the open
systems model; the bureaucratic model and the rational goal model. In
the following scheme we combine our research results with the findings
from Quinn.

Table 2: A provisional model of organizational effectiveness

	Organization theory			
	Human relations	Open system	Rational goal	Bureaucracy
	Organizational climate			
Own dimensions	little dynamism, little control	much dynamism, little control	much dynamism, much control	little dynamism, much control
Harrison character	person-oriented	task-oriented	power-oriented	role-oriented
Handy's God	Dionysus, indivi-dualist	Artemis, chase	Zeus, omnipotent	Apollo, rationality
	Output			
Criterium for effectiveness	Are human relations developed?	Are new needs discovered and fulfilled?	Are there goals and are they realized?	Are the procedures followed?
	person-oriented	organization-oriented	organiza-tion-orien-ted	person-oriented
	flexibility	flexibility	control	control
Danger	Club	Chaos	Narrow scope	Rigidity
	Structure			
Communication form	oral	oral + written	oral, directives	written
direction	upwards	all directions	downwards	upwards and downwards
Structure itself	cluster, informal	matrix, network	web, unclear	tempel, hierarchy
Authority	more decentralisation of authority			clearly defined
	Policies			
Activities	informal, few meetings	wandering around	give directives	alone and in own office
Leadership	relation-oriented	task + relation	task-oriented	procedure-oriented
Reddin's style	relation	integration	dedication	separation
	Personnel variables			
Number of personnel			less personnel per bed in general hospitals	
		more personnel per bed in psychiatric hospitals		
Seniority	has influence	no influence	has influence	no influence

(continued next page)

	Contextual variables
Size	larger hospitals (psychiatric)
Length of stay	shorter stay (general)

In this provisional model we see how a number of elements from organizational psychology and organizational theory come together to a more coherent whole. Until now there were a lot of theories about different aspects. Now those different theories are integrated in one overall model. Whether all parts are already at their right place will need further research and the model can certainly be completed. But this approach seems to have a lot of possibilities. The organizational climate research has always promised to realize a more global and integrated approach of organizations. In this way the organizational climate research tries to fulfil the promises.

7. CONCLUSION

Starting from the research on the relationship between organizational climate and managerial activities and communication structures we developed a provisional model of organizational effectiveness.

The further development of this model is important both from a theoretical point of view as well as from a practical perspective. From this model we may formulate hypotheses which may be tested in coming research projects. This is already done at our center. In practice it is generally accepted that the success of management methods depends on the organizational climate. For instance, management by objectives may be easily introduced within a goal oriented climate, while in the other types of climate a complete turnaround of the climate is necessary for the successful introduction of this management method. The model and the instruments we developed permit the practitioner to make a diagnosis which may predict the chances for the introduction of new methods of management, personnel policies, ... At last the model gives an indication in which direction organizational variables must be changed in order to realize the desired organizational effectiveness and organizational climate.

REFERENCES

(1) French, W. & Bell, C.: Organizational development. New Jersey, Prentice-Hall, 1973, 15.
(2) Payne, R. & Pheysey, D.: G.G. Stern's Organizational Climate Index: a reconceptualization and application to business organizations. Organizational Behavior & Human Performance, 1971, 6, 77-98.
(3) Guion, R.M.: A note on organizational climate. Organizational Behavior and Human Performance, 1973, 9, 120-125, 120.
(4) Cameron, K.: Construct space and subjectivity problems in organizational effectiveness. Public Productivity Review, 1981, 105-121, 105.

(5) De Witte, K.: Organisatieklimaat in ziekenhuizen. Studie over het verband van organisatieklimaat met het funktioneren van direkties en de overlegsstrukturen. Unpublished doctoral dissertation (Promotor: Prof. G. De Cock), Faculty of Psychology and Pedagogical Sciences, K.U. Leuven, 1985, 32–33.

(6) Likert, R.: The human organization. New York, McGraw–Hill, 1967, 137.

(7) Gypen, J. & Schiepers, M.: In de directeursstoel: een exploratieve studie in organisatiegedrag. Onderzoeksrapport Centrum voor Organisatie- en Personeelpsychologie en Stichting Industrie-Unversiteit, 1984.

(8) Porras, J.I. & Berg, P.O.: Evaluation methodology in organization development: an analysis and critique. Research paper 336, Graduate School of Business, Stanford University, 30.

(9) Hunt, J.G. & Osborn, R.N.: Towards a macro oriented model of leadership: an odyssea, In: Hunt, J.G., Sekaran, V. & Schriesheim, C.A. (Eds.), Leadership: beyond establishment views. Carbondale, Southern Illinois University Press, 1982.

(10) Stewart, R.: A model for understanding managerial jobs and behavior. Academy of Management Review, 1982, 7, 7–13.
Kotter, J.P.: The general manager, New York, Free Press, 1982.

(11) Mintzberg, H.: An emerging strategy of "direct" research. Administrative Science Quarterly, 1979, 24, 582–598.

(12) Handy, C.B.: Understanding organizations. Hammondsworth, Penguin Bocks, 1981, 25–41.

(13) Harrison, R.: Understanding your organization's character. Harvard Business Review, May–June 1972, 119–128.

(14) Quinn, R.E. & Rohrbaugh, J.: A competing value approach to organizational effectiveness. Public Productivity Review, 1981, 5, 122–140.

II.4. Personnel Selection, Career Planning and Development

THE PSYCHOLOGY OF WORK AND ORGANIZATION
G. Debus and H.-W. Schroiff (Editors)
© Elsevier Science Publishers B.V. (North-Holland), 1986

ADVANCED TESTING STRATEGIES AND RESPECTIVE ITEM REQUIREMENTS

FOR PERSONNEL SELECTION

Lutz F. Hornke

1. INTRODUCTION

Assessment procedures in personnel selection often do suffer from two closely related problems. One may be identified with the way tests are administered and the other centers around the way tests are constructed. To address the first, one is often caught by the experimental paradigm which demands that tests are administered in just that fashion in which they were developped. This asks for adhering to strict time limits and to item order in the test booklet. However, it seems awkward to administer very easy items to high performing testees just because the test booklet contains them at the beginning and they do fall in anybody's test time limit. Leaving them out and adding some bonus constant would do as well, but less testing time is wasted and testing stress might be reduced, too. The same argument holds for low performing testees. Only those testees in the middle of the scale range will have to be mildly bothered with items too easy and too hard for them. The harder ones will represent a true challenge in some cases at the risk of some easy filler items. Again, some harder items may not even be attempted by average testees because of too rigid time limits. On the whole present test programs ought to be blamed for being suboptimal. They are geared towards an average member of the population as far as difficulty ranges and time limits are concerned. However, they fall short of arriving at valid and reliable differential information in that they deemphasize low and high performing applicants.

Test application, consequently, ought to be able to challenge any testee at any level of the ability or trait in question. This can be achieved by flexible test administration strategies. They are discussed under the headings of "sequential" testing, "adaptive" testing, "tailored" testing or the like. This contribution will demonstrate basic ideas of such testing strategies and discuss necessary item construction rationales for them.

2. TESTING STRATEGIES

Two different approaches are discussed in the literature. One is called "sequential" testing and the other "adaptive / tailored" testing. They will be described here in some detail.

2.1 "Sequential" Testing

This approach follows closely an idea in sampling techniques -or better sequential t-tests- where information is gathered as long as no decision whether to reject or accept -respective hypotheses- regarding type I and type II errors is possible. For testing programs this would mean that a testee will be presented one item after the other until a "reject" or "accept" decision is warranted. The number of items does vary from testee to testee, and testing is a more or less lengthy item sampling process.

SPRT (p_2=.6, p_1=.2 ; alpha=.05, beta=.1)
$\underline{u}_i$ = {010001000}; m_i=9, r_i=2, f_i=7

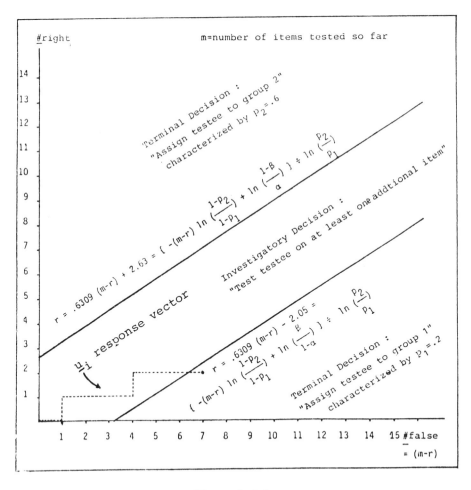

Figure 1 (a)
True Sequential Probability Ratio Format

The advantage of this approach is quite obvious: testees with low or high
performance levels will be discovered after but a few items and testing
is ended then. Only those testees in the middle of the ability range do
have to take quite a few number of items before a final decision can be
made. This might be regarded as "fair" since low performers experience
their failure rate, high performers experience their success rate, and
mid performers might want to have another chance, thus lengthening their
test program. However, in order not to overdo a good thing and finally
end up taking item after item the theoretically open ended sequential
program was cut short, i.e. "curtailed". However, loss of prespecified
decision risks will result, but it remains a theoretical and an empirical
question to evaluate how many testees in an applicant population are hit.
(Figure 1a and 1b represent two sequential approaches)

$$(\; p_1=.4, \; p_2=.775; \; \alpha=.01, \; \beta=.001)$$

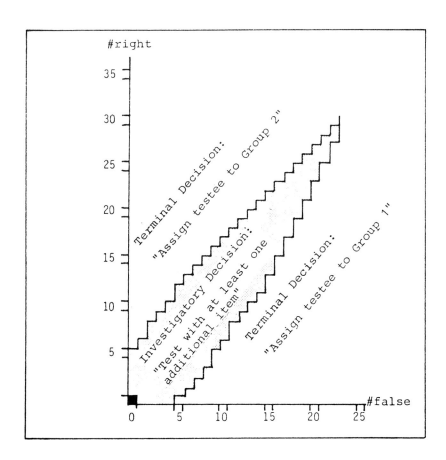

Figure 1 (b)
Curtailed sequential testing format
For details see Hornke, 1982, p. 151(a) and p. 149(b)

It ought to have become clear that sequential testing optimizes testing by administering to any testee as many items as are needed to warrant a final decision considering type I and type II decision errors. For a testee within the "can't decide"-region the consequence is quite clear: he and his personnel psychologist will have to suffer from additional items to be taken. Test time limits do not make any sense! The number of items defines a random variable itself. On the average anyone will gain from this approach since low and high performing testees are screened out rather soon.

2.2 Adaptive Testing

The sequential testing approach optimized "number of items" but disregarded the quality of any item. Quality might mean here the level of difficulty or the trait level represented by the item in question. One might think of an optimal strategy of presenting items that are as close as possible to the testee's trait level, performance level, ability level, or the like. Thus item parameter and person parameter are points on a common psychologically meaningful scale. Accordingly, a testee is tested on an item that minimizes the item/person-parameter distance. Testing then is highly individualized since anyone gets just that subset of items that represents his level of the trait in question. One might achieve this by intelligently retrieving items from a large bank in regard to item quality, i.e. degree of trait relatedness. Hence, item numbers can be held variable, too, by resorting to confidence intervals depending on the degree of information obtained from any individual response vector.

In this respect using optimal items (quality- and quantitywise) to obtain a small confidence interval, i.e. test reliability, makes adaptive testing a very flexible strategy. Due to these facets it clearly optimizes an overall personnel decision strategy where reliability is an issue that has to be settled beforehand and made to conform with an organization's value system.

Adaptation may be achieved differently. One way might be to organize similar items in blocks or kind of graded subtests. A testee is started with the first item of the middle block and any response gets evaluated on the spot. Depending on his answer he is shifted one block up for a correct response and one block down for an incorrect response. After a while he ought to zigzag between to adjacent blocks thus indicating his ability level. A stopping rule might be defined to end testing. (cf Weiss, 1973, Stradaptive Testing; Hornke & Nauels, 1979, Pyramidal Testing). This testing format will work fine on computers. Here item responses are evaluated immediately and item retrieval from blocks is easy to program. However, paper-pencil-versions are possible, too, using instructions like "go to next unused item of block #" printed in invisible ink as response. The testee just overstrikes the number-to-go-to-section with a special pen which renders invisible print visible (Hornke & Sauter, 1981).

However, to make full use of item parameter information a very flexible strategy might profit from intermediate person parameter estimates. This means that after any item the entire response vector is reanalyzed to yield an intermediate person parameter estimate. The latter is taken to

find the next -presumably best- suited item within the bank by searching
for the smallest difference between person -intermediate- estimate and
item parameter. This item will contribute most to what is already known
about the testee in question, i.e. reduce measurement error. As simple as
it sounds the entire optimization is quite complex and depends heavily on
the underlying measurement model. 2- or 3-parameter logistic models (cf.
Lord, 1980; Weiss, 1976; Hornke, 1976) were used. It became quite obvious
that in order to have a fully satisfying adaptive test quite a large
number of items is necessary. Where there are only few items there are
not many degrees of freedom to sample from when measurement in the extremes is of interest. Too small an item set will be exhausted after but
a few items tested. Additional items might not yield reasonably small
item parameter person estimate differences that justify their presentation. (Figure 2 displays the latter dilemma)

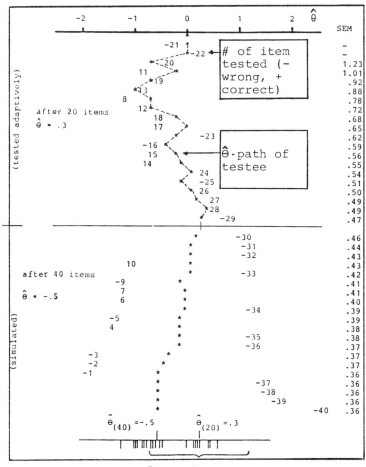

Figure 2
Dangers of retrieving less and less informative items
(from Hornke, 1983, p. 329)

The requirements of an adaptive testing strategy are twofold: (1) it will be best managed by means of a computer programmed to evaluate a testee's intermediate record in the light of maximum-likelihood estimation procedures and retrieve items according to person parameter estimates, (2) it presupposes a reasonably sized set of homogeneous items to draw from. The first requirement is easy to meet since today's Personal Computers are fast enough to handle programs well. However, some intelligence has to be invested into the program as such to cut short otherwise exhaustive computing and item retrieving times.

The requirements for a useful item set are by far harder to meet. "Homogeneous" items are called for since person standing and item location are necessarily interchangeable concepts. Test interpretation ought to be done in terms of item demand and not in terms of percent of persons passing. It is the item content that defines test score interpretation. This was clearly recognized by Klauer (1984) who stressed content validity recently. However, to obtain a fairly large number of homogeneous items item writing rules might help and are discussed in the next chapter.

3. ITEM REQUIREMENTS / ITEM WRITING

"In test making one moves back and forth in continuous interaction: clarifying the definitions of an attribute as one undertakes to develop assessment procedures and modifying assessment procedures as one's conceptions of the attribute is clarified. Of course, the conception of an attribute emerges not simply from a single test maker's thinking but rather from the whole history of research dealing with the construct in question", (Thorndike, 1982, 15). This fine statement, however, lacks quite a bit of clarity that will enable any psychologist to sit down at his desk an write a test for his organization's needs. For the sake of the argument let the Thorndikian notion be challenged. It is true, that there is a historical dimension in test making, but it ought to be one of a useful kind. Here it is stressed that close inspection of previous test making attempts and even results from previous research will yield a set of rules by means of which any -psychological- expert ought to be able to design a new test. This test then will be theory oriented because of the item writing rules set forth. Many published tests might not be of this kind because idiosyncratic item writing approaches were used. All too often numbers took over in item assembly as results of item analysis. Test makers forgot all too often about the back and forth movement and above all about the clarification of the construct in question Thorndike is talking about (see above). They put items together, tried them out on a fair number of guinea pig testees, and let item statistics decide about the final test. Shouldn't it be the other way around? Item writers sit down to explore the trait of interest and then put down a miniature theory of trait-kernels. From their intelligent combination it ought to be possible to design rules and write rule based items which closely relate to the theory established. Any item response then can be traced back to the trait-kernels and testee behaviour interpreted likewise. Also it ought to be possible to write a large set of items using trait kernel combinations whatsoever.

This loosely described idea led to an attempt to write a large set (quantity argument above) of items for use with computerized adaptive testing. A broad range of difficulties was sought by combining aspects (quality argument above) that were known from the literature. The item type happened to be of the matrix format.

In matrix type items there are circles, squares, triangles, etc. which are shaded, or left blank. They are organized in columns, rows, or just vary across patterns. One item had circles, squares, and triangles organized rowwise but had the figures filled with dots, hatches, and texture columnwise. (See figure 3).

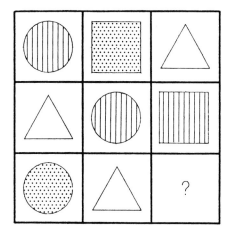

Figure 3
Sample Matrix Type Item

Here two different design rules were used independently, one for figures and the other for "paint". If one were to design a "figure item" and a "paint item" separately each of them ought to be easier than their combination. On part of the testee it is this additional mental labour to pull things apart and systematize them that will make a composit harder. Item solving is just the reverse of item writing, namely finding rules instead of applying rules. So the rule for the item presented in figure 3 would read : "Choose SHAPEs (three different ones --- from a set of shapes) and organize them in SERIEs (one scheme --- from a set of organizing schemata) of three ROWWISE (one direction --- from a set of directions), choose PAINTS (dots, hatches, blank in this case), and organize them in SERIEs of three COLUMNWISE". Using other regular geometric forms or other paints should not make any difference as far as mental demand is concerned.

Attributes as described above were put together for item construction and it seems plausible to use a measurement model that uses this kind of addition as well. The linear logistic test model seems to be appropriate in this case. Here one has one parameter for person ability, θ, and a sum of parameters which represents the items intellectual demand, So. The probability of a correct response to an item may then be written as:

$$P(+) = 1 \: / \: (\: \exp \: (\: \theta - \Sigma o \:) \:)$$

It is the So that represents the difficulty or intellectual demand of an item, hence it is quite obvious that one will want to arrive at item writing rules by specifying what someone has to put together. Each individual feature of an item or cognitive operation to be used in solving

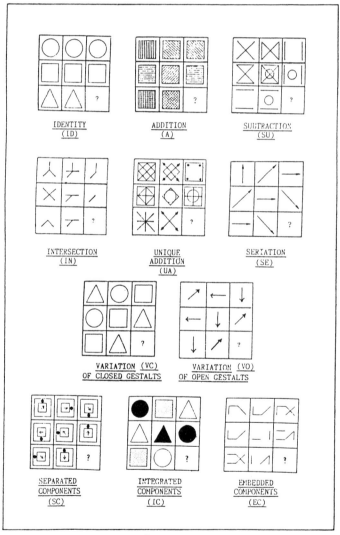

Figure 4
Set of cognitive operations to be used in item construction

it, so to speak, Σo, is thought to contribute to an item's overall difficulty. However, previous studies by Formann (1979), Nährer (1980), or Habon (1981) either used too few operations or two few items to fully explore possible advantages of rule based item construction. A close look through the cognitive research literature dealing with matrix type items led to the following rules:

"(1) Eight rules to compose item features are defined (identity, addition, subtraction, intersection, unique addition, seriation, variation of open gestalts, variation of closed gestalts – exemplified in one component items in figure 4 (Further details see Hornke & Habon, 1984) (For analogy items Hornke, Habon & Mispelkamp, 1984, put similar rules together).

"(2) Single item components may be separated, integrated, or embedded. Here separation means that the two components are clearly discernible, whereas in integration the distinction is achieved by using different component dimensions like shape for one and paint for the other. However, embedded components do require additional mental search operations as to which part of a gestalt might be one or the other component following its own rule. (see lower part of figure 4)   ·

"(3) Relations might hold rowwise, columnwise, or row- as well as columnwise. (See upper part of figure 4, example 1 for rowwise, example 2 for columnwise, and example 3 for row- as well as columnwise).

An item "population" of 648 items would result if one were to use any combination of the above mentioned rules for two component items. However, 32 combinations were impossible to realize due to "identity". A set of 616 items was drawn, distributed in a systematic fashion across 35 test booklets, and administered in a multiple matrix like design to about 7400 recruits of the German Armed Forces. On the average each item was worked on by 7400/35 testees. (For design details see Hornke & Habon, 1984).

Results show that some items did not comply to the homogeneity assumptions for various reasons. One reason being printing flaws, another one had to deal with testees or test administrators not following instructions. After discarding 360 testees for obvious forging behaviour a total of 134 items were found to be inhomogeneous. A close inspection of item content revealed that various sources could be identified which led probably to inhomogeneity (see. figure 5).

However, "Subtraction", was realized as "row 1 minus row 2" and "row 2 minus row 1", yielding virtually two subtraction rules instead of one. The problem here is to find the proper minuend in relation to outcome. Hence "Subtraction" is merely two rules. Dropping items using the second rule finally yielded an entire set of 446 homogeneous items. Decomposing their overall difficulty estimates into operation contributions led to the following distribution: (see Figure 6).

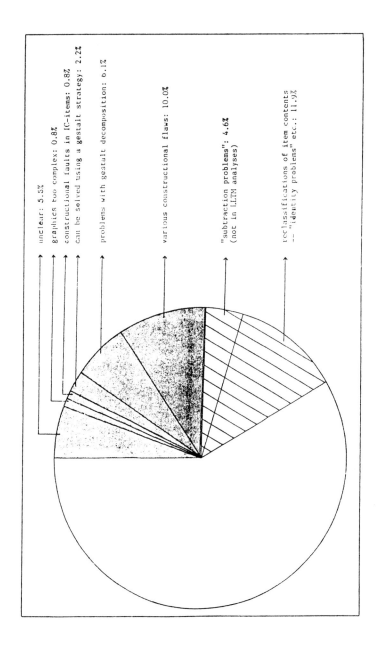

Figure 5
Relation of homogeneous to inhomogeneous items

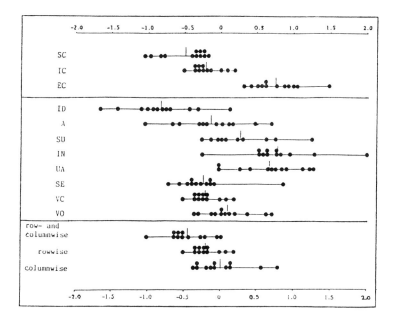

Figure 6
Distribution of operation parameter estimates within test subsets

From the dense cluster on some operations it can be seen that operation parameters were estimated quite satisfactorily. Their mean can be regarded as generalizable contribution to item difficulty. – "Intersection", however, reveals that instead of 60 items constructed only 27 were left over after person and item deletion.

Thus the number of data points from which to estimate operation contributions is quite unfavourable and will explain the larger variance here. However, overall about 40% of the item difficulty variance is explained by cognitive operations used in item construction. This is just a lower bound of what was achieved in writing items according to prespecified rules. Whether this is large or small is an open question and awaits competing studies using different rule based item writing approaches. However, it seems quite an acceptable figure since all individualized testing strategies mentioned above will profit from the large number of homogeneous items at hand. Whether automatized item writing is warranted using specified operations and the corresponding set of parameters from this study is worth an investigation. Newly written items then ought to yield difficulty indices quite close to their estimates using the o's from this study as So. If that were the case to a reasonable degree one might consider personnel testing programs where items are presented that are assembled from operation parameters only without prior (statistical) item analysis.

Test results do require that item embedded operations are valid, i.e. have something to do with the trait or criterion to measure. Synthetical tests as such will be "operation valid" or "content valid" in the proper sense. Test, psychological theory, and personnel decision criterion are linked together in testable manner. This represents the major yet futuristic message of rule based item writing.

4. CONCLUSION

Psychological testing for personnel selection or evaluation suffers from unreasonable restrictions which stem from all-purpose tests. To overcome these drawbacks in any individual case a flexible test presentation and evaluation scheme seems to be called for. However, all strategies discussed above and in the literature demand a fair number of homogeneous items. To achieve this by well grounded item writing rules might be seen as a fruitful step.

5. BIBLIOGRAPHY

Formann, A.K., Die Konstruktion eines neuen Matrizentests und die Untersuchung des Lösungsverhaltens mit Hilfe des Linearen Logistischen Testmodells. (Unveröffentl. Diss., Univ. Wien, 1979)

Habon, M.W., Sprachfreie Tests in der pädagogischen Diagnostik: Regelgeleitete Aufgabenkonstruktion durch formale Modelle (Unveröffentlichte Diplomarbeit, Universität Marburg 1981)

Hornke, L.F., Grundlagen und Probleme antwortabhängiger Testverfahren (Haag + Herrchen, Frankfurt, 1976)

Hornke, L.F. Testdiagnostische Untersuchungsstrategien. In: Groffmann, K.J. & Michel, L. (Hg.), Enzyklopädie der Psychologie, Band 2: Grundlagen psychologischer Diagnostik (pp. 130-172). (Hogrefe, Göttingen, 1982)

Hornke, L.F., Computerunterstütztes Testen – Eine bewertende empirische Untersuchung, Zeitschrift für Differentielle und Diagnostische Psychologie 4 (1983) 323-344

Hornke, L.F. & Habon, M.H., Erfahrungen zur rationalen Konstruktion von Testaufgaben. Zeitschrift für Differentielle und Diagnostische Psychologie 3 (1984) 203-212

Hornke, L.F. & Habon, M.H., Regelgeleitete Konstruktion und Evaluation von nichtverbalen Denkaufgaben (Wehrpsychologische Untersuchungen, Heft 4, 1984)

Hornke, L.F. & Habon, M.W., Evaluation einer rationalen Itemkonstruktion. In: OLECHOWSKI, R. (Hrsg.): Braunschweiger Studien zur Erziehungs- und Sozialwissenschaft, Bd. 10 (Braunschweig, 1983)

Hornke, L.F., Habon, M.W. & Mispelkamp, H.B., Verbale Analogien als

Aufgabe für eine rationale Itemkonstruktion. (Wehrpsychologische Arbeitsberichte, Nr. AL-4-84, 1984)

Hornke, L.F. & Sauter, M.P., Adaptives Testen im Englischunterricht – empirische Untersuchungen zur diskriminanten und konvergenten Validität eines adaptiven Leseverständnistests, Anglistik und Englischunterricht 2 (1981) 147-162

Hornke, L.F. & Nauels, H.-U., Adaptive Verkürzung eines Eignungsdiagnostikums in der Berufsberatung, Diagnostica 25 (1979) 287-298

Klauer, K.J., Kontentvalidität. Diagnostica 30 (1984) 1-23

Lord, F.M., Applications of item response theory to practical testing problems (Lawrence Erlbaum, Hillsdale, N.J., 1980)

Nährer, W., Zur Analyse von Matrizenaufgaben mit dem linearen logistischen Testmodell. Zeitschrift für experimentelle und angewandte Psychologie 27 (1980) 554-564

Thorndike, R.L., Test theory and test construction, Applied Psychometrics (Houghton and Mifflin, Dallas, 1982)

Weiss, D.J., Computerized ability testing: 1972-1975. (Final report. Department of Psychology, University of Minnesota, Research Report Final, 1976)

Weiss, D.J., 1973, The stratified computerized ability test. (Department of Psychology, University of Minnesota, Research Report 73-3)

THE PSYCHOLOGY OF WORK AND ORGANIZATION
G. Debus and H.-W. Schroiff (Editors)
© Elsevier Science Publishers B.V. (North-Holland), 1986

ASSESSING MANAGERIAL POTENTIAL

Ivan T. Robertson

University of Manchester Institute of Science and Technology,
U.K.

Abstract

This paper provides a review of research concerning the validity of various
methods for assessing management potential. A gap between research and
practice is identified and future research needs are proposed.

1.   CURRENT RESEARCH AND PRACTICE

Managerial selection is a topic of considerable interest to both
researchers and practitioners within occupational psychology, and it is
interesting to examine the extent to which current research and practice
correspond.

As far as research is concerned Schmitt et al (1984) surveyed all personnel
selection validity studies published in the Journal of Applied Psychology
and Personnel Psychology between 1964-82. Their data indicate the number
of validity coefficients for managers using various specific predictors.

Table 1. Validity studies from Personnel Psychology and Journal of
Applied Psychology 1964-1982 (From Schmitt et al 1984).

Predictor	No. of Validities*
Biodata	4
Assessment Centres	15
Personality	17
Cognitive tests	22
Supervisory/Peer Assessment	24
Work Sample	3

*Based on averages across independent samples

From the point of view of usage, Robertson and Makin (In Press) have
conducted a survey of the use of predictors for management selection in a
sample of UK organizations.

Table 2.   Usage of predictors for management selection in a sample of
           UK organizations.

	Usage % Never	% Less than 1/2 of Applicants	% 1/2 of Applicants	% More than 1/2	% Always
Interviews	1.0	9.8	4.9	2.0	81.4
References	3.7	14.0	2.8	11.2	67.3
Cognitive tests	70.8	19.8	3.1	1.0	5.2
Personality	64.4	23.8	3.0	5.0	4.0
Assessment					
Centre	78.6	14.6	4.9	1.9	–
Biodata	94.2	2.9	1.0	–	1.9

Comparing research with practice is often a salutary experience – and
proves to be so in this case. References and interviews, are extremely
popular with practitioners. Researchers appear to have almost entirely
ignored references (see Muchinsky 1979) and demonstrated time and time
again that interviews are very poor selection instruments (e.g. Reilly &
Chao 1982). It is only in the use of Assessment centres that research and
practitioner interests seem to coincide. A UK survey in 1973 (Gill,
Ungerson and Thakur) reported 7% usage of assessment centres. Bridges
(1984) in a survey designed specifically to examine assessment centres
found usage of 19% in the UK with 65% of user organizations having begun to
use assessment centres on the last 5 years.

2.   VALIDITY OF PREDICTORS

I should like to suggest a classification system for predictors based on
the principle that future work behaviour is based on three factors: Past
behaviour of the person, current behaviour and personal attributes and
expectancies concerning future behaviour.

2.1.   Predictors based on the past

Predictors focussing on the individual's past are Biographical data,
References and Supervisory/Peer evaluations.

2.1.1. References

The validities reported for references are based on a relatively small
number of studies. Reviews by Muchinsky (1979) and Reilly and Chao (1982)
reveal low average validities of .13 and .18 respectively. In a recent
meta-analysis study Hunter and Hunter (1984) calculated a mean coefficient
for reference checks, against supervisory rating criteria of .26.

2.1.2. Biodata

In general biodata has produced consistently good prediction. Reilly and Chao (1982) examined 58 studies using biodata and report an overall average validity of .35. Schmitt et al (1984) report an average overall validity of .24 and Hunter and Hunter report mean validities varying from .26 to .37 against various criteria. Asher (1972) compared the predictive power of biodata with other predictors, revealing that biodata compares very favourably.

As far as managers are concerned Korman (1968) showed that the validity of biodata for predicting managerial performance was generally lower than for other measures such as peer ratings. Reilly and Chao (1982) however calculate an average validity for managerial jobs of .38 and this is very similar to Schmitt et al's calculation of an overall validity of .34 averaged across all predictors for managerial groups. In practice the number of studies using biodata on managerial groups is quite small. (Reilly and Chao for example identified only 7 coefficients for biodata with managerial groups). Recent work in the UK (Savage, 1985) should provide further evidence for managerial groups.

For all occupational groups the best predictive validity for biodata (.53) is obtained for salary (Schmitt et al 1984).

Much of the reported work on biodata is based on the work of Owens (1976) although other approaches have been developed. Hough and colleagues (Hough, Keyes and Dunnette, 1983; Hough, 1984) have for example developed an alternative approach using information about past behaviour, known as the 'accomplishment record'. The accomplishment record method is based on self-reported description of past accomplishments in job related behavioural dimensions. Hough (1984) reports that accomplishment record scores appear unrelated to traditional psychological measures (e.g. aptitude tests) and correlate with job performance (.23). So far no reports of using this approach for managers are available.

2.1.3. Supervisor/Peer evaluation

Schmitt et al (1984) report an average validity of .43 for supervisory/peer evaluations across all occupational groups. Peer evaluation alone produces an average validity of .49 (Hunter and Hunter 1984). It is interesting that the validities for peer and supervisory and supervisory & peers combined are so similar. On an intuitive basis it would seem likely that there might be differences between peer and supervisory evaluations. Peer evaluation studies concerned specifically with managers are those of Kraut (1975), Roadman (1964) and Weitz (1958).

The average validity of .43 for supervisory/peer ratings given by Schmitt et al was based on 31 validities of which 24 came from managerial groups. Supervisory/peer evaluations show most predictive power with status change as the criterion (average validity = .51), performance ratings are also predicted reasonably well (.32) (both coefficients from Schmitt et al 1984).

2.2.   Predictors based on the present

Predictors focussing on the present are: Interviews, Psychometric tests,
Work-sample tests, Self-assessments, Assessment centres.

2.2.1. Interviews

Successive studies of the validity of interviews suggest that interviews
have little predictive power (see Reilly and Chao, 1982; Arvey and Campion
1983; Hunter and Hunter, 1984). The most promising recent developments
seem to be the potentially good validities of panel interviews (Arvey and
Campion, 1982) and situational interviews (Latham and Saari 1984).
Situational interviews are discussed in a later section.

2.2.2. Tests

Ability tests have well-established validities for a range of occupations.
Schmitt et al (1984) report average coefficients of .27 for aptitude and
general mental ability tests respectively. Ghiselli (1973) reported
average validity coefficients for ability tests (intellectual, perceptual,
spatial and mechanical abilities) for managers varying from .21 to .31 (for
job proficiency). Tests have been used to predict a wide range of
criterion measure (ratings, status change and turnover), the best specific
validity (.44) is obtained for general mental ability with
achievement/grades as criterion (Schmitt et al 1984). Hunter and Hunter
(1984) calculated the mean validity of an ability composite, for entry
level jobs on which training will occur after hiring to be .53.

For personality tests Schmitt et al (1984) report an average validity of
.15 and Ghiselli (1973) reports an average for managers of .21. A popular
personality-based method for predicting management performance involves the
use of McClelland's work on achievement motivation (see McClelland and
Boyatzis, 1982; and Stahl, 1983). The leadership motive pattern (L.M.P. :
moderate to high need for Power, low need for Affiliation and high activity
inhibition) has been shown to be significantly associated with managerial
performance. Gough (1984) has developed a managerial potential scale for
the California Psychological Inventory.

2.2.3. Work sample tests

Work sample tests require applicants to perform a sample of the job in
question. Validities for work sample tests are good. Robertson and
Kandola (1982) report median validities ranging from .24 to .44. Schmitt
et al (1984) report an average validity of .38. Work-sample tests have
however been used predominantly with non-managerial jobs. The major
exception here appears to be the use of situational decision-making
exercises - in particular in-trays and group discussions. Gill (1979)
reports validities for in-trays ranging from .27-.44. For group
discussions Robertson and Kandola report a median validity of .35 (with job
performance criteria).

Work sample tests show good validities across a range of criteria including
performance ratings and achievement/grades. The best validity (.44) is
obtained with Wages as a criterion. Hunter and Hunter (1984) report a mean
validity of .54 when used for promotion/certification and where current job
performance is the basis for selection. Work-sample tests are not

particularly convenient to administer in general, often requiring special
equipment. For managerial groups the requirements are probably much less
and it is perhaps a little surprising that research with work-sample tests
has so far focussed on psychomotor tasks, rather than managerial.

2.2.4. Self-assessments

Many reviews of the value of self-assessment in industrial and
organisational settings (e.g. Thornton, 1980, Reilly and Chao,1982)
conclude that there is little to recommend their use. The criticisms of
self-assessments centre on three main issues (see Levine, Flory and Ash
1977). First it is expected that people will produce an inflated i.e.
lenient picture of their own abilities. Second, that people are unable to
make accurate or reliable self-assessments. Third, that this leniency and
low reliability will lead to poor validity.

Makin and Robertson (1983) examined the literature on self-assessment and
concluded that peoples' self-assessment corresponded more closely with
objective assessments when the factor being assessed was straightforward
and well understood (e.g. simple copy typing ability). For more complex
skills (e.g. typing tables) the self and objective assessments corresponded
less well. It seems clear from this and some of the other studies
mentioned above that self-assessments may be more accurate for well
understood and familiar aspects of behaviour. Mabe and West (1980) provide
a review of the literature relevant to self-assessment and provide guidance
on important factors to consider.

Relatively few studies have examined the value of self-assessment in
selection situations. Reilly and Chao (1982) review 8 studies 4 of which
involved attempts to estimate the predictive validity of self-assessments.

2.2.5. Assessment centres

Assessment centres represent the most comprehensive and specific method for
attempting to predict managerial performance. Schmitt et al (1984) report
mean validity of .41 for assessment centres. Hunter and Hunter (1984)
report a mean of .43 for studies where current performance is the basis for
promotion/certification.

Assessment centres produce best validities for promotability (see Turnage
and Muchinsky, 1984; Schmitt et al; 1984). Supervisor's ratings are also
predicted reasonably well.

2.3. Future orientated predictors

Research on future-orientated predictors is much less comprehensive.

One promising approach is the use of situational interviews (Latham et al,
1980, 1984). This technique uses the results of systematic job analysis to
produce job-related incidents. Incidents are turned into interview
questions in which job applicants are asked to indicate how they would
behave in a given situation. Latham et al report a validity coefficient
(for foremen) ranging from .28 to .35. No studies are available for this
technique with managers.

A second future-orientated approach has as yet received no attention from personnel selection specialists. This involves the use of a self-efficacy scale. Bandura (1982) has defined self-efficacy as,

> "how well one can execute courses of action required to deal with prospective situations" (p. 122)

We are currently working to develop and evaluate a self-efficacy scale for managers.

3.   FUTURE NEEDS

As material in the first part of this paper revealed there is something of a gap between research and practice as far as the selection of managers in the UK is concerned. What is needed to help close that gap? The short answer is that researchers and practitioners need to pay more attention to each other. Researchers have not, so far, offered practitioners much help towards using the methods that are most popular: Reference and Interviews.

Research for example investigating the use of situational interviews for managers would be helpful, as would some research and development work designed to assess and improve the validity of references. In view of their ease of administration and consistent validity, psychological tests of ability appear to be underutilised by practitioners.

Biodata could benefit from the attention of both researchers and practitioners. More research evidence is needed for managerial groups and although development needs are relatively high biodata systems are administratively convenient and should appeal, for example, to organizations recruiting large numbers of trainee managers. Work-sample tests and Assessment Centres seem to serve the purpose for which they have been designed and we might expect a steady growth in their use.

Research needs concerning assessment centres involved investigating the validity of the separate component parts of Assessment Centres.

For work-samples the development and validation of much wider range of managerial work-sample tests than the ubiquitous In-Tray and group discussion represents a challenge to researchers and practitioners.

Taken overall based on current evidence, the best method of managerial selection, is the assessment centre incorporating psychological tests, though, if large numbers of external candidates are involved, biodata, plus psychological tests may be more appropriate. For the selection and placement of internal personnel, peer and supervisory evaluations have similar validities, are easier to administer and have less development costs than assessment centres. If assessment centres are used in a diagnostic way and have a genuine impact on staff development their use for internal candidates has added benefits over and above supervisory/peer ratings.

REFERENCES

Arvey, R.D., & Campion, J.E., The employment interview: A summary and review of recent literature, Personnel Psychology (1982) 35, 281-322.

Asher, J.J., The biographical item: Can it be improved? Personnel Psychology, (1972) 25, 251-269.

Bandura, A., Social Learning Theory, Englewood-Cliffs: Prentice-Hall, (1977)

Bandura, A., Self-efficacy mechanism in human agency. American Psychologist, (1982) 37, 122-147.

Bridges, A, Assessment Centres: Their use in industry in Great Britain. Unpublished MSc Dissertation (Department of Management Sciences, UMIST 1984)

Ghiselli, E.E., The validity of aptitude tests in personnel selection. Personnel Psychology, (1973) 26, 461-477.

Gill, R.W.T., The in-tray (in-basket) exercise as a measure of management potential. Journal of Occupational Psychology,(1979) 52, 185-197.

Gill, D., Ungerson, B., & Thakur, M., Performance Appraisal in Perspective: A Survey of current practice. (London: Institute of Personnel Management 1973)

Gough, H.G., A managerial potential scale for the California Psychological Inventory. Journal of Applied Psychology,(1984) 69, 233-240.

Hough, L.M., Development and evaluation of the "Accomplishment Record" method of selecting and promoting professionals. Journal of Applied Psychology,(1984) 69, 135-146.

Hough, L.M., Keyes, M.A., & Dunnette, M.D., An evaluation of three "alternative" selection procedures. Personnel Psychology,(1983) 30, 353-361.

Hunter, J.E. and Hunter, R.F., Validity and utility of alternative predictors of job performance. Psychological Bulletin,(1984) 96, 72-98.

Korman, A.K., The prediction of managerial performance: A review. Personnel Psychology, (1968) 21, 295-322.

Kraut, A.I., Prediction of managerial success by peer and training staff ratings. Journal of Applied Psychology, (1975) 60, 14-19.

Latham, G.P., & Saari, L.M., Do people do what they say? Further studies on the situational interview. Journal of Applied Psychology, (1984) 69, 569-573.

Levine, E.L., Flory, A. III, & Ash, R.A., Self assessment in personnel selection. Journal of Applied Psychology, (1977) 62, 428-435.

Mabe, P. and West, S., Validity of self evaluation of ability: A review and meta-analysis. Journal of Applied Psychology, (1980) 67, 280-296.

Makin, P.J. & Robertson, I.T., Self assessment, realistic job previews and occupational decisions. Personnel Review, (1983) 12, 21-25.

McClelland, D.C., & Boyatzis, R.E., Leadership motive pattern and long-term success in management. Journal of Applied Psychology, (1982) 67, 737-743.

Monahan, C.J., & Muchinsky, P.M., Three decades of personnel selection research: A state of the art analysis and evaluation. Journal of Occupational Psychology, (1983) 56, 215-225.

Muchinsky, P.M., The use of reference reports in personnel selection: A review and evaluation. Journal of Occupational Psychology, (1979) 52, 287-297.

Owens, W.A., Background data. In M.D. Dunnette (Ed) Handbook of Industrial and Organisational Psychology (Chicago: Rand-McNally,1976)

Reilly, R.R., & Chao, G.T., Validity and fairness of some alternative employee selection procedures. Personnel Psychology, (1982) 35, 1-62.

Roadman, H.E., An industrial use of peer ratings. Journal of Applied Psychology,(1964) 48, 211-214.

Robertson, I.T., & Kandola, R.S., Work sample tests: Validity, adverse impact and applicant reaction. Journal of Occupational Psychology, (1982) 55, 171-183.

Robertson, I.T., & Makin, P.J., Management selection in Britain: A survey and critique. Journal of Occupational Psychology, (In Press)

Savage, A. Personal Communication. (1985)

Schmitt, N., Gooding, R.Z., Noe, R.A., & Kirsch, M., Metaanalysis of validity studies published between 1964 and 1982 and the investigation of study characteristics. Personnel Psychology, (1984) 37, 407-422.

Stahl, M.J., Achievement, power and managerial motivation: Selecting managerial talent with the job choice exercise. Personnel Psychology,(1983) 775-789.

Sneath, F., Thakur, M., & Medjuck, B., Testing People at Work, London: Institute of Personnel Management, 1976

Thornton, G.C., III Psychometric properties of self appraisals of job performance. Personnel Psychology, (1980) 33, 263-271.

Turnage, J.J., & Muchinsky, P.M., A comparison of the predictive validity of assessment center evaluations versus traditional measures in forecasting supervisory job performance: Interpretive implications of criterion distortion for the assessment paradigm. Journal of Applied Psychology, (1984) 69, 595-602.

Weitz, J., Selecting supervisors with peer ratings. Personnel Psychology, (1958) 11, 25-36.

THE PSYCHOLOGY OF WORK AND ORGANIZATION
G. Debus and H.-W. Schroiff (Editors)
© *Elsevier Science Publishers B.V. (North-Holland), 1986*

QUALITATIVE PERSONNEL PLANNING
EXPERIENCES, METHODS AND RESULTS FROM A LARGE COMPANY

Manfred OETTING

Personalentwicklungs-Systeme, Oelixdorfer Straße 89,
D-2210 Itzehoe, Federal Republic of Germany

In the Federal Republic of Germany an increasing number of companies are introducing systematic methods of qualitative personnel planning for their executive staff. The methods has three components: the devices for planning, diagnosis of potential and development of staff. The purpose of qualitative personnel planning is the more reliable recognition of qualified and qualifiable members of staff within a company and their systematic and well-planned training with a view to employing them in difficult and responsible leading positions. This way the chronic lack of executive staff is counteracted. At the same time the motivation of executives is strengthened by offering capable executive staff a fairer chance of promotion. This report is a case study of the practical implementation of such a system in a company.

1. EXPERIENCE AND METHOD IN PERSONNEL DECISIONS

The degree to which eductionalists in charge of training are accepted in a firm increasingly depends on their ability to understand and represent personnel development as a comprehensive system. Today a merely reactive eductional service runs the risk of being regarded as a low priority cost factor whose budget will be ruthlessly cut, if necessary. Wherever a convincing overall system is being offered, personnel development is regaining its high priority in the company.

In many cases line managers are overtaxed and occasionally at a loss if qualified knowledge of internal personnel resources is required to make decisions of considerable import. It is regrettable that, especially in the selection of personnel and the assessment of potential, decisions of vital significance for a company are based on relatively unsuitable methods, even though great emphasis is placed on the importance of such decisions for the overall goal of "economic efficiency". As a consequence, too many and too weak applicants or candidates are given too many opportunities of rising into positions whose demands they cannot adequately meet. On the other hand, genuinely able junior staff often go unrecognised - a nightmare for every personnel manager, who knows from many interviews with junior staff and with applicants that it is at present extremely difficult to find able executive staff (few companies excepted).

To give an example: During a "qualification stock-taking" we learned that one of the most talented participants had been transferred from one of the largest branches of the company to a subordinate position in a relatively insignificant branch in the country, because his superior had problems with him. Thus decision-makers may fail to appreciate existing potential because of limited diagnostic means. In the same investigation we also came across a member of staff who ranked among the most incapable of a group of 70 managers, but who, at the same time, had been employed at about 150% of the customary salary.

Today personnel development systems provide the methodological know-how
that allows an effective elimination of sources of error in the filling
of vacant promotion or leading positions. There is, however, a great
number of obstacles to the use of such systems. One of these is perhaps
the unshaken conviction of many executives that the experience of many
years has given them a sense, or, as the expression goes, a "hunch" for
the right man.

1. case study: the company
This report is about a company with a staff of approx. 3.500. We are
concerned with the third level (approx. 20 heads of main departments,
HMD) and the fourth level (approx. 150 heads of departments, HD) of the
hierarchy. For this firm a special problem in the recruiting of junior
staff for leading positions was the regionalisation of a large part of
the HMD-level and their filter function in the nomination of staff
members deserving promotion: the profit center organisation resulted in
a number of cases — for reasons humanly understandable — that on the one
hand staff capable of promotion were not nominated in order to make use
of their abilities in their own profit center, while, on the other hand,
staff incapable of promotion were nominated to make place for more able
staff.

We work in close cooperation with the company's personnel development
division, which prefers methodic procedures and also has a talent for
dealing both with management and with staff. This proves an inestimable
help in our work.

Our work began in 1981 and, as far as the development of systems is
concerned, it may be regarded as completed. At present, advisory activities consist in continuing checks and the occasional methodological and
practical adaptation of the instruments, as well as the continual examination of the potential of internal and external junior executive staff.
The main basis for our cooperation in this extremely sensitive area is
the mutual trust that has grown over the years.

2. HOW WE STARTED

In our experience the elements and instruments of systematic personnel
development are usually introduced by the personnel division without any
prior consultation of the line management. The implementation of the
assessment centre, a particularly impressive device, will finally
convince the line of the usefulness of personnel development devices: as
a rule, acceptance of the assessment centre by the line management is
fairly high.

The introduction of qualitative personnel planning in the company under
investigation began with a series of conferences of the training
division, which we attended as external consultants. These conferences
aimed at the development of a plan to be presented to the board of
directors.

Our task was to develop devices which were simple and easy to maintain
and which would improve the motivation and development of executives. At
the same time the methodological sophistication of these devices had to
be such as to make an effective contribution to personnel development
and the success of the company as a whole.

As a result of our presentation to the board, we were instructed to discuss the new concept of personnel development in one-day seminaries with all executives from levels 2 to 4 and to adapt it to the requirements of the line management.

This procedure fully corresponds to our idea of personnel development: we view the selection and promotion of staff as a non-delegable managerial task. Personnel division and consultants ought to be aware of the fact that they are performing a service, that it is their duty to facilitate the tasks of the line management by offering them qualified methodological assistance. As we see it, the attempt to leave decisions regarding executive positions to the personnel division is utterly unacceptable.
We thus designed a series of seminaries for all senior executives of the company, the so-called "working-sessions".
At the start of each working session (10-12 participants) we inquired which services, related to the recruiting and promotion of junior executive staff, line managers expected from the personnel division.
The answers were arranged in groups of similar content to enable the development of devices for a qualitative planning system.
In discussions with the participants, the devices developed were subjected to detailed scrutiny in order to gain deeper insight into the advantages and problems of qualitative personnel planning.

On the basis of the needs of the managerial staff, our knowledge of the literature and our large practical experience in consultative work for other companies, we developed with each group its own personnel development plan. The results from the different groups were rather similar. Thus there was little difficulty in integrating the individual concepts into the final plan to be implemented.
The advantage of this procedure is that the whole plan is directly rooted in and accepted by the line management. Furthermore, it ensures an optimal adaptation to the actual needs.

3. SELECTION OF DEVICES/ELEMENTS OF QUALITATIVE PERSONNEL PLANNING

The integrated system for qualitative personnel planning, as worked out by the managerial staff, consists of the following devices/elements.

3.1 (Institutionalised) Dialogue with the Staff

This form was consciously chosen as an alternative to the formal assessment of employees: it avoids a number of problems associated with the latter. Dialogues, taking place at one- or two-year intervals, serve the purpose of discussing with a given employee his performance, state and aims of development, and to generally reflect on his occupational situation. In spite of good intentions, dialogues with employees are often neglected for reasons humanly understandable and thus they ought to be "institutionalised". A proven type of "institutionalisation" is the obligation of a superior to notify the personnel division that a dialogue has taken place. He writes an abstract of the talk, which he passes to his own superior for his information. This abstract is then filed separately from the employee's personal file. After a certain period of time it is destroyed.

A superior should merely judge the performance of a subordinate at his place of work. The agreed aims are to form the standard for such an assessment. Any judgements concerning character or potential of a subordinate cannot but overtax a superior: as a rule he lacks training in this matter and is thus not even able to recognise how weak his basis is for such judgements.

3.2 Defining Personal Characteristics Required in Managers

One main component of any systems for qualitative personnel planning is the definitive setting-up of personal requirements top executives must meet. These must be established prior to the implementation of qualitative personnel planning.

To establish these requirements, we followed the usual method: In a first step, holders of a position and their superiors describe critical incidents that arise in this position. In a second step they describe suitable behaviour for adequately coping with such critical incidents. The catalogue of requisite characteristics, derived from these in a third step, takes the shape of concrete descriptions of behaviour.

3.3 Diagnosis of Potential by Promotion Seminaries (Assessment Centre)

We introduced participants to various diagnostic techniques (performance test, personality test, questionnaire, interview, assessment centre, etc.).
We recommended that line managers should be involved in the diagnosing of potential. This resulted in an assessment technique oriented on systematic observation of behaviour rather than on tests (nevertheless, we generally use performance tests as an important source of information for diagnosis of potential).

We have always rejected a company's demands for "complete solutions" that fail to include managers in the diagnostic process. Such solutions would save much time, managers only carrying out a superficial and unsystematic interview before a contract is signed. It cannot be stressed enough that leadership includes non-delegable duties, and the selection and promotion of junior staff is, in our opinion, one of them. It is true, there are plenty of colleagues who are far more adept at the systematic observation of behaviour than managers, be they ever so well-trained. These colleagues do, however, lack knowledge essential for well-founded decision-making, viz. detailed knowledge of the specific working conditions in a given firm, especially the style of management. This knowledge is, in our view, a precondition for responsible decision-making. In our experience, it certainly outweighs the methodological subtleties of scientific behaviour observation techniques.

The participants unanimously voted in favour of the assessment centre, mainly, as it seems, because of the transparency of the technique and its well-known prognostic precision. The (historically unfounded) English term, which sounds rather harsh, was replaced by the term "Promotion Seminary". Its purpose is the systematic diagnosis of potential, i.e. the potential development and suitability of applicants and staff. The results of this seminary are intended to be a contribution to the planning of individual and collective developmental measures, but also of individual careers and of provisions for the filling of potential vacancies.

Besides the diagnosis of the qualifications of an individual, this "stock-taking of potential" can also serve the purpose of an overall analysis of training required with respect to specialist knowledge and skills. It can also be employed in assessing the abilities of applicants within or without the company.

This technique – if applicable and used by qualified staff – is very suitable for making precise predictions on the prospective performance of a person on the basis of factors inherent in his personality. As "performance" depends in great measure on the present and future working conditions, institutional and personal knowledge of insiders can, in our experience, greatly help to improve the validity of a performance prognosis.

Performance prognosis concerns the prediction of a candidate's future performance in a position in which he had as yet no opportunity to prove himself or about whose performance in this position no reliable inform-ation is available. It must not be employed to assess an employee in his present position (this would mean replacing the value of a factual criterion "performance in a position" by an estimate of "performance in a position").

When choosing a method for diagnosing potential, the assessment centre offers a number of advantages. From the point of view of managers and personnel development experts the most important are:
a) The line management recognises and acknowledges the work of personnel development experts, because managers can understand the method and because they gain a valuable tool for decision-making.
b) The participants feel that they are assessed as objectively and fairly as possible and consequently most of them will accept the system.
c) The high transparency of criteria and methods gives the participants scope for self-presentation. They do not feel exposed to and unmasked by an obscure and all-powerful system.
d) Insight into the method allows the company to recognise its value. At the same time it realises that assessments are largely independent from subjective impressions of superiors.

Two important problems must be mentioned:
a) A relatively large amount of time must be devoted to observation. This may cause problems and lead to unsatisfactory compromises. Methodo-logical compromises will eventually jeopardise the whole system.
b) The quality of the method must be maintained whenever it is employed. The first prerequisite is therefore an expert with excellent methodolo-gical know-how who has sufficient experience and confidence to be able to convince weathered line managers of the concept. This task (and role) is best performed by an external consultant – last but not least to circumvent potential problems with the hierarchy.

3.4 Documentation of Personnel Resources in a Promotion File

The results of "stock-takings of potential" should be documented in a file. Collecting and filing assessment centre results (final assessment, test result, short appraisal) in the personnel development division have proved useful. They are to be kept separate from the personal file. The personnel development division can advise the line management on person-nel decisions. In this particular firm, an electronic file would have created problems. Nevertheless, the use of data bases for personal computers would be an excellent and up-to-date means of following up the development of staff and of controlling developmental measures.

3.5. General Careers Plan

This is a method for establishing planned "standard careers" in horizontal and vertical direction. Its aim is the development of employees on the job, based on a systematical and comprehensive exhaustion of all possibilities. Junior executives gain a wide experience in as many areas as possible. Moreover, they make personal contacts, which may, for instance, help to counteract the rigid bureaucratic flow of information within a company. The employment of junior staff, usually oriented on a company's needs, now also takes into account the goal of systematic development.

3.6. Individual Careers Plan

This is the result of consultative talks between a superior and an employee. The objective is the planning of his (preliminary) career – horizontal and/or vertical. It is based on the general careers plan, but it must take into account developmental needs of an employee with respect to his personality and his position.

3.7 Measures for Development "off the Job"

General and individual career planning, i.e. development on the job must be complemented by special measures of promotion, e.g. seminaries. At present, the company in question uses a module system of standard seminaries for junior executives. In individual cases we also recommend participation in certain external seminaries.

3.8 Succession Plan

This is the designation of a documentation system which provides a preliminary succession plan for every executive position. It contains information on the state of development and (also systematised) developmental measures required of potential successors. If there are two or more potential successors for a position, the succession plan should be publicised, as this will give additional impetus for the development of persons concerned.

4. THE IMPLEMENTATION

After completion of the working sessions, the overall result was submitted to the board of directors, whereupon the personnel division was instructed to implement the proposed system.

The implementation of the "institutionalised dialogue with subordinates" and the "general careers' plan" involved a great deal of effort, the former because of the necessity of extensive training, the latter because of the company's complicated career structure (divided into expert and management careers).

To introduce succession planning it was necessary to convince the managers in question. This was not always easy – and, no doubt, partly due to subjective fears arising from the concrete consideration of a successor for one's own position. Generally it was, however, this component that lead to an intensive concern with the personal development of junior executives.

"Promotion seminaries" (assessment centre) were a subject of lively discussion, even during their first implementation. By now, these seminaries (above all, the objective improvement of the participants' performance) have contributed most to the positive attitude of the line management towards the whole system of qualitative personnel planning in this company.

THE PSYCHOLOGY OF WORK AND ORGANIZATION
G. Debus and H.-W. Schroiff (Editors)
© Elsevier Science Publishers B.V. (North-Holland), 1986

VOCATIONAL TRAINING AND OCCUPATIONAL SUCCESS

Rolf Jansen

Bundesinstitut für Berufsbildung (The Federal Institute for Vocational Education and Training),
Fehrbelliner Platz 3, D 1000 Berlin 31, Germany

The paper presents a method to compare 69 recognized qualified
occupations (Ausbildungsberufe) according to eight indicators,
which intend to measure occupational success. The analysis has
been made with data of a survey of about 30.000 interviewed representatives of the working population of the Federal Republic
of Germany in 1979. The most important findings are highlighted
in the following extract.

1. INTRODUCTION: THE AIM OF THE ANALYSIS

I would like to present an analysis which I carried out together with my
colleague Thomas Clauss, based on one of the most interesting and representative surveys of the working world in the Federal Republic of
Germany [1]. Interesting, since both the number of variables and of persons interviewed were quite large and consequently disaggregative. In
1979 on commission of the Federal Institute for Vocational Education and
Training (BIBB) and the Institute for Employment Research of the Federal
Employment Institute (IAB) approximately 30.000 members of the German
work force chosen on a representative basis were interviewed as to their
training, particular stations of their careers and their working and employment situations. The questionnaire was compiled by both institutes.
The chief area of interest centered on structural information about occupational research as well as research on vocational training. The Federal Institute for Vocational Education and Training supplied several
analytical reports, mainly referring to individual occupational fields.
A brochure containing the synopses of the reports published by the institutes was distributed during the conference [2].

The data set is available for the secondary analytical purposes of the
academic public through the Central Archive for Empirical Social Research in Cologne.

The analysis wants to provide in condensed form information about occupations which require formal vocational training [3]. It presents on one
hand structural information about those persons in the work force who
have completed such an in-plant training or industrial training. The
main emphasis, though, is on the descriptive and evaluative indicators,
which should give insight into occupational success and consequently
into the career prospects of those occupations examined.

This work should not be understood as competition for the ABC-Handbook of Occupations published by the Institute for Employment Research of the Federal Employment Institute. It is, rather, an extension of the concept long adhered to by that institute of subtly differentiated informa- tion [4]. It contains, then, additional aspects to the data presented in the handbook.

In the social reality of our society, it is important how an occupation is evaluated. This is clearly shown by the differing incomes earned in the respective occupations. In labor contracts, especially those pertai- ning to trades and crafts, various factors are often used to enable a differentiated work evaluation (e.g. qualification, strain). This analy- sis will proceed in a similar way. The various evaluative standards for assessing the prospects of selected occupations will be presented.

In particular, they refer to the following aspects (dimensions) of occu- pational activities:

- job security
- promotion, career prospects
- income
- flexibility
- physical work load, strain
- psychological demand, stress
- variety of work vs. monotony
- satisfaction

2.   METHODS

For the purposes of this analysis the occupational situation of those who had in earlier times passed a formal occupational training will be examined. Conclusions will be made based on the present employment si- tuation pertaining to the various career prospects, which are linked to the vocational training in a particular occupation. The basic assumption is that the choice of an occupation which requires training also deter- mines occupational and employment opportunities later in life. Occupa- tional success is influenced essentially by the entrance info an oc- cupation, in other words, by vocational training.

Thus, this analysis includes only those from the survey conducted by BIBB/IAB, who completed an in-plant or industrial training program. In 1979 that was 60 % of the working population, that is approximately 13.3 million; the size of this subsample is 19.787 persons. Those occupations which require a full-time school education were not considered.

The individual occupations requiring vocational training will be classi- fied according to the 4-digital register (modified) of recognized train- ing occupations. The statements made by all who have completed a parti- cular training program (for example, bakers) will be summarized. To en- sure the statistical accuracy of the results, only those occupations we- re evaluated, which are represented by at least 50 persons in the sample survey. Sixty-nine individual occupations were included in the analysis, which represented 84 % of the working population who have completed training programs; the remaining 16 % are listed under "Other".

Our reasons for contenting ourselves with - for a representative study -
relatively small groups in this analysis, are: First, that our natural
interest as employees of the BIBB is in obtaining information about as
many occupations as possible. None the less, the number of occupations
evaluated totals only 69. Considering that there are just over 400 acc-
redited occupations requiring training, this demonstrates how great the
number of relatively seldom occurring specialized occupations there are.
Even such a large survey as this one does not permit reliable conclusions to be made about these. Secondly, we believe that even for occupations which are infrequently represented in the survey, rather reliable
information is to be obtained. This statement is based on the construction of the indicators upon which I will comment briefly a little
later.

Indicators will be calculated based on the information given by those
trained in respective vocations, which will permit a direct comparison
of occupations. Roughly, two types of indicators can be distinguished.

First, there are relative frequencies, that is, percentage values. These
will enable the determination of important structural characteristics
of the trainees in the respective occupations (among the working population of the year 1979). In particular, the following reference numbers
will be shown in one chart[5] summarizing this information:

- Percentage of those who had changed occupation
- Percentage of those who have completed their vocational training
  within the last 10 years
- Percentage of the 50- to 60-year-olds (referring to those active in
  occupations requiring training, but without having changed occupa-
  tion)
- Percentage of those who received their training in a small establish-
  ment (up to 9 employees)
- Percentage of those who work in a small establishment (up to 9 em-
  ployees)
- Percentage of women
- Percentage of self-employed (referring to all trained in occupations)
- Percentage of self-employed (referring to those active in occupations
  requiring training, but without having changed occupations)
- Percentage of those with an additional vocational education
  (specialized technical school, higher technical college, university)

Thus, these are values which are clear and comprehensible and do not require additional explanation or transformation.

Somewhat more complicated, however, are the indicators, which serve to
describe the quality of the present employment situation and occupational success. By way of an additive combination of several characteristics gained through the interviews to form indices, a comparison of the
occupations will be made possible.

Referring to "job security" this means: The percentage of those losing
their jobs within the last five years is an indication of the risk of
losing one's employment. This must, then, have a negative effect on the
evaluation of job security. It points in the same direction, if someone
estimates the risk of losing his present employment or being placed in

another job. Conversely, the percentage of those who assess the danger
as small is a positive measurement of job security. Finally, when dealing with job security, it is to be considered similarly, when someone
states as a reason for changing occupations, that he became unemployed
or the danger of losing his job could have existed or that the new employment was more secure.

From a variety of questions or respectively possible answers, those were
sought out, which could be seen as either a positive or negative contribution to one of those aspects of recognized importance to an evaluation
of "career prospects" of vocations requiring training. If such a characteristic was applicable according to the interview, it was designated
either + 1 or - 1. For each person interviewed an index was calculated
by means of an additive combination of individual characteristics per
indicator. For these indices, then, the mean was calculated to each occupation requiring vocational training. This was done, first, for all
persons trained for an occupation and second, for all those remaining in
this occupation (in other words, without changing their occupation). The
means are raw values for the indicators of each occupations.

To facilitate the interpretation of occupation-related information in
the tabels and especially to transform the values for each indicator to
comparable levels of measurement two ways of standardization where
chosen. First, the z-value-transformation was processed from the distri-
butional statistics known to us.

An even simpler way of the presentation of the data consists of forming
a ranking order for the occupations relating to each individual indicator. The indicators will be replaced by the ranking of the occupations.
In this case, rank No.1 stands for the best position pertaining to that
indicator, whereas rank Nr. 70 corresponds to the worst position. This
also applies to those indicators which, because of the very connotation
of the term, indicate rather negative aspects.

To determine the effect of a change of occupation, differences were calculated relating to both the z-values and the ranking order between the
values obtained for all persons having completed a vocational training
program for a certain occupation and those values received from persons
remaining in the occupation for which they were trained (without change
of occupation). Finally, the different indicators can be combined into
partial or total values.

The indicators of the occupations pertaining to the various descriptive
and evaluative dimensions, and the indices for the structural characteristics, were placed in relation to one another (calculation of
correlations). In this context, I must remind that we are dealing
here with the contemplation of aggregates (occupations). The indices say
something about the occupations requiring training, represented by, it
is true, but abstracted from individuals who were trained in this occupation.

3.   RESULTS [6]

Job Security: This describes the danger of or respectively the security
from being fired or compulsory transfer and unemployment. The occupations which require training in the public sector, e.g. post office

workers, employees of the telephone service company, the technical semi-
skilled occupations of the Federal Railway and public administrative
white collar workers score positively here. Also among the top-ranking
in this group are bank and insurance businessmen. Occupations with a
high percentage of persons changing their occupations are at the other
end of the scale (e.g. gas station attendant, blacksmith, seamstress or
druggist).

Promotion, Career Prospects: The occupations with the best chance of
promotion are craft/technical occupations, especially electricians. Typical occupations for women - where the percentage of women is 90 % or
more - rank without exception lower on the scale; here we are dealing
with assisting occupations, which is frequently expressed in the name
for the occupation. A change of occupation often leads to employment below the level of a skilled worker and, therefore, to a loss of qualification. There are, however, some occupations (for example, typesetter,
mechanician, employees of the telephone service or bank businessmen) in
which those changing their occupation contribute to a favorable overall
picture of that occupation.

Income: There is a clear correlation between the chances for promotion,
career opportunities and the potential income. Occupations which are
mainly trained in large scale enterprises have better chances for higher
income than those found most frequently in small establishments. It is,
however, especially conspicuous that occupations for women without exception rank at the lower end of the pay scale.

Flexibility: This means, the possibility of working in other occupations
than in those for which one was trained without, however, a loss of qualification or status. A broad, basic education which can also be used in
other occupations is a point in favor of greater flexibility (for example, in metallurgical and office occupations). Trade and craft occupations rank at the lower end of the scale. In the past, these lost their
significance and their qualification profile has few overlappings with
other occupations.

Physical Work Load, Strain: Besides the physical demands due to working
conditions, this term also encompasses environmental factors such as
noise, wetness, cold, heat and dust. The strain situation is extremely
favorable in office occupations. At the lower end of the scale are construction jobs, locksmiths (grobschlosserische Metallberufe), as well
as miners and butchers. These are partly, then, the occupations which
have rather lost significance in the past few years, for which the percentage of those changing occupations is above average; but a change of
occupation only rarely improves the physical work load in a fundamental
way.

Psychological Demand, Stress: It is not the case, that blue collar jobs
are physically demanding, while white collar and service occupations are
mentally demanding. There is, rather, a clear connection between these
factors. The pressure to achieve and to keep the schedule can especially
be found in industrial occupations - less often, by contrast, in commercial and service occupations or in trade and craft occupations.

Variety of Work vs. Monotony: The highly qualified commercial occupations must be regarded as the least monotonous. Monotony is to be found
mainly in such trade and craft occupations in which a great part of the

trainees, because of the reduced chances in these occupations, have changed to unskilled industrial work. These are also the occupations considered least flexible. The monotony is not to be found in the actual occupations requiring training, but rather in those occupations available to the trained worker after being compelled to change his occupation.

Satisfaction depends greatly upon the aspiration level of the individual. Job security and opportunity for promotion have a favorable influence on occupational satisfaction. Satisfaction is the result of identification with one's occupation.

Whereas the other steps of the analysis and data processing either should trace the relative position of the occupations in the individual dimensions of measurement or should examine the correlations between individual dimensions for all occupations, the cluster analysis intends to examine the similarities of profile among the occupations. The occupations offer quite different opportunities for occupational success, in spite of the formal equality of the certificates. Based on the similarities of profile, four types of occupations can be distinguished.

- Administrative Commercial Occupations, for which the entrance requirement is frequently a higher school level, are the most successful (income, promotion, job security). Some trade and craft-technical occupations are counted among those in which, like administrative commercial occupations, the physical work load is insignificant (e. g. precision mechanic, typesetter or draughtsman).

- The classical skilled industrial occupations: Metal Worker, Mechanic or Electrician which are employed primarily with upkeep, maintenance and repair, are also above average in terms of success. The lower management are often recruited as a rule from these occupations (foreman and master). Contrary to the group of occupations described above, the working conditions in these are especially burdensome. They are typified by great physical strain as well as by extreme pressure (stress).

- For Commerce, Office and Service Occupations the working conditions are hardly strenuous at all. However, these occupations provide rather unfavorable opportunities for earning money and being promoted. Many occupations for women are typically to be found in this group.

- The occupations causing the greatest problems are predominantly Craft Occupations with Main Emphasis on Construction and Nutrition, which have partly lost their significance. Because of the imbalance of trained workers and the demand for such skilled workers, many are obliged to change occupations. Since the content of the vocational training very seldom overlaps that of other occupations (little flexibility), often only a change to employment in industrial production remains, where under relatively strenuous working conditions rather monotonous work is to be carried out. The migratory effect caused by the loss of significance in the 60's and 70's has led to the situation, that those who have remained in their occupations are significantly better off than those changing their occupations. However, it must be considered, that this positive depiction is determined by a relatively high percentage of self-employed.

A graph has been prepared to clarify how one can continue working
with this concept. A profile comparison of a (according to our analysis)
quite favorable occupation, the administrative white collar worker, will
be compared to the shoemaker. In addition, the shoemakers who stuck to
their occupations will be compared to all shoemakers having completed a
training program.

Graph: Indicator Profiles for Selected Qualified Occupations

- Standardized Z - Values -

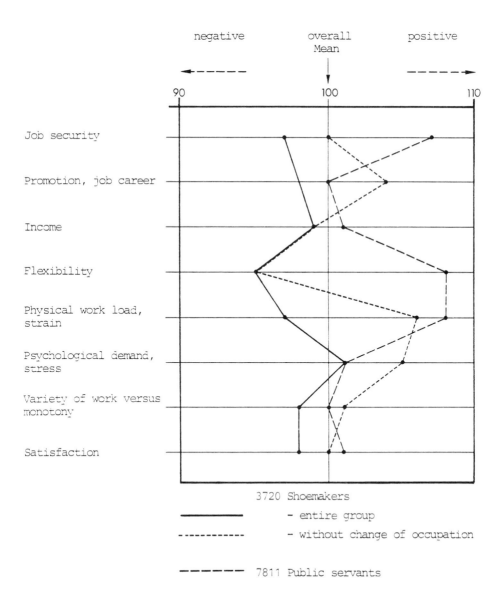

The administrative white collar workers received no negative ratings (below average). They score especially favorably in terms of job securi- ty (public sector), flexibility and physical work load. When referring to flexibility, which can only be measured by persons changing occupa- tion, one must consider that only certain people change their occupa- tion. Because of the favorable (that is, secure) employment situation, those changing jobs are persons who hope for a substantial improvement of their occupational situation (positive selection). The chances for promotion and the variety of work are average, but also income, psycho- logical demand/stress and satisfaction are just barely above average.

And now to the shoemakers: On the whole, trained shoemakers in the wor- king population received negative ratings in all dimensions (except psy- chological demand/stress), especially low in terms of flexibility. For trained shoemakers, who in spite of the loss of occupational significan- ce in the 1950's and 60's, "stuck to their last", staying in their trai- ned occupation has apparently paid off. In a series of measurement va- lues, which encompass the various aspects of occupational success, they clearly outrank their colleagues who changed occupation. Sixty-three percent of the working persons who completed an apprenticeship as shoe- maker indicated that they had since turned their backs on this occupa- tion. Many of them could find no work as shoemakers. Or else they did not earn enough in comparison to other occupations. Industrial enterpri- ses were offering enticingly good wages. As a result, many trained shoe- makers are employed as unskilled or semi-skilled workers in industrial manufacturing. And such industrial work is typified by great physical strain, by pressure to achieve and by monotony. Very few succeed in ad- vancing to a supervisory position. And because of increased implementa- tion of effeciency measures, these are the jobs which are most endange- red.

FOOTNOTES AND REFERENCES

[1]   Clauß, T., Jansen, R., Betriebliche Berufsausbildung und berufli-
      cher Erfolg - Die Bewertung von Ausbildungsberufen mit Hilfe von
      empirisch gewonnenen Indikatoren, Berichte zur beruflichen Bildung
      No. 65, Berlin 1984; this report ist available for 18,-- DM at:
      Bundesinstitut für Berufsbildung, Fehrbelliner Platz 3,
      D-1000 Berlin 31.
[2]   This information on project 1.036 is available free of charge from
      the author.
[3]   It deals with recognized training occupations of the German Dual
      System.
[4]   IAB (Ed.) ABC-Handbuch (Handbook of Employment Prospekts for Train-
      ing, Occupational and Specifically Economic Branches), Nuremberg
      1974; an up-date of this data can be found in: MatAB Special issue,
      December 1976, MatAB 1/1978 and BeitrAB 60 and 61.1. Concerning the
      concept: Chaberny, A., Schober, K., Risiko und Chancen bei der
      Ausbildungs- und Berufswahl - Das Konzept der differenzierten In-
      formation über Beschäftigungsaussichten, in: Mertens, D. (ed.),
      Konzepte der Arbeitsmarkt- und Berufsforschung, BeitrAB 70 (pp.
      659-687), Nuremberg 1982.
[5]   See Clauß, T., Jansen, R.: op.cit. Table 5, p. 25; a reproduction
      of several tables that had been available to the listeners is not
      possible for technical reasons.
[6]   This chapter gives a broad overview of the results. For more de-
      tailed information see the original report.

THE PSYCHOLOGY OF WORK AND ORGANIZATION
G. Debus and H.-W. Schroiff (Editors)
© Elsevier Science Publishers B.V. (North-Holland), 1986

TURNING POINTS, TRAPS AND TUNNELS: THE SIGNIFICANCE OF WORK
ROLE TRANSITIONS IN THE LIVES OF INDIVIDUALS AND ORGANISATIONS

Nigel Nicholson

MRC/ESRC Social and Applied Psychology Unit,
University of Sheffield,
Sheffield S10 2TN, UK.

ABSTRACT

The notion of the Transition Cycle is used to show how work role
transitions are frequent and important events in people's lives.
Research from three major projects at the Social and Applied
Psychology Unit has shown how they vary in their origins,
processes and outcomes. Nine properties of transition cycles are
proposed to explain these differences, summarise our current
state of knowledge about job changing, and aid future analysis
for theory building, research, and application.

1.   INTRODUCTION

Work role transitions can be broadly defined as any major change in a
person's work duties. This definition thus encompasses not just major
career transitions and employer changes, but also instances of radical
job redesign or reorganisation of responsibilities. Transitions should
command our attention for three reasons: (1) they are ubiquitous, everyone has experienced at least one; (2) they are frequent, many people
experience them repeatedly throughout their working lives; and (3) they
are important, they have theoretically and practically significant consequences.

Transitions may be turning points in the lives of individuals and organisations, representing genuine new beginnings for both. They may also be
traps for the unwary or the powerless; some transitions lead nowhere, in
the sense that they just present the person with more of the same, or
some work situation from which there is no retreat or escape. They may
be tunnels for those people (decreasing in number!) for whom transitions
represent orderly steps along a career track towards predictable ends.

In this paper I shall be summarising the main themes and issues in the
study of work role transitions that have emerged from recent research
conducted by the Work Role Transitions, Innovation and Career Development
team at the Sheffield Social and Applied Psychology Unit*. The following
projects have been completed:

---

*   Research reports and papers on which this review is based are
      available on request. Interested readers are invited to write to
      the author for a list of these.

a.   A British national survey of middle and senior managers, with
      particular concentration on women in management. The repeat
      survey design has provided extensive career history and last-
      transition data on 2300 managers (including 800 women) at time 1
      and also longitudinal data from a 1100 subsample one year later.

b.   An intensive study of 180 recent graduate entrants to a major oil
      company. The study design is multi-method and longitudinal, and
      explores process issues in adjustment to work role transitions.

c.   A case study of the promotion system in a Police Force. This
      interview and questionnaire study focussed on 122 Police
      Inspectors (the "middle management" of the police), and evaluated
      the dysfunctional consequences of one kind of career development
      system.

2.   THE NOTION OF THE TRANSITION CYCLE

The notion of The Transition Cycle (see Figure 1) will be used in this
paper to summarise our state of knowledge about job change.

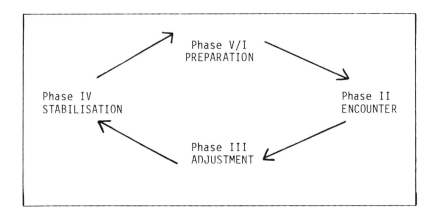

Figure 1:   The Transition Cycle

The notion of the process as a cycle conveys three important truths about
transitions:

a.   It suggests perpetual motion - each one of us is at some stage of
      one (or more) transition cycles. No sooner have we completed
      adjustment to one change than the next is visible on the horizon,
      through to the final work role transition of retirement. When
      one has reached a stabilised relationship with the new job and
      environment (if this stage is reached at all!) then one's
      experiences are a form of preparation for the beginning of the
      next possible transition.

b.   The cycle shows that there are distinctive phases to transitions; the processes and qualities of experience are different at each stage. In the preparation or anticipation stage expectancies and motives predominate. In the encounter phase (the first few days or weeks) the individual is preoccupied with cognitive sense-making and affective stress-coping. The adjustment phase involves the assimilations and accommodations the person makes to reach an acceptable "fit" between themselves and the role, i.e. changes in identity and initiatives to alter the work role. The stabilisation phase connotes the pattern of discretionary and controlled performance that is reached through adjustment. This may yield successes and failures, conformity and deviance, isolation or involvement.

c.   The cycle contains the implication that what happens at one stage affects what happens at the next. Failure to prepare adequately for change increases the likelihood of a "shock" reaction at the encounter stage. How one copes with the shocks and surprises of encounter may set the pattern for the person's longer term adjustment strategy. How adjustment is achieved determines what kind of stabilised working relationship will become established. How satisfactory is the stabilisation will colour the individual's attitude towards their next possible transition.

3.   PROPERTIES OF TRANSITION CYCLES

If we think of the transition as a building block, we can see how careers can be conceived as chained sequences of them, and how organisational climates might be described in terms of the kinds of cycles people experience in them. For the notion of transition cycle to have this constructive analytical purpose we need to look at the different types of transition people may experience. It is proposed that nine dimensions can be used to characterise properties of any transition cycle.

3.1.   Speed

How fast is the cycle turning? Our research, and comparable work in North America, show that the rate of movement is increasing. Fewer than one in ten British managers has only had experience of a single employer in their working life and most experience a major work role transition every three years. For young managers in large corporations the rate of change seems to be even faster - in our oil company study transfers took place on average once every nine months. What determines speed? There are three causes: (1) organisational turbulence: moves are enforced by such events as company reorganisations; (2) individual motives: many people are restlessly seeking job change to enhance their career opportunities and satisfactions; (3) company policies: many companies deliberately rotate people through a variety of jobs at a rapid rate as a means of "training". Some might cynically say that the real motive here is control, and that one of the best ways of maintaining the status quo is not to leave anyone in a job long enough to achieve control or the power, knowledge and motives to make changes. High speed can operate as a kind of gyroscope - achieving organisational stability through movement.

3.2.   Amplitude

How radical is the transition, or how novel are its demands on the person? This is another way of asking how well prepared are people for change. Preparation may be general as well as specific. One's state of readiness comes partly from anticipating the particular demands that await one, and partly from one's much longer history of prior training and experience: one's "anticipatory socialisation". Thus it can be that someone may be well forewarned about a coming transition but be unready to face its demands, or, alternatively, one can have little or no warning about a change and yet find the new demands call upon one's familiar and practised skills. So we might expect amplitude to be highest early in one's career, and to decrease thereafter. This would be true if people had orderly career patterns. In general though our research shows that managers at all career stages are likely to be confronted by demands for which they are untrained and unprepared. Indeed, amplitude is often heightened by people acquiring false expectations about coming changes. This can be observed frequently in the recruitment process where organisations are more concerned with selling themselves than in conveying a realistic image of what will await the new recruit. High amplitude can also be generated by organisational practices that result in unplanned or random transfers.

3.3.   Symmetry

What "shape" is the transition cycle? How much time is spent at each stage of the cycle? A symmetrical cycle is one where all stages are fully experienced, and an asymmetrical one is where one or more stages are missed out, the cycle is terminated prematurely, or one stage predominates over all others. For example, if the contrasts experienced at the encounter phase are highly traumatic, no other adjustment than coping with stress may be possible. In other cases, assimilation of the newcomer into complex or conflictual group settings may mean that adjustment processes are consuming and perpetual, and no stabilisation is achieved. The opposite case is where a transition takes place into some highly practised and undemanding new role performance. Then encounter and adjustment are achieved with extreme rapidity and a stabilised working pattern is immediately formed. Transitions into simple and highly routinised jobs often have this asymmetry. Indeed, symmetry usually varies as a consequence of the amount of adjustment that will be required - from simple jobs where the emphasis is all upon performing and little on learning, to highly complex jobs where lengthy learning and enculturation are necessary. From the foregoing it will also be apparent that the "shape" or symmetry of transition cycles changes over the typical life/career history. During the early career period encounter and adjustment are major challenges. Stabilisation is often missed out because of the rapid job changing of many young people in their early years of employment. In mid-career, as one becomes more practised in handling transitions, the emphasis is likely to switch to the bridge between adjustment and stabilisation. Late career is dominated by the later phases of the cycle, with greater emphasis on stabilisation and preparation for one's last job moves and impending retirement. This is a "typical" pattern, but our research shows that decreasing numbers of people have "typical" patterns. Future research could usefully evaluate how the symmetry of transition cycles departs from these norms, and shed fresh light on life/career adjustment trends.

3.4. Continuity

Are transition cycles logically sequential? Does each one follow its predecessor in a predictable or orderly fashion? In other words, when we look at an individual's lifetime sequence of transition cycles do we see what is conventionally thought of as a "career" or do we see a work history of largely unconnected employment experiences? The determinants of continuity are often environmental. Job change takes place against a background of turbulence and upheaval in industrialised societies. Careers, if they can be found, have to be driven against the prevailing tides of uncertainty and change. Company reorganisations, takeovers and mergers, the sudden departure of key people, and rapidly changing economic fortunes are all commonplace in modern organisations and frequently thrust upon employees the imperative of sudden and unexpected job change. Planned careers become difficult under such circumstances and people accept quite radical changes if they feel under sufficient external constraint. Our research confirms that not only are managers making radical moves more often than "conventional" career moves, such as simple promotions, but they have very little ability to predict either type. Of course discontinuous career patterns are also internally motivated, and our research also shows that managers often make radical moves out of dissatisfaction with their previous situation. Discontinuous careers seem to be created by managers' repeated searching for challenging and fulfilling work; each new move bringing fresh frustrations and opportunities for further change. Indeed, so common is radical job change that we are close to the point where the conventional notion of career should be abandoned, and some broader notion of work history be connoted by the term.

3.5. Discretion

Who controls progress through the transition cycle? How much opportunity do individuals have to shape the qualities of their experience at each stage of the cycle? Preparatory socialisation may be tightly scheduled, as in much technical training, or entirely at the individual's discretion, as in many managerial job changes. What happens at the encounter phase may be fixed and programmatic or it may be left to chance. In the adjustment phase the nature of tasks may compel the person to adopt particular strategies, or they may find considerable freedom in how tasks may be defined and performance constructed. In the stabilisation phase, performance may be tightly or loosely controlled by supervisors and evaluation systems. Discretion typically comes from three sources. By default: when control systems simply neglect the individual and the job. Through planning: when some particular degree of control or latitude is purposefully scheduled by personnel or line management. By demand: when the individual deliberately challenges and tries to alter the boundaries of discretion. The predominant values, norms and practices of organisations as "cultures" embody the amount of discretion that will be encountered, and the chief instrument for its expression is usually the supervisor. In general, the higher the status of the role into which transition is being made, the greater the discretion, though this is less a planned phenomenon than a reflection of increases in trust and ambiguity which accompany the broadening responsibilities of higher level tasks. However, even at graduate entrant level, discretion can be surprisingly high for the newcomer, more often by default than by planning. Dropping graduates "in at the deep end" may be justified by

managers as the best way to learn, but in reality it is often because
people are too busy to think of and plan any other strategy.

3.6.   Complexity

How clearly or easily can the tasks of the transition cycle be defined?
For lower level roles what needs to be done at each stage can often be
reliably predicted, even to the point of being linked to reward and
control systems, e.g. employment contracts being provisional upon newcomers making "the grade" in training and early performance.   More
complex transitions involve multiple encounters and adaptations - cycles
within cycles.   Transition is made not just to a set of role requirements
but also to work groups, subordinates, client populations and so on.
Where transitions involve geographical relocation, there will also be
important adjustment tasks in relation to the community, and for spouse
and children.   How stressful is transition will be a direct function of
complexity, and successful coping will depend upon how effectively the
various tasks of transition can be synchronised.   Some powerful interactions can be expected.   Adaptive failures in one sphere are likely to
spill over into others, turning the transition into a crisis.   One way of
researching the complexity of transition cycles is to observe the
critical events and tasks that are encountered.   The more varied and
unexpected these are is an indication of complexity.

3.7.   Propulsion

Who is driving the transition cycle, the person or the system?   It is
likely to make a considerable difference to how the cycle is experienced
whether it was initiated by the person or determined by outside forces.
This is less a dichotomy of alternatives than a continuum of influences,
since many transitions fall into an intermediate zone;   for example, the
offer that cannot be refused, the opportunity that cannot be ignored, or
the forced move that is subsequently directed by the individual.   A move
to self-employment after enforced redundancy is a typical example of the
latter type.   Even when moves seem totally constrained, people often
approach them with the spirit and intent of controlling the process.
Clearly, how much the person feels a proactive agent or a reactive victim
of change will determine the kind of commitment they have to the process.
Where career systems are designed so that all job moves and placements
are hierarchically determined, then problems of frustration, mismatch,
powerlessness, alienation and deviance become more likely.   People who
feel self-propelled are more likely to take risks, overcome obstacles and
experience fulfilment.   Note, that it is whether the person feels self-
directed that matters, rather than how an outside observer might judge
them.   Self-propulsion or directedness can be seen to shift the basis for
commitment away from both organisation or profession.   When interviewing
graduates to establish whether their orientation was of the
"cosmopolitan" or "local" type, we found that neither model seemed to
apply to many self-directed individuals who said that their primary
commitment was "to myself".   Any loyalty to their organisation or
profession is provisional - they will stick with either as long as they
feel that they are achieving what they want or feel they deserve.   So we
can see that propulsion is one of the most critical dimensions of transition, and reflects both the type of environment in which change is taking
place and the personality disposition of the job changer.

3.8. Facilitation

Who or what helps progress through the cycle? Where a transition involves even a moderate degree of novelty or complexity in its demands, the task for the person is one of path-finding. This task is made easier by having reliable information and insights at the preparation stage, supportive informants and good "maps" of the new social and technical environment at the encounter stage, dependable feedback and empowering relationships at the adjustment stage, and relevant evaluation and reward systems at the stabilisation stage. Job descriptions and organisational charts are among the documented information sources that may be used, and appraisal, counselling and training practices are among the formal organisational systems that may apply. Supervisory relations and local group dynamics are the informal means for facilitating adjustment to change. Family and friends outside work may also be highly important. Our research shows the first two of these, i.e. the formal systems, are seriously deficient in most organisations. Thus how satisfactory are informal and personal relationships is critical to how much support people have in adjustment. In the work environment the boss is a key figure, though through pressure of work, competing demands, or just a lack of awareness of what they can do to help, supervisors are often unhelpful and therefore circumvented as help is sought from colleagues and others. The uncontrolled reliability and direction of these informal supports can mean that informal socialisation leads to deviant or dysfunctional adjustment patterns rather than effective performance and organisational integration. There is much that organisations could do to improve the formal information and resources available to people, and to aid the speedy formation of supportive working relationships. In the encounter phase, newcomers should not be placed initially in socially isolated work roles, and they should be encouraged to explore their new environments in a climate of freedom and safety. Having a real job to do at an early stage, which involves genuine challenges but low failure costs, is the best way to ensure satisfactory and satisfying adjustment processes. Well managed performance review and goal-setting methods help to maintain trust, commitment and effectiveness at the stabilisation phase, and can incorporate the kinds of counselling and planning that will prepare people for their next transition.

3.9. Significance

What are the outcomes of transition for the person and the organisation? Do they result in "replication" - enhancing the situational status quo or reinforcing the person's identity? Are the changes that occur a form of "gradation" - some evolutionary growth or decline of organisational functions or personal attributes? Or are they a kind of "revolution" - resulting in some radical change in job or organisational operations or in some fundamental shift on an identity parameter? Are they traps, tunnels or turning points? This is the question of surpassing importance in the study of transitions, and is why they present an urgent challenge and opportunity for research. What happens in the adjustment phase supplies the answer to this question, though, as we have seen, this is largely determined by what has happened in previous stages of the cycle and, indeed what has happened in previously experienced transition cycles. So taking the adjustment phase as a primary focus immediately requires us to broaden our attention to encompass the history of the individual's past experience and the characteristics of the organisational cultures that generate opportunities for change and the events

that influence the process of change. Our research shows that the outcomes of transitions are commonly left to chance, intuition or instinct,
to the extent that neither the individual nor the organisation is usually
approaching adjustment analytically or planfully. Empirical evidence
confirms that personal change is an outcome of adjustment, though during
any one cycle it may be hard to detect; change occurring suddenly or
gradually after a sequence of certain cycles. There are also many
dimensions to personal change and some, such as self-image or esteem,
seem to be more labile than others, such as values and needs. Innovation
seems to be a more widely detectable adjustment outcome in our management
samples, who often re-form the roles they are in to fit their skills and
requirements.

4.   CONCLUSIONS

So research is confirming that many transitions have great personal and
organisational significance. They can reveal the small beginnings from
which larger and longer term developments stem, and they can be seen to
have immediately important personal and social consequences.

This analysis has sought to reveal the varied forms that transitions
take, where and how they originate, and how they are experienced. The
nine dimensions discussed above have been proposed as a potential
descriptive and analytical system for the future study of transitions.
It may also have practical application as an agenda for self-analysis or
counselling about how people prepare for and experience change. There
has been insufficient space in this presentation to consider the effects
of interactions between dimensions. For example, it is evident that
speed x complexity yield "short-circuiting" of the cycle, i.e. failure to
reach the conclusion of the adjustment phase. Many other subtle and
important interactions can be proposed. It will be for empirical
research in the future to identify what combinations of features are
critical to the occurrence of significant outcomes.

There are already theoretical and research literatures that can shed
light on transitions - in the areas of lifespan development, careers and
counselling, occupational socialisation, job redesign, and organisation
development - but these bodies of knowledge have remained separate and
uncommunicating. The importance of the microprocesses of adjustment to
work role transitions has not been recognised widely by scholars in these
areas, yet what happens in the transition cycle is an issue of common
concern to them. Research on transitions offers a new way of bridging
these disciplinary interests and synthesising their knowledge and ideas.

REFERENCES

Recent papers by members of the SAPU Work Role Transitions, Innovation and Career Development team:

(1) Alban-Metcalfe, B. and Nicholson, N. (1984). The Career Development of British Managers. London: British Institute of Management. (Summary: SAPU Memo No 680).

(2) Arnold, J. (1984). Tales of the unexpected. Surprises experienced by graduates in the early months of employment. British Journal of Guidance and Counselling, 13, 308-319. (SAPU Memo No 671).

(3) Arnold, J. (1985). Getting started: Graduates adjusting and developing during their first year of employment. Personnel Review, in press. (SAPU Memo No 726).

(4) Cawsey, T.F., Nicholson, N. and Alban-Metcalfe, B. (1985). Who's on the fast track? The relationship between career mobility, individual and task characteristics. Paper presented to Academy of Management Annual Conference, San Diego, August 1985. (SAPU Memo No 703).

(5) Glowinkowski, S. and Nicholson, N. (1985). The promotion pathology: A study of British police inspectors. Personnel Review, in press. (SAPU Memo No 659).

(6) Nicholson, N. (1984). A theory of work role transitions. Administrative Science Quarterly, 29, 172-191. (SAPU Memo No 487).

(7) Nicholson, N. (1986). Work role transitions: Processes and outcomes. In P.B. Warr (ed), Psychology at Work, 3rd edition, in press. (SAPU Memo No 743).

(8) Nicholson, N., West, M.A. and Cawsey, T.F. (1985). Future uncertain: Expected vs attained job change among managers. Journal of Occupational Psychology, in press. (SAPU Memo No 709).

(9) West, M.A. and Nicholson, N. (1984). Role innovation and creativity in the world of work. Paper presented to the BPS Annual Social Psychology Section Conference, Oxford, September 1984. (SAPU Memo No 670).

(10) West, M.A., Nicholson, N. and Arnold, J. (1985). Identity changes as outcomes of work role transitions. In T. Honess and K. Yardly (eds), Self and Identity: Individual Change and Development. Routledge and Kegan Paul, in press. (SAPU Memo No 663).

(11) West, M.A., Nicholson, N. and Rees, A. (1985). Transitions into newly created jobs. (SAPU Memo No 707).

THE PSYCHOLOGY OF WORK AND ORGANIZATION
G. Debus and H.-W. Schroiff (Editors)
© *Elsevier Science Publishers B.V. (North-Holland), 1986*

TRAINING AND INTERVENTION WITHIN ORGANIZATIONS

Report of the chairman
G. PITHON
Laboratoire de Psychologie Sociale,
Université de Montpellier III,
F-34032 Montpellier Cédex, France.

Participants: Pithon, G.; Brouillet, D.; Costalat, A.M.;
Goguelin, P.; Thionville R. (all France).

The planning of tomorrow's society is prepared from training systems
that today's society sets. This stake is particularly important for
developing societies because of the fast de-multiplication of knowledges
and know-how they really need, but also for post-industrial societies
which stagnate in a crisis of growth that is badly controlled (bad
adaptation to new techniques, to a necessary recycling and industrial
modernization, to youth unemployment, creation of new jobs etc.).
In France, since the national interprofessional agreement of July   9,
1970 and the vote of law of July 16, 1971, various measures have come to
strengthen and complete the legal and contractual devices, "making of
the permanent professional training a national obligation".
Therefore, training is a right for all salaried employees; social
partners and the work's council are consulted. The employee can ask for
a training clearance certificate, distinct from the training plan of the
enterprise (law of July 17, 1978).
Annual or pluri-annual contracts between the government and enterprises
or professional branches can be signed after agreement from trade unions
and salaried employees (law of February 24, 1984). Therefore training
objectives and means must be discussed by the partners. Finally,
trainings which alternate with practice are offered to young people
between 18 and 25 in order to complete their education thanks to
training courses which objectives are qualification and adaptability to
employment.
Within the frame of this workshop of the West European Conference on the
Psychology of work and organization, various questions are raised:
− How to intervene by the means of training, and taken as a whole, to
make changes easier within organizations?
− How to take into account the trainee's social needs, particularly
anxiety?
− How to recruit trainees for a training program in a standard and
efficient way?
− How to work out carefully regular training contracts thanks to
educational methods based on objectives and training assessment (or
formative evaluation)?

1. HOLISTIC APPROACH OF ADULT TRAINING IN ORGANIZATIONS

In this lecture, P. Goguelin stands up for a "holistic", or global
approach of training in organizations opposed to traditional, analytic
approaches.
Indeed, in a very cartesian concern of rationalization the officials of
these organizations often make up homogeneous training groups, either in
a "vertical" (technicians, accountants etc.) or "horizontal" way (pro-

duction, supervisors, executives etc.). Such practices make the work of training staff easier as far as a group having identical problems and aims is concerned. However, they contribute to put a brake on the organizational and personal change of workers: caste feeling, segmentary vision of problems and even crystallization of oppositions develop, and they are a prejudice for the working of the organization.

Creating heterogeneous training groups including persons working on the same production line, should limit these "perverse effects". Moreover, the holistic approach proposed by Goguelin tries to integrate positive aspects of various practices in fashion (management participation by objectives, semi-independent groups of management, quality circels, enrichment of tasks etc.). The training pattern he proposes (see fig. 1) integrates some vertical and horizontal groups who successively meet, and as often as it is needed, to formulate and solve the problems they think necessary to retain. Vertical groups, composed of representative persons from various hierarchical levels, establish a list of difficulties they have to cope with, and a list of all their possible causes. Horizontal groups who are composed of representative persons concerning all stages of the production process, and who have already been part of vertical groups, must look for solutions to the problems compiled by vertical groups, ask for information, propose trainings etc. Vertical groups meet again to examine the solutions, study their applicability or bring up new difficulties.

Members of vertical and horizontal groups then adjust their solutions and regulate by themselves the speed concerning the evolution of meetings.

R. Thionville illustrates this approach by describing an intervention in a building enterprise which rallied all employees. Until that time, the enterprise was proposing trainings to its employees taken from standard catalogues it received. The intervention, focused on the enterprise plan, allowed to develop the motivation, the responsibility spirit of each worker, and to decrease the dependence of workers from the hierarchy.

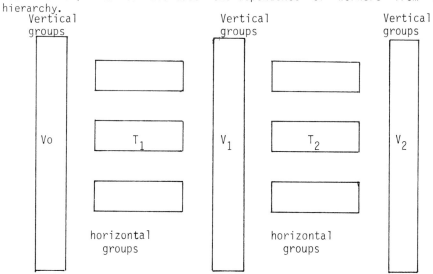

Figure 1

The discussion on those two lectures was essentially about the changes induced by such a practice, changes that anyone undertakes to do at his level without only wishing that "the other will do it"! It also permitted to underline the limits of "expression groups" planned by the Legislator in French enterprises. Finally, it was above all pointed out that such a practice could develop the "culture of enterprise".

2. TAKING INTO ACCOUNT AFFECTIVE OR COGNITIVE NEEDS IN TRAINING SITUATIONS

A.M. Costalat discusses the problem of taking into account social needs and emotional states in which trainees are, while they are trained. The field study focused on middle executives from the tertiary sector in enterprises. Indeed, there is a relation between social needs which are developed by future trainees before they go to the training course and their state of anxiety. The latter is defined as "an anxiety of situation" whose cause is known by the trainee, opposed to the "diffuse and chronical anxiety" linked to complex variables of the personality.
If people are free to constitute a group, anxious ones will prefer the company of people they know and non-anxious will get together with unknown persons.
Then, this study allows to reveal that the affiliation interpreted by Schachter (1) as a response to anxiety corresponds to an affective need for anxious persons and to a cognitive need for non-anxious ones.
The group that is imagined and desired represents for anxious persons a need of affective cohesion realizing harmony and therefore the "social rest", when for non-anxious persons it rather represents a field for cognitive exploration, structuration and social differentiation.
This analysis gave rise to various reactions in the group of participants. Which procedure should be used to orientate the trainees into their trajectory of training respecting their socio-affective needs (practices of information, of selection and of composition of groups in the process of education)? Can the affective needs be "saturated" to make the development of cognitive needs easier?
In social psychology these questions re-introduce the need to take into account the personal variables in the situation of training.

3. STANDARD INTERVIEWS FOR THE CHOICE OF CANDIDATES TO TRAINING COURSES

When the demand of training is higher than the supply, it becomes essential to carry out the selection of the candidates.
D. Brouillet suggests an original procedure of selection interview. It consists in standardizing the situation by giving the means to objectivize the expectations of the training staff and in building up a "reference profile". To that effect he uses the technique of the semantic differential scale (Osgood, 1957) (2). The trainers establish by dialogue a reference profile corresponding to the final objectives of the training considering the semantic space determined by the trainers; the candidates must situate themselves on each dimension of the differential scale. During the interview, the jury asks them to argue their positions (especially the ones presenting divergences with the profile of reference) which they are not aware of.
The results obtained seem to be particularly instructive. In front of the difficulty to objective their representations and because of the false idea they have got of the interviews of selection, professionals

(men and women) are brought to appeal to specialists, who, for most of
them, assess behaviours according to a psychological theory and not
according to professional objectives. Thus this procedure institutes a
dialectic between training and selection.
Actually, the selection based on the finality of the training can,
because of the product it puts in, retro-act on the training process.
Without contesting the originality of the process, the participants
underlined the need to set up a "profile of reference", not only from
the point of view of the trainers, but also from the demands of the
employers and the possible users (administration of hospitals, doctors
and patients for the training of nurses, for example). Actually, the
last mentioned can propose duties, constraints and obligations which
adhere to the job and which would be badly defined by the responsibles
of training.
Moreover the confrontation of profiles of reference could be a means to
provoke changes in politicies about training and professional practices.

4. PARAMETERS OF A REGULAR TRAINING CONTRACT: PEDAGOGY BY OBJECTIVES AND FORMATIVE EVALUATION

In a time when we are confronted to a growing "contractualization" of
social relationship within post-industrial societies, G. Pithon tries to
define some paramters essential to the setting of regular training
contracts in adult educational methods.
There is a training contract as soon as a link associates trainers to
trainees: "In this way, communication seems to be a contract because,
like every contract, it obeys to rules and carries stakes" (Ghiglione)
(3). Rules and parameters of this system of communication can be more or
less explicit (Elkind) (4). Training stakes can be shared by partners or
may be independent or opposed.
Educational methods based on objectives and formative evaluation are,
among others, essential practices in order to establish new contractual
relationships between the trainers and the trainees. They are part of a
theory concerning training systems where they are linked in an interplay
of mutual influences: analysis of the needs, determination of objectives, study of psycho-social features concerning the trainees, setting
of homogeneous or heterogeneous groups, elaboration of training plans
and programs, choice of appropriate educational methods and techniques,
and finally setting of various evaluation procedures.
Formative evaluation must be situated among other evaluation proceedings
(informative, diagnostic and summative) and G. Pithon summarizes their
main functions: information about the functioning of a training system,
the forecasts about the abilites of success or failure of persons,
sanctions about achieved works.
The training assessment, or formative evaluation is apart from these
because it is a micro-system leading to regulate educational strategies
of trainers and apprenticeship of trainees, by the means more particularly of self-assessment proceedings.
An experiment realized in a natural situation which was done in collaboration with C. Estrabunt, studies the effects of various training contracts in a training course sanctioned by a written test (essay type)
that ends the training program.
In one group (I) the objectives and the evaluation proceedings are
explicit, opposite, and integrated thanks to a confrontation of the
trainer's assessment with the self-evaluation of the trainees concerning an intermediate task: the writing of a report. The clarifying of

objectives is realized thanks to a precise grid of corrections which is used for evaluations.

In another group (II), the same process carried on for an oral lecture, that is to say according to objectives less relevant considering the requirements of the written test that sanctions the training course.

Finally, in four groups (III) there is neither precise explication of the objectives nor use of formative evaluation practices. From the results obtained to the final test, corrected by the trainers of group III, it appears that an educational method based on objectives associated to formative evaluation practices contributes, among others, to the setting of regular and efficient training contracts. The relevance of objectives is fundamental. Group II, which has less good results than group I, seems however able to transfer its methodological acquisitions in oral expression to a written test because it has better results than group III. Contrary to group I, group II does not seem to be able to correctly forecast its final results concerning the form and quality of expression.

At the time of the discussion that followed this lecture the necessity of inscribing educational methods in particular social relationships that bring them up was pointed out; that is to say, various kinds of contracts of communication (implicit or explicit) which associate the trainers to the trainees.

There remains the hard task to make a synthesis of the synthesis!

The change in organizations is easier thanks to a global approach that combines vertical and horizontal groups. In these conditions, each one can participate in the detection and formulation of problems as well as the setting of solutions, contrary to traditional training groups, created on a sectorial or socio-professional basis that reinforce opposed interests and a "bitty" sight of the organization.

Taking into account social needs (affective and cognitive) before, during and after the training course allows to adapt and optimize intervention, as well when the preliminary information is given concerning actions to be undertaken, as when the setting of groups is done, and actions are followed.

The conception of standard interviews concerning the choice of candidates to a training course allows the training staff, employers, even the users, to build an "ideal profile" of the candidate. These processes insert a dynamic of changes in training organizations because it makes it compulsory for the partners who often do not meet each other, to confront their various demands. It also inserts a greater equity for candidates who are too often subjected to the hazards of the selective interview which "rules of the game" vary between the members of a same board of examiners and, a fortiori, between different boards.

Finally it appears that the relationships between the trainers and the trainees must be studied as a particular contract of communication whose objectives, stakes and rules are more or less explicit as far as the tasks are concerned. Their clarifying and appropriateness, thanks to pedagogy by objectives and formative evaluation, seem to make training contracts more regulated and efficient.

The lectures given at this workshop show that each social and educational intervention can dynamise, at various levels, the "synergy": "training of people-organizational changes".

REFERENCES
(1) Schachter, S., The Psychology of Affiliation, Stanford: Stanford University Press, 1959.

(2) Osgood, C.E., Suci, G.J. & Tannenbaum, P.H., The measurement of meaning, Urbana, Ill.: University of Illinois Press, 1957.
(3) Ghiglione, R., Le contrat de communication, le jeu et les enjeux, Champs éducatifs. 1981, 2, 11-19.
(4) Elkind, D., Teacher-child contracts, in: Readings in Educational Psychology: Contemporary perspectives, New York: Murphy and Row, 1976.

THE PSYCHOLOGY OF WORK AND ORGANIZATION
G. Debus and H.-W. Schroiff (Editors)
© Elsevier Science Publishers B.V. (North-Holland), 1986

THE SKILLS OF LEADERSHIP

Ian E. Morley & Dian M. Hosking.*

Department of Psychology, University of Warwick, Coventry CV4
7AL, England.

1. INTRODUCTION

A salient feature of the social psychological literature on leadership is
the gloomy pessimism with which critics judge past progress and likely
achievements. Amongst the criticisms are the claims that:

1.1. Leadership is equated simply with intended influence, which makes
leaders no different from other members of a group. Attention has
focused on a very narrow range of leader behaviours which occur in interactions between a leader and a relatively small group (Child & Hosking
[1]; Hosking & Morley [2]).

1.2. The variables studied have been unimportant, accounting for little
variance in the performance of individuals or social units (Hosking &
Hunt [3]).

1.3. Much of the social psychological literature is not social at all.
To quote Katz & Kahn [4],, it is only beginning to consider "the operation of leadership processes in the real world, namely within social
systems" (p. 536). The current state of the art may be seen in the
macro-oriented model of Hunt & Osborn [5].

1.4. The attempt to study leadership has meant that knowledge has been
divorced from action (Argyris[6]). Hosking & Morley [2][7][8], have
argued that macro models such as those of Hunt & Osborn [5] emphasize the
condition of being organized rather than acts of organizing. That is,
they treat aspects of organization as if they were fixed physical
entities rather than emergent properties which reflect social actions,
interactions, and evaluations. If Clark [9] is correct (and we think he
is) what is required is a shift from mechanistic to non-mechanistic views
of knowledge. Thus, to understand leadership we have to understand its
"cognitive, discretionary, and politically problematic aspects" (Clark
[9], p.376).

1.5. Research on leadership does not add up. To quote Stogdill [10],
"the endless accumulation of empirical data has not produced an integrated understanding of leadership" (p. vii).

Criticisms of this kind are well known, and deserve to be taken seriously. Some would conclude that the concept of leadership should be

---

* Dr Hosking is Lecturer in Organizational Behaviour, University of
Aston, Management Centre, Gosta Green, Birmingham B4 7DU, England.

abandoned (Miner [11]). We could not disagree more. In our view
organizations take the form they do because leaders, whether formal
(appointed) or informal (emergent) choose to exercise certain kinds of
social skill (Hosking & Morley [7][8]). What is required is the
development of a social psychological theory which makes it possible
systematically to articulate the nature of the skills involved.

2. LEADERSHIP, ORGANIZATION AND SOCIAL SKILL

As a discipline social psychology needs to integrate models of actors,
models of processes, and models of social systems (or contexts) (Morley
[12]; Hosking [13]; Mugny [14]). If the integration is to be successful
it will be necessary to describe actors, processes, and contexts in ways
which are mutually supportive or commensurate. Ideally, we would like to
describe actors, processes and contexts in the same kinds of way.

In the context of leadership it is clear that an adequate theory should
satisfy four additional constraints. First, it should link talk
about leadership to talk about skill. Clearly, the outcomes of social
processes (including what is learned) depend upon the skills of the
participants (Mills [15] , pp. 17-18). Second, it should recognize that
leaders have a special position within a social system or organization
(Mugny [14]). In our view the leader is the person with the top rank in
the status hierarchy of the group. He or she has a special responsibility for organizing in the sense of Weick [16]. Third, it should
treat leadership as involving a series of role relationships, within and
between groups (Morley & Hosking [17]). Social psychologists have
focused on the former to the detriment of the latter (Hosking & Hunt
[3]). We prefer the emphasis in Sherif & Sherif [18], namely that:
"Leadership involves the role relationships between the leader and other
members and instrumentalities for coordinating interaction" (p. 170).
Leadership is a special kind of organizing activity. It is political
decision making, construed in the widest possible sense. It is, thus, a
process in which issues are framed and handled inside and outside the
group. Finally, it should treat leadership as an intelligent performance, requiring an organized system of values and beliefs (Dehn &
Schanck [19]; Bales [20]).

3. SOCIAL SKILL AS AN INTEGRATING CONCEPT

The literature on leadership has not been informed by attempts systematically to articulate the nature of the skills which make leaders
effective. The main purpose of this paper is to introduce a model of
social skill based on the work of Morley [12][21] and Hosking [22][23]
[24]. An important part of our argument is that in many respects the
skills of leaders are the skills of negotiators. Following Morley [21] we
regard the skilful leader as someone who, through an understanding of the
threats and opportunities in the environment of work, and of the resources he/she can bring to bear, is able to take active and effective
measures to protect or pursue the values and interests seen to be at
stake.

Most research looks at managers, or other appointed officials. It is more or less assumed that the way to understand leadership is to follow the officials round and examine what they do. We have two reservations about this. First, it is important to establish that the officials are acting as leaders in some clearly defined sense. Second, it is not enough to study what leaders do, in the style, say, of Luthans & Lockwood [25]. What is required is a focus on problems or issues. To quote Hosking & Morley [2] "what is central is that leaders recognize certain issues as important, and ignore others; that issues are defined by scripts which identify threats and opportunities, and suggest guidelines for action; and that effectiveness is what makes sense collectively in certain social and political environments".

Let us try to spell out some of the implications of this point of view. Notice, first, that the language we have used is the language of politics. Organizations are systems in which people with different values negotiate and renegotiate the terms on which they will do business (Morley & Hosking [17]). Whatever else may be involved, leadership is politics at work; it is power in use (Lee & Lawrence [26]; Kanter [27]). Those who say that research on leadership has a disembodied, non-organizational quality are not just making a comment about levels of analysis. They are recognising, implicitly or explicitly, that the study of leadership has been divorced from the study of social action.

We have said that leadership is organizing activity, in the sense of Weick [16]. To quote Weick [16], it is activity in which "reality is selectively perceived, rearranged cognitively, and negotiated interpersonally" (p. 164). We shall call this activity sense-making. Leaders are expected and perceived to take a more central role in this activity than others. They help others to make sense of their environments in ways which contribute to their identities as members of a social order (Hosking & Morley [2][7]). They construct a social order in which certain kinds of change are seen to make sense historically (Hosking & Morley [2]; Kanter [27]).

To understand sense-making of this kind it is necessary to understand how people describe their worlds, and recognize threats and opportunities within them (Hosking & Morley [2]). From this point of view it is important to link work on leadership with work in cognitive science, political science, and personality theory, dealing with the structure and function of systems of value and belief (Carbonnell [28]; Axelrod [29]; Bales [20]; Davies [30]). We assume that, to understand leadership we have to understand something of leaders' outlooks (Davies [30]), operational codes (George [31]), and theories in use (Argyris [6]). Broadly speaking, we have to understand their view of the world, and how it works.

It follows from this that leadership is a matter, primarily, of macro rather than micro skills. The crucial issue is whether leaders "know their way around" (Hosking & Morley [2]). If they do they will be able to organize the core values of members of their groups. That is, they will be able to help others to understand how the social system works and how to operate within it.

Talk about skill implies talk about control and talk about organization
(Hosking & Morley [2]). The control is control of social order. The
social order is based on systems of power and systems of value. The
control mechanism is negotiation, within and between groups. The organization comes from knowledge of the social system, and what is possible
within it.

Burns [32] has described the essence of leadership as "the interaction
of persons with different levels of motivations and of power potential,
including skill, in pursuit of a ... joint purpose" (p. 19). We believe
that such interactions are best described as negotiations. The outcome
of the negotiations are sets of rules. They determine the kinds of
business people will try to do, and how they will try to do it. However,
the rules of the game have to be <u>viable</u>, to work within a given social
system. Skilful leaders are, thus, sensitive to the power structures
within the organization (Wrapp [33]). This means, in turn, that leaders
must keep in touch with a wide range of people, inside and outside the
groups they lead (Kotter [34]). It also means that the concept of sense
making must be broadly defined to include the social processes by which
leaders generate purpose and commitment, within and between groups.

Let us summarise some of the main points we have made in this section of
our paper. First, we are looking for a concept of social skill which
will integrate the literature on leadership and the literature on management. Second, when we speak of social skill we have in mind the skills
of action in an environment which is inherently political. Third, we
hope to integrate the literatures on leadership and negotiation. In
particular, we think the concept of social order is central to the study
of leadership: and we think social order is negotiated order. Fourth,
a concept of social skill should be informed by work in individual
psychology and political science. Finally, the concept should recognise
that there are different kinds of problems. To anticipate a little,
leadership construed as political decision making includes the core
problems of identification, development and choice. (Strictly, speaking,
perhaps, we should add implementation).

4. A GENERAL MODEL OF SOCIAL SKILL

We adopt a decision making approach to leadership. We assume that
decision making begins when actors identify an <u>issue</u>. We assume, further
that what counts as an issue depends on the ways actors perceive actual
or potential changes in the social system to which they belong. What is
crucial, in our view, is whether actors perceive such changes as <u>threats</u>
or <u>opportunities</u> (Morley & Hosking [17]). A psychologically adequate
model of the actors within social systems should show how they obtain
knowledge of their environment, organize it, and use that knowledge to
guide intelligent action.

The first component in our model of social skill therefore concerns the
<u>knowledge base</u> of the actors. We have set out our position in detail,
elsewhere (Morley [12]; Hosking [13]; Hosking & Morley [2]). Here, we
will simply sketch the outline of the main argument.

Effective leaders manage the process by which issues are defined, and
accepted by others as the basis for action. That is, leadership

involves the management of meaning (Smircich & Morgan [35]). What makes this possible is that skilled leaders are skilled perceivers. They are skilled perceivers because they have available higher order constructs which give them a distinctive outlook, or world view.

First, they have systems of values and beliefs which allow them to define threats and opportunities, in ordinary language. Second, they have a great deal of specific knowledge about the social system in which they work. Third, they understand the process of decision making. More precisely, they recognize certain dilemmas inherent in the choices they make. They are, therefore, able to select tactics and sequence be-haviour in a coherent and orderly way. Finally, they have their own models of man. In particular, they recognize that people have limited capacities for processing information and performing mental work. Accordingly, they make moves designed to reduce ambiguity, clarify communications, and generally slow things down.

The second component in our model concerns the ways in which leaders move around the social system. Leaders are effective, in our view, because they shape networks in the sense of Kotter & Lawrence [35]. They build relationships with those they cannot directly control, based on the exchange of information, resources, and support. This means that they are able to recognize when they have ideas which are plausible, but false, or incomplete. It also means that they learn what makes sense collectively, and what does not.

It is important to emphasise, in the present context, that skilled leaders participate in close relationships with high status members of other groups (Batstone, Boraston & Frenkel [36]). There is an exchange of information about political activity within the groups, and in the wider social system. There may also be an exchange of activities in which each helps the other to solve political problems. In particular, each may help the other to construe the past in ways which correspond to the needs of the present (Kanter [27]).

The final element in our model concerns the core problems of the decision process. These are the identification of issues, the develop-ment of solutions, and the selection of policies. We believe that each of the core problems is handled through a process of negotiation, or bargaining. What is most evident, however, is a contrast between two kinds of bargaining (Morley [12]).

On the one hand there are processes which are cognitive, primarily. Leaders use these to help themselves, and others, organize their intellectual activity, and think clearly about the issues. On the other hand, there are processes which are political, primarily. Leaders use these to manage differences between themselves and others, considered as representatives of social groups. The differences may be generated by conflicting goals, or by basic differences in outlook.

Cognitive processes predominate during the stages of identification and development. The bargaining is, perhaps, integrative bargaining, in Walton & McKersie's [37] sense. It is also rational bargaining, in the sense of Snyder & Diesing [38]. Political processes predominate during the stage of selection. The bargaining is pressure bargaining. It is distributive bargaining, in Walton & McKersie's sense.

Thus, leaders, considered as decision makers, need two kinds of skill. They use cognitive activity to remove unnecessary obstacles in the way of decisions which promote social identity and social order. They help others to work out what is going on, and why. At the same time they are not afraid to disagree. Rather, they organize disagreement to reflect the strength in party positions. In this way they make salient (and validate) their roles as representatives of groups.

5. CONCLUSIONS

Leadership has not been considered in relation to the cognitive and social (political) processes of organizing. The skills involved have not been systematically studied. Consequently, we do not have an adequate social psychology of leadership.

We have attempted to show the kinds of move which need to be made if we are to build adequate models of leaders and of the process of leadership. A major implication of our argument is that leadership is organizing activity in which leaders negotiate rules which make sense collectively.

We believe that the concepts we have outlined are necessary for the analysis of leadership and negotiation in any political context. At the same time, we believe that they will be part of a model of the wider context, or social system. After all, if we are to move away from mechanistic views of organizations it is essential that we include the knowledge and skills of the actors as significant parts of such social systems.

As we have argued elsewhere, the skilful performer is someone whose behaviour follows naturally from the key characteristics of the tasks they undertake (Morley & Hosking [17]). It follows naturally because skilful performers understand the nature of the cognitive and political processes required.

The study of leadership used to be a central part of social psychology. It is not any more. It used also to be a central part of the literature on organizations. It is not any more. We would like to bring the study of leadership centre stage once more, in both disciplines. To do so we need to pay more attention to cognitive and social aspects of the problems of political descretion and choice. That is, we need to pay more attention to leadership, considered as a set of social skills.

REFERENCES

[1]   Child, J. and Hosking, D.M., Model Building and Contributions to Understanding, in: Hunt, J. and Larson, L., (eds.), Crosscurrents in Leadership (Southern Illinois University Press, Carbondale and Edwardsville, 1979) pp.148-156.
[2]   Hosking, D.M. and Morley, I.E., The Skills of Leadership, Eighth Biennial Leadership Symposium, Texas Tech University, Lubbock, Texas, U.S.A., 1985.
[3]   Hosking, D.M. and Hunt, J.G., Social Psychological Contributions to the Study of Leadership, International Workshop on Social Psychology and Social Policy, University of Kent, Canterbury, 1980.

[4] Katz, D. and Kahn, R., The Social Psychology of Organizations (Wiley, New York, 1978).

[5] Hunt, J.G. and Osborn, R.N., Toward a Macro-oriented Model of Leadership: An Odyssey, in: Hunt, J.G., Sekaran, U. and Schriesheim, C.A., (eds.), Leadership: Beyond Establishment Views (Southern Illinois University Press, Carbondale and Edwardsville, 1982).

[6] Argyris, C., How Normal Science Methodology Makes Leadership Research Less Additive and Less Applicable, in: Hunt, J.G., and Larson, L.L., (eds.), Crosscurrents in Leadership (Southern Illinois University Press, Carbondale and Edwardsville, 1979).

[7] Hosking, D.M. and Morley, I.E., Leadership and Organization: Processes of Influence, Negotiation and Exchange, Working Paper, Department of Psychology, University of Warwick, 1985.

[8] Hosking, D.M. and Morley, I.E., Leadership and Organization: The Negotiation of Order, University of Aston Management Centre Working Paper Series, (1983), Number 249.

[9] Clark, P.A., Part 5 Integrative Comments: Leadership Theory: The Search for a Reformulation, in: Hunt, J.G., Hosking, D.M., Schriesheim, C.A., and Stewart, R., (eds.), Leaders and Managers: International Perspectives on Managerial Behavior and Leadership (Pergamon Press, Oxford, 1984) pp.375-381.

[10] Stogdill, R., Handbook of Leadership: A survey of Theory and Research (Free Press, New York, 1974).

[11] Miner, J., The Uncertain Future of the Leadership Concept: An Overview, in: Hunt, J.G. and Larson, L., (eds.), Leadership Frontiers (Comparative Administration Research Institute, Kent State University, Kent, Ohio, 1975).

[12] Morley, I.E., Negotiation and Bargaining, in print.

[13] Hosking, D.M., Leadership and organizational skills, in print.

[14] Mugny, G., The Power of Minorities (Academic Press, New York, 1982).

[15] Mills, T.M., The Sociology of Small Groups (Prentice Hall, Englewood Cliffs, N.J., 1967).

[16] Weick, K., The Social Psychology of Organizing (Addison-Wesley, Reading, Mass., 1979).

[17] Morley, I.E. and Hosking, D.M., Decision Making and Negotiation: Leadership and Social Skills, in: Gruneberg, M. and Wall, T.D., (eds.), Social Psychology and Organizational Behaviour (Wiley, Chichester, 1984) pp.71-92.

[18] Sherif, M. and Sherif, C.W., Social Psychology (Harper and Row, New York, 1969).

[19] Dehn, N. and Schanck, R., Artificial and Human Intelligence, in: Sternberg, R.J., (ed.), Handbook of Human Intelligence (Cambridge University Press, Cambridge, 1982) pp.352-391.

[20] Bales, R.F., Personality and Interpersonal Behaviour (Holt, Rinehart and Winston, New York, 1970).

[21] Morley, I.E., Negotiation and Bargaining, in: Argyle, M., (ed.), Social Skills and Work (Methuen, London, 1981) pp.84-115.

[22] Hosking, D.M., Leadership and Organizational Skills, Working Paper, Department of Psychology, University of Warwick, 1985.

[23] Brown, H. and Hosking, D.M., Distributed Leadership and Skilled Performance as Successful Organization in Social Movements, in print.

[24] Grieco, M.S. and Hosking, D.M., Networking, Exchange and Skill, 7th E.G.O.S. Colloquium, Stockholm, Sweden, 1985.

[25] Luthans, F. and Lockwood, D.L., Toward an Observation System for Measuring Leader Behavior in Natural Settings, in: Hunt, J.G., Hosking, D.M., Schriesheim, C.A., and Stewart, R., (eds.), Leaders and Managers: International Perspectives on Managerial Behavior and Leadership (Pergamon Press, Oxford, 1984) pp.117-141.

[26] Lee, R. and Lawrence, P., Organizational Behaviour: Politics at Work (Hutchinson, London, 1985).

[27] Kanter, R., The Change Masters: Corporate Entrepreneurs at Work (George Allen and Unwin, London, 1984).

[28] Carbonnell, J., Politics, in: Schank, R. & Riesbeck, C.K., (eds.), Inside Computer Understanding (Lawrence Erlbaum Associates, Hillsdale, N.J., 1981) pp.259-307.

[29] Axelrod, R.J. (ed.), Structure of Decision: The Cognitive Maps of Political Elites (Princeton University Press, Princeton, 1976).

[30] Davies, A.F., Skills, Outlooks and Passions: A Psychoanalytical Contribution to the Study of Politics (Cambridge University Press, Cambridge, 1980).

[31] George, A.L., The "Operational Code": A Neglected Approach to the Study of Political Leaders and Decision Making, International Studies Quarterly XIII (1969) 190-222.

[32] Burns, J.M., Leadership (Harper and Row, New York, 1978).

[33] Wrapp, H.E., Good Managers Don't Make Policy Decisions, Harvard Business Review July-August (1984) 191-212.

[34] Smircich, L. and Morgan, G., Leadership: The Management of Meaning, The Journal of Applied Behavioral Science 18 (1982) 257-273.

[35] Kotter, J. and Lawrence, P., Mayors in Action: Five Studies in Urban Governance (Wiley, New York, 1974).

[36] Batstone, E., Boraston, I. and Frenkel, S., Shop Stewards in Action (Blackwell, Oxford, 1977).

[37] Walton, R.E. and McKersie, R.B., A Behavioral Theory of Labor Negotiations: An Analysis of a Social Interaction System (McGraw-Hill, New York, 1965).

[38] Snyder, G.H. and Diesing, P., Conflict Among Nations: Bargaining, Decision Making and System Structure in International Crises (Princeton University Press, Princeton, N.J., 1977).

II.5. Work Values

WORK VALUES AND PERSONALITY: EVOLUTION AND DIFFERENTIATION*

Jacques PERRON

Département de Psychologie
Université de Montréal
C.P. 6128, Succursale A
Montréal, P.Q., Canada, H3C 3J7

1.   INTRODUCTION

In the field of vocational psychology, theorists such as Ginzberg, Ginsburg, Axelrad and Herma [1], Super [2], Tiedman, O'Hara and Baruch [3] and Zytowski [4] consider work values as a dimension of personality which plays a determinant role in the process of career choice. As a matter of fact, a review of the literature by Descombes [5] shows that work values have been studied over the past sixty years. They are operationally defined by the degree of importance that a person attaches to different modes of being and behaving which are relevant to the reality of work.

If this concept of work values is useful in the study of career choice and development, is it relevant to the psychology of work and organizations? Various contributions from this field of research indeed tend to support this point of view.

Peters and Waterman [6] in analyzing successful organizations refer to the law of shared values to illustrate one of their "secrets". They mention that these successful organizations make sure that employees adhere to their value system, their "culture" or quit. The authors conclude that each of the organizations they analyzed was paying a great deal of attention to the value process and clearly stated its leading values.

According to Locke [7], values should be considered among the determinants of work satisfaction. Perceived work situation in relationship with the values of the individual represents the most immediate determinant of work satisfaction. This position is singled out by Staw [8] in his recent review of the literature on work satisfaction. After noticing that research on work satisfaction in the last thirty years has been a-theoretical, this author stresses that Locke's point of view represents one of the few conceptual models derived from discrepancy and social comparison theories.

In this interactionist paradigm, outcomes of personal adjustment (e.g. development, productivity, satisfaction) are considered as resulting in part from an adequate relationship between personal attributes and characteristics of the human environments in which workers are involved.

---

*
  This research was supported in part by a grant from the Québec Ministry of Education (FCAC).

The contribution of values to personality then consists in detecting, decoding and assessing essential aspects of the environment which correspond to the features the individual perceives in him/herself and places at the core of his/her identity.

Based on this assumption, this research aims at establishing, in a developmental framework, the evolution of the link between work values and a personality typology essentially derived from vocational interests.

2.   A PERSONALITY TYPOLOGY

As reported in recent reviews of the literature by Borgen [9], Brown and Lent [10] and Walsh and Osipow [11, 12], Holland's [13] theory, because of its numerous empirical supports as well as practical applications, stands as a very sound explanatory system of career choice and development. One of the basic propositions of this theory is that by the personal characteristics they evoke and the aptitudes and skills they require occupations can be reduced to six categories which refer to as many personality types. In order to describe these six types, Holland [13] uses vocational interests, personal attributes, values, and actual or envisaged occupations. For the aims of the present research, only the last two criteria are retained.

Realistic (R). Has conventional values; more specifically attaches much importance to economics and less to aesthetics. Occupations: policeman, welder, plumber.

Investigative (I). Holds theoretical values which underlie interest for symbolic activities and explanatory systems; sometimes not inclined toward aesthetic values. Occupations: biologist, physician, mathematician, air pilot.

Artistic (A). Non conformist and intuitive; has primarily aesthetic rather than economic or political values. Occupations: musician, architect, writer.

Social (S). Predominant values are social, sometimes religious, and primarily oriented toward helping or educative interpersonal relations. Occupations: practising psychologist, personnel director, recreation services director.

Enterprising (E). Attracted by influence and persuasion; holds economic and political values, and attaches less importance to theoritical and aesthetic values. Occupations: administrator, lawyer, insurance salesman.

Conventional (C). Conformist, orderly, and perseverant; primarily oriented toward economic values and attaches less importance to aesthetic and religious values. Occupations: financial expert, accountant, secretary, bank officer.

It is noticeable that values assigned to each type are derived from the **Study of Values** of Allport, Vernon, and Lindzey [14]. The nature of this instrument is well adapted to Holland's definitions since, as many authors consider, it probably measures interests better than values.

On the other hand, very few researches have been designed to test the relationship of Holland's personality types to values typically relevant to the world of work. Recent results obtained by Larcebeau [15] indicate significant factorial links between these two networks of variables. The author concludes that among adolescents, personal values hierarchy manages choices and attitudes which are characteristic of work and occupations.

Research done by the present author over the past ten years has been aimed at developing and testing an instrument designed to measure work values.

3.   A MEASURE OF WORK VALUES

The **Questionnaire de Valeurs de Travail** (QVT) by Perron and Dupont [16] has been developed in an American francophone context and administered to more than 5,000 subjects (mainly students).

The QVT contains 68 items corresponding to the most commonly measured aspects of work. Subjects answer each item using a six point Likert-type scale (1: **Practically no importance**;   6: **Very high importance**). Ten (10) items constitute an empirical deviation scale. The 58 others measure the five following categories of values.

Status: 14 items dealing with being admired, popular, and socially recognized, having responsibilities, being influent, and earning a high salary.

Realization: 11 items referring to creativity, discovery, utilization of personal resources, self-knowledge and expression, perseverance, active participation.

Climate: 10 items relating to understanding and acceptance on the part of others, being in a pleasant and well-organized environment and with pleasant co-workers.

Risk: 12 items pertaining to difficulties to overcome, unpredictable, unknown or dangerous situations as well as competitive relationships.

Freedom: 11 items related to independence, freedom, self-determination, individualism and being different from others.

Corrected item-total correlations vary from 0,44 to 0,69 (Status), 0,39 to 0,58 (Realization), 0,40 to 0,53 (Climate), 0,39 to 0,64 (Risk), and 0,33 to 0,57 (Freedom). Inter-scale correlations range from 0,05 to 0,53 and show that each scale has a specific contribution to the instrument. Scale reliability (alpha coefficient) is 0,89 (Status), 0,82 (Realization), 0,78 (Climate), 0,84 (Risk), and 0,79 (Freedom). Convergent and discriminant validity of the QVT is supported by various studies confirming logically expected differences and similarities between numerous groups of subjects.

4.   METHOD

Data in the present research have been collected from three samples of

French-speaking male and female students in the province of Québec
(Canada). The first sample contains 1,385 junior high school students;
the second, 1,579 senior high school students; the third, 1,929 college
students representing 10% of the population of first year students at the
University of Montreal, and registered in 42 different departments.

Besides answering the QVT, all the subjects indicated their preferred
occupations. Three judges using a one-letter code (R,I,A,S,E,C)
classified each occupational preference in one of the six personality
types defined by Holland [13].

Table 1 gives a breakdown of subjects according to educational level
and personnality type.

Table 1

Table 1: Repartition of subjects (N: 4,609) according to educational
level and personality type

Educational level	Personality type*						Total
	R	I	A	S	E	C	
Junior High	249	242	137	259	113	247	1247
Senior High	91	487	193	355	128	179	1433
College	109	797	151	533	292	47	1929
Total	449	1526	481	1147	533	473	4609

* R: Realistic; I: Investigative; A: Artistic; S: Social;
  E: Enterprising; C: Conventional

Scores obtained on each scale of the QVT - they vary from 10 to 60 -
are submitted to a multivariate analysis of variance (Manova) using a 3
(educational level) by 6 (personality type) factorial design. If
significant, this analysis is followed by a discriminant function analysis
as suggested by Bray and Maxwell [17]. The underlying hypothesis of this
research is that the relationship between work values and personality
types will increase according to educational level. Thus, a significant
interaction effect is expected.

5.   RESULTS

As shown in Table 2, the interaction effect reaches a 0,00001 level of
significance, thus indicating that, in terms of work values, personality
types do not differ uniformly at each educational level.

Further analysis shows that two discriminant functions respectively
accounting for 36% and 31% of the variance prove to be significant in
explaining the relationships between subject variables and dependent
variables (Table 3). For the sake of this presentation only the results

Table 2

Table 2: Multivariate analysis of variance results on work values by
educational level and personality type

Source	Wilks	Approx. F	df	p
Personality (A)	0,89828	19,96676	25;17037	0,00001
Educational level (B)	0,78379	118,81249	10;9172	0,00001
A x B	0,97549	2,28394	50;20919	0,00001

Table 3

Table 3: Standardized coefficients of significant discriminant functions

Variable	Function 1	Function 2
Status	- 0,89423	- 0,03461
Realization	0,58885	- 0,61883
Climate	- 0,17470	- 0,10496
Risk	- 0,19111	0,28490
Freedom	0,52349	0,94700

from Function 1 are analyzed in more detail. This function is interesting since discrimination of the groups is produced by Realization and
Freedom on the one hand as opposed to Status on the other. In order to
illustrate these discriminant effects, the means involved in the
comparisons were weighted by the standardized discriminant coefficients,
thus generating discriminant scores for each personality type at each of
the three levels of education. Figure 1 shows the position of each group
on a bipolar continuum ranging from Status on the one hand to Realization
and Freedom on the other.

Observations to be derived from Figure 1 are the following. First, at
each educational level, the distance separating the two most apart
personality types is practically the same (Junior High: 7,08; Senior
High: 7,74; College: 6,56).

Second, Junior High subjects attach more importance to Status and less to
Realization and Freedom than do Senior High and College subjects.

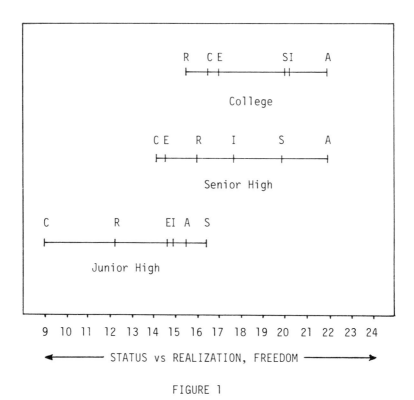

FIGURE 1

Figure 1: Work Values (weighted means) for Personality Types (RIASEC) at
          Three Levels of Education (Junior High, Senior High, College).

Third, in terms of work values, a pattern of personality types becomes
more precise from one level of education to the other. Indeed, at the
Junior High level types C,R, and E are clearly distinct from one another
(5,47) on the work values continuum whereas types I, A, and S are less
different (1,44) and, at the same time, very close to type E. At the
Senior High level, types C, E, and R are homogeneously grouped (1,66)
whereas types I, A, and S are relatively distant one from the other
(4,25); at the same time the two sets of types are more distant (1,83)
from one another than they are at the Junior High level. Finally, it is
at the college level that the pattern of personality types is more
clearly defined. Types R, C, and E are homogeneously grouped (1,51) as
well as types S, I, and A (1,91) and both sets of types stand from one
another (3,14). This last configuration based on work values corresponds
exactly to what Holland [13] designates as the two metatypes to which the
six types can theoretically be reduced.

6. DISCUSSION

The results of this study show that three of the five QVT scales (Status vs Realization and Freedom) contribute to differenciate, in a variable way according to educational level, the six personality types described by Holland and based on the occupation envisaged by the subject. In this sense, they replicate those obtained by Larcebeau [15] and confirm, although in a more operational way, Holland's intuition that values are a significant element of his personality typology.

The increasing strength of the relationship between work values and personality according to educational level probably coincides with a maturation process accompanied by an increment in the realism, the specification, and the crystallization of vocational interests which culminate at the college level.

On the other hand, the double pattern of personality types which charac-terizes the evolution of the relationship between work values and personality is based on a value dichotomy with an external (Status) and an internal (Realization and Freedom) frame of reference. What basically differentiates types R, C, and E from types S, I, and A is the fact that the former put more emphasis than the latter on the social recognition, influence, and monetary rewardings offered by work; at the same time they value to a lesser degree work dimensions like creativity, personal growth, freedom, and individuality. Because values have an incidence on occupational choice, one may expect that youth will seek for work environments which represent these two types of "culture". This is why it seems important that the world of work and organizations clearly defines itself in terms of values in order to enrich functions like recruitment, promotion, management, and productivity.

From another point of view this research contributes to support the validity of the QVT. It would still be increased by studies done in organizational settings. The instrument could also be used to measure perception of working environments using the same value contents. Then, as recommended by Staw [8], it could serve as a way of studying phenomena like work satisfaction and quality of work life in a precisely defined theoretical framework.

REFERENCES

[1] Ginzberg, E., Ginsburg, S.W., Axelrad, S., & Herma, J.L. (1951). Occupational Choice: An Approach to a General Theory. New York: Columbia University Press.
[2] Super, D.E. (1957). The Psychology of Careers. New York: Harper.
[3] Tiedeman, D.V., O'Hara, R.P., & Baruch, R.W. (1963). Career Development: Choice and Adjustment. Princeton, N.J.: College Entrance Examination Board.
[4] Zytowski, D.G. (1970). The Concept of Work Values. Vocational Guidance Quarterly, 18, 176-186.
[5] Descombes, J.-P. (1980). Cinquante ans d'études et d'évaluation des valeurs professionnelles (1925-1975). Revue de psychologie appliquée, 30, 1-104.
[6] Peters, T.J., & Waterman, R.H. (1982). In Search of Excellence. New York: Harper.

[7] Locke, E.A. (1976). The Nature and Causes of Job Satisfaction.
      In M.D. Dunnette (Ed.): Handbook of Industrial and Organizational
      Psychology. Chicago: Rand McNally.
[8] Staw, B.M. (1984). Organizational Behavior: A Review and
      Reformulation of the Field's Outcome Variables. Annual Review
      of Psychology, 35, 627-666.
[9] Borgen, F.H. (1984). Counseling Psychology. Annual Review of
      Psychology, 35, 579-604.
[10] Brown, S.D., & Lent, R.W. (1984). Handbook of Counseling
      Psychology. New York: Wiley.
[11] Walsh, W.B., & Osipow, S.H. (Eds.) (1983a). Handbook of Vocational
      Psychology, Volume I: Foundations. Hillsdale, N.J.: Erlbaum.
[12] Walsh, W.B., & Osipow, S.H. (Eds.) (1983b) Handbook of Vocational
      Psychology, Volume II: Applications. Hillsdale, N.J.: Erlbaum.
[13] Holland, J.L. (1973). Making Vocational Choices: A Theory of
      Careers. Englewood Cliffs, N.J.: Prentice-Hall.
[14] Allport, G.W., Vernon, P.E. & Lindzey, G. (1970). Study of Values
      Manual. Boston: Houghton - Mifflin.
[15] Larcebeau, S. (1983). Motivation et personnalité. L'orientation
      scolaire et professionnelle, 12, 215-242.
[16] Perron, J., & Dupont, R.M. (1974). Questionnaire de Valeurs de
      Travail. Document inédit, Université de Montréal.
[17] Bray, J.H., & Maxwell, S.E. (1982). Analyzing and Interpreting
      Significant MANOVAs. Review of Educational Research, 52, 340-367.

THE PSYCHOLOGY OF WORK AND ORGANIZATION
G. Debus and H.-W. Schroiff (Editors)
© Elsevier Science Publishers B.V. (North-Holland), 1986

THE IMPACT OF CHANGES IN WORK ETHICS UPON ORGANIZATIONAL LIFE

Eric ROSSEEL

Vrije Universiteit Brussel, Center for Organizational and
Consumers' Psychology.

1. INTRODUCTION

In the seventies, it was almost generally accepted that a new work ethic
was emerging among the young generations (Rousselet, 1974, Yankelovich,
1974). It was stated that this new work ethic emphasized autonomy in
work, anti-bureaucratical attitudes, an anti-career mood and a preference
for leisure. Our research into the evolutions of the work ethic started
from the assumption that the economic crisis should have undermined this
evolution towards a new work ethic, especially among lower educational
levels. Indeed, the core of the new work ethic, the need for self-expres-
sion in work, has been associated with higher educational levels since
Centers' Psychology of Social Classes (Centers, 1949). The emergence of
a new work ethic in the sixties can in this sense be   interpreted as a
correlate of the general rise of the cultural and educational levels of
the population as a whole. The actual economic crisis has stopped this
trend, so putting barriers upon the proliferation of a new work ethic.

Within this general framework, three studies were undertaken to explore
new trends in the work ethic of the young generations. We will briefly
review these studies and comment the results in the light of the possible
impact of changes in the work ethics upon organizational life.

2. WORK ETHICS OF FLEMISH ARMY RECRUITS (Rosseel, 1983)

A first study tested the *homogeneity* of the various elements associated
with the 'traditional' and the 'new' work ethic and the hypothesis that
only the high-educated young people would express the new work ethic.
A representative sample of 663 Flemish (male) army recruits was administered a questionnaire tapping to aspects of 'traditional' and 'new' work
ethics and to life-style preferences. Work ethics were measured by a list
of 26 Likert-type items and life-style preferences by rating and rank-
ordering five life-styles presented in the form of a prosaic text of some
80 words and labeled Adventurous (A), Family-Oriented (B), Career-making
(C), Selfrealization in 'Craftmanship'(D) and Aversion of Work (E).

A Smallest Space Analysis (Lingoes, 1973) upon the 26 work ethic items
and the five life-styles shows undoubtfully that the items can be regrouped into two regions (Fig. 1). The left region of 'traditional' work
attitudes can be divided up into three clusters : Conservative Careerism,
Negative Attitudes towards Unemployed and Work as a Habit/Family-oriented-
ness with rather modest alpha-coefficients (.50, .49 and .32).

Vrije Universiteit Brussel, Center for Organizational and Consumers'
Psychology, Pleinlaan 2, 1050 BRUSSEL.

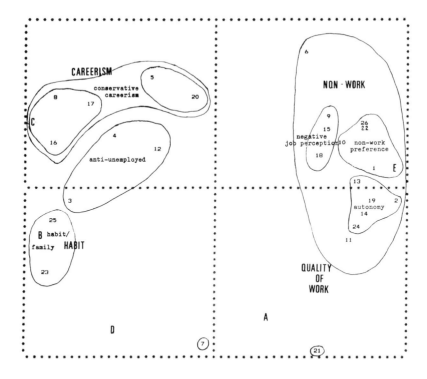

Fig. 1   SSA-configuration Work Ethic items

The correlation between "Habit" and "Conservative Careerism" is of low
significance ($p < .10$), confirming our hypothesis that 'traditional' work
orientations do not combine to a homogeneous 'traditional work ethic'.
The group of 'new' work ethic items shows two emphases : an *aversion of
work in general* (top of right SSA-region) and a need for personal autonomy
and *quality of work and life*. Three clusters can be distinguished :
'Negative Job Perceptions', 'Non-Work Preference' and 'Personal Autonomy
in Work and Creative Life Activities' (alpha-coefficients : .49, .65 and
.62). As a single scale the three clusters reach an alpha value of .76,
which is rather deceptive. Thus, the homogeneity of the different elements
of the 'new work ethic' can also be questioned.

In general, the sample did not tend towards adherence to a new work ethic.
Traditional attitudes such as work as a 'natural' habit and an 'uncritical'
acceptation of the quality of available jobs prevail. The most preferred
life-styles concern Family-Orientedness/Job Security (B) and Selfrealisation in (technical) Craftmanship (D). Modernistic life-styles (A and E)
are less popular.

The hypothesis that lower-educated people express more 'conservative'
attitudes was fully confirmed. A two-factor ANOVA of the six work ethic
scales by educational level and social status shows that differences in
work ethics are especially explained by reference to educational level.

Lower levels stress 'conservative' careerism ($F_{3,619} = 18.2$; p $<$ .001) and higher levels 'personal autonomy and need for creative life activities' ($F_{3,619} = 17.3$; p $<$ .001). Differences in social status have no effects upon work ethics, except that unemployed have less anti-unemployed attitudes ($F_{2,608} = 10.2$; p $<$ .001).

3. LIFE ASPIRATIONS AND WORK ORIENTATIONS OF PEOPLE-ORIENTED AND TECHNOLOGY-ORIENTED STUDENTS

A detailed inspection of the data of the army recruits study furnished indications that led us to question the uniformity of the work ethic of higher educated young people. A pilot study among a sample of 87 university and non-university students, all following higher education, revealed us the nature of important differences *within* higher educational levels. These 87 students were interviewed and they completed a questionnaire composed of a short list of open questions concerning their life goals and professional ambitions for the next 10 years, and a list of some 80 attitudinal statements (among which the 26 items of the army recruits study) concerning work ethics, life priorities, work facet priorities, use of strategies for professional success, the fear for unemployment and the attitude towards the future. Analysis of the data showed significant differences between students 'working with people' and students 'working with things'. So a systematic study was designed to explore these differences in a more elaborated way.

For a systematic comparison of *people-oriented* and *technology-oriented* students, all Flemish 'industrial high-schools' (engineers, electronicians, etc.) and 'social schools' (social workers) in Brussels were contacted. All first-year and last-year students were invited to participate in the research program. These samples were supplemented by 120 first-year and last-year university students in psychology and communication sciences (people-oriented) and informatics (technology-oriented). The total sample consisted of 621 respondents : 345 technology-oriented and 276 people-oriented. 405 are freshmen. Male students are mostly technology-oriented and females people-oriented. The respondents were administered the same questionnaire as the one used in the pilot study.

Analysis of the answers to the open questions unfold the basic pre-occupations of the students : professional selfrealisation and social-affective security and intimacy. Conventional values of work and family seem very popular. Work is a way to realize one's potentials, a means for building up one's own family and a means for being inserted in society.

The attitudinal statements could be recombined into 12 scales. Computed scale scores range from 1 (low) to 5 (high). Alpha-coefficients all exceed .60, except for the scale "Unproblematic Life".

The mean scores of these scales (see Table 3) generally confirm the answers to the open questions. A Smallest Space Analysis of the twelve scales allows to distinguish six 'life-styles' : Critical Work Ethic, Professional Involvement, Conventional Social Success (Work and Family), Individualistic Careerism, Enjoying Life and Rejection of the Actual Social System (Fig. 2).

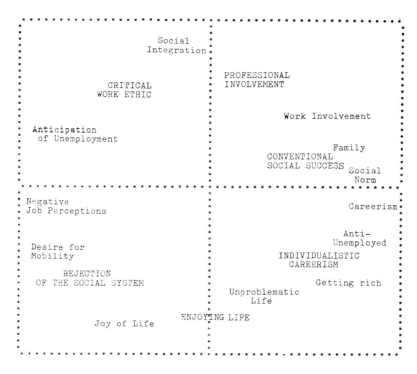

Fig. 2   SSA-configuration Work Ethic Scales

The differences in attitudes and aspirations between people-oriented and technology-oriented students are very obvious. We can illustrate them by comparing life priorities and work facet priorities for the two groups of students. (Table 1).

Table 1   Life priorities of people-oriented and technology-oriented students

	Total sample % imp (% 1st rank)		people-oriented	technology-oriented
Professional Activities	97	(12)	97	97
True Friends	93	(13)	96	91
Relation Partner	86	(22)	84	87
Stable Job	80	(2)	70	84
Family Life	77	(35)	65	87
Fight for Ideals	61	(7)	67	57
Leisure Time	55	(2)	53	56
Have own House	43	(-)	28	54
Earn much Money	39	(1)	27	48
Make a Career	39	(3)	24	51

Table 2   Work Facet Priorities of people-oriented
          and technology-oriented students

	Total Sample % imp (% 1st rank)	people- oriented	technology- oriented
Interesting Activities	94 (29)	94	94
Recognition	84 (18)	77	90
Job Security	82 (14)	76	87
Social Contacts	77 (8)	92	63
Helping Others	76 (11)	86	68
Achievements	75 (5)	71	79
Autonomy	68 (8)	70	66
Responsibility	66 (3)	65	66
High Earnings	40 (4)	27	50
Power	19 (-)	12	25

Results   clearly indicate that technology-oriented students put a lot
more emphasis upon the conventional values of home, family and career
whereas people-oriented students stress values such as friendship and
affective relations. These results are confirmed by an analysis of work
facet priorities (Table 2). People-oriented students appreciate social
contacts and helping other people through their job, unlike technology-
oriented students who attach more value to career aspects (job security,
recognition by superiors).

Nearly all 12 constructed scales succeed in discriminating the two groups
of students   (Table 3). The results can easily be described in terms of
the SSA-configuration. People-oriented students occupy the left region of
the mapping expressing a Critical Work Ethic and technology-oriented
students the right region of the Conventional Values of Family and Career.
These differences between people- and technology-oriented students do not
seem to be an effect of the educational training itself : they are as
obvious for first-year students as for last-year students.

Table 3   Differences in orientation scales between
          people-oriented and technology-oriented students

	Total Sample Mean	people- oriented	technology- oriented	t_{619} value
Social Integration	4.0	4.2	3.8	7.8 $p < .001$
Work Involvement	3.9	3.8	3.9	1.3 N.S.
Family-Orientedness	3.8	3.6	4.0	7.1 $p < 001$
Careerism	3.3	3.0	3.5	8.3 $p < 001$
Joy of Life	3.1	3.1	3.1	.5 N.S.
Anti-unemployed	3.1	2.6	3.4	12.9 $p < 001$
Unproblematic Life	3.0	2.8	3.1	4.5 $p < 001$
Anticipation of Unemployment	3.0	3.4	2.7	15.9 $p < 001$
Negative Job Quality Perception	3.0	3.1	2.8	6.7 $p < 001$
Desire for Mobility	3.0	3.1	2.8	4.3 $p < 001$
Getting Rich	3.0	2.6	3.2	11.4 $p < 001$
Social Norm	2.6	2.4	2.8	9.1 $p < 001$

(1 = low; 5 = high)

This, however, should not tempt us to the conclusion that the attitudinal differences themselves drive the students to a particular educational and professional choice. We are rather inclined to state that a definite educational choice based upon initial vocational interests entails a rapid integration in a specific professional subculture and an anticipative socialization of values and norms of that subculture during the months between the final choice and the effective entry into higher education.

Social background, i.e. the father's profession, explains only minor differences in orientations. Sex differences overlap those of the educational 'subculture', but a two-factor analysis of variance shows that most of the differences between people- and technology-oriented students do not have a sex-basis. The remaining sex-differences seem to polarize along the top-bottom dimension of the SSA-configuration. Male students stress "a-social" values (Rejection of the System, Getting Rich); female students are more oriented towards social integration and conformistic values (Work Involvement, Social Integration, Family-Orientedness).

In each way, this study confirms our hypothesis that important differences in orientations and aspirations exist within the category of high-educated people. They seem to be associated to particular professional subcultures characterized by specific values and traditions and by net differences in job and career opportunities : people-oriented professions are a lot more threatened by unemployment than technology-oriented professions among which a happy few still can realize their American Dreams.

4. WORK ETHICS AND FUTURE PERSPECTIVES OF A SAMPLE OF LAST-GRADE HIGH-SCHOOL CHILDREN (HIGHER SECONDARY EDUCATION)

The previous study showed that orientations to work and life are established before entry into a final educational training. Therefore, the study was replicated with a sample of high school children in order to determine : 1. to what degree differentiations in work orientations and future perspectives are present at the age level before the final educational choice or the transition to work; 2. to what degree the day by day preoccupations of those children converge into a structured and coherent life and work orientation.

An accidental sample of 209 school children was composed with the collaboration of three teachers, appointed to the two last grade classes of the Higher Secondary Education in five Flemish schools. They were trained to administer a short questionnaire and to lead a group discussion of their classes about the topics of life goals and work ethics. The questionnaire consisted of some open questions (plans and projects after termination of the present studies, reactions upon possible unemployment), a list of life and work facet priorities and some 40 attitudinal statements, covering topics such as the image of the future, the fear for unemployment, the perceived cause of unemployment of individuals (Furnham, 1982), the adherence to a traditional or a "new" work ethic and attitudes towards "new technologies" (computer and robot).

The life and work priorities and the attitudinal statements could be regrouped into 8 scales (scores from 1 = high to 3 = low) : 1) Family-orientedness (Lack of Career Ambitions) (mean = 1.52); 2) Pessimism (Negative Attitudes towards New Technologies) (mean = 1.71);

3) Action-orientedness (Personalized Way of Life) (mean = 1.73); 4) Power-lessness (mean = 1.77); 5) Achievement Orientation (Careerism) (mean = 1.85); 6) Joy of Life (mean = 2.12); 7) Self-confidence (Individualistic Optimism) (mean = 2.15); 8) Positive Attitude towards New Technologies (mean = 2.23). (Alpha's range from .56 to .76).

A traditional orientation of family-orientedness (Lauwers, 1984) remains very popular among the school children of this sample and confirms the stagnation of the changes in values associated with the Golden Sixties (Gadourek, 1982). Pessimism and powerlessness dominate the moods and feelings. The proliferation of new technologies is experienced as threaten-ing rather than offering new hope for a better future. Of course, even if this sample is heterogeneously composed, it is in no way representative of the population of Flemish school children.

The SSA-structure of attitudes unfolds the basic dimensions of the pre-vious study : conventional vs. critical, individualistic vs. social-inte-grative, acceptance of the social system vs. rejection of the social system. Differences in aspirations and attitudes, however, are not as con-centrated to one factor. Differences concern sex, parents' occupational activities, ideological or religious affiliation ('humanistic' vs. 'catho-lic'), study curriculum options (Sciences, Social Sciences, Vocational Training). Sex and father's occupation "cause" more differences in aspira-tions than curriculum options (which anticipate   the "professional subcultures" that were distinguished in the previous study). Girls are more study-motivated and more family-oriented but they feel themselves more threatened by the job-killing effects of new technologies and they are generally more pessimistic. Children from high-status families tend more towards the values of the New Work Ethic. Children form salaried employees feel themselves more powerless,whereas children from self-employed middle-class people manifest more self-confidential and indivi-dualistic attitudes. In general, differences in aspirations and attitudes reflect differences in realistic social opportunities that are open to specific categories of young people.

Group discussions with the children confirmed the pessimistic mood that prevails among the contemporary youth. Long-term plans and goals are scarcely formulated. Making plans is experienced as irrealistic and frus-trating. So, day by day issues occupy the minds of these children : money, love affairs, weekend activities, and so on. Most of them are not pre-occupied by their future after their studies, even not by the perspective of unemployment. The incertainty of the future induces in this way a very marked "here and now" orientation (du Bois-Reymond, 1984).

5. DISCUSSION

Throughout the reported studies, some important conclusions emerge. First of all, the polarizing dimensions reappear in each of the separate studies. They concern : 1) conventional vs. critical; 2) individualistic vs. social-integrative and 3) acceptation vs. rejection of the social system. So, the orientations can be ordered in a circumplex of six life-styles. (Fig. 3).

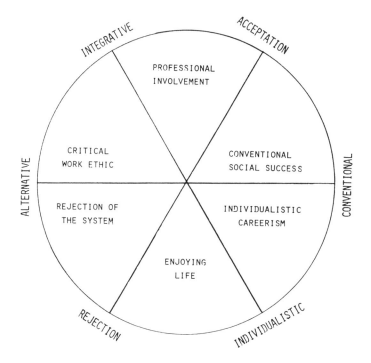

Fig. 3   Circumplex of Life Styles

The results indicate further that for most young people the core of the
work ethic consists of rather 'traditional' and conformistic values of
work, home and family. Higher-educated adolescents tend more towards a
critical work ethic, especially adolescents who prepare themselves for
'Working with People'-professions. They stress the social usefulness of
their future jobs. Adolescents who engage in 'Working with Things'-profes-
sions supplement their conventional orientation with striking individualistic and meritocratic elements.

Generally speaking, a New Work Ethic, as defined in the sixties and seventies, is not predominant. Young people feel themselves dependent on 'society' for getting work, i.e. a life perspective. This seems especially clear
for female students : girls are no longer looking for personal emancipation
in work but they express a need for paid work in order to build up a happy
family life. Most boys and girls are willing to take the jobs that will be
offered to them. In this sense, our results confirm the notion of the
flexibilized subject who restrains himself from formulating precise professional plans and goals (du Bois-Reymond, 1984).

It is not easy to infer the implications for organizational life from our
findings. We tentatively suppose that the young work force of the eighties
will not manifest the exigent but work-committed and work-involved attitudes of the sixties and the seventies. In their condition of social dependence most young people will develop a more apathic or calculative attitude : no criticisms but also no real job or organizational commitment.

This orientation of 'simply doing the job' will foster the already visible come-back of authoritarian and paternalistic management. Despite the superficial popularity of pseudo-Japanese Quality Control Circles and Work Consultation Groups, management styles can become more firm and tough without resistance.

At the same time, talented and dynamic young professionals have to develop a more individualistic and merciless attitude in order to pick up the few interesting careers that are open to them. Envy and distrust will disturb cooperation among managers or professional staff personnel. The spirit of self-disclosure that characterized the group-dynamic approach of the seventies, cannot keep its ground in a situation of reduced opportunities (Levine & Cooper, 1976). The individualistic touch favours small enterprises where ambitious and talented young people can make their way without dashing against bureaucratic barriers. Individualistic and meritocratic attitudes can also form the source of a 'new entrepreneurship'.

In the sixties and seventies work was presented as a place for self-development and self-realisation. Even if the quality or working life in the foregoing decades must not be idealized, times have changed since the economic crisis has effected people's attitudes and behaviour. As work remains the source of income and social status, it will become more like an arena with proud winners and embittered losers.

REFERENCES

du BOIS-REYMOND, M.   Jongeren en hun toekomst (Young people's Future).
          Conferentiebundel Zesde Onderwijssociologische Conferentie.
          Amsterdam, SISWO, 1984.

CENTERS, R.   The psychology of social classes.
          Princeton NJ, University Press, 1949.

FURNHAM, A.   Explanations for unemployment in Britain.
          European Journal of Social Psychology, 1982, 12, 335-352.

GADOUREK, I.   Social change as redefinition of roles.
          Assen, Van Gorkum, 1982.

LAUWERS, J.   De Belg aan het Werk (Belgians at work).
          in : Kerkhofs, J. & Rezsohazy, R. De stille ommekeer Tielt,
          Lannoo, 1984.

LINGOES, J.C.   The Guttman-Lingoes Nonmetric Program Series.
          Ann Arbor, Mathesis Press, 1973.

LEVINE, N. & COOPER, C.L.   T-groups : Twenty Years on.
          Human Relations, 1976, 29, 1-23.

ROSSEEL, E.   Work ethic and Orientations to Work of the Young Generations.
          The impact of educational level. Social Indicators Research, 1985
          (in press).

ROUSSELET, J.   L'Allergie au Travail.
          Paris, Le Seuil, 1974.

YANKELOVICH, D.   The New Morality.
          New York, Mc Graw-Hill, 1974.

THE PSYCHOLOGY OF WORK AND ORGANIZATION
G. Debus and H.-W. Schroiff (Editors)
© *Elsevier Science Publishers B.V. (North-Holland), 1986*

RELATIONS BETWEEN WORK AND CONSUMPTION ORIENTATIONS

Roland PEPERMANS[*]

Generale Bank, Social Studies 02/A, Montagne du Parc 3
B-1000 Brussels, Belgium.

Although few empirical findings exist, four hypothetical
relationships between work and comsumption orientations were
delimited. After different research steps, questionnaire-data
were gathered on 9 work and 9 consumption orientations. Using
canonical correlation analysis, smallest space analysis and
confirmatory monotone distance analysis, four empirical
relationships were discovered, which agreed partially with the
hypotheses. They were called <u>Traditionalism, Individualism,
Desinterest</u> and <u>Consumption as Compensation for Work</u>, and showed
cross-validity.

1. INTRODUCTION

Given the steady growth of economic psychology (e.g. Van Raaij, 1981),
it may surprise to see that no empirical study exists of how psychological variables concerning work and consumption are related. Such a
research, which has motivational implications, could join Lewin's (1952)
<u>Life Space Theory</u>, and can be seen as a specification of the <u>work/non-
work research</u> (Pepermans, 1986).
Psychological (and sociological) literature provides few information
concerning a total view on relationships between work and consumption.
But adjacent to other research objectives some partial information is
published. First, a possible compensatory effect of consumption is
suggested, in terms of an attitude of conspicuous consumption given an
instrumental work orientation: alienating effects of the work place may
be compensated through extra attention to the consumption domain
(Chinoy, 1955; Gorz, 1966; Seeman, 1971).
On the other hand, low hierarchical employees often show desinterest in
both the work and consumption domain, and place most emphasis on the
family and the local neighbourhood (Crozier, 1965; Belleville, 1978).
Only very few studies present information of a more complex nature on
this subject. Wilensky (1960) in a sociological study of work, leisure,
career possibilities and stratefication data, proposes a three level
typology of possible connections between work and consumption behaviour,
parallel to a social status hierarchy. Strumpel (1976) deals with three
economic orientations each incorporating specific aspects of work and
consumption behaviour. Mitchell and MacNulty (1980), as part of a
marketing oriented segmentation, present eight types of consumers (as
well as their relative share of the population), a majority of which is
spread over three types. These parallel the other groups (in the other
studies) very well in terms of relating work to consumption. Finally, a

_____
[*] Thanks go to Prof. Dr. J. Borgers for his stimulating interest and his
helpful comments, and to the Belgian National Fund for Scientific
Research for enabling this research while under contract as a Research
Assistant.

preliminary project to the present study (Pepermans & Boehringer, 1982) also showed results in agreement with the previous findings in the literature, even including the so called compensatory effect. Hence, four hypothetical relationships could be deduced from the empirical data, also including the already mentioned Desinterest-relationship (as a matter of fact, this appeared in the four studies):

1. Traditionalism: The work domain is characterised by a high work involvement. Concerning consumption, it seems as if one shows withdrawal behaviour, although one has the financial means to buy anything that one would like.

2. Ambition: One's aspiration is to belong to the previous group, hence one is very ambitious. In the meantime, one concentrates on acquiring a snobistic materialistic status. People are especially interested in so called welfare symbols.

3. Desinterest: Both the work and consumption domain get a low involvement. One concentrates on security and rather passive work behaviour and shows a rather submissive consumption behaviour.

4. Consumption as Compensation for Work: Consumption is considered to be the reward for negative work experiences and for the efforts in the work domain. Work is only a means for getting an income.

According to Wilensky (1960) and Strumpel (1976), the foregoing relations go together with a status hierarchy, starting with a high social status at Traditionalism, and ending with a low social status for consumption as Compensation for Work.

To limit our interests, orientations were chosen as the behavioural variable which could reveal the foregoing hypothetical relations, although these are still in very general terms and need researchable specification. This decision was made since all studies at least presented information concerning domain specific behavioural objectives. As a result, orientations were defined as indications an individual gives about his/her behavioural goals.

In this study, work will be considered as employment, as activities of man producing goods and services for others on a contractual basis. Consumption has been limited to spending money because previous research has shown this to be most central to the meaning of consumption for a great majority of people (Pepermans, 1984a).

Given these definitions, the main purpose of this study becomes the investigation of the existence and the type of relationships between work and consumption orientations. However, before being able to operationalise and test the hypotheses, necessary work and consumption orientations have to be determined.

2. METHOD

Work orientations

Although known under different names (e.g. Rosseel, 1981; Walker & Tausky, 1982; Tziner, 1983) work orientations are generally considered part of one's work behaviours. Starting with Rosseel's (1981) Likert-type scales measuring different work orientations, and after several qualitative and quantitative steps and tests of validity and reliability, and also after having cross-validated the instrument using different samples, we ended up with 9 mearurable work orientations: 1. Desengagement, 2. Financial Motives, 3. Positive Habit, 4. Career as Source of Identity, 5. Organisational Commitment, 6. Promotion and

Power, 7. Autonomy, and Refusing Organisational Control, 8. Social Contact, and 9. Unionism (alpha-reliability ≥ .60; item test-retest reliability p ≤ .05.).

Consumption orientations

Instead of a partial view on consumption and possible orientations, such as product-specific or shopping orientations (e.g. Boote, 1981; Gutman & Mills, 1982), a more general approach was considered valuable, namely taking total consumption behaviour into account. Again different qualitative and quantitative research steps made us accept valid and reliable Likert-type scales for the measurement of 9 general consumption orientations (also showing acceptable cross-validity): 1. Personal Distraction, 2. Showing Off, 3. Personal Sensation, 4. Aversion – Avoidance, 5. Aversion – Acceptance, 6. Price(reduction), 7. Consumption as Lifegoal, 8. Social Contact, and 9. Publicity Oriented (alpha-reliability ≥ .60; item test-retest reliability p ≤ .05).

Operationalisation of the hypotheses

Based on various sources of information (in-depth interviews, literature, a.o.) an attempt could be made to express the four hypothetical relations in terms of work and consumption orientations which are expected to go together (unfortunately due to lack of space one should contact the author for more information). This is presented in Table 1.

Table 1:   The four hypothetical relations in terms of work and consumption orientations

1. TRADITIONALISM
   - work: 4. career as source of identity
   -                5. organisational commitment
   - consumption: 4. aversion – avoidance

2. AMBITION
   - work: 5. organisational commitment
   -                6. promotion and power
   -                7. social contact
   - consumption: 1. personal distraction
   -                2. showing off
   -                8. social contact
   -                9. publicity oriented

3. DESINTEREST
   - work: 7. autonomy, and refusing organisational control
   -                9. unionism
   - consumption: 5. aversion – acceptance
   -                6. price(reduction)

4. CONSUMPTION AS COMPENSATION FOR WORK
   - work: 1. desengagement
   -                2. financial motives
   -                9. unionism
   - consumption: 2. showing off
   -                7. consumption as lifegoal
   -                9. publicity oriented

Relations between work and consumption orientations
Procedure: Subjects had filled in both questionnaires on work and
consumption orientations, as well as provided data on several socio-
demograp ic variables. Summative scores were computed for each
individual and for each scale. These data were used to analyse the
relationships.
Samples: A first sample (S0) consisted of 458 subjects (Ss) from one
firm and was used to determine the main results. Three other, smaller
samples (S1, S2 and S3) from different organisational backgrounds participated also in this investigation in order to cross-validate the
results from S0. A summary of a few socio-demographic characteristics of
the different samples is presented in Table 2.

Table 2: Major sample characteristics of the four samples

	S a m p l e s			
	S0	S1	S2	S3
N	453	45	57	41
AGE				
-25	121	10	10	9
26/45	235	29	30	23
46+	102	6	17	9
EDUCATION				
primary	44	1	15	2
low sec.	218	2	12	7
high sec.	167	7	12	19
univ. ers.	23	35	14	13
no resp.	6	–	4	–
INCOME (in 1000 BF)				
-/29	181	–	2	11
29/39	183	18	24	10
39/49	70	13	21	12
49/+	13	13	6	8
No resp.	6	1	4	–
PROFESSION				
manager	27	27	12	16
cler. work	82	16	9	1
blue coll.	340	1	34	4
no resp.	9	1	2	1

Statistical techniques: The most obvious technique to determine relationships between two sets of variables is canonical correlation analysis (CCA). The results of CCA can be expressed in terms of different
canonical variates for which each variable (orientation) gets a
canonical loading. As such, each variate shows a possible relationship
between the work and consumption orientations (the two sets of
variables) of declining importance (canonical correlation). These can be
interpreted in view of the highest loadings. Yet a problem arises due to
the ordinal nature of our data. Ordinal CCA does exist (Van der Burg &
de Leeuw, 1983), but inaccuracies seem still likely. Therefore it was
decided to test the results of a metric CCA onto the outcomes of a

nonmetric analysis of a different nature, and in this way taking account of the ordinal features of our data, yet respecting the credits of CCA. For this purpose nonmetric Smallest Space Analysis (SSA) was employed (Guttman, 1968), starting from a matrix of gamma coefficients between the different scales (e.g. Pepermans & Boehringer, 1982). SSA results in a multidimensional space. The deviation between the original data (gamma matrix) and the accepted configuration is given by the coefficient of alienation (Guttman, 1968). A regional interpretation of the SSA-space (Lingoes, 1979) can be tested upon its acceptability using Confirmatory Montone Distance Analysis (CMDA) (Lingoes & Borg, 1983). Using this procedure the relations between work and consumption orientations, resulting from CCA, were tested in the SSA-space based on their regional representation. Afterwards, the main CCA-results (for sample S0) were cross-validated using the CCA-outcomes for the smaller samples and using second order CCA (Pepermans, 1984b), as well as using distinct CMDA's (Pepermans, 1984b).

3. RESULTS

Most important are the CCA-results. Table 3 presents the first four highly significant variates (p $\leq$ .000) as well as the different loadings for each variable (orientation) for the main sample S0.
The first variate agrees very well with the hypothetical relationship called <u>Consumption</u> <u>as</u> <u>Compensation</u> <u>for</u> <u>Work</u>. It is characterised by an important instrumental work orientation and work desengagement. This apparently goes together with consumption viewed as a lifegoal, and an orientation towards low prices.
The second variate has been interpreted as <u>Individualism</u> because of the importance of a personal distraction and personal sensation view on consumption. Social contacts remain very important in both the work and consumption domain. But contrary to our hypothesis of Ambition, promotion is not a main work orientation. Therfore, the hypothesis of Ambition was not accepted, but was changed into Individualism, stressing the personal (egocentric) nature of most orientations.

Table 3: Canonical variates and loadings after the analysis of the 9 work and 9 consumption orientations for the main sample S0.

	orientations	variates			
		1	2	3	4
W1.	desengagement	<u>-.78</u>	.14	-.02	-.05
W2.	financial motives	<u>-.75</u>	-.04	.12	<u>.36</u>
W3.	positive habit	-.02	<u>.44</u>	<u>-.52</u>	.08
W4.	career as source of iden.	-.08	<u>.42</u>	<u>-.57</u>	<u>.34</u>
W5.	organis. commitment	.04	<u>.17</u>	<u>-.84</u>	.05
W6.	promotion and power	.04	<u>.33</u>	.03	<u>.70</u>
W7.	autonomy, refus. org. contr.	-.14	<u>-.10</u>	.11	<u>.59</u>
W8.	social contact	-.03	<u>.86</u>	-.04	.02
W9.	unionism	<u>-.31</u>	<u>.15</u>	-.12	.03
C1.	personal distraction	-.20	<u>.74</u>	-.09	.04
C2.	showing off	<u>-.50</u>	<u>.04</u>	.09	<u>.66</u>
C3.	personal sensation	.01	<u>.40</u>	.06	<u>.64</u>
C4.	aversion - avoidance	-.14	<u>-.12</u>	<u>-.64</u>	-.06
C5.	aversion - acceptance	-.09	-.31	-.13	<u>.44</u>

(cont. next page)

C6.	price(reduction)	-.36	.01	-.11	-.17
C7.	consumption as lifegoal	-.81	-.05	.13	.25
C8.	social contact	-.19	.47	.61	.29
C9.	publicity oriented	.08	.01	-.23	.42
canonical correlations		.58	.38	.33	.29

The third variate is interpreted as being a confirmation of the hypothesis of Traditionalism. One notices a central work and organisational involvement. Consumption does not get much attention. The impression is that consumption is important because one has to stay alive, but it is not considered to form a life domain which allows for pursuing important life goals; consumption gets a rather negative image. The fourth and last variate which has been interpreted, remains rather tentative. In accordance with our hypotheses, a Desinterest-relationship was expected. Instead, a complex set of orientations was found. Hence, the operationalised Desinterest-relationship ought to be rejected. Yet it has to be remembered that Desinterest can be seen as an expression of the independence of both the work and comsumption domains. This may indeed have caused the somewhat unexpected correspondence between some work and consumption orientations in the CCA-results (see fourth variate in Table 3). When both domains are considered to be unrelated, a rather random relationship between orientations may result. Therefore, it is not impossible that the fourth canonical variate is indeed an expression of the hypothetical Desinterest-relation, or more exactly, of a non-relationship.
The unexpected content of the fourth variate may also have been caused by sample characteristics (a CCA is rather sensitive to it), or by our cutting off the analysis after the fourth variate (due to less significant canonical correlations). Yet the latter explanation could be rejected, using the information from further analyses (Pepermans, 1984b), while the possibility of sample related results is tested in the cross-validation part of this investigation.
Of course, measurement errors may have had an influence too. But in view of the positive results concerning validity and reliability of the different scales, and the coherent structure of the empirical relationships which agree rather well with the hypotheses (and the scarce literature), measurement errors are considered to have had a minor influence.
Concerning the Desinterest-relation in the fourth canonical variate, finally attention has to be drawn to the fact that one work and one consumption orientation already appear in the operationalisation of this relation.
The proposed relationships following the CCA-outcomes, could be transposed in the form of regions to the space resulting from an ordinal SSA. The acceptability of these regions for partitioning the space could be tested using CMDA.
Although these results, for a three-dimensional SSA-space, were highly acceptable for the main sample, problems were discovered when trying to cluster the orientations for the Desinterest-relation. It seemed that they were not within acceptable distances of each other. Therefore a solution for Desinterest was tested where the spatial region consisted of only the two orientations which appeared not only in the fourth canonical variate but also in the hypothetical expression of Desinterest i.e. W7. Autonomy, and Refusing Organisational Control, and C5. Aversion – Acceptance. In the same three-dimensional space CMDA showed this to be

highly acceptable too, and provided a coefficient of alienation of .166. At the same time, no problems were encountered when trying to cluster both orientations (for Desinterest) in the SSA-space.

Therefore, the latter solution was accepted as a definite result concerning relations between work and consumption orientations for the main sample. In Table 4 these results are presented in more explicit terms (but considering the Desinterest-relation as a tentative conclusion, given the foregoing considerations):

Table 4: Four empirical relations between work and consumption orientations

1. TRADITIONALISM
   work: 3. positive habit
                  4. career as source of identity
                  5. organisational commitment
   consumption: 4. aversion – avoidance

2. INDIVIDUALISM
   work: 3. positive habit
                  4. career as source of identity
                  6. promotion and power
                  8. social contact
   consumption: 1. personal distraction
                  3. personal sensation
                  8. social contact

3. (DESINTEREST)
   work: 7. autonomy, and refusing organisational control
   consumption: 5. aversion – acceptance

4. CONSUMPTION AS COMPENSATION FOR WORK
   work: 1. desengagement
                  2. financial motives
                  9. unionism
   consumption: 2. showing off
                  6. price(reduction)
                  7. consumption as lifegoal

The spatial representation of the relations in SSA clearly revealed the opposite character of the relations Traditionalism and Consumption as Compensation for Work, both in terms of work and consumption orientations. The same accounts for Individualism and Desinterest. On the other hand, related work orientations emphasize similarities between Traditionalism and Individualism, and between Desinterest and Consumption as Compensation for Work. Related consumption orientations are a characteristic of similarity between Traditionalism and Desinterest, and between Individualism and Consumption as Compensation for Work.

Cross-validating these results with CCA, SSA and CMDA, showed no important differences in the content of the four relations. But, unless the general agreement, some differences were discovered in the importance of each relationship for the different samples. The fact that Consumption as Compensation for Work is found to be the first variate for the main sample SO, is probably due to the high number of blue collars in SO. Sample S2 showed a similar result for this matter. Traditionalism or Individualism seemed, considering the distinct CCA's, more important for S1 and S3.

This finding is confirmed when testing the social status hypothesis. Using data on education, personal net income and professional prestige, the relationship between social status and the four empirical relations was investigated using nonmetric Kruskal-Wallis one-way analysis of variance.

It could be concluded that the compensation function of consumption is most important for the lowest status people. Desinterest for workers with a somewhat higher status, and Traditionalism showed a great affinity for workers with a high social status. Individualism however, showed no significant relationship with our social status variable.

These results were cross-validated and it was found that only Consumption as Compensation for Work is significantly related to social status for the smaller samples, similar to the result for the main sample.

The connection between low social status and the compensation function of consumption agrees with a suggestion often found in the literature which states that alienated workers dislike work and seek compensation in the consumption domain (Chinoy, 1955; Gorz, 1966; Seeman, 1971). However, the assumed causality was not investigated in our study.

Finally it was possible to describe each empirical relation using socio-demographic variables, but due to lack of space, that matter will not be elaborated on here.

As a conclusion, it may be stated that four relations between work and consumption orientations were delimited. It became clear that the traditional labels used in the work/nonwork studies did not entirely suit the purpose of specificly describing the content of each relation. Next to two possible spill-over relations (Desinterest and Individualism), at least one compensation relation was found, although Traditionalism may also be seen as compensation. Or the latter may, as well as Desinterest, also be considered a segmentation relation. Given these problems, we plead for more specificity when characterising relations between two or more life domains (Pepermans, 1986), and for more attention to different life domains which constitute the life space, as an important step to get to know more about human behaviour.

REFERENCES

(1) Belleville, P., 1978, Attitudes culturelles et vie quotidienne des travailleurs manuels. Futuribles, 17, 555-568.

(2) Boote, A.S., 1981, Market segmentation by personal values and salient product attributes, J. Advert. Res. 21, 1, 29-35.

(3) Chinoy, E., 1955, Automobile workers and the American dream. Gordon City (N.Y.): Doubleday.

(4) Crozier, M., 1965, Le monde des employes. Paris: Editions du Seuil.

(5) Gorz, A., 1966, Work and consumption. In: Anderson P. & Blackburn R. (Eds.), Towards socialism. London: Collins, 317-353.

(6) Green, P.E. & Rao, V.R., 1972, Applied multidimensional scaling: a comparison of approaches and algorithms. New York: Holt, Rinehart & Winston.

(7) Gutman, J. & Mills, M.K., 1982, Fashion life style, self concept, shopping orientation, and store patronage: an integrative analysis. J. Retailing, 58, 64-86.

(8) Guttman, L., 1968, A general nonmetric technique for finding the smallest coordination space for a configuration of points. Psycho-metrika, 33, 469-506.

(9) Lewin, K. 1952, Field theory in social sciences. London: Tavistock Publications.

(10) Lingoes, J.C., 1979, Identifying regions in the space for interpretation. In: Lingoes, J.C., Roskam, E.E. & Borg, I. (Eds.), Geometric representations of relational data. Ann Arbor (Mich.): Mathesis Press.

(11) Lingoes, J.C. & Borg, I. (1978), CMDA-U: Confirmatory Monotone Distance Analysis – Unconditional. J. Market. Res., 15, 610-611.

(12) Mitchell, A. & MacNulty, C., 1980, De veranderingen in levensopvattingen en levensstijl. In: Wissema, J.G. & Eppink, D.J. (Red.), Toekomstanalyse voor managers: basis voor actie. Deventer: Kluwer, 33-42.

(13) Pepermans, R., 1984b, Relatives tussen consumptie – en arbeidsorientaties: een survey-onderzoek met across-validatie (Relations between consumption and work orientations: a survey research with cross-validation). Brussels: Vrije Universiteit, unpublished doctoral dissertation.

(14) Pepermans, R., 1986, Over de noodzaak tot herbezinning van het arbeid/niet-arbeidsonderzoek. Ned. Tijdschr. vr. Psychol., 1986 (in press).

(15) Pepermans, R. & Boehringer, J.-Cl., 1982, Some hypotheses on the relationships between work and consumption experiences, with an empirical comparison of factor analytical and multidimensional scaling results. In: Proceedings Report. The third national symposium on human factors and industrial design in consumer products. Columbus (OH): Ohio State University, 229-245.

(16) Rosseel, E., 1981, Arbeidsorientaties. Een conceptuele analyse en een empirisch onderzoek. Brussels: Vrije Universiteit, unpublished doctoral dissertation.

(17) Seeman, M., 1971, The urban alienation: some dubious theses from Marx to Marcuse. J. Person. & Soc. Psychol., 19, 135-143.

(18) Shimmin, S., 1980, The future of work. In: Duncan, K.D., Gruneberg, M.M. & Wallis, D. (Eds.), Changes in working life. Chichester: Wiley, 1-15.

(19) Strumpel, B., 1979, Economic life-styles, values and subjective welfare. In: Strumpel, B. (Ed.), Economic means for human needs. Ann Arbor (Mich.): University of Michigan, ISP, Survey Research Center, 19-65.

(20) Tziner, A., 1983, Correspondance between occupational rewards and occupational needs and work satisfaction: a canonical redundancy analysis. J. Occup. Psychol., 56, 49-56.

(21) Van der Burg, E. & de Leeuw, J., 1983, Non-linear canonical correlation. Brit. J. Mathem. & Statist. Psychol., 36, 54-80.

(22) Van Raaij, W.F., 1981, Economic psychology. J. Econ. Psychol., 1, 1-24.

(23) Walker, J.E. & Tausky, C., 1982, An analysis of work incentives. J. Social Psychol., 116, 27-39.

(24) Wilensky, H.L., 1960, Work, careers and social integration. Intern. Soc. Sci. J., 12, 543-574.

SUBJECTIVE THEORIES ON WORK, LEISURE, AND CONTROL

Ernst-H. HOFF

Max Planck Institute for Human Development and Education

The relationship between work and leisure in the thinking, feeling and action of the individual as conceptualized and studied by scientists to date will be outlined. Analogous subjective theories that people themselves develop about the relationship between the central areas of life will be discussed as they pertain to their own lives. In further analogy to scientific patterns of explanation, the subjective concepts of control pertaining to self-control and control by others in work and leisure can be described by way of conclusion.

1. SUBJECTIVE THEORIES

It is necessary to begin by explaining why "subjective theories" are the topic. Theoretical considerations in everyday life are called *"subjective"* only because they are formulated in everyday terms. For subjectivity, that is, for differences between people with their individual characteristics, the language of everyday life permits greater leeway than more formal scientific language does. However, the purpose of this chapter is not to emphasize fundamental differences between subjective and scientific theories, for that misleads one to devaluate subjective thinking in daily life, as could be the case with the equally common term of "naive" theory (Laucken, 1974). In the areas of social science research addressed here, one cannot speak of "theories" in a strict, nomothetic sense. At most, studies on work and leisure contain "quasi theories" (Hecker & Grunwald, 1981). By the same token, some of these scientific quasi theories seem "naive," i.e., not very self-reflective, from the perspective of comparatively reasonable everyday thinking.

What, then, do subjective *"theories"* refer to? As just mentioned, the purpose of this chapter is to identify similarities rather than differences between subjective and scientific theories. To that extent the features below apply to both types of theories and can therefore also be used to differentiate scientific patterns of thinking. The term of subjective "theories" is intended primarily to distinguish them from the otherwise customary psychological descriptions of atomistic, interindividual differences with the help of personality and attitudinal dimensions.

The *first* and probably most important feature of such theories is, therefore, the formation of *relations* between individual substantive elements. A person's conceptions, experiences, attitudes, perceptions, or evaluations are not simply related to individual factors, events, or processes but also to their interrelationships, and they, in turn, are linked through relations that represent a pattern. For this reason, it is also possible to speak of conceptual *patterns*. The seemingly old-fashioned language of Gestalt psychology is well-suited to express this. Every subjective theory can be termed "Gestalt." In other words, the Gestalt is not simply the additive collection of individual elements, but rather it represents a structural whole in itself. Subjective *valence* or meaning therefore cannot possess individual elements as such. Their meaning is derived from the relations and interactions with other parts within the Gestalt or the subjective theory.

A *second* determining feature of subjective theories can be called the explanatory function of relations. Subjective theories contain conceptions about the *causality* of factors, events, or processes. (Note that causality is understood very broadly. It does not refer merely to conceptions of mono- and multicausal determination but also to reciprocal interaction.)

A *third* feature of subjective theories is that they contain assumptions about consistency--the occurrence, duration, variability, or development of factors, events, processes, or relations over time.

2. SCIENTIFIC APPROACHES TO WORK AND LEISURE

In nearly all the social science literature on work and leisure or, more precisely on the relationships between the thinking, feeling, or acting of the same person in the two different main areas of life, the term "work" is understood to mean *paid* work, by which is meant all clearly-defined occupational activities regulated institutionally (through a labor contract, course of training, certificate, and the like) for securing the material necessities of life. In this way, agreement on the contexts or settings of work in time and space is straightforward for the majority of the employees in our society (those persons in industry and office work, for example). And in empirical studies it makes clear for these large populations a priori that leisure time in the sense of "nonwork" can be clearly distinguished in terms of time and space from paid work in a factory, company, or office. The features identified above allow the most important scientific approaches to be surveyed and depicted as in Figure 1.

1. "Generalization" (a) W_+ -----------------► L_+

                        (b) W_- -----------------► L_-

2. "Compensation"   (c) W_- -----------------► L_+

3. "Neutrality"   (d) W   no relationships   L

Fig. 1. Main scientific theses about the relationship between work and leisure. (Relationships between work (W) and leisure (L) are symbolized by connecting lines. Subjective valences originating in these relationships are differentiated only very generally into positive (+) and negative (-) valences. Types of causality or the directions of determination are represented by arrowheads. Consistency over time is not represented because scientific assumptions about it are not explained.)

If relations between work and leisure are explored in the research (Wilenski, 1962; for a survey, Ulich & Ulich, 1977; Staines, 1980), it is the thesis of a *"generalization,"* a "spillover," or an "extension" that dominates (Meissner, 1971; Form, 1973; Torbert & Rogers, 1973; Rousseau,

1978; Miller & Kohn, 1983). It is postulated that behavioral patterns and experiences have the same positive or negative valence in both areas of life. (In some of the studies, however, it is difficult just to establish whether a scientifically founded "positive" or "negative" assessment by the researcher is involved or whether it is a matter of the scientific depiction of the respondent's own subjective valence and thus a part of subjective theories.) The explanation for the identity of the two is primarily what is sought in the work, a circumstance most aptly expressed in the title of the well-known study by Meissner (1971): "The long arm of the job." The constraints imposed on behavior by work, and the negative experiences linked with it overshadow leisure as well being manifested as restricted, strongly receptive behavior and generalized negative experiences. By the same token, the active organization of work induces equally active and positive leisure.

The same direction of determination applies to a competing thesis, that of *"compensation"* (Miller & Weiss, 1982). According to the compensation thesis, however, the valences of the two areas are seen in contrast to one another. If work is experienced as restrictive, leisure will be used as positive compensation for it. Again, though, in many cases one cannot often really tell in the empirical studies whether these judgements stem from the researcher (or the researcher's operationalization) or whether subjective valences of the respondent are involved.

Lastly, *"neutrality"* or "segmentation" is put forward as an explanation (Kabanoff, 1982). Empirically, this thesis is gaining acceptance as the one that is best substantiated. Particularly in the German-speaking countries, all studies generally seem to support the thesis that the behavior in the two main areas of human life in our society is independent of the experiences (Schaginger, 1960; Hanhart, 1963; Wippler, 1970; Fröhlich, 1978, Hecker & Grunwald, 1981; perhaps the most interesting German study, that by Schlösser, 1981, is an exception in every respect-- in its theoretical and historical foundations and in its qualitative methodology).

Instead of making a detailed presentation of the evidence according to random samples, operationalization, and analytical methods at this point, I shall now discuss a few fundamental research problems. The first and most important one lies in what seems to be the most solid piece of evidence for neutrality. It appears as if it is an outright artifact of research, or better, it seems that a great, but actually unnecessary effort has been mounted to research a specious question. Of course the objective demands for a person's action can be quite independent of each other in work and leisure. But one could argue in utterly orthodox behaviorist terms that actual, subjective behavior transpires only in specific situations and is determined by the situation. The same goes for the corresponding unlinked cognitions (if they are permitted as subjects of research at all). Key, holistic concepts in psychology like "personality" or "identity" are invalidated if one imagines the human being to be something of a chameleon completely divided into a working person and a private person. In all theoretical approaches claiming to have an interactional paradigm (Hoff, 1981, 1984), it seems to be unthinkable from the outset that one and the same person does not mentally compare his or her behavior or action in different situations. The cognitive linkage concerns emotions, too, and even if modes of action turn out to be incomparable or impossible to transfer, this still indicates a previous cognitive process of comparison.

The question remains, how the empirical evidence can be explained. In this chapter it is argued that the thesis of neutrality does indeed seem to be much scientific nonsense, but that it makes very good sense in terms of subjective conceptual patterns. When persons suffer from behavioral constraints in their work, it is understandable that they try "to tune out." The subjective segmentation of areas of life can thus be interpreted as a compensatory strategy whose goal is to avoid having contraints, negative thoughts and feelings carry over into ostensibly "free" time, to allow the person to be able to think, feel, or do something quite "different." The studies cited above probably reflect primarily the respondents' *subjective* neutrality thesis, which, for its part, could be interpreted *scientifically* in terms of the compensation thesis. In past research, then, the extremely equivocal cliche "work is work and play is play" has erroneously been taken as gospel truth without being "properly" classified according to its compensatory function.

Of a number of other research problems, only one is to be taken up in this chapter. As early as 1958, Habermas differentiated considerably more types of relationships between work and leisure than those mentioned above. He was later reproached because his distinctions were not mutually exclusive and thus not useful for empirical study. In these terms, the forms or theses of generalization and compensation mentioned above are conceived to mutually exclusive. It is easy to see, however, that one fails to appreciate reality in this way, for in reality it can very well happen that the same leisure activity or the same cognitions can be understood simultaneously in terms of generalization and compensation. The argument that different interpretations can be entertained simultaneously now brings the element of time into play. At the very point when one would conduct temporal microanalysis of a single day in the life of a person, none of the usual theses would be tenable as the only one to occur. Rather, the thesis that there is permanent *reciprocal interaction* would presumably seem to be appropriate as a *global* description of the relationship between work and leisure: Work behavior and leisure behavior affect each other; cognitions or emotions relating to one area surface in the other or influence the cognitions related to it and vice versa. This complexity grows as time goes on. Of course, that does not preclude the possibility of there being a long-term *trend* toward a "generalization" or toward compensatory behavior, especially when no drastic changes occur in the person's occupation or leisure (and in research there is a tacit assumption of consistency over time).

3. SUBJECTIVE THEORIES ON WORK AND LEISURE

As a rule (to which, of course, there are exceptions, such as those in the research on central-life interests), in social science research measurements of time budgets and satisfaction and the like are made separately for work and leisure. The values for the two areas of life are then correlated. Thus the fact that people *themselves* very clearly think about a relationship (or equally clearly about a nonrelationship) is in no way trivial. In my own case studies (Hoff et al., 1983), they do not do this just in response to prompting by the researcher or interviewer; they often do it quite on their own. This indicates that thinking in terms of relationships does not have to follow tediously from individual judgments but rather that relationships per se are conscious subjects of everyday thinking.

The theses cited above, which have been discussed in the relevant scientific literature (see Figure 1) cover only a fraction of all the combinations that can be imagined on the basis of the aforementioned charac-

teristics and questions about valences and directions of determination.
They can be presented graphically as illustrated in Figure 2.

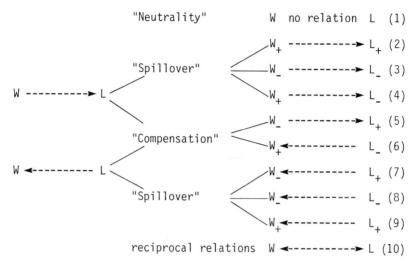

Fig. 2. The heuristics of subjective conceptual patterns. The direction of a determination is indicated by arrows, and the valence
of an experience or an action in work (W) or leisure (L) is characterized as positive (+) or negative (-).

Unlike on the scientific level, all of the hypothetical relationships
in Figure 2 are dealt with on the level of subjective theories. The heuristics presented here therefore prove to be empirically fruitful. Subjective descriptions of the relationship between work and leisure can be
treated by content analysis and unambiguously classified according to the
features introduced. It is not possible to treat all the relationships
represented in Figure 2 individually here and to document them with such
descriptions or classified interview passages (see Hoff, 1984). However,
the findings below are particularly interesting.
There really are cases when the subjective *neutrality thesis* (form 1
in Figure 1) is very persistently asserted. Employees who hold a subjective view like that, however, argue on a relatively high (or abstract)
level of temporal and spatial aggregation. For them, in other words,
work as a whole has nothing to do with leisure. In such cases in-depth
interviews may lead to contradictions between this global level of evaluations and that of situation-specific, definitive descriptions. When
the areas are separated according to the motto "work is work and play is
play," then it often remains unclear whether the actual state or a desired
state of the person is being described. In the last analysis, one thing
is particularly conspicuous: People who do *not* immediately prefer the
neutrality thesis but one of the other forms (2-10) instead often preface
their choice with a negative definition. They say that separation into
a work person and a private person is absolutely not possible, either for
themselves or for anyone else. The argument that the neutrality thesis
is scientifically untenable--i.e., not "true," unthinkable--is therefore
expressed in everyday language, too, and that with intense, totally unconditional conviction.

The most important interindividual difference in views therefore seems to be characterized by the extreme of a total dichotomy on one hand (form 1 in Figure 2) and all other forms on the other, ranging from form 2 all the way to reciprocal interaction at the other extreme, form 10.

As mentioned above, all relationships occur--not only the determination of leisure through work, but also the determination of work through leisure (forms 6-9). However, all *deterministic relations* (forms 2-9) are temporally specific, meaning that they refer to the subjective linkage between very specific factors, events, processes or people in time and space in both areas of life. Afterwards, such concrete, situation-specific conceptualizations can also be generalized (but not necessarily).

People who interpret their everyday lives in terms of *interactional relationships*--the conception of a permanent, mutual influence process between thinking, feeling and acting in work and leisure (form 10 in Figure 2)--also do so on a high (or abstract) level of spatiotemporal aggregation and speak broadly of work and leisure as overall areas. Later, in concrete descriptions of temporally specific situations, a variety of many monocausal relationships appears (2-9). Thus, it is actually only this interactional form that involves a generalized conceptual *pattern* of far greater theoretical complexity, a pattern in which temporally specific, mono- or multicausal determinations eventually cancel out each other. Besides the fact that the abstract interactional pattern seems to result from the sum of very concrete, situation-specific determinations running in the opposite direction, another more extensive qualitative difference is to be noted: This pattern differs from the others in that circular processes are prominent rather than isolated cause-and-effect relationships. Functionally speaking, for example, leisure as "recreation" is seen not only as a result of specific stresses from the past workday, but also as the cause for one's coping with them on the following workday, etc. In terms of everyday speech, this indicates an understanding of the theoretical relation that is described scientifically with the help of the twin concepts of "production" and "reproduction."

4. CONTROL IN WORK AND LEISURE

The concept of *valence* has not yet been made quite clear in this chapter. What does it mean when the two areas of life are judged "positively" or "negatively"? Or what else does it tell us when work is experienced as "negative" and leisure as "positive"? Particularly when work and leisure are concerned, such judgments refer primarily to the degree of self-determination in human action (positively judged) or to the degree of its determination by others. That, in turn, is true for science and everyday life. In terms of the compensation thesis, work is usually regarded as "constraint" and leisure as time that is "free" of this constraint, as the realm of personal "freedom."

A causal relationship is also expressed in the twin concepts of pressure and freedom, of control by others and self-control. The question is whether the person's behavior is determined by the "external" world--whether he is an object of his environment--or whether he is master of his own behavior and thereby the subject of his environment (or whether both are true at the same time). Here, too, *scientific approaches* and entire families of theories can be distinguished according to the paradigmatic causal relationships they favor (Endler & Magnusson, 1976). In nativistic, organismic, or personalistic theories of personality, internal characteristics of the human being are considered to be the sole or dominant

factors determining his or her behavior. Such theories are countered by
an environmental, deterministic, or situational position to be found, for
example, in orthodox behavioralism. The concept of human beings that dominates is one in which the individual's behavior is seen as a reaction to
primarily external stimuli. For some time, however, approaches rooted in
action theory have been discussed in psychology, and an interactional
paradigm is considered to be the only reasonable one. Individuals are simultaneously seen as subject *and* object of their environment. The question as to whether inner traits *or* the external environment, the individual *or* the situation, unilaterally determines behavior (or, through the
behavior, the other side) is recognized as incorrectly posed. Instead,
the reciprocal interaction of both of these sides is emphasized. In contrast to a concept of behavior as *reaction* (be it to internal drives or to
external stimuli), the concept of behavior as an exchange process of simultaneous reaction (to the environment) and action (of the person) is becoming the center of scientific interest.

The same patterns of thought on which scientific theories are based
are now encountered in psychological concepts of control. They focus
on *subjective concepts*, convictions, or "beliefs" of individuals that
they are the subject or the object of their environment. Clearly, the
concept introduced by Rotter (1966) on the locus of control has the
closest affinity to the above-mentioned scientific paradigms. An extremely personalistic view in science corresponds to an "*internal Locus of Control*", in other words, to the subjective conviction that one's own behavior (and its impacts) is determined by internal factors, by one's own powers, efforts, capabilities, or inherited traits. And the opposite conviction postulating an "*external Locus of Control*," namely, that one's own
behavior (and its impacts) is determined by external forces, other people,
etc., can almost be described as extreme "situationism" in everyday life.

As mentioned, the scientific discussion now considers the question of
whether individuals *or* the environment determine behavior to be incorrectly posed. Instead, the paradigm of reciprocal interaction is taken for
granted. It is all the more surprising that researchers pose this incorrectly formulated question to people in daily life and then expect answers
that they themselves would consider untenable or, in extreme cases, incorrect. (This is not to deny that such subjective conceptions do occur.) It
is just striking that an *interactional conceptual pattern* in everyday life
is not also considered possible and scientifically discussed over and
above this. All scientific reasons and my own empirical case studies
(Hoff, 1982; Hohner, 1984; Hoff & Hohner, 1986) indicate that such a concept of being subject *and* object simultaneously in one's own environment
really does exist. And in analogy to the scientific paradigm, this subjective paradigm can be considered as the most realistic, most differentiated, and most rational.

This proposal of a new conception does not, however, refer exclusively to the interactional form itself. It makes the customary distinction,
too, seem less important to the judgment of interindividual differences.
In contrast to the interactional quality, the common *deterministic quality*
of control or exertion of influence is more important than the internal
or external "Locus" of Control is. Incidentally, persons with deterministic convictions of control have not expressed them in a solely external
or solely internal way in our own case studies either, but rather both
types of the "Locus" are stated depending on the specific area: In work
they see themselves as the object of their environment, in leisure, as the
subject, without this being subjectively felt as contradictory. It is entirely possible to combine the notion of strictly unilateral and unchang-

ing, intensive determination with the notion of determination running in
the opposite direction, of a contrary "locus" of control. One can even put
it this way: The more restrictive and controlled by others strong work is
experienced the more necessary it is to interpret leisure as being completely independent of work and just as unilaterally determined by oneself.

   To conclude, this point of view clarifies the connections between subjective concepts of the relationship between work and leisure on one hand
and control on the other. In retrospect, it also becomes clearer that it
makes sense to speak of subjective "theories" in terms of complex, interrelated conceptual *patterns*. Concepts of a strictly unilateral determination (either that of the person through the work environment or that of the
leisure environment through the person) give rise to concepts of dichotomy
or segmentation of the areas of life and vice versa. The same is true for
the relationship between interactional concepts of control and the concept
of reciprocal interaction of one's own work and leisure. Even (or precisely) when work is experienced in general terms as being restrictive vis-a-
vis leisure, it makes sense in that area of life to continue seeking and
developing latitudes for action. Unlike the view that behavior is unilaterally determined by external *or* internal factors, the notion of interactional conceptual patterns links these sources of influence causally: *Because*
external pressures are perceived, one must exhaust one's capabilities in
action or efforts to overcome or get around these restrictions. And vice
versa, degrees of freedom are not all that is perceived in leisure time
(and if so, then the perception is illusory); pressures are perceived, too.
In the context of these complex subjective theories, self-determined action
means that inner powers, predispositions, capabilities, impulses, or motives can no longer have an effect exclusively and unilaterally; they can
have an effect only according to external circumstances.

ACKNOWLEDGEMENTS: A much longer German version of this chapter can be
obtained from the author upon request. I am indebted to Heike Jacobsen
and Wolfgang Lempert for their helpful comments.

Translated by David Antal.

REFERENCES

Endler, N. S. & Magnusson, D. (Eds.) (1976). Interactional Psychology and
      Personality. Washington D.C.: Hemisphere.
Form, W. H. (1973). The Internal Stratification of the Working Class.
      American Sociological Review, 38, 697-711.
Fröhlich, D. (1978). Innerbetriebliche Arbeitssituation und Teilnahme an
      freiwilligen Vereinigungen. Zeitschrift für Soziologie, 7, 56-71.
Habermas, J. (1958). Soziologische Notizen zum Verhältnis von Arbeit und
      Freizeit. In G. Funke, Konkrete Vernunft. Festschrift für
      E. Rothacker (pp. 219-231). Bonn, Germany: Bouvier.
Hanhardt, D. (1973). Arbeitszufriedenheit und Freizeit. In R. Schmitz-
      Scherzer (Ed.), Freizeit (pp. 327-339). Frankfurt, Germany:
      Akademische Verlagsgesellschaft. (First published: 1963).
Hecker, K. & Grunwald, W. (1981). Über die Beziehungen zwischen Arbeits-
      und Freizeitzufriedenheit. Ein theoretisch-empirischer Beitrag.
      Soziale Welt, 32, 353-368.
Hoff, E.-H. (1981). Sozialisation als Entwicklung der Beziehungen zwischen
      Person und Umwelt. Zeitschrift für Sozialisationsforschung und Er-
      ziehungssoziologie, 1, 91-115.

Hoff, E.-H. (1982). Kontrollbewußtsein: Grundvorstellungen zur eigenen Person und Umwelt bei jungen Arbeitern. Kölner Zeitschrift für Soziologie und Sozialpsychologie, 34, 316-339.

Hoff, E.-H. (1984). Gesellschaftlicher Zwang und individueller Freiraum? Naive und wissenschaftliche Theorien zum Verhältnis von Arbeit und Freizeit. In H. Moser & S. Preiser (Eds.), Umweltprobleme und Arbeitslosigkeit. Gesellschaftliche Herausforderungen an die Politische Psychologie. Vol., 4 (pp. 167-190). Weinheim, Germany: Beltz.

Hoff, E.-H. & Hohner, H.-U. (1986). Occupational Careers, Work, and Control. In M. M. Baltes & P. B. Baltes, Aging and the Psychology of Control (in press). Hillsdale, N.J.: Erlbaum.

Hoff, E.-H., Lappe, L. & Lempert, W. (1983). Methoden zur Untersuchung der Sozialisation junger Facharbeiter. Materialien aus der Bildungsforschung, Vol. 24. Berlin, Germany: Max-Planck-Institut für Bildungsforschung.

Hohner, H.-U. (1984). Kontrollbewußtsein und berufliche Restriktivität. Entwicklung und empirische Erprobung eines integrativen Modells. Doctoral Thesis. Berlin, Germany.

Kabanoff, B. (1982). Occupational and Sex Differences in Leisure Needs and Leisure Satisfaction. Journal of Occupational Behavior, 3, 233-245.

Laucken, U. (1974). Naive Verhaltenstheorie. Stuttgart, Germany: Klett.

Meissner, M. (1971). The Long Arm of the Job. A Study of Work and Leisure. Industrial Relations, 10, 239-260.

Miller, L. E. & Weiss, R. M. (1982). The Work-Leisure Relationship: Evidence for the Compensatory Hypothesis. Human Relations, 35, 763-771.

Miller, K. A. & Kohn, M. L. (1983). The Reciprocal Effects of Job Conditions and the Intellectuality of Leisure-time Activities. In M. L. Kohn & C. Schooler, Work and Personality. An Inquiry into the Impact of Social Stratification (pp. 217-241). Norwood, N.J.: Ablex.

Rousseau, D. M. (1978). Relationship of Work to Nonwork. Journal of Applied Psychology, 63, 513-517.

Schaginger, E. M. (1974). Arbeit und Freizeit. In R. Schmitz-Scherzer (Ed.), Freizeit (pp. 317-326). Frankfurt, Germany: Akademische Verlagsgesellschaft. (First published: 1960).

Schlösser, M. (1981). Freizeit und Familienleben von Industriearbeitern. Frankfurt/New York: Campus.

Staines, G. L. (1980). Spillover versus Compensation: A Review of the Literature of the Relationship between Work and Nonwork. Human Relations, 33, 111-129.

Torbert, W. R. & Rogers, U. P. (1973). Being for the Most Part Puppets. Interactions between Men's Labor, Leisure and Politics. Cambridge, Mass: Schenkmann.

Ulich, E. & Ulich, H. (1977). Über einige Zusammenhänge zwischen Arbeitsgestaltung und Freizeitverhalten. In Th. Leuenberger & K.-H. Ruffmann (Eds.), Bürokratie - Motor oder Bremse der Entwicklung? (pp. 209-227). Bern: P. Lang.

Wilensky, H. L. (1962). Labor and Leisure: Intellectual Traditions. Industrial Relations, 23, 1-12.

Wippler, R. (1973). Freizeitverhalten: ein multivariater Ansatz. In R. Schmitz-Scherzer (Ed.), Freizeit (pp. 91-107). Frankfurt, Germany: Akademische Verlagsgesellschaft. (First published: 1970).

II.6. Safety and Prevention
of Accidents

THE PSYCHOLOGY OF WORK AND ORGANIZATION
G. Debus and H.-W. Schroiff (Editors)
© Elsevier Science Publishers B.V. (North-Holland), 1986   323

MEASURING ACCIDENT LIABILITY INDEPENDENTLY OF ACCIDENT OCCURRENCE

N.P. Sheehy and A.J. Chapman

Department of Psychology, University of Leeds, Leeds LS2 9JT, UK

1. INTRODUCTION

1.1. Human Error

This paper considers the relationship between accident liability and
accident occurrence. An approach is outlined which permits the study of
accident liability independently of, but in relation to, accident
occurrence. In outlining this approach a method for studying covert error
and relating covert error to overt, injury-producing error is described.

The view of human error adopted here is similar to that outlined by
Reason (1). Human error is seen, not as rooted in irrational and
maladaptive tendencies, but in non-trivial psychological processes.
Norman (2) and Reason (3,4) have argued for treating action slips and
lapses differently from mistakes. Slips and lapses are considered to be
failures to correctly execute a particular action sequence. Mistakes have
their origins in planning failures. However, more recently Reason (1) has
suggested that this dichotomy may obscure a more fundamental distinction:
that between errors emerging from resource-limited conscious processes and
errors emerging from the apparently unlimited capacity of unconscious
processors or knowledge structures.

An important feature of Reason's treatment of human error is that it shows
how systematic error may often go unnoticed, especially when the error
does not lead to physical damage. Also his treatment emphasizes a
difficulty in relating overt consequences to covert antecedents. It is
possible systematically to repeat a planning error or 'mistake' but avoid
self-injury by adopting a 'safety margin' and tactfully proceeding through
a large number of 'near-miss' encounters. Under such circumstances the
occurrence of an injury-producing accident may not motivate an examination
of habitual, faulty work practices. More likely, people will attribute
the accident to an unfortunate combination of unfavourable factors and
justify this by pointing out that a similar incident has never before
happened to them.

2. ACCIDENT LIABILITY

2.1. Incidence and Liability

Evidence of repeated accidents is usually taken as evidence for accident 'proneness'. The practice of comparing high-accident with low-accident groups is common and it presumes a linear relationship between accident liability and accident occurrence (cf. Sheehy and Chapman (5)). Frequently the inference is drawn that those who have the most accidents are those who are most liable to accidents. This may be true in a simple statistical sense, but Eysenck (6) has argued that a psychological approach to accident liability must go beyond statistical analysis. The statistical approach is primarily descriptive, whereas the psychological approach generates hypotheses about the effects of individual differences. For example, it might be predicted that locus of control is related to accident occurrence and, by implication, accident liability (cf. Jones and Wuebker (7)). However, accident liable, or 'at-risk' individuals might not necessarily be those with the greater accident history. To be repeatedly involved in accidents one has to be exposed to circumstances in which accidents have a good probability of happening. Also, one should need ineffective coping strategies in order to increase the likelihood that threatening circumstances will lead to accidents. This suggests that a liability is a multivariate multidimensional concept and not as simple as has commonly been supposed (cf. McKenna (8)). Thus, Boyle (9) has pointed out that the observed distribution of accidents in a population may be an aggregate of many smaller distributions of accidents for sub-groups with different accident liabilities.

Investigations of near misses are a partial response to the need to study accident liability independently of accident occurrence. Usually, the purpose of such investigations is to get a more thorough understanding of accident antecedents. Although strong correlations have been observed between events preceding accidents and near misses there are good reasons for treating these as separate kinds of incidents. The strongest reason is that many researchers have witnessed near-misses but hardly any have seen a near-miss transformed into an accident (cf. Sheehy (10)). It is possible that an individual's history of near-misses will not be related in simple linear fashion to his/her accident biography.

It is possible that near-misses, both observable and unobservable kinds, constitute a better measure of liability than does accident occurrence. A difficulty with observational studies of near-misses and minor slips is that usually they can only be accurately identified through an analysis of physical injury and property damage. Frequently, minor slips in an action sequence can be 'let go' if remedial action can be taken later in the sequence. These kinds of error, which are usually attributable to planning mistakes, can only be revealed through an analysis of subjective reports. Thus, the development of non-intrusive methods for eliciting reports should be a major objective in further studies of accident liability.

2.2. Methods for Eliciting Records

There is a number of methods and techniques available for eliciting records of error. They can be classified as on-line or off-line and as verbal or nonverbal. On-line methods exploit people's capacity to provide verbal commentaries on their behaviour as it is performed. Protocol analysis is used to relate verbal commentaries to observable behaviour. Off-line methods involve the use of diaries to record and comment on incidents after they have happened. Questionnaires designed to measure liability to accident also fall into this category. Both on-line verbal commentary and off-line verbal recollection rely on the ability of people to verbalize their plans and actions. Frequently this is a difficult task, especially when one is examining skills which are usually performed sub-consciously. Nonverbal techniques attempt to elicit records of errors by permitting people to record an occurrence and nothing more. There is a number of advantages to using nonverbal techniques. Most importantly they are less distracting than verbal techniques and they minimize the risk that, in attempting to provide a verbal report of a near-miss or a failure-in-progress, a person's task will actually be made more difficult and more dangerous.

Nonverbal techniques for eliciting records make use of event recording devices to obtain cumulative frequency measures. Their use is restricted because, usually, it is difficult to obtain information additional to the fact that an incident occurred. In the Department of Psychology at the University of Leeds a device has been designed and built which will partly overcome this difficulty. It measures approximately 20cms by 12cms. Up to nine pre-defined events can be recorded and this increases the number and complexity of incidents that can be recorded. Pressing any of the keys places a time code in a memory register so that, in addition to simple frequency counts, the device permits time-series analysis, including time-of-day analysis. Up to 999 events can be recorded. The device can then be connected to a standard dot-matrix printer and the contents of the memory registers printed for subsequent analysis. Thus, the device can be used as a 'diary'. It is planned to use the instrument to conduct detailed studies of near-accidents, slips and mistakes and to relate analysis of these kinds of events to accident occurrence. One prediction is that the relationship between slips, mistakes and 'accidents' is not linear and that individual coping strategies help people to moderate the levels of threat to which they may routinely be exposed while working. The development of the instrument and of methods to investigate slips and mistakes will require a more thorough analysis of the relationship between accident occurrence and accident recording.

3. ACCIDENT RECORDING

One argument of Reason's theory states that there is likely to be a poor correlation between covert error (planning failures) and overt error (execution failures). We would add that there is also likely to be a poor correlation between the occurrence of both kinds of error and reports of their occurrence. This is especially true of covert errors because, by definition their consequences are never revealed directly in action failures. One implication of this is that reports of covert error may reveal little about overt, injury-producing error. Thus, error reports cannot be used directly to test hypotheses about covert error processes. However, there may be a strong correlation between event reporting and

overt error. The method described here attempts to maximize the
correlation between self-reports of error and observable behaviour.

It is conceivable that skilled actions are the result of mental activity
related to the primary task and event reporting is the product of a
separate activity associated with the production of an event record. This
suggests a need to consider two theories: one to account for task error
and another to account for error reporting. People readily confuse memory
for doing things with memory for imagining doing things. This is
particularly so where routine or trivial tasks are concerned. A trivial
action sequence may be planned consciously, but never executed. Such
planned action sequences are often executed unconsciously and
recollections usually do not discriminate accurately between the plan and
its execution. The difficulty associated with recalling whether one
locked the door to one's house is an example of this. Accidents in
industrial environments often occur while performing routine tasks.
Accident investigation is made difficult by the fact that victims and
witnesses frequently are forced to conjecture that they acted in
particular ways. Errors of mis-remembering, or recording errors, need to
be distinguished from memory errors where an action is simply forgotten.
Recording errors reflect confusion in the interpretation of information in
memory, not simply the forgetting of a propositional activity tag. Thus,
one cannot conclude that those who most frequently make errors will also
be most likely to forget to record their errors. The processes are
different and poor performance in the one does not necessarily imply poor
performance in the other.

The need for two theories, one to account for error generation and the
other to account for record generation, means that discrepancies between
action and report do not imply that one's action error theory is faulty.
From the point of view of studying error recording this seems a
pessimistic conclusion. However, error records can be used as a source of
hypotheses about error generation. For example, Reason's earlier work has
provided hypotheses about the aetiology of accidents which have shaped
more recent formulations of his theory 1 . More importantly, the
correlation between error generation and error recording may be
sufficiently strong to warrant using error records to understand accident
occurrence. A primary research task should entail the development of
methods to facilitate report generation and maximize the correlation
between error-generation and error-recording. Thus, it will be necessary
to validate error records against on-line verbal reports, on-line
behaviour and off-line verbal reports. Figure 1 summarizes the
connections between the different kinds of recording. There is a small
amount of empirical data which relate to the relationships described
therein.

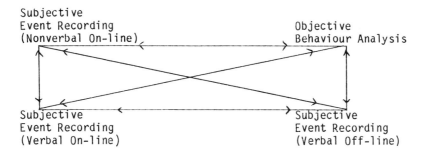

FIGURE 1
Relationships between four kinds of record analysis.

Bainbridge (11) has reviewed the evidence which suggests that on-line verbal reports of activities are frequently wrong. Often people report doing things that they are observed not to do and they report effects of variables which were not present. Thus, the correlation between subjective on-line verbal records and objective behaviour analysis is weak. Bainbridge noted also that the correlation between off-line verbal records and observable behaviour tends to be weak. For example, people have theories about how accidents happen (cf. Sheehy and Chapman (12)) and tend to select and emphasize aspects of behaviour which confirm their theories. Often they are oblivious to the importance of variables which do not feature in their theories. Hermann (13) has reviewed the use of off-line verbal recording measures, such as questionnaire and diary techniques. He concluded that although these measures have high internal validity they do not predict performance. For example, Wilkins and Baddeley (14) attempted to predict the degree to which people forget to press a button on a portable event recording from scores elicited on the Cognitive Failures Questionnaire. They found a small, positive non-significant correlation. Thus, the correlation between on-line nonverbal records and off-line verbal reports seems also to be weak. There appear to have been no studies of the remaining relationship pairs: (1) on-line nonverbal event recording and observable behaviour; (2) on-line nonverbal event recording and on-line verbal event recording; and (3) on-line verbal event recording and off-line verbal recording.

4. CONCLUSION

The development of methods and techniques for investigating human error through record analysis requires further studies of the relationships between the various recording forms available. Nonverbal techniques have not been used effectively and they deserve serious consideration for two reasons. First, as on-line recording devices they are less intrusive than verbal methods. Second, they are particularly effective for recording incidents which have been recognized as having gone wrong, but which are difficult to verbalize. Both verbal and nonverbal methods can be used to obtain a better understanding of the antecedents of industrial accidents. Specifically, they can help investigate the relationship between accident liability and accident occurrence and they permit the study of the former independently of the latter. The most efficient use of both methods will be realized in studies which attempt to combine the advantages of both. However, it is also essential to conduct more thorough analyses of the relationships between the various recording methods independently and in combination, in order to validate them individually.

REFERENCES

  (1) Reason, J.T., Slips and Mistakes - A Consequence of Human Error?, in: Oborne, D.J., Contemporary Ergonomics (Taylor and Francis, London, 1985).
  (2) Norman, P.A., Categorization of Action Slips, Psychological Review, 88 (1981) 1-5.
  (3) Reason, J.T., Actions Not as Planned: The Price of Automization, in: Underwood, G. and Stevens, R. (eds.), Aspects of Consciousness (Academic Press, New York, 1979).
  (4) Reason, J.T., Lapses of Attention, in: Parasuraman, R., Davies, R. and Beatty, J.B. (eds.), Varieties of Attention (Academic Press, New York, 1981).
  (5) Sheehy, N.P. and Chapman, A.J., Accidents and Safety, in: Gale, A. and Chapman, A.J. (eds.), Psychology and Social Problems: An Introduction to Applied Psychology (Wiley, New York, 1984).
  (6) Eysenck, H.J., Fact and Fiction in Psychology (Penguin, Harmondsworth, 1965).
  (7) Jones, J.W. and Wuekker, L., Development and Validation of the Safety Locus of Control Scale, Perceptual and Motor Skills, 61 (1985) 151-161.
  (8) McKenna, F.P., Accident Proness: A Conceptual Analysis, Accident Analysis and Prevention, 15 (1983) 65-71.
  (9) Boyle, A.J., "Found Experiments" in Accident Research: Report of a Study of Accident Rates and Implications for Future Research, Journal of Occupational Psychology, 53 (1980) 53-64.
 (10) Sheehy, N.P., The Interview in Accident Investigation: Methodological Pitfalls, Ergonomics, 24 (1981) 437-446.
 (11) Bainbridge, L., Verbal Reports as Evidence of the Process Operator's Knowledge, International Journal of Man-Machine Studies, 11 (1979) 411- 436.
 (12) Sheehy, N.P. and Chapman, A.J., Children's Accidents as Children See Them, in: Oborne, D.J. (ed.), Contemporary Ergonomics (Taylor and Francis, London, 1985).
 (13) Hermann, D.J., Know Thy Memory: The Use of Questionnaires to Assess and Study Memory, Psychological Bulletin, 92 (1982) 434-452.
 (14) Wilkins, A.J. and Baddeley, A.D., Remembering to Recall in Everyday Life: An Approach to Absent-Mindedness, in: Gruneberg, M.M., Morris, P.E. and Sykes, R.N. (eds.), Practical Aspects of Memory (Academic Press, New York, 1978).

THE PSYCHOLOGY OF WORK AND ORGANIZATION
G. Debus and H.-W. Schroiff (Editors)
© Elsevier Science Publishers B.V. (North-Holland), 1986

ACCIDENTS TO YOUNG PEOPLE ON THE UK YOUTH OPPORTUNITIES PROGRAMME

A Ian GLENDON

A R HALE

Applied Psychology Division
Aston University, UK

University of Delft
The Netherlands

Reports of 1700 accident injuries to young people were coded using a model for data collection and analysed to determine patterns of accident injuries. More serious injuries were found to be associated with situations not involving normal work activity. To reduce the large amount of unexplained variance in such data more structured collection techniques are recommended as an aid to greater understanding which could aid prevention activity.

1. INTRODUCTION

The Youth Opportunities Programme (YOP) was the immediate predecessor of the UK Youth Training Scheme (YTS) and ran from April 1978 until March 1983. Like the YTS, YOP was run by the Manpower Services Commission (MSC) who sponsored the research to be described. Details of the studies may be found in Hale and Glendon [1] and in Glendon and Hale [2].

2. DATA COLLECTION AND ANALYSIS

Accidents which resulted in injury to young people on YOP - most of whom were aged between 16 and 18 years, were reported directly to the MSC. A sample of 1700 accident injury report forms - representing six months complete data was selected for analysis. To assist in the coding of data under the 'description of accident' heading, a model was drawn up from a content analysis of a sample of 60 of the accident reports to represent an idealized accident injury sequence. This is shown in Figure 1.

All the cases were computerized, checked for logical errors and a sample was tested for coding reliability (inter-coder reliabilities for the variables considered in this chapter were between .72 and .92). The data were analysed using the Statistical Package for the Social Sciences (SPSS) version 9.

3. CHARACTERISTICS OF THE SAMPLE

Data were obtained on around 30 variables and the breakdowns are given in full in Glendon and Hale [2]. However, in this paper only some of the descriptive statistics are presented in order to provide some basic information on the sample.

Just under 82% of the sample were male and the mean age of those injured was 17 years and 1 month with a standard deviation of 8 months. 65% of the cases were from the SIC categories ⌊3⌋ 'Professional and Scientific', 'Distributive Trades', 'Public Administration' or 'Miscellaneous Services'. Thus, accident injuries reported from YOP schemes were very much a phenomenon of the service industries. The pattern probably broadly reflects the distribution of young persons among the various sectors although there are no data to confirm the validity of this supposition. However, there is a rather different pattern of accident injuries among employees in the same age group within the working population making any comparisons between these groups problematic.

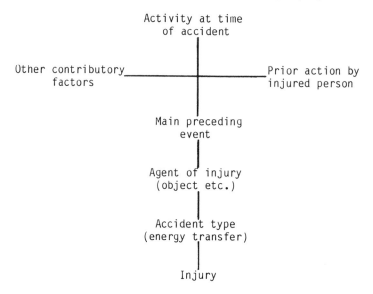

FIGURE 1   Model of accident injury sequence used for
data collection

The main locations from which accident injuries were reported were: factory (19.5%), education or training establishment (18%), shop, hotel or restaurant (13%), park or garden (7.5%) and construction site (7%).

The main types of injury sustained were: laceration or other wound (31%), crushing or bruising (22.5%), fractures (18%), strains and sprains (13%), burns and scalds (4%), other injuries (11%). There were six fatal injuries in the sample.

Over 26% of reported injuries were to fingers or thumb and a further 15% were to the hand or wrist. Eleven percent were injuries to toes or foot, 9.5% were to the head or neck and 5% were eye injuries.

The Regulations in force at the time of the study were used as a basis for coding injury severity ⌊4⌋. Besides the six fatal accidents, just under 4% were classified as major injuries and 73% involved more than three days lost time. The remainder resulted in 3 or fewer days absence.

A breakdown by accident type showed that just under 22% of cases involved being 'struck by object', with 'fall to lower level' and 'caught or trapped between objects' each accounting for just under 12% of cases. Main agents of injury were 'physical objects' (21%), surfaces (16%) and hand tools (16%).

While 84% of accident injuries were reported as having occurred during normal work activity, a further 8% occurred during non-work activities such as workbreaks or outside work (e.g. road traffic accidents) and a further 8% were associated with improper behaviour such as horseplay or unauthorised work.

4. RESULTS

Of particular interest was the relationship between activity at the time of the accident and injury severity using the Notification of Accidents and Dangerous Occurrences Regulations 1980 (NADOR) criteria [4]. The proportions of cases under each severity category occurring during normal work activity and other types of activity are shown in Table 1.

TABLE 1   Summary crosstabulation of accident injury
severity and activity at time of accident

ACCIDENT INJURY SEVERITY	ACCIDENTS OCCURRING:	
	DURING NORMAL WORK	OUTSIDE WORK,DURING WORKBREAKS OR FROM IMPROPER BEHAVIOUR
Fatal	2 (33%)	4 (67%)
Major	50 (64%)	28 (36%)
Over 3 days absence	1038 (85%)	189 (15%)
Under 4 days absence	323 (86%)	53 (14%)
Overall	1413 (84%)	274 (16%)

(Data were missing for 13 cases)

Table 1 shows that there is a gradient effect such that the more severe the injury the less likely is it to have occurred during normal work, although these differences are not statistically significant. However, this finding is consistent with those of Powell et al. [5] on workplace accident injury severity and work activity.

Crosstabulation of the categories of the variables shown in Figure 1 with activity at the time of accident revealed a large number of significant relationships and these are summarized in Table 2. Table 2 shows that there are marked differences in the accident injury characteritics reported between accidents occurring at work and those associated with activities which are not part of normal work.

TABLE 2   Summary of prevalence of accident injury characteristics crosstabulated with activity at time of accident

ACCIDENT INJURY CHARACTERISTICS	ACTIVITY			
	NORMAL WORK	OUTSIDE WORK	WORKBREAKS	IMPROPER BEHAVIOUR
INJURY TYPE AND SITE	Eye, fingers, trunk, foot. Open wound.	Multiple and head injuries of a serious nature. Internal, trunk, leg, bruises.	Multiple and head injuries of a serious nature. Internal, arm, ankle. Fractures. Burns.	Multiple and head injuries of a serious nature. Burns and scalds.
ACCIDENT TYPE AND AGENT OF INJURY	Caught between. Cut/sharp object. Awkward movement. Hand tool. Container.	Falls. Moving machinery. Transport.	Falls. Heat. Contact with people.	Struck by flying objects or by people. Heat.
PRECEDING EVENT	Loss of grip or control. Object drops. Stack collapse. Loss of attention.	Jump. Lose balance. Collision, emergency stop (vehicle).	Slip, trip. Lose balance. Pushed. Leak/explosion.	Object thrown. Pushed. Adjust machinery (unauthorised).
PRIOR ACTION	Normal by victim.	Wrong by others.	Wrong by others.	Wrong by victim or others.
CONTRIBUTORY FACTORS	Work methods. P.p.e. poor or not used. Lack of skill.	Personal protection. Equipment (P.p.e) not used.	Design or condition of work area. Supervision.	Supervision.

5. FURTHER ANALYSIS OF FINDINGS AND DISCUSSION

In attempting to improve upon the model used as a basis for data collection, variables and categories were selected on the basis of whether these had shown interesting relationships from earlier analyses and whether they could be considered as part of a theoretical accident injury sequence.   In order to retain cell sizes large enough for statistical analysis, categories were collapsed so that there was a maximum of seven for each variable including a miscellaneous category of less common cases which could be theoretically important in the analysis.   Inevitably this process involved some loss of data.   The collapsed categories of the main accident sequence variables are shown in Table 3.

TABLE 3   Variables and collapsed categories within the main accident injury sequence

VARIABLE	CATEGORIES
Injury severity (dependent variable)	fatal and major over 3 days absence under 4 days absence
Injury type	cuts or lacerations crushing or bruising fractures or dislocations strain or sprain injuries miscellaneous injuries
Accident type	contact with objects falls - all types caught or trapped exertion or strain energy - heat, chemical, etc. miscellaneous accident types
Agent of injury	physical objects as agent ground or surface hand tools - all types plant, building etc. transport - all types person or animal agent miscellaneous agents
Activity at time of accident	normal work - moving normal work - static all non-work activities

The variables shown in Table 3 were inter-correlated to produce a new model which is shown in Figure 2.

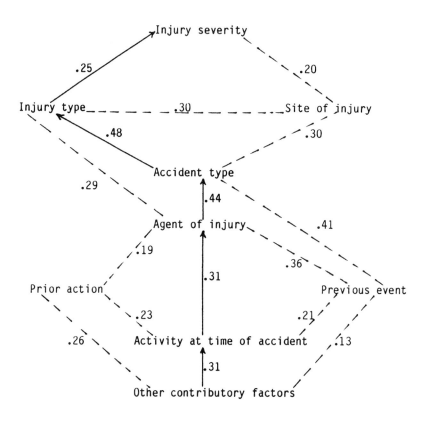

FIGURE 2   Accident sequence model derived from inter-correlations of the
main variables

It should be noted that Figure 2 represents only a correlational model
(the correlations are values for Cramer's V test for categorical data) and
that the 'causal' sequence has been imposed from the inherent logic of the
process.   While all the correlations shown are statistically significant
($p < 0.05$ or better) all are relatively low so that at no point in the
sequence is as much as 25% of the variance at a later stage explained by
reference to a single variable at a previous stage.   Thus, there is
considerable unexplained variance in the data.   Notwithstanding these
caveats it remains possible to trace a main pathway through the data
which suggests that the variables shown in Table 3 are more central to the
accident injury sequence than are others.

The model also suggests a basis for further analysis using the
collapsed categories of the five main accident injury sequence
variables shown in Table 3.   In order to explore further the nature of
the relationship between the dependent variable injury severity and the
other variables in the sequence, discriminant analysis of the data was
undertaken to determine whether the predicting set of new variables (the
21 categories in Table 3) could discriminate between the three groups of
cases using the NADOR classification [4] as a basis for the dependent
variable groups:

```
1 - fatal and major injury cases,
2 - cases resulting in more than three days absence,
3 - cases resulting in less than four days absence.
```

The twenty-one collapsed categories (factors) of the variables in the main accident sequence path shown in Table 3 were entered as dummy variables into a stepwise discriminant analysis. Six of the factors did not enter the analysis because they added too little to the discriminating functions already present. A further six had low standardized canonical discriminant function coefficients on both of the discriminant functions which emerged as statistically significant. The factors which had high coefficients on one or both discriminant functions are shown in Table 4.

TABLE 4 Main factors contributing to the discriminant functions

FACTOR	STANDARDIZED CANONICAL COEFFICIENT	
Fractures and dislocations	.90	
Miscellaneous injuries	.36	Function 1
Non-work activity	.31	
Falls - all types	.56	
Contact with objects	.52	
Miscellaneous injuries	.51	
Miscellaneous accident types	.46	Function 2
Strain and sprain injuries	-.45	
Person or animal agent	.37	
Physical objects as agent	.35	

The two significant discriminant functions account for just over 20% of the total variance within the data with over 87% of the explained variance attributable to the first function. The first function appears to be related to injuries which tend to be in the more serious categories and which are more likely to occur during activity which is not directly connected with work. The second function is more diffuse and harder to interpret but seems to be related to some of the more common and less serious types of injuries, accident types and agents of injury. Function 1 discriminates between the most and the least serious injury cases (groups 1 and 3) but much less well between groups 2 and 3. Function 2 does not discriminate well between any of the groups.

With prior probabilities assigned on the basis of group size, 72% of cases were correctly predicted by the discriminant classification. However, while over 97% of the over-3-day absence cases were correctly classified, predictions for cases in the two smaller groups were poor. The analysis suggests that cases in groups 2 and 3 are hard to distinguish from one another in respect of the variables on which information was available, but that it is possible to identify characteristics of cases in the most serious injury group.

6. CONCLUSIONS

One of the main problems in using accident injury data as a basis for targetting resources towards improved prevention activities is the unstructured way in which such data are usually collected. This study has demonstrated the usefulness of a model for coding descriptions of accident injuries. With an adequate number of cases it was possible to improve upon the initial model used for data collection. The revised model indicated that while it was possible to find significant relationships between some of the main variables used in the analysis, it was clear that much of the variance remained unexplained. Thus, there remains a large random element in accident injury aetiology as revealed by these data. Analysis of data based upon reported accident injuries would be improved if procedures were adopted in which a logical structure such as that in Figure 2 were used as a basis for data collection.

Analysis revealed two main general types of 'accident scenario'. Most accidents were associated with normal work activity and resulted in 'common' types of injury which required a few days absence. Of particular interest was the finding that 16% of accident injuries reported were associated with activities which were not part of normal work - particularly during workbreaks, through horseplay or unauthorised work. Serious (major and fatal) injuries were disproportionately associated with non-work activity. This finding presents a dilemma for accident prevention activities related to the employment of young people - whether on the one hand to target the more common but less serious types of injury accidents, or whether on the other hand to attempt to tackle the factors which are associated with the much less common events which tend to have more serious injury outcomes.

ACKNOWLEDGEMENT

The authors acknowledge the sponsorship and support of the UK Manpower Services Commission in carrying out the research upon which this chapter is based. The views expressed in the chapter are entirely those of the authors.

REFERENCES

[1] Hale, A.R. and Glendon, A.I., Accidents on the Youth Opportunities Programme: Pilot study report (Manpower Services Commission, Sheffield, 1984)

[2] Glendon, A.I. and Hale, A.R., A study of 1700 accidents on the Youth Opportunities Programme (Manpower Services Commission, Sheffield, 1985)

[3] UK Central Statistical Office, Standard Industrial Classification revised 1968 (HMSO, London, 1968)

[4] UK Health and Safety Commission, Notification of Accidents and Dangerous Occurrences Regulations 1980 (HMSO, London, 1980)

[5] Powell, P.I., Hale, M., Martin, J. and Simon, M., 2000 accidents: A shop floor study of their causes (National Institute of Industrial Psychology, London, 1971)

THE PSYCHOLOGY OF WORK AND ORGANIZATION
G. Debus and H.-W. Schroiff (Editors)
© Elsevier Science Publishers B.V. (North-Holland), 1986

THE EFFECT OF A VIDEO-TAPED SAFETY PROGRAM ON THE ATTITUDE TOWARD
SAFETY: A FIELD EXPERIMENT

Jef SYROIT

Tilburg University, Department of Psychology P700,
P.O.B. 90153
5000 LE Tilburg, The Netherlands

This study has been carried out in the main distribution center of
a supermarket chain in order to evaluate the effect of a film about
safety on the attitude toward safe behavior, using a Solomon-Four-
Group design and the attitudes being measured by means of Thurstone
scales. Analysis of variance on the posttest measures revealed a
significant main effect for the Film factor, and a significant
Testing x Film interaction effect. Subjects who attended the film
showed more positive attitudes toward safety than those who did
not. The interaction effect could be indicative for a pretest sensitization effect. Analyses of differences between pretest and
posttest attitude scores revealed that subjects who attended the
program changed toward a more favorable position, while the other's
attitudes did not change. An analysis of the film showed that the
persuasive characteristics of the message fitted well to the
characteristics of the audience.

1. INTRODUCTION

This study reports changes in employees' attitudes toward safety at work
as affected by attending a video-taped film about safety. Employees of a
Belgian supermarket chain were made sensitive to safety problems by means
of a film that had been recorded in different units of the firm. Before
distributing the safety program throughout the company questions had been
raised about the possible impact of that program on workers' safe behavior
and their attitude toward safety. Since the safety records of the firm
were neither reliable nor valid - only those accidents were recorded for which
medical assistance was asked - and given the urge with which the program
had to be distributed, only attitudinal effects were examined.

On the basis of persuasion literature (McGuire,1969) it was expected that
a message should have the following characteristics in order to be effective.
A message containing only arguments pro safety is preferable to a two-
sided message, assuming that the audience is not highly intelligent, and
that it already has a positive attitude toward the subject (Hovland,1957).
Since most of the employees were directly or indirectly involved in a big
accident (a gas explosion), and all of them occupy low level positions,
performing unskilled jobs and having low educational levels, both assumptions were met.
The strongest arguments should be presented at the end of the message. Although the literature about persuasion is far from conclusive about the
conditions under which recency and primacy effects occur, it seems that

recency effects do occur more frequently than primacy effects (Zimbardo &
Ebbeson,1969).
The message should make an appeal to fear. Janis (1970) has shown that there
exists a curvilinear relationship between amount of fear evoked and attitudinal change. Low and high fear appeal have less effect on attitudes than
a moderate level of fear appeal.
Finally, the program should be produced and sponsored by the Personnel
Research Unit of the company because of its high status position in the
firm and because it is considered by the employees as occupying an independent, neutral position between the employer and the employees.

The attitudinal change has been studied in a field experiment, using a
Solomon-Four-Group design (Campbell & Stanley, 1963). Attitudes were measured by means of two parallel Thurstone scales (Edwards, 1957). The time
interval between the pretest and the presentation of the program was two
weeks, and between the presentation of the program and the posttest ten
days.
This field experimental design has advantages as well as disadvantages.
Most problematic in this design is the control of variables that might influence the attitude during the time interval between the pretest and the
posttest measurement of the attitude. The major advantage of this design
lies in its high external validity as compared to the external validity
of laboratory experiments.

2. METHOD

2.1. Subjects

Subjects were 88 male employees working in the loading and discharging
berth of the central warehouse of the company. All employees voluntarily
participated in the experiment, which was introduced to them   by the
Personnel Research Unit as an investigation about the perception of work
and of the work environment.

2.2. Design

The subjects were assigned to one of the four conditions of the Solomon-
Four-Group design. The organization of the work in this unit did not allow
for a random assignment of subjects to conditions. Each condition contained
employees from one shift only.

Half of the subjects were pretested, and the other half did not receive
the pretest measurement. From both groups approximately one half attended
the program (24 and 23, respectively); the others (20 and 21, respectively)
did not see the film. All subjects received a posttest measure of their
attitude toward safety.

2.3. The message

The message consisted of a video-taped film showing pictures of accidents
on the job and on the way from home to work, and consequences of accidents
such as: the capsizing of a fork-lift truck, a car accident, somebody stepping in a nail, a surgical intervention, etc... The film lasted 20 minutes.
The video recording was judged on a number of characteristics derived from
McGuire's review on persuasion. Twenty students were asked to indicate on
11-point scales whether the given characteristics were present or absent

in the message. The scales ranged from -5 (not characteristic at all) to +5 (very characteristic). Table 1 contains the mean scores and standard deviations for each item. The mean scores were tested against the zero point of the scale by means of z-tests. These z-values are given in the last column of Table 1. Inspection of the means and of their corresponding z-values reveals that the message is one-sided pro safety; that the strongest arguments do not appear in the beginning but rather at the end of the film, and that the film is fear appealing.

Table 1: Characteristics of the message

item	mean	s.d.	z
- use of rational arguments	-3.70	.98	-16.84
- strong arguments first	-3.35	2.13	- 6.84
- makes appeal to feelings	+3.20	2.07	+ 6.75
- containing irrelevant elements	+2.70	2.15	+ 5.46
- only arguments contra safety	-2.70	2.20	- 5.34
- fear appealing	+2.35	2.13	+ 4.80
- only arguments pro safety	+1.50	2.69	+ 2.43
- conclusions to be drawn by audience	+1.45	3.32	+ 1.91
- makers of the film are competent	-1.15	2.76	- 1.82
- strong arguments at the end	+1.20	3.02	+ 1.73
- dynamical	+1.05	2.54	+ 1.70
- containing arguments pro and contra	-1.15	3.10	- 1.62
- ambiguous	+0.90	2.90	+ 1.35
- clear presentation	-0.95	3.27	- 1.27
- conclusions given to audience	-0.50	3.28	- .66

2.4. Attitude measurement

The attitude toward safety was measured by means of two parallel scales. Fifty items were judged by 50 judges on 11-point scales ranging from (1) 'extremely favorable' to (11) 'extremely unfavorable'. Twenty-three items met the necessary criteria: small Q-values, and scale values ranging from 1 to 11. Two parallel scales were constructed. Subjects' attitude scores consisted of the medians of the scale values of the items to which they agreed. Examples of items are:
- Safety is somebody else's business; not mine.
- All the time, all possible risks should be taken into account.
- If one is careful, it isn't dangerous at all to transport people with a fork-lift truck.

3. RESULTS

Means and standard deviations of the pretest and the posttest measures of the attitude toward safety are given in Table 2. The posttest scores were analyzed by means of an analysis of variance according to a 2 X 2 design. Table 3 contains a summary of the analysis of variance results.

The analysis of variance shows a significant main effect for the Film factor. Subjects attending the safety program show a significantly more

Table 2: Means and standard deviations of pretest and posttest attitude
         scores

condition		n	pretest mean	sd	posttest mean	sd
pretest	film	24	8.61	.75	9.19	.37
pretest	no film	20	8.55	.57	8.46	.42
no pretest	film	23			9.29	.35
no pretest	no film	21			8.03	.54

favorable attitude toward safety than subjects who did not attend the film.
However, we also found a significant test X film interaction, which is
mainly due to the significant difference between the means of the two conditions who did not attend the safety program. Pretested subjects show a
more favorable attitude toward safety than subjects who did not receive a
pretest. The opposite result holds for the two conditions who attended the
videofilm.

Table 3: Summary of ANOVA on the posttest scores

Source	Df	MS	F	p
pretest (A)	1	.56	3.01	.09
film (B)	1	21.51	115.92	.001
A X B	1	1.52	8.20	.005
error	84	.19		

In order to test changes in the attitude toward safety, differences between
the pretest and posttest measures of the attitude were tested by means of
t-tests for correlated means. These tests reveal that the difference between the pretest and posttest means is significant in the Film condition
($t = 3.08$, df = 23, $p < .01$), and that this difference is not significant
in the No Film condition ($t = -.64$, df = 19). Thus, attendance to the film
resulted in a change toward a more favorable attitude from pretest to posttest. The slight change toward a less favorable attitude among subjects who
did not see the film is not significant.

4. DISCUSSION

The difference between the attitudes of employees who attended the film and
of those who did not attend the film is remarkable. Employees who have seen
the film show a significantly more favorable attitude toward safety than
employees who have not seen the program. Furthermore, the data support the
conclusion that attending the film resulted in a change toward a more

favorable attitude toward safety at work. The difference between the pre-test and the posttest measures of the attitude toward safety were only significant for those employees who attended the film.

The significant pretest X film interaction might be indicative for a pretest sensitization effect. However, according to Lana (1969) pretest sensitization does not frequently occur when unidirectional communication serves as the treatment, as in this case (see Table 1).

The strong effect of the film on the attitudes of the employees must be, at least partially, attributed to the correspondence between the characteristics of the message and of the sender on the one hand, and of the audience, on the other. It is plausible to assume that the attitude of the sender - the Personnel Research Unit - toward safety at work is (very) positive. The initial attitude toward safety of the subjects is also positive, as can be derived from the pretest scores (overall mean = 8.40). The characteristics of the message fit well to those of the audience. The film does not contain rational arguments; it is a one-sided message in favor of safety; it is fear-evoking, and the strongest arguments are given at the end of the film and not in the beginning.

Summarizing, it can be stated that the use of a filmed program on safety is an effective means toward changing employees' attitudes about safety. One may wonder to what extent employees will behave more safely after attending a video-taped safety program. And even if they behave more safely the question remains to what extent these behavioral changes can be explained by the attitudinal changes. This study does not allow for making speculations about the complex relationship between attitude and behavior (see e.g. Jaspars, 1981).

ACKNOWLEDGEMENTS

I should like to thank Mr. D. Lories and Drs. W. De Hertog for their practical assistance during the execution of this study.

REFERENCES

Campbell, D.T., & Stanley, J.C. (1963). Experimental and quasi-experimental designs for research. Chicago: Rand McNally.

Edwards, A.L. (1957). Techniques of attitude scale construction. New York: Appleton-Century-Croft.

Hovland, C.I. (Ed.)(1957). The order of presentation in persuasion. New Haven: Yale University Press.

Janis, I.L. (1967). Effects of fear arousal on attitude change: Recent developments in theory and experimental research. In L. Berkowitz (Ed.), Advances in experimental social psychology (Vol. 3, pp. 166-224). New York: Academic Press.

Jaspars, J.M.F. (1981). Attitudes en attitudeverandering [Attitudes and attitude change]. In J.M.F. Jaspars & R. van der Vlist (Eds.), Sociale psychologie in Nederland: Vol. 1. Het individu (pp. 193-234). Deventer: Van Loghum Slaterus.

Lana, R.E. (1969). Pretest sensitization. In R. Rosenthal & R.L. Rosnow (Eds.), Artifact in behavioral research (pp. 119-141). New York: Academic Press.

McGuire, W.J. (1954). The nature of attitudes and attitude change. In G. Lindzey & E. Aronson (Eds.), The handbook of social psychology (Vol. 3, pp. 136-314). Reading, Mass.: Addison-Wesley.

Zimbardo, P.G., & Ebbeson, E.B. (Eds.)(1969). Influencing attitudes and changing behavior. Reading, Mass.: Addison-Wesley.

THE PSYCHOLOGY OF WORK AND ORGANIZATION
G. Debus and H.-W. Schroiff (Editors)
© Elsevier Science Publishers B.V. (North-Holland), 1986

VISUAL INFORMATION PICK-UP
IN A SIMULATED DRIVING SITUATION

Hans-Willi SCHROIFF & Werner MÖHLER
Department of Psychology/Department of Traffic Engineering

Rheinisch-Westfälische Technische Hochschule Aachen
Jägerstr. zwischen 17 und 19
D-51 Aachen, Federal Republic of Germany

Within the general aim of identifying the cues by
which speed-regulation actions are initiated we
assessed the eye movements and speed-regulation
actions of 50 subjects while viewing series of
consecutive road scenes in the laboratory. We
observed an increased eye-movement activity with
scenes showing built-up areas that is not correlated with speed changes. However, speed changes
are highly correlated with "road redundancy
changes" as obtained by a quantitative image
analysis. Looking at aggregated group data we
could not identify road-scene elements that
clearly mediate speed regulation. It is hypothe-
sized that the perceptual-motor feedback loop of
speed regulation is influenced by more general
characteristics of a road scene.

1. INTRODUCTION

Compared with a number of other activities car-driving still bears a
considerable risk. West-German official reports state that about 47% of
all accidents outside built-up areas with personal injuries are caused
by an inadequate regulation of driving-speed. This percentage is even
increased in areas with low or medium traffic density.
In spite of road safety campaigns, improved road conditions (e.g.
straightening of curves) and an increased number of warning signs
drivers still approach danger zones with a high driving speed (see e.g.
figure 2). Obviously the problem consists in influencing the drivers'
decision in a more unobtrusive way. A key to the solution of this
problem may lie in the observation that characteristic speed changes are
registered at specific points of a driving route (see Kayser, Möhler &
Otten, 1985). We have been concerned with the question which characteristics of a road scene cause the driver to slow down at these points. Is
it possible to identify these cues by means of an analysis of visual
information pick-up? Are speed changes associated with different strategies of visual information pick-up? In our studies we are trying to
answer these questions tentatively by analyzing empirical evidence from
laboratory and field data.

2. THEORETICAL BACKGROUND

Senders (1983) has attacked the problem from an information-theoretical perspective. He argued that the choice of driving speed can be

regarded a function of "route uncertainty". Uncertainty can be influenced by a number of variables like wiggliness of the road, the overall density of significant objects or the probability that some new object will enter the road. The joint influence of all these factors can be expressed in an uncertainty estimate per unit length of road. If we assume that each road has a certain information rate built into it it follows that the higher the driving speed the more bits per time unit will have to be processed -- resulting in a lower redundancy per unit of time. Senders (1983) argues that the selection of driving-speed depends on a "psychological speed-limit" -- i.e. the point where the joint task demands of visual information processing and programming motor actions match the information processing capability of the driver. The driver adapts her/his driving-speed to the "psychological speed limit" -- otherwise she/he has to bear risk.

Increased uncertainty may lead to general changes in the strategy of visual-information pick-up and/or to a change of driving-speed. Within an information-theoretical framework it seems reasonable to assess objective redundancy changes in consecutive road scenes (as an independent variable) and to evaluate the effects of route redundancy on driving speed and eye-fixation behaviour as dependent variables.

Within general redundancy changes it is plausible that the driver reacts to specific (visual) cues in the road scene ("discriminative stimuli", see Fuller, 1984). It seems necessary not only to identify the cues, but also the probability of an adequate reaction to these stimuli: A discriminative stimulus (school bus at bus stop) can readily be identified without taking the adequate action (slowing down) to avoid negative consequences (injuring a child).

If one wants to map speed changes onto redundancy changes and to identify discriminative stimuli two methodological problems have to be solved:

A quantitative image analysis of consecutive road scenes should result in a description of redundancy changes of a driving route.

The reliable assessment of visual information pick-up requires a registration device maintaining high-precision measurement in the driving situation. Though enormous improvements have been made in the last decade most commercially available devices do not seem to meet even minimal precision standards. The NAC registration system e.g. already shows a spatial error of up to 4 degrees of visual angle in laboratory settings. In our laboratory and field studies we have employed a more precise registration device ("Demel DEBIC 80-84") -- a corneal reflection back-lit pupil system with an average spatial error of +/- .7 degrees of visual angle. Although originally designed for laboratory use the system can be employed in field studies in the driving vehicle (see Schroiff, 1983; Möhler, in preparation).

3. METHOD

3.1. Selection of driving routes

A number of village entrances were selected as driving routes which could be characterized by maximal changes in road scene contents. Each route was photographed on slides with a distance between the pictures of 50 m (route series). A road scene is one picture out of a route series. Each road scene consists of constellations of road elements (e.g. houses, fences, crash barriers etc.; for an example see figure 3).

3.2. Quantitative image analysis

Consecutive road scenes were analyzed by determining the relative share of road elements in defined image segments. Overall image changes could be computed based on estimates of the relative area density of the single road elements. The following parameters were computed (for a detailed description see Kayser, Möhler & Otten, 1984):

- "relative road scene redundancy"

Relative road scene redundancy was computed by matching corresponding area segments of successive road scenes. The lower the overall change in the image segments the higher the resulting redundancy value. The following figure shows an example for route No.12:

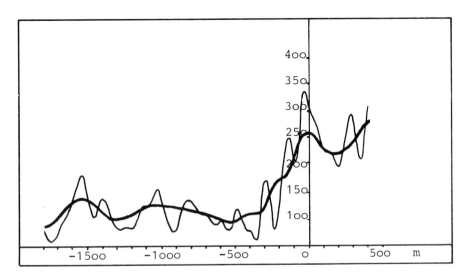

FIG. 1   Changes in road scene redundancy for route No. 12 (X-axis: distance from village entrance; Y-axis: redundancy value). Smoothed values are indicated by a thick line.

- "relative road scene coherence"

An index of road scene coherence was based on the analysis of the area segments covered by the various road elements thus describing the changes in the variety of elements in consecutive road scenes.

3.3. Speed profiles

Speed profiles were assessed by following cars at a constant distance with a car equipped with a speed-measuring device. The resulting continous speed profiles were cross-validated by radar speed-checks at various points of the route.

3.4. Eye-movement parameters

In the eye-movement laboratory of the Institute of Psychology the eye-movements of 50 student subjects (all experienced drivers) were registrated during the presentation of the series of successive route scenes. X-Y-coordinates of the point of regard were analyzed by data reduction programs based on algorithms developed by Kliegl (1982). In addition to the standard summary statistics the following eye-movement parameters were derived from the raw data for each route scene:

– "attentional centres of gravity"
Attentional centres of gravity were defined as those areas of a road
scene with a relative increase in the product of fixation duration and
fixation frequency.
   – "moment of inertia of the scan path"
This parameter corresponds to the physical moment of inertia. Smaller
values indicate a higher variability of looking behaviour for each road
scene .
   – "deviations of scan path from vanishing point"
Pilot studies indicated that subjects preferred to fixate the point of
intersection of the left and right roadside ("vanishing point").
For the computing algorithms of the eye-movement parameters we refer to
Kayser, Möhler & Otten (1985).

3.5. Subjective ratings
Subjects had to rate consecutive road scenes on a number of dimensions
like "clearness", "degree of built-up area" etc. Although our subjects
were not in a real driving situation and the presentation rate of
successive road scenes remained constant they were required to indicate
speed regulation actions by stepping on an "accelerator" and a "brake
pedal" while viewing road scenes.

4. RESULTS

Results will be reported for route No. 12 only. The data collected on
other routes yielded comparative results.

4.1. Speed profile
Figure 2 shows the speed profile for route No.12:

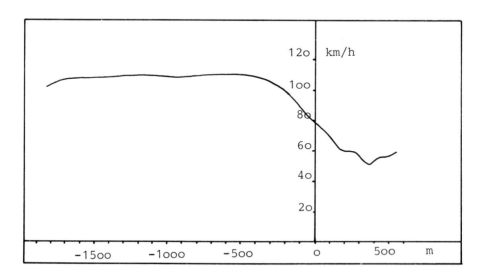

FIG. 2 Average speed profile of 48 drivers for route No. 12 (X-axis =
        distance from village entrance; Y-axis = speed in Km/h).

4.2 Eye movement parameters

In the following figures eye-movement parameters are plotted continously for route No. 12. Figure 3 gives an impression of the distribution of visual attention for the total group of subjects for a road scene inside and outside a built-up area. Figure 4 shows the average "moment of inertia" (see next page). There is a tendency towards lower values for road scenes inside the village thus indicating larger interfixation distances. Figure 5 shows the average "deviation from vanishing point": here we observe only minor changes with road scenes inside the village (see next page).

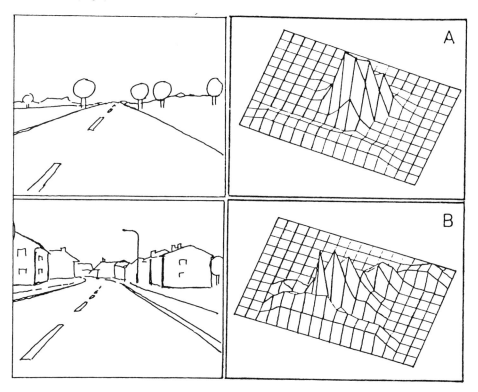

FIG. 3 "Attentional centers of gravity" for different road scenes (Fig. 5A: outside built-up area; Fig 5B: inside built-up area).

4.3 Subjective ratings

Due to the space limits we have to refer to Kayser, Möhler & Otten (1985) for details concerning this point. In general one may conclude that the results of the individual ratings on the proportion of road scene elements correlate significantly with the results of the quantitative image analysis. We also observed an almost linear relationship between the "braking"-reactions in the laboratory and the values of the actual speed profile (see figure 6). The "negative percentage"-parameter was chosen to facilitate the comparison with the speed profile. The resemblance between the two curves is striking. This indicates that subjects in the laboratory situation are able to assign a realistic "speed"-value to an individual road scene.

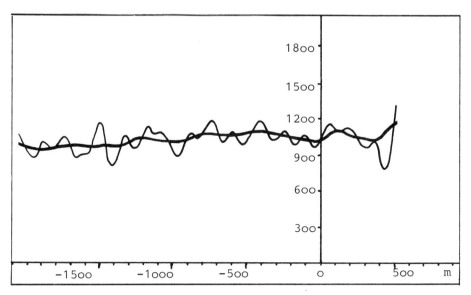

<u>FIG. 4</u> Average "deviation of fixation point from vanishing point"
(X-axis: distance from village entrance; Y-axis: deviation-
value). Smoothed values are indicated by thick line.

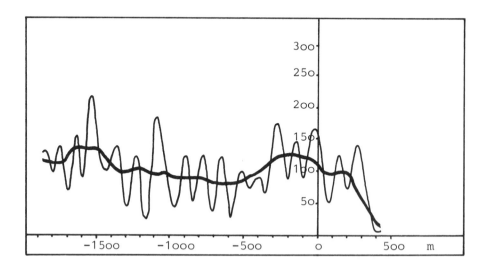

<u>FIG. 5</u>   Average "Moment of inertia of scanpath" for route No. 12
(X-axis: distance from village entrance; Y-axis: inertia-
value). Smoothed values are indicated by the thick line.

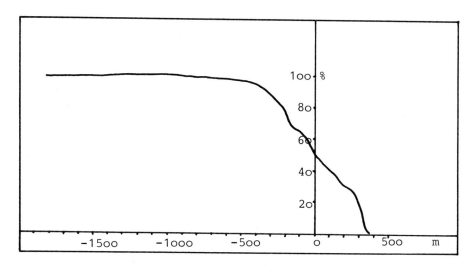

FIG. 6 Negative percentage of "braking"-reactions in the laboratory
(X-axis: distance from village entrance; Y-axis: "braking"-
reactions).

5. DISCUSSION

The discussion of results will have to be restricted to route No. 12.
For details concerning other routes we again have to refer to Kayser,
Möhler & Otten (1985).
A first discussion point concerns the question whether the redundancy of
a driving route can be evaluated by means of a quantitative image analysis. The procedure proposed by Kayser, Möhler & Otten (1985) offers a
tedious but effective way to describe a driving route with respect to
the degree of continous image changes. We have repeatedly observed a
substantial relationship between the redundancy values obtained by means
of this method and the values of the speed profile. According to our
data this more global parameter accounts for a major part of driving-
speed variance. We believe that this finding could represent somewhat of
a starting point for future studies.
On the other hand we did not find any interpretable relationships
between driving speed and more global parameters of eye-movement
activity. What we can conclude from the results of our laboratory study
is that (a) eye-movement activity is increased in built-up areas and
that (b) the "vanishing point" is the area with the highest fixation
probability -- probably because of its relatively high information
density.
Apart from this more global analysis we have tried to identify specific
elements in the "critical region" of the route where speed changes are
observed. Our results are negative so far: looking at aggregated group
data only did not result in the identification of areas with a general
"attentional value" (e.g. a traffic sign). Further investigations should
rather be based on the evaluation of single-case studies.
For a general evaluation of our results it must also be taken into
account that laboratory data were collected and despite of the high

correlations between actual speed and ratings the external validity of the results should be cross-checked by the results of a field study.

In summary we may conclude that speed changes can best be predicted by more global redundancy changes in consecutive road scenes as assessed by quantitative image analysis. However, at the moment we do not know enough about the specific cues and mechanisms that mediate speed-regulating actions. To gain information here it seems necessary to observe the perceptual-motor feedback loop of car-driving directly by registrating eye-movements and speed-regulating actions in the real driving situation (see Möhler, in preparation). This should also clarify the role of parafoveal and peripheral visual perception about which we can only speculate in the present investigation (see also Kayser, Möhler & Otten, 1985).

REFERENCES

(1) Fuller, R. (1984) A conceptualization of driving behaviour as threat avoidance. Ergonomics, 27, 1139–1155.
(2) Kayser, H.-J., Möhler, W. & Otten, N. (1984) Quantitative Erfassung des Straßenraumes (unter Berücksichtigung bebauter Stadtrandge-biete). Schlußbericht zum Forschungsauftrag FA 02.85 G 82 E. Insti-tut für Straßenwesen, Erd- und Tunnelbau der Rheinisch-Westfälischen Technischen Hochschule Aachen.
(3) Kliegl, R. (1981) Automated and interactive analysis of eye fixation data in reading. Behavior Research Methods and Instrumentation, 13, 115–120.
(4) Möhler, W. (in preparation) Visuelle Analyse des Fahrraumbildes und Geschwindigkeitsregulation. Dissertation, Fakultät für Bauwesen, Rheinisch-Westfälische Technische Hochschule Aachen.
(5) Schroiff, H.W. (1983) Experimentelle Untersuchungen zur Reliabilität und Validität von Blickbewegungsdaten. Dissertation, Philosophische Fakultät, Rheinisch-Westfälische Technische Hochschule Aachen.
(6) Senders, J. W. (1983) Visual scanning processes. Dissertation, Department of Psychology, Katholieke Hogeschool Tilburg, The Nether-lands.

PART III

PROFESSIONAL PROBLEMS

THE PSYCHOLOGY OF WORK AND ORGANIZATION
G. Debus and H.-W. Schroiff (Editors)
© *Elsevier Science Publishers B.V. (North-Holland), 1986*

TOWARDS SUCCESSFUL PSYCHOLOGICAL ASSOCIATIONS

Th. JONKERGOUW

c/o Nederlands Instituut van Psychologen/EFPPA
Postbox 5362
NL-1007 AJ Amsterdam, The Netherlands

This article raises the question of how to organise associations of psychologists in such a way that they will be successful in the nineties. Form the point of view of a sociologist of work and organisation by discipline and experience the importance of the use of different types of power to obtain compliance of the association's membership is stressed (§1). The process of organisationbuilding is treated in §2. Attention is paid to the functions that associations have to fulfill for their members in order to be and remain influential (§3). The association's policy is influenced itself by organisational dynamics, consequence of the segmentation process in society and profession and the accompanying shift in power relations (§4). The best way to handle a number of professional issues (§5) is by choosing for a strategic policy (§6). The article is concluded (§7) with a list of 20 commandments to ensure that one's association will be successful in the next decade.

1.   INTRODUCTION

Most people spend most of their lives in organisations. They are born in the micro organisation of a small family and some hours later by their parents are made members of a certain state. Many of them are some days later enriched with another membership, e.g. that of a hugh world wide organisation, the Vatican based Roman Catholic Church. At the age of about four years they start a long organisational career, spending many years (sometimes 20) in school systems of all kinds, varying form the Kindergarten to the university, with primary and secondary schools in between. Usually males are enlisted into the army. All these and several other organisational memberships are thrust upon people. There is in fact not much free choice, and where such free choice exists, it has to be exercised within the boundaries of the social system just mentioned. For instance: one can choose to be a boy scout, a member of a sporting club or a students association; one can work in a factory to earn one's living. Once one starts working, serious life begins. On the basis of economic necessity one begins to choose the organisations to which one wants to belong and to be an active participant in. One chooses an organisation in which to work in order to earn money for better living standards. One becomes a member of a political party and of a trade union, and can obtain active roles in them, working as a voluntary or honorary official. If one makes grave mistakes, one is sent to prison. One starts a family oneself and initiates a new organisational circle.

All organisations impose pressure or strain on its participants, because all organisations demand compliance of their members as Amitai Etzioni (1975) pointed out in his "Comparative analysis of complex organisations". He distinguishes between coercive, utilitarian and normative organisations. And many organisations do have a dual compliance structure; they develop compliance structures in which two patterns occur with the same or similar frequency. Professional associations, especially those that fulfill several trade union functions, can be arranged somewhere on the normative-utilitarian continuum, according to the relative degree of renumerative compared with normative (pure of social) compliance. The middle section of the continuum constitutes of course a balanced (dual) type.

The main difference between dual and other types of compliance in professional associations (and unions) is that in dual structures increased deviation from organisational norms and directives is followed by activation of a different Type of power, while in other types it tends to activate more power of the same type. On the other hand, in the dual normative (social) utilitarian type, two powers are applied, usually not at the same time, but alternatively, depending on the specific kind or degree of behaviour. Most people belong to many organisations at the same time, occupying different positions in them, being exposed to different patterns of compliance, having a commitment to them and attempting to obtain benefit from them in exchange for their work, fee or any other resource that they spend on them.

2.   FROM PROFESSION TO PROFESSIONAL ASSOCIATIONS

Professional associations arose – mostly on a local scale – and are still founded, for several reasons like the need of company or of a society for studying certain problems, especially the possibility for exchanging information about new developments in the professional field. Membership of a professional association, which is open only to those who are qualified to practise the profession, is an expression of the recognition of personal competence (Carr-Saunders & Wilson, 1964). This is especially important in a market that is characterized by intrasparency, which makes it impossible for the demanders of certain services to judge the competence of individual professional practitionners. In such a situation a guarantee of constant quality is being offered by membership of a professional society (Lulofs, 1981).

Although started on a local scale, professional associations are transformed into a national organisation when there is an external motive, usually the opinion that separate partial markets on a local level can no longer be protected. The national society is pre-eminently the instrument to reach marketcontrol. The first step of such a nation-wide association will be a striving for the recognition of the rights of the organised professional group to the profession's practice. The founding of a national society is often an important step in obtaining a public and legal recognition of the exclusive position of the professional group regarding the activities it considers as being within its domain. If it succeeds in securing this position of exclusiveness, it will try to derive rights and privileges. An important prerequisite for the realisation of this nation-wide type of promotion of its interests is the existence of a clearly defined and unanimously recognized object, that can be controlled by the members of the organised profession in a more or less exclusive manner (Mok, 1973). Generally speaking, a profession has to meet three conditions to be able to control the market:

1. Knowledge: the profession can only be practised after a long formal training;
2. Power: having the disposal of means and sources, of power to obtain the goals that are aimed at with the practice of the profession;
3. Rendering of services: at the level of professional activities, the needs of the consumers have to be taken into account in the very first place.

The concept of profession has both an analytical meaning and a symbolic value. The latter, which is used by professionals themselves, is rather ideological by nature in that it legitimizes the privileges of the profession in society. The analytical meaning of the concept "profession" refers to the so-called characteristics-approach; professions are considered as occupations that share a number of basic features which distinguish them from other, consequently non-professional occupations (Van der Krogt, 1981). Two examples illustrate this approach.

a. Klinkert (1978) distinguishes in his study of the medical profession between empirical and theoretical features. Empirical characteristics are: a long training, legal discipline, medical ethics, the role medical specialists play in the determining of government policy in the health care field and at medical examinations in enterprises, army, insurance companies. This last point is of course an expression of the autonomy of physicians in defining health and illness. As theoretical characteristics he considers:
   - institutionalisation: the profession's activities have been crystallized completely and they show a certain degree of permanency. All the parties involved share a considerable degree of consensus and a clear view regarding these activities.
   - legitimation: the activities of the profession are supported by a clear amount of knowledge and a clear system of values, inside the profession as well as outside.
   - a legally supported autonomy, regarding the domination of the internal social control, the control of the profession's recruitment, the power to define by itself the nature and the extent of that part of reality to which the professional activities are oriented (i.c. health and illness).

b. The second example (Ritzler, 1972, cited by Pool, 1979), mentions as the predominant features:

   - general and systematic knowledge, acquired through a relatively long period of education and training and through informal contacts with colleagues;
   - authority over clients: the professional defines the client's needs and judges the quality of the service he himself rendered. The client's behaviour knows very few alternatives;
   - the ideal of servitude: the profession is in the interest of society;
   - self regulation, including internal grievance

procedures and ethical discipline.
- a legal basis.

Speaking about the building of a profession, it might be useful to distinguish between two types of institutionalisation (Mok, 1973):

a. domain institutionalisation: this is the degree to which the environment permits a profession to consider certain activities as its domain and to develop within that domain a fixed pattern of activities and a consensus about values.
b. social institutionalisation: this is the degree to which the environment permits a profession to develop an internal pattern of interactions with clear boundaries with respect to outsiders and to use this pattern as a means for the normative integration of professional colleagues.

As far as psychology is concerned there are considerable differences between European professional associations with respect to trade union functions, legislation, ethical code, criteria for full membership, membership fees etc. (Kjolstad, 1983).

3. FUNCTIONS OF PROFESSIONAL ASSOCIATIONS

A professional association is formed by incumbents of occupation positions with similar exchange problems, who unite on a voluntary basis to realise goals and interests that are connected with their professional position. According to Daheim (1969), the main goal of association is to facilitate for the individual member a "profitable" exchange ratio between performance and rewards. The members can direct their joint efforts to two subgoals:

1. assisting each member to acquire and improve the cognitive and normative orientation which allows him to perform the expected role, i.e. procuring and transmitting to each member the required technical knowledge and, to a certain degree at least, articulating the more general norms of role performance.
2. acting collectively toward the exchange partners and other relevant segments of the social environment to maximize the rewards, e.g. money and prestige, for the individual member. Exchange partners are work organisations, associations of work organisations, single clients, organised clients, and the political organisation of society which provides a legal framework for the exchange relationship; all of them make up the social environment of the occupational or professional association.

Daheim speaks of occupational associations in a general category which can be classified on a continuum according to the goal or the function they have for their members. On the one hand there are organisations whose predominant goal is the improvement of their member's occupational qualification, Millerson's study association (1964). On the other hand there are organisations which predominantly function to augment the material rewards for their member's occupational role performance, Caplow's expansive union (1954). In between are occupational associations like the professional association. In every association both subgoals are pursued, but the emphasis is always on one of them, sometimes leading to a neglect of the other. On the level of the association the same fundamental conflict of interests appears which can be observed on the level of the individual incumbent of an occupational position. If the exchange partner gets the impression that the incumbents of a certain occupational position do not perform as expected, e.g. because their qualifications do not keep up with the change of their tasks, the incumbents collectively loose prestige with the exchange partner. The immaterial rewards decrease as the criticism of the exchange party becomes publicly known. If the lack of efficient performance is regarded by the exchange party as very grave, the power equilibrium is disturbed: the other side refuses to grant the rewards as before or to increase the rewards as usual, and it depends mainly on the possibility of replacing the incumbents of the occupational position and their willingness to put effective pressure on the exchange partner, at what point the new equilibrium in the exchange relationship will develop. The loss of power manifested in reduced success of the occupational association, has secondary consequences, as some of its members are no longer willing to participate in the organisational activities. This, in turn, further weakens the power in the exchange relationship on the collective level.

According to Millerson (1964), the main fuctions of the professional association for its members are:

- study: broadening of knowledge of a certain field;
- qualification taking care of basic and continued training;
- control: maintaining norms of behaviour by means of an (ethical) code of conduct;
- protection: promotion of material and legal status interests.

Parry and Parry (1976) summarize all these functions to a common denominator by saying that collectivisation of promotion of interests in a broad sense, e.g. in the form of a professional association, reduces uncertainty at the individual level. A professional association will consequently last or grow to the degree it succeeds in controling the uncertainty of individual occupational incumbents.

Of course the meaning of a professional association for occupational incumbents and the aims that are pursued will vary with the phase of development of the organisation. Later in this article I will pay attention to some fundamental questions professional associations have to cope with.

4.   ORGANISATIONAL DYNAMICS

Occupational and professional associations can be more successful as they meet more two processes of control: (1) control of uncertainty of the individual and (2) control of the external market (through knowledge, power, authority, rendered services). Both processes are very narrowly connected with one another. The effectiveness of these processes is mainly dependent on a. the characteristics of the profession as discussed above, and b. the segmentation of the profession.

Once there is a nation-wide association of professionals, existing problems can be dealt with, but new problems arise. One of them is the so called segmentation. According to Bucher and Strauss (1961) segments are groupings of professionals who share an organised identity. These segments change permanently consequent on external changes. Bucher and Strauss compare them in a way with social movements. Segments within an occupational or professional group are different from one another in several respects: specific activity, methodology and techniques, clients, interests (i.e. the exchange value and the value of its use).

Segmentation can be caused by a great many factors such as specialisations leading to other clients, other technology, etc.; different markets, differences in professional practice; lack of consensus about important features of the profession (e.g. the stucture of salaries). Segmentation is a continuing or renewed way of collectivisation. In fact there are again some individual occupational incumbents who are of the opinion that their specific interests are not promoted sufficiently by the existing association. These individuals will seek support to create a new collective actor. There are several possibilities for this actor to manifest himself, be it in an informal or a formal way. One possibility is playing a role as an action group or as a suborganisation within the existing occupational association. Another possibility, which will be chosen in case of very serious conflicts of interests, is that segmentation leads to withdrawal or a split off and the founding of an alternative association. Which way will be chosen depends mainly on the circumstances (Van der Krogt, 1981).

Segmentation is a continuous sociological process, which contributes largely to the dynamics of the organisation. Sometimes it is not very radical and might be welcomed by all parties involved for reasons of efficiency. But when segmentation is caused by profound differences in view on fundamental questions, it involves a fierce struggle for power. It depends on the power (internal as well as external) of the segments involved, how the struggle will end.

What I intend to make clear in this part of this article is the following: The process fo collectivisation is aimed at acquiring power and a powerful position for the collectivum in order that the power position of the individual members can be enlarged and improved. By way of his association, the individual becomes part of a collectivum that has a position of power in a network of relationships with other organisations, and that tries to influence the making and the execution of decisions in that network. Through collectivisation the individuals can operate on a higher level of steering and management. But an occupational or professional association is not one happy family. It is in fact a complexity of (horizontal) segments. From this point of view the profession is the consequence of conflicts of interests and struggle between the segments (Mok, 1973). The association represents mainly the dominant segments within a profession. But the other segments will, we might expect, not be sleeping; at least they had better not. What they should do is to use their own power resources and develop new products, find new markets and try to change the balance of power within the national association.

5.   PROFESSIONAL ISSUES

In their "Professional's Guide to the American Psychological Association", Kilburg and Pallak (in Sales, 1983), write: "In a sense, the
major issues confronting professional psychology in the 1980s are identical to those faced by the earliest professionals". The questions they
are pondering include:

1. Who are we as a profession?
2. How do we compete successfully in the marketplace?
3. How do we organise so as to perform our functions
   effectively?

"All roads lead from an individual's or an organisation's identity. The
identity of professional psychology represents the fusion of the collec-
tivity of applied psychologists and is best seen through the concerted
action of their major institution", the professional association.

The first question refers to the consensus that is needed about what
constitutes an educational program in psychology. Every association must
have a method to clearly determine which training programs are truly
psychological.

The second major issue confronting organised psychology focuses on
further elaborating its ability to function in a free and open market
place. Important is of course the establishment of the status of our
discipline before the law, via licensing. But licensure only gets our
professional foot in the door. Therefore it is necessary to modify many
laws in order for psychologists to be able to practice their profession
fully in a given country. A related set of issues concerns the structure
of several major markets for psychological services, especially health
and education. We think of course of the monopolous position of the
physicians and the reimbursement of psychologists.

The third issue of Kilburg and Pallak concerns how the professional
association is to be organised to advocate, educate and regulate discipline. Central to the concerns of the association should be questions
like: (1) Who speaks on behalf of Dutch, French etc. psychology?; (2)
How shall resources be allocated within the organisation to meet the
needs of the organised groups of members?; (3) How can the most effective and efficient type of organisation be retained?

A fourth major issue for European professional psychology must be how to
create new fields of employment for psychologists and how to reduce the
influx of students into the psychological departments of universities.

There is thus a magnitude of work to be done to enhance a successful
existence in the 90s.

6.   TOWARDS A STRATEGIC POLICY

In Europe in almost every country there exists an association of professional psychologists. They differ of course in many respects for
reasons of history, tradition, culture, economic and sociological conditions, etc. But all will have sooner or later to face questions such as
those mentioned before. This paragraph will therefore give a general

approach to focus and tackle the issues from the point of view of the
association.

Because of changes in society and the continuous segmentation in the
association we must commit ourselves to a so-called developmental model
in which an organisation as a whole changes as the result of a change
between its component elements. The nuclear process in this model is the
formation of the organisational regime. This is formed as a consequence
of the way different internal and external parties are behaving to one
another in the defining of three critical moments: strategy, structuring, manning (Jonkergouw, 1983). I give you a short clarification of
each of these important concepts.

Strategy of the organisation: implies the formulation of its goals and
the giving of a concrete form to them by the choice of external social
bases that the different parts of the organisation can direct their
actions to: markets, opponents, coalitionpartners or other points in
their environment. The strategy includes the operational targets. At
this level we can see changes in an organisation's policy and a shift in
its aims: an organisation can specify its aims and set bounds to its
field of action; it can broaden its goals, maintaining the already
existing ones; it can renew its goals by replacing existing ones.

Structuring of the organisation: this means the division of labor and
power between the different parties inside and outside the organisation.
Let us look first at the division of labor: one or more parties specia-
lise in one or more tasks; one or more parties cooperate with other
parties in the execution of certain tasks; one or more parties get rid
of old tasks and replace them by new ones. So there are three modes of
choice-specification, enlarging and renewal of tasks. The other element
in the structuring process is the division of power. Here three alternatives can also be distinguished: 1. hierarching – an existing party
tries to impose its will upon one or more other parties; 2. formation of
a coalition – two or more parties agree on a community of interests
without involuntarily restricting each other's relative autonomy; 3.
taking over of power – two or more parties mutually change their positions without interfering with the positions of the other parties.
Manning of the organisation: this means that there is a change in the
circle of parties involved in the "ingroup". Here again there are three
possibilities: "curtailment, extension or replacement. This point concerns of course the elite positions in the organisation.

To finish this paragraph I distinguish between three so-called projections of the associations future:

1. ideological projections – they imply an ongoing
   institutionalisation of the dominant regime, in which a
   certain party is already predominant;
2. pragmatic projections – they foresee a certain adaptation
   to the development, e.g. co-operation of a rising elite
   with the dominant one;
3. utopian projections – they foresee a clear renewal of the
   organisation.

The analysis of the future perspectives foreseen for the organisation
from the position of each party involved, supplies an overview of all
the possible alternative regimes that are open to the organisation. Each

organisation consequently has as many alternative options for its future as there are interested parties. Theoretically speaking in every alternative there will be different views on the "key commitments" of the organisation.

From my earlier thoughts about the ongoing process of segmentation and its effect on the power equilibrium in the association, I hope to have given some clear idea of the importance of the frame of reference I presented, to prepare your association for a successful future in the 90s. Especially work and organisational psychologists can be expected to make a valuable contribution to da democratic as well as efficient road to the next decade.

7.   TASKS TO BE DONE: 20 COMMANDMENTS

Psychologists professional associations will adopt a wise policy by choosing a two track policy. On the one hand side one has to "view with alarm" and develop a long-term oriented policy; on the other hand one has to "spit against the wind" that's blowing from government and employers who are cutting their budgets for psychological services. So action has to be taken, there is urgency for it.

With respect to this required action that has to be taken in a twofold way, one for the immediate future, the other for the preparation of a successful existence in the 90s, I will give you a series of suggestions that might benefit your association.

1. Psychology's underline{credibility} must be promoted, both as a science and as a profession. Psychologists should become more active as social advocates. Only by addressing itself to social issues can the association enhance its image (e.g. Payton, 1984).
2. Psychology must make clearer its relevance and social utility. Psychologists should develop a growing concern with the decisions and policies that are part of social reality. This point concerns the issue of a disciplinary shift toward interfacing psychology and social policy. The concern is with science's understanding of the public. This understanding requires an ongoing appraisal of the latent or manifest social implications of research and would be enhanced by efforts to develop or clarify such implications. These efforts are in no way incompatible with the business or objectivity of psychology as a science and can only enhance its validity as an important domain of inquiry (e.g. Masters, 1984). In this respect referring should be made to APA's Psychology in the Public Forum (Pallak, 1982).
3. Psychology must also make clearer its economic utility. "We are living in an age of increasing accountability and limits. If psychology is to live up to its code of ethics and orient itself toward the public welfare as well as maintain its fiscal viability, it is now time to plan the use of our diminishing resources in a much more systematic, explicit and rational manner" (Fishman and Neigher, 1982). Decision-makers and their advisors in all kinds of organisations must be convinced that they

will benefit from the use of psychology and by the employment of psychologists. To underline the importance of this issue of costs/effectiveness of psychology the European Federation of Professional Psychologists Associations (EFPPA) is preparing a conference on the benefits of psychology in Lausanne, 1986.

4. Psychologists must be made more aware of "the extent to which laws, government administration, health insurances practices, and various health service delivery models affect and will continue to affect both the discipline and profession of psychology" (Dörken, 1976). Because psychology is no longer a small, predominantly academic discipline, it is no longer insulated from the legal, economic, and political realities that influence the practice of any profession. Until now our general professional behavior has been extremely naive. It is too easy to think that delivering good services to clients automatically creates a wide social and political support for laws in favor of psychology. "As a profession psychology no longer can afford the luxury of assuming that someone else will represent its unique interests. As individual citizens, it is a societal responsibility we must no longer ignore" (DeLeon in Sales, 1983). In the USA it is only recently that psychologists have, in any organised or systematic sense, begun to ask how they can have a meaningful impact on their nation's various legislative bodies as they make decisions affecting their profession and society. Psychology's potential contribution is a most significant one.
In a nutshell, the legislative process is the political process. "Legislative processes are complex and to be successful, require a measured balance of public interest, professional objectives are delineated, sponsorship is gained, compromises are considered, and selective maneuvring guides each bill through to its destination" (Shapiro a.o., in Dörken and Associates, 1976; also Simon, in Sales, 1983). Especially this point of participation in the political and legislative process is in fact a rather long-term activity. At the same time one has to be informed properly on what is going on in politics and legislation from day to day, to be able to intervene effectively.

5. Make an inventory of all psychologists' relevant knowledge and contacts as far as they can be of any use in the process of influencing in one phase or another the decision making process of the political and bureaucratic machinery.

6. Encourage your members to apply for jobs in bureaucracies of governmental departments and of important advisory bodies. They can be very useful eyes and ears for the profession and take an active but secret part in the building of thoughts and the writing of certain documents.

7. Encourage psychologists, members of your association, to participate in expert-advisory and program-committees of political parties and of similar groups of their

parliamentary representatives.

8. Encourage psychologists to become <u>members of boards</u> of insurance companies, broadcast companies and all other kinds of organisations that usually play some role either in decision making about, or in financing, psychological activities. Don't forget the so-called secret societies, where elites of all societal circles meet and do transactions.

9. Use all other <u>resources and means of power</u> of the individual professionals to enlarge the power position of the association in order to control successfully its members uncertainty. Also the members who work in the field are important as eyes and ears to play a part in the great monitoring process that the association has to develop. At the same time they can function as a primary care facility for colleagues who need support.

10. <u>Define or redefine</u> your collective or segmental <u>professional identity</u>, make clear th core and the boundaries of the domain you want to develop, possess and defend and make a plan of action that might direct your concerted efforts.

11. Don't forget to <u>analyse your association</u> in its weak and its strong points, doing this with respect to the threats and chances in its environment. In fact there exists no environment as such but only a multitude of complexly interrelated organisations that are bearers of developments and trends in society.

12. Create and develop <u>interorganisational networks</u> and coalitions for transactions of commodities and resources you don't dispose of yourself but are in need of. Join those whom you are not able to beat.

13. Create so many <u>selective incentives</u> that individual psychologists are disadvantaged when they don't belong to the association, parasitic behavior is eliminated and the organisations membership runs up to a hundred percent of its potential (Olson, 1965). This is also of importance from a financial point of view.

14. Make your association's <u>structure as flexible</u> as possible to control the ongoing conflict of interests between the segmentation-groups, so that they experience the importance of added value of a prestigious organisation as a whole to the relative small political weight that is represented by a part.

15. Add to this flexible structure a <u>dual compliance</u> pattern of normative and utilitarian nature.

16. Enlarge your <u>budget</u> by other means than annual fees, selling of books or interest on your bank account.

17. Define <u>budgets for certain priorities</u> you want to invest much energy in. Especially lobbying usually is an expensive affair.

18. Optimize the <u>employment-dimension</u> which can be found in nearly every document that is published by government.

19. Enrich yourself by <u>international co-operation</u> in the European Federation of Professional Psychologists Associations (EFPPA), the International Association of Applied Psychology (IAAP) and the International Union of Psychological Science (IUPsyS).

20. And finally, on a very personal level, sometimes it
    helps psychology's interests enormously if <u>one important
    person</u>, who belongs to an elite circle, is married to a
    psychologist or has had in his near social circles a
    very positive experience with a psychologist.

For psychology much is at stake if we wish a prosperous future in the
90s. I hope to have made clear to you what crucial role I impute to
professional associations. And I hope you will have discovered that the
contribution of work and organisational psychologists can be a strategic
one, that simply can't be missed.

References

(1) Bucher, R. & Strauss, A.: Professions in process. American Journal
     of   Sociology, 1961, 66, 325-334.
(2) Caplow, Th.: The sociology of work. University of Minnesota Press,
     Minneapolis, 1954.
(3) Carr-Saunders, A.M. & Wilson, P.A.: The professions. London, Cass,
     1964.
(4) Daheim, H.: Outline of a theory of occupation associations. Mens en
     Maatschappij, 1969, 44, 1-14.
(5) DeLeon, P.H.: The changing and creating of legislation: The politi-
     cal process. In: B.D. Sales, (ed.). The professional psychologist's
     handbook. Plenum Press, London, 1983.
(6) DeLeon, P. a.o.: How to influence public policy. A blueprint for
     activism, American Psychologist, 1982, 476-485.
(7) Dörken, H.: Avenues to Legislative Success. American Psychologist,
     1977, 738-745.
(8) Etzioni, A.: A comparative analysis of complex organizations.
     Revised and enlarged edition. The Free Press (Macmillan), New York,
     1975.
(9) Fishman, D.B & Neigher, W.D.: American psychology in the eighties.
     Who will buy? American Psychologist, 1982, 37, 533-546.
(10) Jonkergouw, Th.A.J.M.: Strategie en leiding van de vakbeweging in
     Nederland, Ordeman, Rotterdam, 1983.
(11) Kjolstad, H.: Professional psychologists Associations. An EFPPA
     report, EFPPA, Amsterdam, 1983.
(12) Klinkert, J.J.: Huisarts en professie, in Huisarts en wetenschap,
     nr. 21, 1978, 6-10, 43-47, 93-96.
(13) Krogt, T. van der: Professionalisering en collectieve macht, een
     conceptueel kader. Vuga, Den Haag, 1981.
(14) Lulofs, J.G.: Een markttheoretische benadering van professies, Mens
     en Maatschappij, 1981, 56, 349-377.
(15) Masters, J.C.: Psychology research and social policy. American
     Psychologist, 1984, 39, 851-862.
(16) Millerson, G.: The qualifying associations - A study in professio-
     nalisation. Routledge and Kegan Paul, London, 1964.
(17) Mok, A. L.: Beroepen in actie; bijdrage tot de beroepensociologie.
     Boom, Meppel, 1973.
(18) Olson, M.: The logic of collective action; public goods and the
     theory of groups. Harvard University Press, Cambridge, 1965.
(19) Pallak, M.S.: Psychology in the Public Forum. American Psycholo-
     gist, 1982, 37, 475.
(20) Parry, N. & Parry, J.: The rise of the medical profession: a study
     of collective social mobility. Croom Helm, London, 1976.

(21) Payton, C.R.: Who must do the hard things? American Psychologist, 1984, 39, 391–397.
(22) Pool, J.J.: Professionaliteit bij artsen en verpleegkundigen. Mens en Maatschappij 54, 1979, nr. 3, 292–306.
(23) Ritzer, G.: Professionalism and the individual. In: Freidson, E. (ed.), The professions and their prospects, Sage, Beverly Hills, 1971.
(24) Shapiro, A.E. a.o.: The legislative process, in H. Dörken and Associates, The professional psychologist today, New developments in law, health insurance and health practice, London, Jossey-Bass Publ., 1976.
(25) Sales, B.D. (ed.): The professional psychologist's handbook. Plenum Press, London, 1983.
(26) Simon, G.C.: Psychology, professional practice and the public interest. In B.D. Sales (ed.), op. cit., 1983.

THE PSYCHOLOGY OF WORK AND ORGANIZATION
G. Debus and H.-W. Schroiff (Editors)
© *Elsevier Science Publishers B.V. (North-Holland), 1986*

367

WHAT ORGANIZATIONAL PSYCHOLOGISTS SAY THEY DO
AND WHAT THEY REALLY DO

Gaston DE COCK

Department of Psychology
University of Leuven/Louvain
Tiensestraat 102
B-3000 Leuven, Belgium

1. HIGH GROWTH RATE OF PSYCHOLOGISTS

Thirty years ago, when I mentioned that I would like to study psychology, people were astonished and asked a little bit suspicious: "Psychology, what's that? What can you do with it? Psychology was rather unkown and people did not know what psychologists could do.
In order to understand this astonishment of 30 years ago we can refer to the number of psychologists at that time. The number was small and only a few people had contact with psychologists. The last 30 years a rapid increase in the number of psychologists took place.
In the following statistics I will limit myself to the Belgian situation, not only because of my resources, but also because what happened in Belgium is not a typical Belgian phenomenon but a European one or even a worldwide one, with only slight differences in the time-period and the numbers.

In the following tables I will give you an idea of the rapid growth of the number of students in psychology at the Belgian Universities. Students in psychology and educational sciences are included in the number of students. Both kinds of students are studying in the same faculties and the national statistics take the faculty as the smallest unit. From 1950 - 1968 the statistics do not differentiate the French and Flemish speaking students in Leuven and Brussels. From 1969 on there were separate statistics.

Table 1: Growth rate of the number of students in the Faculties of Psychology and Educational Science 1950-1965 (Belgium).

Year	Gent	Leuven Louvain	Brussel Bruxelles	Luik Liege	Total	Growth rate 1949=100
1949-50	45	155	118	54	372	100
1954-55	68	327	113	51	559	150
1959-60	174	560	139	118	991	266
1964-65	355	1018	461	228	2062	554

In table 1 we can see that in 15 years, between 1950 - 1964 the number ob students increased five times.

Table 2: Growth rate of the number of students in the Faculties of
          Psychology and Educational Sciences at the French- and
          Flemish speaking universities between 1970-1984.

YEAR	FLANDERS TOTAL	FLANDERS %	WALLONIA TOTAL	WALLONIA %	BELGIUM
1970	1973	60%	1335	40%	3308
1975	2616	64%	1471	36%	4087
1980	3543	65%	1930	35%	5473
1985	3703	63%	2178	37%	5881

In the 15 years, between 1965 and 1979 the growth rate was smaller than
it was between 1950 – 1965. But even then, the number of students in
1979 was 2,65 times higher than it was in 1965. Compared with 1950 we
have 15 times more students in 1984.

In order to complete the information and to give you a better idea about
the distribution of the students over the different universities we
calculated the percentages of the students in the faculties.

Nearly 2/3 of the students are studying in Flanders (63%). We observe an
unequal distribution of students over the different universities. The
university of Leuven (Flemish) has 38 % of the total number, the
University of Louvain (French) and Ghent (Flemish) have 18 % and 19 %
followed by Liege (French) 11 % and than Brussels with less than 10 % of
the students in Psychology.

The increase of students, as is shown by the tables, can partially be
explained by referring to the normal expansion that took place in all
universities, but the expansion in Psychology was higher than in other
study orientations, especially for the number of female students (as is
shown in table 3).

In table 3 (see next page) we can see a higher growth rate of female
students, compared to that of the male students. The majority of
psychology students in Flanders are female and in Wallonia even 2/3 are
female students.

Table 3: Increase in male and female students in the Faculties of Psychology and Educational Sciences between 1970-1984.

| YEAR | MALE | | FEMALE | | |
	TOTAL	%	TOTAL	%	TOTAL
1970	1646	49%	1662	51%	3308
1975	1806	44%	2281	56%	4087
1980	2256	41%	3217	59%	5473
1985	2328	39%	3553	61%	5881

During the same period 1950 - 1984 we can also observe a rapid growth of psychology as a science and the development of a society relevant approach of its object: human behavior.
When in 1950 the question "What does psychology mean and what do psychologists do?" was relevant because psychology was unknown, the same question can be asked in 1985.
This question is still relevant because on the one hand the people did not follow the rapid evolution of psychology while on the other hand they have more contacts with this science and with many kinds of psychologists. This diversity of contacts and the wide range of activities of psychologists contribute to a lack of clear understanding of what psychology means and what psychologists do.

2. WHAT DO PSYCHOLOGISTS DO?

Psychology students are trained for a wide range of occupations, as can be inferred from the various options the universities offer them. Although the names given to these options may differ from one university to another, the options for psychologists can be classified in four main categories:

1. Work-, community- and organizational psychology.
2. Psychology in schools and educational and vocational guidance.
3. Clinical psychology.
4. Theoretical psychology.

We will limit ourselves to the work-, community- and organizational psychologists.
The "Careers Advisory Services" at the Universities of Leuven and Ghent carry out regular surveys among psychology graduates in order to ascertain the fields in which they are employed. The results of these surveys are published in brochures or in articles in reviews.

1. Occupational- community- and organizational-psychologists endeavour to resolve the psychological problems which arise in the working environment, whether in industry, ministerial departments, public utility services, agriculture, commerce, transport or any other type of organization. These sectors still continue to offer a growing number of

opportunities to psychologists. This development is attributable to the
fact that society as a whole (via official regulations, even at international level) and all industrial organizations individually show an
increasing concern for human problems and feel responsible for them.
Consequently, there is an increased need for specialists in psychological sciences. Their task is to put forward solutions taking account of
sometimes contradictory demands: on the one hand, the demands for a high
rate of productivity and on the other the demands – which are just as
compelling, if not more so – fed by a need to create an atmosphere
conducive to human selffulfilment in and through work. The actual field
of activities will obviously vary greatly, depending on the firm, the
psychologist's personal qualities and competition with other universitiy
graduates (legal experts, economists, sociologists etc). Moreover, for a
large number of problems the psychologist will need to work in close
cooperation with other specialists, such as doctors and engineers. This
means that depending on the concrete field of action, his activities may
relate to personnel psychology, ergonomic psychology, organizational
psychology, economic psychology and community psychology.

The personnel psychologist works within the framework of the personnel
or research and development departments of organizations, industrial
firms, banks, department stores, hospitals etc. He is responsible for
selecting employees (who is suited to which jobs and duties), for
drawing up job descriptions, for analysing recruitment and promotion
criteria, for seeking solutions to profitability and transfer problems.
The work of these psychologists not only fosters the firm's economic
expansion but also improves the employees' whole working environment. As
the people responsible for training, they head the team which devises
and carries through specialization and retraining programmes, trains the
firm's managerial staff and attend to career schemes.

The ergonomic psychologist's objective is to design or devise, to
construct or to change machines, equipment, tasks, the working method
and environment, in such a way that they are suited to the employees'
psychological characteristics. Firms which are developing difficult
control devices will seek the psychologists' advice as to the way in
which the instruments might be best adapted to observation and handling
capacity. Ergonomic psychologists will also be able to study the
influence of lighting, noise and the sharing out of work on employees.
In addition, they can play a great part in fostering better
understanding of the human problems which arise within an organization
and in seeking solutions in conjunction with the organization.

The organizational psychologist seeks, for instance, means of increasing
job satisfaction, of resolving conflicts or tensions within the organization and of creating better relations between fellow-workers and
subordinates. He also seeks to provide adequate training, to reconcile
employees' individual motives with the organization's objectives and to
play the role of mediator in trade union action. The organizational
psychologist is increasingly tending, however, to approach the organization as an entity, with its own identity and specific scope for growth.
In this connection it should be noted that the organizational psychologist plays a part in devising and following through the organization's
development schemes focusing on better health and effectiveness; he also
examines the atmosphere reigning within the organization, as such examinations often reveal important basic facts about the organization's
overall policy. As the organization is located in a wider environment it

can be said that community psychology is a source of considerable enrichment for the organizational psychologist.

The economic psychologist attempts to gain greater perception of the psychological processes (e.g. perception, information processing, learning processes, methods of change, motivation, expectations, desires, decisions) which determine the economic behaviour of consumers, entrepreneurs, producers, savers, investors, taxpayers and the authorities. With the help of a public opinion analysis, he studies the expectations, motivations, desires and experiences of (potential) consumers of products and adapts advertising campaigns and slogans accordingly. He also seeks the real need for goods and services for consumers and suggests points which might help them to protect themselves more adequately against their purchasing behaviour. Lastly, he seeks the psychological factors which determine the volume of saving, the choice of forms of saving and fluctuations on the stock market. But community psychology inhabits the same research field.

Community psychologists examine behaviour vis-a-vis far-reaching socio-economic issues (hours of work, leisure, division of labour and distribution of income, social services wanted, desirable standard of living and prosperity), with an interest in more effective policies on the part of the public authorities.
Specialist centres or bureaux, with a large team of occupational and organizational psychologists, are also sometimes commissioned to carry out the above mentioned tasks. For instance, there are industrial psychology services, psychological advisory and selection bureaux, centres for increasing productivity, for selecting managerial staff, improving organization and management, advertising and market survey bureaux. Psychologists with sufficient experiences in the older age group may be appointed to posts such as head of personnel or director of an organization's overall policy.

I believe what is said above is true, but it shows such a variety of activities that it becomes difficult to define what a work- and organizational psychologist really is.

In order to have a deeper insight in what the work- and organizational psycholigist does we carried out an investigation at our Center of Organizational psychology of the University of Leuven, with the main question: "How does a work- and organizational psychologist see himself or herself and how does middle management see the psychologist? (De Cock, G., De Witte, K., Langenus S. and Devogelaere E.).

We asked 300 work- and organizational psychologists to fill in a questionnaire in order to find out how they see themselves as psychologists and we asked them to give other questionnaires to people with whom they are working. Only 48 psychologists (16 %) answered the questionnaire. That means we should be very careful with our conclusions especially since the sample consists mainly out of younger psychologists.

The mean age of the sample was 30,5 years and 11 of the 48 are working at a university or another eductional institution; 10 psychologists started their career in personnel selection; 9 started a career outside psychology and later on they came in the fields of organizational psychology and 18 were from the beginning involved in the many

activities of the personnel department. 70 % of them changed once from
job, 50 % changed twice or more and only a few left the typical psychology for more management oriented function.
Because of the small number of respondents, 16 %, and because these were
mainly younger psychologists we may not generlise these results.
Although a few interesting ideas came forward.

3. RESULTS

1. Selfimage

The psychologists see themselves in a helping role. One makes a call on
them, when there is a problem in the field of training, development or
selection. Most psychologists are not involved in the negotiation for
collective agreement nor for ergonomic problems. On a list of 15 occupations the psychologists put themselves very high. The psychologists see
themselves as affiliative and not powerful, as understanding and accepting and they put the emphasis on human relations.
The psychologists are not achievement oriented. The psychologists think
they do not have good technics at their disposal and they do not
consider themselves as experts.
The psychologists are not involved in policy making.

2. Image of middle management towards the psychologists.

Middle management says: the psychologists are unknown that's why we have
a negative image of them. The psychologists are living in their own
world, isolated, unapproachable and inaccessible. Psychologists do not
know enough of the economic organizational problems. Middle management
places the psychologists at a low rank in the list of occupations. In
the opinion of middle management psychologists are power oriented as
well as affiliative and it does not agree with the statement that the
psychologists are understanding and accepting. The middle managers do
not believe that the psychologists put the emphasis on human aspects.

4. IMPORTANT DEVELOPMENTS FOR THE FUTURE

Another survey we did in 1981-82 together with Prof. Sylvia Shimmin
(Great Britain) and Prof. Paul Coetsier (Belgium) was dealing with the
expectations of ENOP members (European Network of Organizational
Psychologists) about: Work and Organizational Psychology in the 1990 and
beyond.
The aim of our survey was to obtain information about the future of
Organizational Psychology and the social forces influencing this field.
Twenty-four respondents from thirteen different countries participated
in this inquiry. We formulated scenarios about possible trends within
organizations and society and asked the participants: will this trend
accelerate, remain or decelerate?

Scenario 1: There is a steady decline in the motivation to work. Many
young people refuse to work, more people benefit from early retirement.
More and more people value freedom and leisure time.

This trend will
     accelerate :   11
     remain   :   6
     decelerate   :   7

Scenario 2: Worktime is becoming shorter, there are more part-time jobs although unemployment is increasing.

This trend will
    accelerate : 17
    remain   :   5
    decelerate :   2

Scenario 3: Laws on employment of members of discriminated groups (sex, race, religion) laws on health, safety and ecology become very stringent.

This trend will
    accelerate : 10
    remain   : 10
    decelerate :   4

Scenario 4: Clerical jobs are being replaced by computers.

This trend will
    accelerate : 22
    remain   :   1
    decelerate :   1

Scenario 5: Due to a breakthrough in the development of software, applications of mini- and micro-computers grow at a high rate. Information gathering and means of communication are becoming more fluent.

This trend will
    accelerate : 24
    remain   :   0
    decelerate :   0

Scenario 6: After a short period of stagnation, industrial democracy and participation is in heavy demand. It is the most important claim by the unions, strongly backed by their members.

This trend will
    accelerate : 11
    remain   :   5
    decelerate :   8

Scenario 7: Third world countries are more and more influencing economics and policies.

This trend will
    accelerate : 16
    remain   :   3
    decelerate :   1

We asked the respondents their view on the demand for organizational and work psychologists in the following domains:

	The demand for org. & work psychologists will		
Domain	Increase	not change	decrease
training	19	5	–
counseling	18	4	2
career planning	15	9	–
research	14	10	–
ergonomics	15	7	2
labour relations	13	11	–
organizat. devel.	16	4	4
health	13	9	2
personnel adm.	13	7	4
consumer behaviour	9	12	3
public relations	7	14	2
selection	5	11	8

Looking into the future is difficult and not always reliable. The forementioned data were gathered in 1981 and it might be interesting to see
where we are in 1985, what would enable us to use additional information
in order to adjust these data and to have a clearer picture of 1990.
The small number of respondents in 1981 neither permits us to
generalise. However, keeping these remarks concerning reliability and
generalisability of data in mind we can still formulate some suggestions
for the future with the forementioned scenarios as our guide:
1. Improving the quality of working life and leisure time opens new
   possibilities for psychologists.
2. Work- and organizational psychologists need to do research on
   structuring and restructuring work conditions in order to improve and
   create possibilities for part-time work. We also need to study the
   problem of very loose ties between individuals and organizations.
3. Training remains an important task but in order to be effective
   several aspects will need special attention:
   - Man-machine interactions and their ergonomical aspects.
   - The relationship between computerized information systems and
     organizational structure.
   - The impact of new forms of information processing on organizational
     decision making.
4. Reviewing the way selection procedures are applied is another task
   for the future organizational psychologist.
5. A closer relationship and collaboration between practitioners and
   researchers is a topic deserving special attention.
6. For the more experienced psychologists there is a need to participate
   in the strategic planning and strategic decision making of
   organizations.
   Too many times psychologists stick too long to a partial approach.
   They avoid the complexity of an organization. As long as we think
   that the focus of organizational psychologists is restricted to the
   behaviour of individuals and groups within organizations, we will
   miss new opportunities and moreover, we will never be real
   "organizational" psychologists.
   More and more we should be willing to deal with the organization as a
   whole, and be ready to cross the bounderies of the personnel
   department. In order to clarify the statement put forward in point 6,
   I will present the results of a survey done by W.H. Hegarty and R.C.
   Hoffman (1983).
   The information for the project was collected from 423 top managers.
   This sample represented the top management teams of 112 manufacturing
   firms. The firms surveyed were located in 10 European countries:

Belgium,   France,   Germany,   The   Netherlands,   Switzerland,   United
Kingdom and the four Scandinavian countries.
The   authors   investigated   the   influence   of   the   departments   on   3
categories of strategic decisions:
1. Product/Market-decisions   about   products   or   markets   and   ways   to
   compete.
2. Technological-decisions concerning the supply of raw materials and
   production technology.
3. Administrative-decisions   about organization structure and systems
   for   resource   allocation,   planning   and   control,   including   human
   resources, management development etc.

They also look for the influence on strategic decisions in general.   The
results are presented in the following figures.

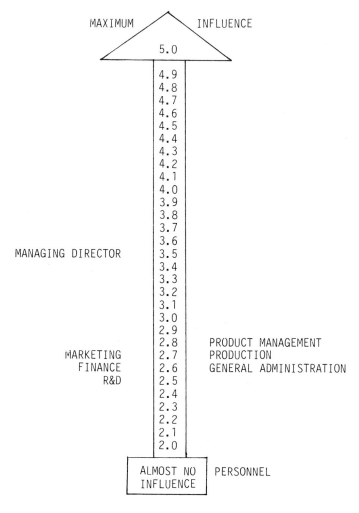

Figure 1: Overall influence on all decisions by different departments

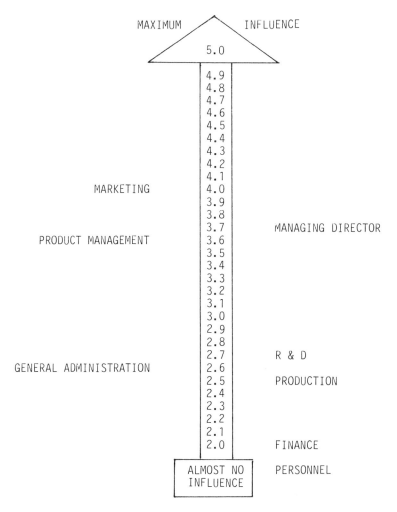

Figure 2: Influence on product/market decisions by different departments

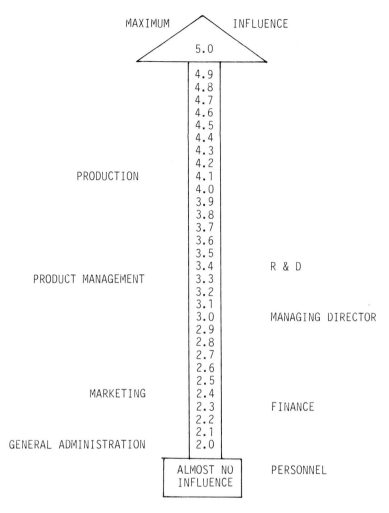

Figure 3: Influence on technological decisions by different departments

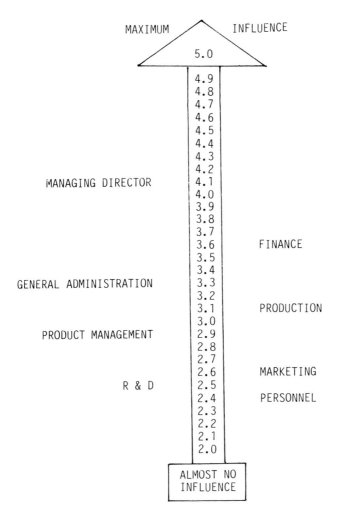

MAXIMUM ◁ INFLUENCE

5.0

4.9
4.8
4.7
4.6
4.5
4.4
4.3
4.2
MANAGING DIRECTOR   4.1
4.0
3.9
3.8
3.7
3.6   FINANCE
3.5
3.4
GENERAL ADMINISTRATION   3.3
3.2
3.1   PRODUCTION
3.0
PRODUCT MANAGEMENT   2.9
2.8
2.7
2.6   MARKETING
R & D   2.5
2.4   PERSONNEL
2.3
2.2
2.1
2.0

ALMOST NO
INFLUENCE

Figure 4: Influence on administrative decisions by different departments

The authors arrived at the conclusion that the areas of responsibility and expertise of the personnel department appear to be too narrow to exert influence over most of the strategic decisions.
Personnel departments do have significant influence over certain administrative decisions. But they are not enough involved in the development of new products, new markets, new work-methods and new technologies.
Personnel management should become "human resource management" and "organization management". The "know-how" is available but should be more visible.
I hope these data will be a stimulus to widen the scope of work- and organizational psychologists.

THE PSYCHOLOGY OF WORK AND ORGANIZATION
G. Debus and H.-W. Schroiff (Editors)
© *Elsevier Science Publishers B.V. (North-Holland), 1986*   379

REFLECTIONS ON THE INTERVENTIONS OF ORGANISATIONAL PSYCHOLOGISTS

Allan P.O. WILLIAMS

City University Business School, London.

1. INTRODUCTION

I should like to draw your attention to three beliefs which we probably
all share: (1) In order to survive and be successful organisations con-
tinually have to adapt to changes in their environments (e.g. economic,
social, political, technological changes): (2) there exists a body of
knowledge and associated technology which is of potential value to
organisations planning change (i.e. organisational psychology): (3) in
our professional role as organisational psychologists we are concerned
in helping organisations to utilise this available knowledge in order to
enhance their effectiveness. The term organisational psychologist is
being used to refer to the consultant who intervenes in organisational
processes; this contrasts with the term occupational psychologist whose
client is primarily an individual seeking, for instance, career guidance.

Now there are a number of problems in this scenario which have concerned
many of us, e.g. Cherns [1], Beyer [2], Williams [3]. For example:
organisations do not necessarily utilise available knowledge; when they
do seek to apply up-to-date knowledge, they may use inappropriate strategies in seeking help from consultants; when appropriate consultants are
approached, their efforts may be seen by clients as a mixed blessing.

In order to try and reduce the frequency of these problems arising there
are steps which we should be taking, such as educating potential clients
on how to use us, marketing our professional skills, and improving the
training of organisational psychologists. But the theme which I should
like to promote is that before applying these solutions, we need to learn
more about the ways in which we are being used as opposed to the ways in
which we would like to be used, the implications which these have for
the training of organisational psychologists and the resources which they
need, and the critical factors which differentiate between the more and
the less successful interventions.

In other words, organisational psychologists need to take time off to
reflect on what they are doing in organisations, and to see what guidelines can be drawn for the future. I should like to share with you my
efforts in this direction, as they relate to the projects carried out by
the Centre for Personnel Research and Enterprise Development (C-PRED).

2.   C-PRED

The Centre was established in 1978 within the City University Business
School to provide consultancy/research services designed to help companies
arrive at more effective decisions relating to personnel and organisational issues. The academic aim was to generate research data which
could be used to increase our understanding of the conditions associated
with effective interventions. By the end of 1984 the research data consisted of a pool of 36 projects commissioned and paid for by client
organisations. Clients consisted of financial institutions, manufacturing
companies, government departments, and professional bodies.

The projects themselves consisted of attitude surveys, evaluation of
training and appraisal programmes, validating selection procedures,
identifying training needs, conducting equal opportunity audits and designing positive action programmes, and evaluating organisational
structures.

The small number and diverse nature of the projects did not allow any
reliable quantitative analysis to be made on the pool of projects, as
carried out for instance by Dunn and Swierczek [4]. The qualitative
analysis undertaken involved a process of comparing each project in the
pool with the others, in order to identify similarities and differences
which could account for their differential outcomes. The outcomes were
the author's judgement as to the value of the project to the client with
respect to its content or findings, and the processes involved in arriving
at these results.

3.   SIX EMERGENT DIMENSIONS

3.1. Innovative or Maintenance Response

Organisation theorists such as Chris Argyris have pointed out that most
change efforts in organisations are maintenance rather than innovative
changes. A project which made an input to a maintenance response was
concerned in evaluating a condensed version of an established realistic
job preview. The organisation was not trying to do something new, merely
introduce a shortened version of something they were already doing. A
project making an input to an innovative response involved carrying out
an attitude survey on employees who were to be moved to a new plant, and
to be introduced to a radically different organisation design. This
innovative/maintenance dimension seems to be a significant contextual
feature in an intervention. An innovative response is much more traumatic
to the social system, and a consultant making an input to this situation
may have to adopt a more participative approach in carrying out his or her
assignment, and be much more aware of the political forces operating.

3.2. Phase of Management Problem Solving Cycle

This dimension refers to a series of events which are associated with a
planned change effort. A four-phased framework for representing the
cycle is the following: (1) Prioritisation and orientation (management
explore situational factors, identify problems and opportunities, determine priorities and lay down guidelines for action); (2) Problem diagnosis
(exploring the nature of the selected problem/opportunity to gain insight

into the underlying factors); (3) Decision-making (generating possible solutions and selecting most favoured follow-up action); (4) Implementation and evaluation (determining detailed objectives, planning and organising, controlling and evaluating progress against plans and objectives).

A client may commission a project to make an input to one or more of these phases, only rarely does an external consultant make an input to all four phases. Even the idealistic action research paradigm often only starts at the second phase. C-PRED has carried out projects making inputs to one or more of the last three phases. Clients usually only approach external consultants once they are well into the first phase.

3.3. Problem or Opportunity Initiated Change

Most changes taking place within organisations can be classified either as being initiated by a problem or crisis (e g. high level of absenteeism), or as an attempt to take advantage of an opportunity for improving performance or competitiveness (e.g. using assessment centres to improve the quality of management trainees). Most projects fell within the problem category. This is not surprising since these were the situations where sufficiently powerful forces for change had been generated to result in external help being sought.

3.4. Project Decision Making Style

Just as one can characterise management decision making styles as being on a continuum ranging from an authoritarian to a participative style, so one can describe the key decisions relating to a project in terms of a similar range of styles. Thus in the attitude surveys we have carried out there are examples of an authoritarian style (decisions made by the managing director and the consultant), a consultative style (decisions made by the personnel manager and consultant, but in close consultation with staff representatives and unions), and a participative style (key decisions made by a committee consisting of management and union representatives, with the advice of the consultants).

The style used in relation to a project did not necessarily reflect the dominant managerial style within the organisation. But recognising the style which management was prepared to accept, and the style which was most appropriate to the dynamics of the situation, were important goals for the consultants. Their understanding of this variable determined the way in which they related to different members of the client system.

3.5. Controlling and Collaborative Role of Acting Client

The acting client is the internal manager of the project, and therefore it is he or she who has immediate responsibility for monitoring and controlling its progress Acting clients may adopt a close or distant approach in this role. The former approach tended to be characterised by the acting client interacting frequently at a formal (e.g regular progress meetings) and informal level (e.g. frequent consultative and social meetings) with the consultants. We had extreme examples of both styles. On one project, after the initial briefing on the project there was minimal contact with the acting client until a draft report had been written. On another there was almost daily contact with the acting client during the course of the project.

3.6. Dominant Role of Primary Consultant

As a researcher the consultant is concerned in helping the client's
problem solving processes by applying a range of research models and
techniques. As an adviser he or she is concerned in helping these processes by suggesting appropriate methods and solutions which have been
successfully applied in other similar situations. As a trainer he or she
helps these processes by enabling individuals or teams to acquire particular attitudes, skills and knowledge.

In the projects to date the primary consultant (i.e. the individual
directly responsible for the conduct of the project) has mainly been in
the role of researcher. The term dominant role is used in relation to
this dimension because each of these roles includes, in practice, an
element of the other two. Thus in carrying out an employee attitude
survey one uses research skills (e.g. questionnaire design, sampling),
advisory skills (e.g. in the light of situational factors one guides the
client on the aims and broad features of the survey), and training or
coaching skills (e.g. helping individual managers learn how attitude
survey results can be most effectively used for management problem
solving). This multiple role of the organisational psychologist or inter-
ventionist does highlight the different goals of the consultant-researcher
who is concerned with an organisation's problems, and the academic-
researcher who is concerned with the development of a discipline or area
of knowledge.

4.   A MODEL FOR THE EFFECTIVE MANAGEMENT OF INTERVENTIONS

Taking into account these six emergent dimensions, and related knowledge
in this field, it is possible to put forward a model incorporating the
key variables and relationships affecting intervention outcomes. Figure 1
is a preliminary attempt at this.

4.1. End Result Variables

In judging the success of an intervention project, there are two criteria
which should dominate: the findings or information generated by a project
should be used and be found useful within the context of the client's
problem solving or opportunity seeking efforts (content criterion); the
process of carrying out the project or intervening in the organisation
should facilitate successful outcomes to the client's problem solving or
opportunity seeking efforts (process criterion). These two criteria are
intertwined, but it is worth separating them if only to highlight the
situation where a project may come up with a high quality solution (e.g.
for designing a selection system), but one which is not used by the client
because the processes involved in arriving at this solution aroused strong
resistance to change.

4.2. Emergent Variables

The utility value of a project is shown as a function of the consultants'
credibility and acceptability (which in turn is dependent upon the client's
perceptions of the consultants' technical skills and resources); the consultants' behaviours and strategies (in turn dependent upon their perception of client needs and expectations, and contextual or situational

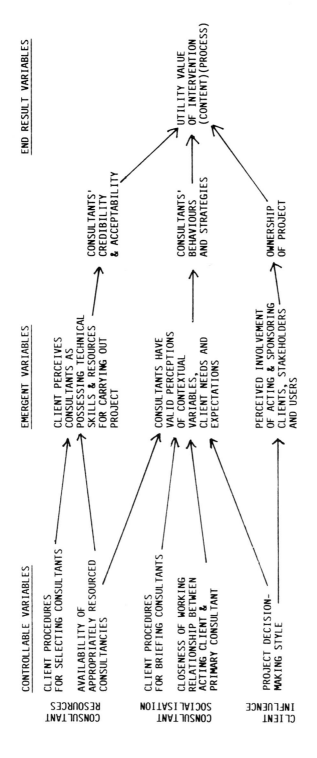

FIGURE 1

A model for the effective management of interventions

variables); and the ownership of the project (in turn the result of the perceived involvement in the project by various groups within the client system).

The relationships implied so far can be defended on rational, psychological (behaviour reflecting perception), and empirical grounds (the importance of the ownership variable in the organisation development literature).

4.3. Controllable Variables

In order to influence the emergent variables there are a number of actions which clients and consultants can and do take. These are the variables over which direct control is voluntary, and in relation to which clients and consultants can be trained to make more effective decisions (i.e. ones which will increase the probability of an intervention achieving a high utility value).

The first two sets of variables refer to consultant resources. Client procedures for selecting consultants will clearly affect the client resources at their disposal. We have come across a wide variation in the competence displayed by clients in this process. They may know whether they are looking primarily for someone with research, advisory or training skills, but few use a systematic approach in matching a consultant's skills with the intervention requirements demanded by the situation. If consultants with inadequate skills or resources for the situation are selected, then this will inevitably be reflected in the project outcomes.

The availability of appropriately resourced consultancies is the responsibility of the directors of consultancies and the trainers of consultants. How effective are we in selecting and training organisational psychologists? Are our consultancy services and resources designed to meet the needs of clients? How effective are we in educating potential clients as to what we are best at? These questions are important because they should make us think of those factors which we in the profession of organisational psychology can influence so as to increase the frequency of successful interventions.

Consultants are socialised into client organisations. Two critical ways in which the client can control this process is through formal briefing sessions, and through the less formal interactions taking place between the primary consultant and the acting client. Where these are effective they will enable consultants to develop valid perceptions of the context of an intervention (i.e. whether part of an innovative or maintenance response, and so on), and thereby be less likely to misunderstand client needs and expectations. Poor briefing and inadequate informal contact between client and consultant often lead to inappropriate behaviour on the part of the latter. Critical information about the client system may only be acquired through casual conversation with the acting client. A close working relationship between the acting client and consultant may become even more important when a project stretches over several months - early notice of impending changes to the client system will allow the consultant to adapt a project so that its value is not diminished by these changes.

The extent to which the acting client, and other interested groups within the client system, can influence the decision making processes associated with a project will affect their feelings of involvement with the project. The enhanced interactions which take place in a participative project decision making style, will also provide additional opportunities for the consultant to learn about the needs and expectations of different interest groups within the organisation.

5.   SUMMARY AND CONCLUSIONS

We need to learn as individuals and as a professional body how we can be of most use to organisations attempting to adapt to changing environments. One way of promoting this learning process is to analyse the projects which we actually carry out for organisations, and to highlight those similarities and differences which appear to affect outcomes.

In attempting this exercise on a pool of thirty-six projects carried out by C-PRED, six dimensions emerged as being potentially significant variables in an intervention. Three of these are contextual variables (innovative or maintenance responses; phase of management problem solving cycle; problem or opportunity initiated change). They refer to antecedent conditions which organisational psychologists or consultants need to be aware of if the content and process of their intervention are to be of value to the organisation.

The three other emergent dimensions are concerned with power and process (project decision making style: controlling and collaborative roles of acting client; dominant role of primary consultant). These are ongoing variables which are changeable during the course of an intervention. Clients and consultants need to be aware of the role of these variables in influencing the outcomes of interventions.

In reflecting on these findings a preliminary model evolved which hypothesises significant relationships which need to be carefully managed for successful interventions. Both clients and consultants have a role to play in managing these relationships.

REFERENCES

[1]   Cherns, A., Using the Social Sciences (Routledge & Kegan Paul,London, 1979).
[2]   Beyer, J.M., The Utilisation of Organisational Research, Administrative Science Quarterly, 27(4), (1982), pp.588-686.
[3]   Williams, A.P.O., Using Personnel Research (Gower, Aldershot, 1983).
[4]   Dunn, W N , and Swierczek, F.W., Planned organisational change: towards grounded theory, Journal of Applied Behavioural Science, 12(2), (1977), pp.135-387.

THE PSYCHOLOGY OF WORK AND ORGANIZATION
G. Debus and H.-W. Schroiff (Editors)
© *Elsevier Science Publishers B.V. (North-Holland), 1986*

RECENT DEVELOPMENTS OF WORK AND ORGANIZATIONAL PSYCHOLOGY IN SPAIN

José M. PEIRO

Departamento de Psicologia General. Facultad de Psicología.
Avda. Blasco Ibañez, 21
46010 Valencia, Spain.

The radical change in political climate in Spain since 1975 has
stimulated research and development in the fields of Work and Organizational Psychology. This research reflects topics of interest
generally in the international field, but more importantly relating
to aspects of Spanish society. The objective of this latter research contributing to the development of Spain as a modern industrial European nation is discussed.

1. THE SOCIAL AND POLITICAL FRAMEWORK

An adequate understanding of the recent developments of work and organizational psychology in Spain needs some references to the economical, political and social factors and changes experienced throughout the last decade.

The Spanish Civil War (1936-1939) led to a dictatorial regime under General
Franco which lasted until 1975. Many years had to pass before the beginning
of an economical and industrial development and a progressive recovery of
scientific activities at the universities. The increase in the standard of
living, as in other European countries, was an important factor which contributed to the modification of the Spanish social structure, building up
a large middle class lacking in its previous history.

The beginning of a democratic state, after Franco's death (1975) was supported by a great majority of Spaniards, and during the last decade Spain
has emerged as a modern and democratic society in the Mediterranean area
with a very prestigious Crown, not very large political parties, and carrying on an administrative decentralization process that gives room to Regional Autonomous Governments instead of the old centralization. Nevertheless, terrorism, a strong economical crisis and a high level of unemployment
(20 per cent of the active population) are the main real problems of present
Spanish social life.

Spanish industries, needing technological and organizational changes and
more competitive structures, are suffering a process of reconversion and
with it high levels of conflict led by new and influential trade unions.
Also noteworthy are the new developments in universities, with the introduction of more technical studies that are creating a new framework for relationships between industries and universities and the development of applied research. All of these events are framing the present activities of
organizational and work psychologists in academical and professional fields.

2. THE TEACHING OF WORK AND ORGANIZATIONAL PSYCHOLOGY

2.1 Training for Undergraduates

The establishment of the bachelor's degree in psychology in 1968 changed the academic profile of Spanish Psychology. The new studies started at the Universities of Madrid and Barcelona. They consisted of five academic years, two of them common to the bachelor's degree of Philosophy and Arts and three specific on psychological subjects. Later changes in the curriculum have favored specialization, and today students of psychology take only psychological subjects during the five academic years. Many other universities have been incorporating the bachelor's degree of psychology in the last decade.

In general, there is no specific curriculum for the specialities, but some optional courses dealing with different fields of application are offered. In Organizational Psychology the courses offered show some common characteristics in all the universities. First, the number of courses offered lies, in most cases, between four and five. Second, the topics covered are, in general, of introductory character; however, we can also notice the presence of some more specific subjects related to an old tradition: Personnel Selection, Training, Ergonomics, Marketing, Work Psychopathology and Mental Health.

During the last few years some Spanish textbooks have been published trying to cover the main topics for these courses. We can mention the well-known work of Siguan (1963) which is oriented in Human Relations. More recently several works have appeared in Work and Industrial Psychology (Mateu, 1984; Quintanilla, 1984) and on general scope of Organizational Psychology (Peiró, 1983-84) together with others of introductory character (Dominguez and Casas, 1979; Mallart, 1981; Ballesteros, 1982). Also noteworthy are the translation activities in Spain and Latin American countries, making available well-known English works to Spanish readers.

Interestingly enough, various surveys about sophomores' preferences have shown that only 6 % would prefer to specialize in Organizational Psychology (Montoro and Quintanilla, 1981). If we consider their preferences when students reach the second level (4th and 5th years of the studies), between 15 and 25 % choose the subjects of Work and Organizational Psychology although this choice does not exclude the training in other specialties.

2.2. The Training of Post-Graduates and the Third Level of University Studies.

The School of Applied Psychology for post-graduate students of the University of Madrid offers a sort of specialization in Organizational Psychology that includes some courses such as Industrial Psychology, Personnel Selection, Organization of Enterprises, Safety and Hygiene at Work, Evaluation and Job Analysis, Personnel Management, Psychology of Commercial and Marketing Activities and Work Psychopathology. In it, the classical questions are well represented but the new perspectives of Organizational Psychology and the new strategies of intervention are barely taken into account.

Nevertheless, a considerable demand for postgraduate training is found among psychologists. Crespo (1982) in a survey carried out on a sample of 868 psychologist members of the "Colegio Oficial de Psicólogos" showed that about 75 % of the sample had "urgent" or "very urgent" needs for training. Among the preferred subjects, in Industrial and Organizational Psychology, people mentioned the Psychology of Organizations, Personnel Selection, studies on Organizational Climate and Personnel Training. These topics were placed at the top by about 5 % of the sample in each case. The author concludes from this study that graduates of psychology feel a great necessity for professional training not to be met with theoretical training but through work and practice. The Spanish Society of Psychology recently facing the problem of postgraduate training in the universities, saw the controversy between the tendency to center the graduate training around basic research and the one centered in the professional and specialized training (Hernández, 1984). In the following years the universities will have to meet the challenge of answering these demands.

2.3. Training Offers Outside the University

Many Management Schools are interested in Work and Organizational Psychology and most of them offer training on management with emphasis on psychological aspects. We shall mention the following ones: EADA (Top Management School), EOI (School of Industrial Organization), ESADE (School of Management), ESIC (School of Marketing), IESE (School of Organizational Studies) and ICAI- ICADE (Institute of Organizational Management). All these centers are characterized by offering applied training for executives and intermediate level managers.

3. RESEARCH AND PUBLICATIONS ON WORK AND ORGANIZATIONAL PSYCHOLOGY

3.1. Main Research Centers and Groups

In recent years *Spanish Universities* have developed some research activities of theoretical and applied interest on this subject matter. First, in the School of Applied Psychology at the University of Madrid some research projects on motivation at work, stress, work satisfaction and organizational change have been carried out under the direction of Profs. Yela and Forteza. In the Department of Social Psychology (headed by Prof. Jimenez-Burillo) some doctoral research on Organizational Development has been made and Prof. Torregrosa has carried out research on unemployment and safety at work.

At the University of Barcelona Dr. Mateu and colleagues have studied Organizational Development, Management Development and other aspects of Quality of Working Life in the frame of the Social Psychology Department headed by Prof. Munné.

At the University of Valencia two doctoral dissertations, one on Traffic and Road Safety Psychology and another on the theoretical perspectives of Organizational Psychology,as reflected by the *Annual Review of Psychology* (1950-1977), have been directed by Prof. Carpintero; the authors are currently doing specialized research; thus Dr. Soler, with Dr. Tortosa, have continued studies on Road Safety and Traffic Psychology and Dr. Quintanilla has developed studies on Work Satisfaction and on Personnel Selection. In the same University Prof. Peiró and colleagues are carrying on research about Role Behavior, Stress at Work, Power and Organizational Structure.

At the Autonomous University of Madrid Dr. Ridruejo, Professor of Social Psychology, has directed some doctoral research on Organizational Conflict, and has developed some research projects on Ergonomics and their usefulness for integrating handicapped people in work and organizations.

At other universities there are also current research programs in the field.

Also in Granada, within the Social Psychology Department, directed by Prof.
Morales, some studies are being done on unemployment problems and work coop-
eratives. In Seville we also find similar efforts at the Department of Social Psychology headed by Prof. Barriga. In Salamanca, Drs. Garrido and Fernández Seara have done some studies on Unemployment, Professional Guidance
and Road Safety. Finally, at the University of La Laguna, Fuertes and Quin-
tana are working on Job Evaluation within the framework established by Mc-
Kormick. As we can see, there is widespread interest in Organizational Psychology in the universities, but time must pass before we can accurately
evaluate their results.

Some *Governmental Agencies*, generally dependent on the Ministry of Labor are
also carrying out applied research. Thus the National Institute of Employment, which enrolls many psychologists from all over the country, studies
problems of youth unemployment, the effects of industrial reorganization,
personnel recruitment, selection and training for workers. Other than this,
the National Institute for Safety and Work Hygiene has developed some studies on Ergonomics, Work Psychopathology (intoxications, alcoholism, etc.)
and Accident Prevention.

It is hard to evaluate the research done by *Enterprises and Consulting Centers*, as their reports are of confidential nature and have very restricted
diffusion. In most cases their research is occasional and not framed in very
strict conceptual lines but this fact does not necessarily lessen their
worth and merit. We detect some of these works through the analysis of the
Proceedings of recent Congresses dealing with these subject matters.

We here mention works related to Health and Work Hygiene and Personnel Se-
lection problems in a time of economic crisis (Iraeta and Zufiaur in Renfe,
Spanish Railways). There are also some studies on Training, Personnel Selec-
tion and Organizational Climate done at the CTNE (Spanish Telephone Co.).
The Spanish automobile industry (FASA-Renault, General Motors, Citroen, Tal-
bot, Ford, and Motor Iberica) has developed psychological work on Quality
Circles. IBM has developed studies on Work Climate, Survey Feedback and
Quality Circles (Cañero); Roberto Zubiri, S.A. has studied Semiautonomous
Groups at work (Poblete); Tecmaton has focussed on Technology and Organizational Change and Learning (Garijo) and Sevillana de Electricidad (with Dominguez) has paid attention to Conflict and Work Accident Prevention. Other
than this, we have to mention Insurance Companies such as Mapfre and Cy-
clops that have developed important activities on Work Psychopathology and
Accident Prevention.

In brief, we can find two large research orientations: the one rooted in
the academic world and the other coming from public and private agencies
and enterprises. Although there are some relationships between both lines
(some people act as academic members and professional psychologists) this
interaction is still weak and not well institutionalized. Efforts are to be
made to establish new research and service contracts between universities
and enterprises.

3.2. Research Subjects and Publications

This information must be completed with the study of the papers presented
on our subject matters at the Psychology Congresses in Spain during the
last decade. The results show an adjusted view of the differential weight
of the main topics (Table 1).

TABLE 1. Topics of Papers on Work and Organizational Psychology presented in Recent Spanish Congresses of Psychology *.

	N	%
Selection, Guidance and Training	44	16.73
Motivation, Satisfaction, Working Life Quality	28	10.64
Behavior at Work, Psychopathology and Work Accidents	40	15.20
Human Relations and Industrial Relationships	27	10.26
Psychological Effects of Unemployment	23	8.74
Organization and its Environments	2	0.76
Psychological Assessment in Organizations	5	1.90
Organizational Development and Change	68	25.85
Specific Areas (Traffic, Military Psychology and Prisons)	26	9.88
Total	263	100.00

The main topic appears to be Development and Change in Organizations. In this domain many papers are influenced by the Organizational Development movement, others by Transactional Analysis points of view and others by the Tavistock approach. There are also papers influenced by the Behavior Modification approach and, recently, by the Japanese Organizational Psychology (especially Quality Circles).

The second area is Personnel Selection and Training, which has a long tradition in Spain. In recent decades new instruments and technologies have been incorporated. Nevertheless, there are no relevant theoretical contributions in the field.

Third, we find the topics related to Work Behavior: absenteeism, productivity, accidents, etc. Here we see the important influence of French work in Psychopathology and Ergonomics (Leplat, Cuny, Sivadon, Dorna, and others).

There is a large number of papers dealing with Motivation and Work Attitudes. In them Humanistic Theories are predominant (Herzberg, Maslow, Alderfer...) but those of Need Achievement (McClelland), Expectancy (Vroom, Lawler) and Goal Setting (Locke) are also present. More recently, studies on Work Climate and Quality of Working Life (Davies, De Cherns) have been developed. The topic of Conflict and Human Relations has also received attention. The study of conflict levels, collective bargaining and the role of third parties herein have been considered within the models of Thomas, Pondy, Walton or Fauvet (Fernández Rios).

A great number of studies are also dealing with the psychological effects of unemployment. Other recent specific developments are the works on Traffic Psychology and Road Safety, Commercial Psychology and Marketing. However, there are very few studies on Organizational Structure, relations between organizations and environments, Decision Making, Power and Communication processes and Networks.

In sum, Organizational Psychology in Spain is being developed in several topics of the field but needs more contributions in others and in this task universities may play an important role.

4.   PROFESSIONAL ACTIVITY IN WORK AND ORGANIZATIONAL PSYCHOLOGY

It is difficult to offer an adjusted view of this point as there are only fragmentary data. Nevertheless, we will offer here a tentative approach. At present the Colegio Oficial de Psicólogos has registered about 14,000 psychologists but only about 4,500 of them are doing professional work (Hernández, 1984). Their estimated unemployment reaches 20% and 50% are carrying out psychological activities only as secondary occupation (Hernández, 1982). This professional group presents the following demographic characteristics; 63% are females and 37% are males; about 40% are younger than 25, and 70% are younger than 30 years old; only 3% are older than 45. With regard to professional areas they show the following preferences: Educational Psychology about 55%, Clinical Psychology about 40% and Work and Organizational Psychology less than 10%.

These data may be compared with those obtained from members of the branch of Industrial Psychology of the Spanish Society of Psychology (Ordoñez, 1981). About 40% in this group are older than 35 and 12% are above 45 years old; furthermore, about 80% are males. That means that psychologists working in organizations are older and more frequently men than in the general sample of psychologists. Industrial psychologists are distributed as follows: working at services (banks, business firms, insurance cos.): 42%; steel companies: 19%; building industry: 11%; governmental agencies: 6% and others: 22%. In more than 90% of the enterprises surveyed the following functions are carried out: scientific personnel selection, conflict resolution, social politics of employees and disciplinary systems; but on the contrary half of the enterprises are not concerned with Job Enrichment or the integration of psychologically or physically impaired people. Some of these functions, however, are not attached to the psychologist' role in most of the cases: salary and pay politics, commercial management techniques, safety and hygiene plans, collective bargaining and disciplinary systems (Ordoñez, 1981).

In short, we generally have an old-fashioned profile of the "organizational psychologist" mainly centered in Psychotechnics and away from decisions on salary politics, organizational structures design and safety and hygiene aspects. All this requires a change or reformulation of the organizational psychologist's role in Spain. Nevertheless, the needs for a new profile are not especially felt by their employers. In a sample of 55 enterprises employing 80 psychologists about 66 % of their representatives considered that the training of the psychologists was well adapted to the demands of their jobs (cited in Hernandez, 1982).

5. THE INSTITUTIONAL FRAMEWORK OF WORK AND ORGANIZATIONAL PSYCHOLOGY

Some societies have contributed to the institutionalization of Organizational Psychology in Spain. First, the Spanish Society of Psychology, founded in 1952; its section of Industrial Psychology has developed some scientific and training activities: the First Seminary on Ergonomics (1974) and a *Study on Perspectives and Realizations of Work Psychology in Spain* (Ordoñez, 1981). In addition, several scientific sessions on Work and Organizational Psychology have been carried out in the National Congresses of Psychology organized by this Society.

The Colegio Oficial de Psicologos (founded in 1980), with a branch of Work Psychology has also played an important role in the institutionalization process of Psychology in Spain.

A First National Congress of Work Psychology was organized by the Colegio

and Spanish Society of Psychology (1983). In it about 650 members participated and more than 150 papers were presented. The topics of the sessions
were the following: Organizational Psychology, Motivation at Work, New
Dimensions of Work Psychology, Psychology of Mental Health, Training and
Organizational Development and Psychology of Conflict.

In 1984 the Colegio Oficial de Psicólogos itself organized the First Congress of the Colegio Oficial de Psicólogos with the general heading of "Human Development and Life Quality". In it one of the general areas was dealing with Work Psychology and 40 papers were presented about the role of the
psychologist in Organizational Development, Change and Design.

The Second National Congress of Work and Organizational Psychology took
place in Tarrasa (Barcelona) in 1985. It was monographically devoted to the
topic of Psychological and Social Interventions in Organizations.The Annual
Meeting of the European Network Organizational Psychology took place in the
framework of that Congress, allowing the mutual improvement of knowledge
and contacts.

Other associations and institutions are closely related to Organizational
Psychology. We include here the Spanish Association of Personnel Management
(AEDIPE) (Aedipe, 1979) , the Association for Training and Development at
Enterprises (AFYDE) (Afyde, 1982), and recently the Group of Professionals
in Organizational Development.

6. THE SPECIALIZED JOURNALS AS A CHANNEL FOR SCIENTIFIC COMMUNICATION

At present only one journal - *Revista de Psicología del Trabajo y las Orga-
nizaciones* - recently appeared is monographically devoted to this discipline. Nevertheless other journals publish relevant material: *Revista de
Psicología General y Aplicada, Sociología del Trabajo, Alta Dirección* and
Revista de la Asociación Española de Dirección de Personal.

7. FUTURE PERSPECTIVES

It is difficult to predict the future of Organizational Psychology in Spain
although some trends could be inferred from the facts already mentioned.
First of all there is a social group of active professionals and trained
psychologists working in the field and promoting the consolidation of this
specialty in Spanish enterprises. The recent transformation of Spanish universities may favor a greater development of teaching and research in the
field, but here we are only at the beginning. The specialized training of
professionals should not be left to centers outside the university. In my
opinion, the dissociation between the academic and professional worlds is
dysfunctional and impoverishing. On the contrary it is necessary to inten-
sify the relationships between the research centers (at universities) and
psychologists working in organizations in order to increase the development
of applied psychology research.

The research in this area should take into account theoretical advances,
new conceptual models and methods and not limiting itself to occasional
efforts. An enlargement of research topics is also needed: some important
aspects are lacking in Spanish research (Communication processes, Decision
Making, Power and Hierarchy, Groups in organizations, Technology and Struc-

ture, Work and Women, etc.). Finally, a close connection of Spanish researchers and professionals with foreign research centers and scientific societies is needed. Without a doubt, the integration of Spain in the C.E. E. will require a closer contact and cooperation between spanish work psychologists and their colleagues from other European countries.

NOTES AND REFERENCES.

*The Congresses considered are VI National Congress of Psychology (Pamplona, 1979); VII National Congress of Psychology (Santiago, 1982); I National Congress of Work Psychology (Madrid, 1983); I Congress of the Colegio Oficial de Psicólogos (Madrid, 1984); I Congress of Psychological Assessment (Madrid, 1984).

AEDIPE: *La humanización del trabajo en Europa*. Madrid. Ibérica Europea de Ediciones, 1979.
AFYDE: *Ponencias y comunicaciones de las Segundas Jornadas Nacionales y Primeras Iberoamericanas de Intercambio de Experiencias sobre la Formación u el Desarrollo de la Empresa*. Madrid. AFYDE, 1982.
Ballesteros, R.: *La psicología aplicada en la empresa*. (2 vols). Barcelona. CEAC, 1982.
Crespo, E.: Necesidades formativas de los psicólogos. *Papeles del Colegio*. 1982, 2, 6, 20-28.
Dominguez, P. & Casas, J.I.: *Introducción a la psicosociología del trabajo*. Madrid. Pablo del Rio. Col. Síntesis, 1979.
Hernández, A.: La situación laboral de los psicólogos(1-2). *Papeles del Colegio*, 1982, 2, 31-49; 6, 42-49.
Hernández, A.: La psicología como profesión. *Papeles del Colegio*, 1984, 16/17, 61-63.
Mallart, J.: *Psicología Industrial y Organizacional*. Cuadernos de Organización Científica y Ergonomía. Asociación Iberoamericana para la Eficacia y la Satisfacción en el Trabajo. Madrid, 1981.
Mateu, M.: *La nueva organización del trabajo*. Barcelona. Ed. Hispano Europea, 1984.
Montoro, L. & Quintanilla, I.: Enseñanza universitaria de la Psicología. Estudio de Preferencias en el alumnado. Trabajo presentado en la Reunión Internacional de Psicología. Alicante, 1981.
Ordoñez, M.: *Realizaciones y perspectivas de la Psicología del Trabajo*. Madrid, Sociedad Española de Psicología, 1981.
Peiró, J.M.: *Psicología de la Organización* (2 vols.) Madrid, UNED, 1983-84.
Peiró, J.M.: Historical Perspectives of Work and Organizational Psychology in Spain. In H. Carpintero & J.M. Peiró (Eds): *Psychology in its Historical Context*. Valencia, Monografías de la Revista de Historia de la Psicología, 1985, 267-282.
Quintanilla, I.: *El hombre en el trabajo: insatisfacción y conflicto*. Valencia. Promolibro, 1984.
Siguan, M.: *Problemas humanos del trabajo industrial*. Madrid, Rialp, 1963.

AUTHOR INDEX

SUBJECT INDEX

The subject index is based on the keywords provided by the authors. The page number refers to the first occurence of the keyword in the contribution .

ABBREVIATIONS

```
A ............ Artistic
ABB ......... Arbeitsbeschreibungsbogen (Job description questionnaire)
ACM ......... Association of Computer Machinery
AD .......... Additional Decrement
AEDIPE ...... Spanish Association of Personnel Management
AET ......... Arbeitswissenschaftliche Erhebungsverfahren zur Tätigkeits-
              analyse (Task analysis questionnaire)
AFYDE ....... Association for Training and Development at Enterprises
AI .......... Artificial Intelligence
A.I.D.A. .... Attention, Interest, Desire, Action
ALS ......... Automated Library System
ANOVA ....... Analysis of Variance
APA ......... American Psychological Association


BIBB ........ Bundesinstitut für Berufsbildung (Federal Institute for
              Vocational Education and Training)
BMS ......... Fragebogen zu Belastung-Monotonie-Sättigung (Question-
              naire for stress, monotoy, saturation)
BOCI ........ Business Organizational Climate Index
BTK ......... Bijzonder tijdelijk kader (temporary emplayment provided
              by the Employment Service))


C ........... Conventional
CAD ......... Computer Aided Design
CADMAT ...... Computer Aided Design, Manufacturing, and Testing
CAM ......... Computer Aided Manufacturing
CAO ......... Collective Arbeidsovereenkomst (wage agreement)
CCA ......... Canonical Correlation Analysis
CE .......... Constant Effort
CG .......... Cooperative Group/Control Group
CIE ......... Commission International d'Eclairage
CIELUV ...... one of several uniform colour spaces agreed upon by the
              CIE
CIG ......... Cassa Integrazione Guadagni
CMDA ........ Confirmatory Monotone Distance Analysis
CNC ......... Computerized Numerically Controlled Equipment
CUI ......... Centrum voor Overheidsinformatica (Governmental Center
              for Computer Science)
CULSET ...... Computer Program for Colour Sets
CPB ......... Central Planning Bureau
```

C-PRED .... Centre for Personnel Research and Enterprise Development
CRT .... Cathode Ray Tube
CTNE .... Spanish Telephone Company

DAC .... Derde Arbeidscircuit (Third labour circuit)
DBAK .... minimal perceived colour difference from a given set and
               the background colour
DENDRAL ...... program for generating explanatory hypotheses in organic
               chemistry
DIN .... Deutsche Industrie Norm (German Institute of Standardiza-
               tion)
DIO .... Decisions in Organisations
DMIN .... Minimal Perceived Distance between Colours
DSS .... Decision Support Systems

E .... Enterprising
EADA .... Spanish Top Management School
EDP .... Electronical Data Processing
EEC .... European Economic Community
EFPPA .... European Federation of Professional Psychologists Associat-
               ions
EG .... Experimental Group
EOI .... Spanish School of Industrial Organization
ESADE .... Spanish School of Management
ESIC .... Spanish School of Marketing

FAA .... Fragebogen zur Arbeitsanalyse (Job analysis question-
               naire)
FBL .... Freiburger Beschwerdeliste (Freiburger Symptom Question-
               naire)
FCAC .... Quebec Ministry of Education

GHQ .... General Health Questionnaire

HMD .... Heads of Main Departments
HD .... Heads of Departments

I .... Investigative
IAAP .... International Association of Applied Psychologists
IAB .... Institute for Employment Research of the German Federal
               Employment Institute
IAM/DTI ...... Institute   of Administration Management/Department of
               Trade and Industry
ICAI-ICADE ... Spanish Institute of Organizational Management
ICS .... Interactive Computer System
IDE .... Industrial Democracy in Europe
IESE .... Spanish School of Organizational Studies
IFIP .... Institute for Information Processing
IG .... Individual Group
IKBS .... Intelligent Knowledge Based System
ISR .... Institute of Social Research
IUPsyS .... International Union of Psychological Sciences

JAR .... Job at Risk
JDI .... Job Description Index

KARL .... Knowledgeable Application of Rule-Based Logic

LG .... Longer Group
LISREL .... Linear Structural Equation Analysis
LMP .... Leadership Motive Pattern

MACINTER ..... Man-Computer Interaction Research
MMI .... Man-Machine-Interface
MSC .... Manpower Services Commission
MYCIN .... Production rule oriented system for medical consultation

NADOR .... Occurrences Regulations

OPS .... Rule based programming language

PPE .... Personal Protection Equipment
PRODOSTA ..... Project Control and Documentation Standards
PROLOG .... Computer Language (especially in Artificial Intelligence)

QVT .... Questionnaire de Valeurs de Travail (Questionnaire for
               Work Values)

R .... Realistic
RGB .... ("red-green-blue") Colour Signals
RVA .... Rijksdienst voor Arbeidsvoorziening (Employment Service)

S .... Social
SAZ .... Skala zur Messung von Arbeitszufriedenheit (Job satis-
               faction measurement scale)
SEM .... Systems Engineering Models
SG .... Short Group
SIMONA .... Studie- en Informatie-Model voor de Ontwikkeling van een
               Nieuw Arbeidsmarktbeleid (A model for the information on
               and Study of the development of a new management for the
               labour market))
SPSS .... Statistical Package for the Social Sciences
SSA .... Smallest Space Analysis

TBS .... Tätigkeits-Bewertungs-System (Task Evaluation System)
TDS .... Task Diagnosis Survey

UCS .... Uniform Chromaticy Scale

VDT .... Video Display Terminal
VDU .... Video Display Unit
VOS .... Vragenlijst Organisatiestress (Questionnaire for stress in
               organizations)

WYSWYG .... "What you see is what you'll get"

YOP .... Youth Opportunities Program
YTS .... Youth Training Scheme